CRACKNELL'S

CONTRACT COMPANION

Cracknell's
Contract Companion

SEVENTH EDITION

BY

D. G. CRACKNELL, LL.B.,

of the Middle Temple, Barrister

Butterworths
London

1989

United Kingdom	Butterworth & Co (Publishers) Ltd, 88 Kingsway, LONDON WC2B 6AB and 4 Hill Street, EDINBURGH EH2 3JZ
Australia	Butterworths Pty Ltd, SYDNEY, MELBOURNE, BRISBANE, ADELAIDE, PERTH, CANBERRA and HOBART
Canada	Butterworths Canada Ltd, TORONTO and VANCOUVER
Ireland	Butterworth (Ireland) Ltd, DUBLIN
Malaysia	Malayan Law Journal Sdn Bhd, KUALA LUMPUR
New Zealand	Butterworths of New Zealand Ltd, WELLINGTON and AUCKLAND
Singapore	Butterworth & Co (Asia) Pte Ltd, SINGAPORE
USA	Butterworths Legal Publishers, ST PAUL, Minnesota, SEATTLE, Washington, BOSTON, Massachusetts, AUSTIN, Texas and D & S Publishers, CLEARWATER, Florida

A CIP Catalogue record for this book is avaiable from the British Library.

ISBN 0 406 50115 7

Typeset by Cotswold Typesetting Ltd, Gloucester
Printed and bound in Great Britain by Billing & Sons Ltd, Worcester

PREFACE TO THE SEVENTH EDITION

First, I must record my gratitude – and, I am sure, that of many students – to Dr Vincent Powell-Smith for preparing the fourth, fifth and sixth editions of this title.

In this edition I have built upon his sure foundation, adding 73 case summaries and sections, at least, of seven Acts of Parliament. Of course, other statutes have been amended or repealed and some cases have been omitted, if only to make room for the new material.

The hope remains that students will continue to find it helpful to have this book at their side, at whatever level they are called upon to read this particular subject.

October 1988   D. G. CRACKNELL

PREFACE TO THE FIRST EDITION

THIS work is not intended to compete with other legal textbooks, but it is hoped that it will be of use as a companion to textbooks, lecture notes and correspondence courses. It is intended primarily for the student who does not have access to or time to take full advantage of a law library and finds it difficult to ascertain the facts of cases or the wording of Acts of Parliament to which he has been referred in the course of his studies. Other students are more fortunate in so far as they have the opportunity to make full use of a law library, but it is thought that even they might find it to be of assistance to have this work at hand, especially when revising for examinations.

An attempt has been made to include those cases and statutory provisions which are of importance to students. The statutes speak for themselves and the case notes contain an outline of the facts and a summary of those points in the judgement which are vital from a student's point of view. Cross-references have been made in order that the student who refers to one case will have little difficulty in finding others in which the same or a similar point arose. There is also a short glossary of Latin words and phrases that a student is likely to encounter during his reading.

This volume is concerned with the general principles of the Law of Contract. In all this work, the author is greatly indebted to the publishers for their patience, encouragement and painstaking preparation of the manuscript for press, including the compilation of the indices.

July 1961   D. G. CRACKNELL

CONTENTS

Preface to the Seventh Edition v
Preface to the First Edition vi
Cases 1
Statutes 151
    Statute of Frauds 1677 [649]
    Gaming Act 1710 [650]
    Statute of Frauds Amendment Act 1828 [651]
    Gaming Act 1835 [652]
    Gaming Act 1845 [653]
    Infants' Relief Act 1874 [654]–[655]
    Bills of Exchange Act 1882 [656]
    Gaming Act 1892 [657]
    Marine Insurance Act 1906 [658]
    Law of Property Act 1925 [659]–[661]
    Law Reform (Frustrated Contracts) Act 1943 [662]–[664]
    Corporate Bodies' Contracts Act 1960 [665]–[666]
    Misrepresentation Act 1967 [667]–[670]
    Gaming Act 1968 [671]–[673]
    Supply of Goods (Implied Terms) Act 1973 [674]–[680]
    Matrimonial Causes Act 1973 [681]
    Unfair Contract Terms Act 1977 [682]–[696]
    Sale of Goods Act 1979 [697]–[710]
    Limitation Act 1980 [711]–[721]
    Public Passenger Vehicles Act 1981 [722]
    Supreme Court Act 1981 [723]
    Supply of Goods and Services Act 1982 [724]–[741]
    Companies Act 1985 [742]–[743]
    Insolvency Act 1986 [744]
    Minors' Contracts Act 1987 [745]–[748]
    Consumer Protection Act 1987 [749]
Glossary 187
Index 197

CASES

Adams v Lindsell (1818) 1 B & Ald 681 [1]

The defendants wrote to the plaintiff to offer to sell some wool and asked for a reply 'in course of post'. The letter containing the offer was wrongly addressed and because of this the letter of reply was posted and received two days later than it would have been reasonable for the defendants to expect. On the day previous to the receipt of the letter of acceptance the defendants sold the wool to a third person, but the letter of acceptance had been posted before the day on which the wool was sold. The plaintiff sued for breach of contract. *Held*, the plaintiff was entitled to recover as the contract was concluded when the letter of acceptance was posted. (See also *Household Fire, etc, Insurance Co Ltd v Grant.*)

Addis v Gramophone Co Ltd [1909] AC 488 (House of Lords) [2]

Addis was wrongfully dismissed from his employment by the defendants, and claimed (a) damages for the manner of his dismissal, and, (b) damages for his injured feelings. *Held*, such damages are not recoverable. Addis was entitled to recover only the commission and salary which he had lost. (See also *Shove v Downs Surgical plc, Cook v Swinfen* and *Cox v Phillips Industries Ltd.*)

Adler v Dickson [1954] 3 All ER 396 (Court of Appeal) [3]

A sailing ticket issued to the plaintiff provided: 'Passengers . . . are carried at passengers' entire risk' and 'The company will not be responsible for and shall be exempt from all liability in respect of any . . . injury . . . of any passenger . . . whether such injury . . . shall occur on land, on shipboard or elsewhere . . . and whether the same shall arise from or be occasioned by the negligence of the company's servants . . . in the discharge of their duties, or whether by the negligence of other persons directly or indirectly in the employment or service of the company . . . under any circumstances whatsoever . . .' The plaintiff was injured and she alleged that her injuries were caused by the negligence of the master and boatswain of the ship. *Held*, the shipping company were protected by the terms of the contract but the plaintiff could proceed with her action against their employees who received no protection, expressly or by implication, under the contract. (See also *Scruttons Ltd v Midland Silicones Ltd.*)

Affréteurs Réunis Société Anonyme, Les v Leopold [4]
Walford (London) Ltd [1919] AC 801 (House of Lords)

A charterparty provided that commission was due to the charterers' brokers on the signing of the charter whereas by custom commission was only payable if hire was earned. *Held*, commission was payable on the signing of the charter as the custom was entirely inconsistent with the plain words of the agreement and therefore, in the circumstances of the case, of no effect. The charterers, as trustees for the brokers, could enforce this provision against the shipowners. (See also *Royal Exchange Assurance v Hope* and *Palgrave, Brown & Son Ltd v Owners of S.S. 'Turid'.*)

1

Agromet Motoimport Ltd v Maulden Engineering Co (Beds)   **[5]**
Ltd [1985] 2 All ER 436

The plaintiffs were Polish tractor manufacturers and the defendants their distributors in England. Under the terms of their contract, a claim for the purchase price of 13 tractors was referred to arbitration and an award was made in the plaintiffs' favour. When they came to enforce the award, the defendants relied, inter alia, on s. 7 of the Limitation Act 1980, arguing that the enforcement proceedings had been commenced more than six years after the original breach of contract. The award had been made within the six-year period. *Held*, the defendants' contention would be rejected. There was an implied term that the arbitration award would be honoured and a breach of that implied term gave rise to an independent cause of action which was not statute barred.

Ailsa Craig Fishing Co Ltd v Malvern Fishing Co Ltd   **[6]**
[1983] 1 All ER 101 (House of Lords)

The appellants' fishing boat sank while berthed in Aberdeen harbour and the vessel was a complete loss. At the time, the respondent security company were required by contract to provide continuous security cover and the appellants' loss resulted from the respondents' negligence and breach of this contract. However, the contract provided, inter alia, that in the event of the respondents incurring liability 'for any loss or damage of whatever nature arising out of . . . or [the] failure in [the] provision of the services' contracted for, such liability was to be limited to £1,000. *Held*, this clause effectively limited the respondents' liability to £1,000 because, inter alia, it applied where there had been a total (as well as a partial) failure to provide the contracted services. 'Whether a condition limiting liability is effective or not is a question of construction of that condition in the context of the contract as a whole. If it is to exclude liability of negligence, it must be most clearly and unambiguously expressed, and, in such a contract as this, must be construed contra proferentem . . . I venture to add one further qualification, or at least clarification: one must not strive to create ambiguities by strained construction . . . The relevant words must be given, if possible, their natural, plain meaning. Clauses of limitation are not regarded by the courts with the same hostility as clauses of exclusion; this is because they must be related to other contractual terms, in particular to the risks to which the defending party may be exposed, the remuneration which he receives and possibly also the opportunity of the other party to insure.' (*per* Lord WILBERFORCE). (But see *Mitchell (George) (Chesterhall) Ltd v Finney Lock Seeds Ltd.*)

Ajayi v R. T. Briscoe (Nigeria) Ltd [1964] 3 All ER 556   **[7]**
(Privy Council)

By two hire-purchase agreements the defendant hired from the plaintiffs eleven lorries valued at over £24,000. The defendant fell into arrears and over £11,000 was still unpaid. He wrote to the plaintiffs saying that he had to withdraw the lorries from use because of lack of repair and servicing facilities, but he did not wish to forfeit the sums already paid, and would contribute for all essential repairs carried out by the plaintiffs' repair organisation, the repairs to be debited to his account and paid for when the lorries were again in service. The plaintiffs wrote back promising to provide these facilities and confirming that they were agreeable to the defendant 'withholding instalments due . . . as long as they are withdrawn from active service'. The defendant then returned eight of the lorries for repair. Two years later the plaintiffs brought an action for payment of the outstanding instalments, and the defendant pleaded the equitable defence of promissory estoppel, on the basis of the plaintiffs' letter. *Held*, the defendant had failed to establish the defence of promissory estoppel for, on the evidence, it had not been proved that the lorries were not made available to him after they had been repaired and he had not altered his position, after receipt of the letter, by not putting forward counter-proposals or by organising his business in a different way, and it could not be inferred that such reorganisation was necessary. (See also *Central London Property Trust Ltd v High Trees House Ltd*, *Combe v Combe* and *Tool Metal Manufacturing Co Ltd v Tungsten Electric Co Ltd*.)

Akerhielm v De Mare [1959] 3 All ER 485 (Privy Council)   [8]

The appellants decided to form a company in Kenya to manufacture 'cold process tiles' and issued a prospectus which stated that: 'About a third of the capital has already been subscribed in Denmark.' This statement was untrue but the appellants honestly believed it to be true at the time at which it was made. The prospectus induced the respondents to subscribe for shares in the appellants' company but when the company went into liquidation they sought damages for deceit in respect of the alleged fraudulent misrepresentation contained in the prospectus. *Held*, their action would fail as, when it was made, the appellants honestly believed the representation to be true. (See also *Derry v Peek*).

Akerib v Booth Ltd [1961] 1 All ER 380 (Court of Appeal)   [9]

The defendants let to the plaintiff rooms on the second and third floors but retained in their possession a water closet on the fourth floor. The agreement stipulated that the plaintiff should give the whole of his packing and forwarding business to the defendants and provided that the defendants 'shall not in any circumstances be responsible for damage caused by . . . water . . . to any goods whether in the possession of the [defendants] or not'. Due to the negligence of the defendants or their servants, water escaped from a cistern in the water closet and damaged the plaintiff's goods. *Held*, the defendants were liable because words, however wide, must be construed in relation to the subject-matter about which they are used and the words upon which the defendants relied applied only to goods which came into their possession for packing and forwarding. 'In a document of this class . . . if there is any doubt as to its meaning . . . the proper construction must be against the defendants' (*per* DANCKWERTS LJ). (But see *Alderslade v Hendon Laundry Ltd*.)

Albazero, The [1976] 3 All ER 129 (House of Lords)   [10]

The plaintiffs chartered a vessel from the defendants under a five-year time charter, and a cargo of crude oil was shipped on board in Venezuela for discharge at Amsterdam. The bill of lading named the plaintiffs as consignees. In the course of the voyage the vessel and her cargo became a total loss. At the time of the loss the property in the cargo was no longer vested in the plaintiffs but in endorsees of the bill of lading, who were now the cargo owners. The plaintiffs claimed damages against the defendants for breach of the charterparty which had resulted in loss, and the question was whether the plaintiffs were entitled to substantial damages, since they had no proprietary interest in the goods. *Held*, the plaintiffs' claim must fail. The general principle that, apart from nominal damages, a party to a contract could only recover the actual loss he had himself sustained, was subject to an exception in the case of a commercial contract concerning goods where it was in the parties' contemplation that the proprietary interest in the goods might be transferred from one owner to another after the contract had been entered into and before the breach, but that exception could not be extended to a contract for the carriage of goods which contemplated that the carrier would also enter into separate contracts of carriage with whomsoever became owner of the goods carried pursuant to the original contract. This was such a contract and the plaintiffs were entitled only to nominal damages.

Alder v Moore [1961] 1 All ER 1 (Court of Appeal)   [11]

The defendant, a professional footballer, received an injury to his right eye and everyone concerned believed that he would never again be able to participate in professional football. In view of this, the plaintiff insurer paid him £500 under a policy of insurance which provided: 'No claim shall be paid hereunder for permanent total disablement unless the claimant shall have given to underwriters a signed declaration to the effect that he will take no part as a playing member of any form of professional football in the future and that in the event of infringement of this condition he will be subject to a penalty of the amount paid him in settlement of his claim'. The defendant made such a declaration, but within four months was a professional with another club. The plaintiff sought to recover £500 from the defendant. *Held*, the plaintiff would succeed as his claim was for the repayment of a sum in circumtances which were entirely equitable.

Alderslade v Hendon Laundry Ltd [1945] 1 All ER 244   [12]
(Court of Appeal)

One of the terms on which the appellants accepted articles for laundering was that: 'The maximum amount allowed for lost or damaged articles is 20 times the charge made for laundering'. Certain of the respondent's handkerchiefs were lost as a result of the appellants' negligence and the respondent claimed damages. *Held*, the appellants had successfully excluded liability for such loss and the claim must fail. (But see *Davies v Collins* and *Smith v South Wales Switchgear Ltd*.)

Alec Lobb (Garages) Ltd v Total Oil GB Ltd   [13]
[1985] 1 All ER 303 (Court of Appeal)

The plaintiffs were a company and a mother and her son who were the shareholders and directors of the company. In 1964 the company borrowed £15,000 from the defendants, on security of a legal charge which contained a tie covenant by the company to purchase the defendants' petrol exclusively for the period of the loan (18 years) and for a further period thereafter; the charge was irredeemable during the loan period. By November 1968 the company was under pressure from other creditors and the parties entered into negotiations, the plaintiffs receiving independent advice. Reluctantly, but in order to preserve the garage as a sales outlet for its petrol, the defendants agreed a lease and lease-back transaction whereby the garage was leased to the defendants for 51 years in return for the payment to the company of a premium of £35,000 and there was an immediate lease-back to the son and mother for a term of 21 years at a rent of £2,250 per annum. This transaction extinguished the existing charge and it was completed in July 1969. The sublease (the lease-back) could be terminated by either party after 7 or 14 years; it contained an absolute prohibition on assignment and tie provisions as to the sale only of the defendants' petrol. The plaintiffs sought – in 1979 – to set aside the lease and lease-back arrangements. *Held*, they could not succeed. Although the doctrine of restraint of trade applied, on the facts the restraint constituted by the lease and sublease was not unreasonable and it was accordingly valid. Further, again on the facts, the defendants' conduct had not been unconscionable or oppressive and, in any case, the plaintiffs' claim in equity was barred by laches. (Applied: *Esso Petroleum Co Ltd v Harper's Garage (Stourport) Ltd*; distinguished: *Lloyds Bank Ltd v Bundy*; but see *Vancouver Malt and Sake Brewing Co Ltd v Vancouver Breweries Ltd*.)

Alexander v Rayson [1936] 1 KB 169 (Court of Appeal)   [14]

Mrs Rayson agreed to take a flat in Piccadilly at a rent of £1,200 pa and this rent was to include the provision of certain services. Mr Alexander, the owner of the flat, sent her two documents, one being a lease of the flat at a rent of £450 and the other was an agreement for the rendering of certain services in consideration of the payment of £750 pa and the services specified in this document were almost identical to those referred to in the earlier agreement. A dispute arose as to whether certain of the services had been carried out and when Mrs Rayson refused to pay an instalment under the service agreement, Mr Alexander brought an action to recover that amount and one quarter's rent payable under the lease which had been tendered but refused. By her defence Mrs Rayson contended that the service agreement was void for illegality as its purpose was to lower the rental value and enable the owners to obtain a reduction in the rateable value which was, in fact, achieved. *Held*, the transaction was fraudulent and Mr Alexander could not enforce either the lease or the service agreement. (See also *Berg v Sadler & Moore* and *Miller v Karlinski*.)

Allan (J.M.) (Merchandising) Ltd v Cloke   [15]
[1963] 2 All ER 258 (Court of Appeal)

The defendants owned a club and hired from the plaintiffs a roulette-wheel, a roulette table and a croupier's rake. Upon the defendants failing to make the second quarterly payment in accordance with the terms of the contract of hire the plaintiffs sued for its recovery, but the defendants maintained that the contract was illegal. It was envisaged by the parties that the equipment hired would be used for the playing of roulette-royale and, although at the time at which the contract was made neither party knew that the game was unlawful, the court found that roulette-royale as it was played to the knowledge of both parties was an unlawful game. *Held*, the contract of hire was illegal and no action lay for the recovery of arrears of rent. 'Where two people together have the common design to use a subject-matter for an unlawful purpose, so that each participates in the unlawful purposes, then that contract is illegal in its formation; and it is no answer for them to say that they did not know the law on the matter' (*per* Lord DENNING MR). (See also *Snell v Unity Finance Ltd*.)

Allcard v Skinner (1887) 36 Ch D 145 (Court of Appeal)   [16]

When Miss Allcard was about 35 years of age she felt a desire to devote her life to good works. She became associated with the Sisters of the Poor and after a few years became a professed member of that sisterhood and bound herself to observe the rules of poverty, chastity and obedience. The rule as to poverty required a member to surrender all her property either to her relatives, the poor or to the sisterhood itself. The rules also provided that no sister should seek advice from anyone outside the order without the consent of the lady superior. Within a few days of becoming a member Miss Allcard made a will bequeathing all her property to Miss Skinner, the lady superior, and in succeeding years made gifts to the value of about £7,000 to the same person. When Miss Allcard left the sisterhood about eight years later she immediately revoked her will but waited a further six years before commencing an action to recover what was left of the money given to Miss Skinner. *Held*, if she had sued to recover the amount of her gifts which had not been expended on the fulfilment of the purposes of the sisterhood at an earlier date she would have succeeded on the ground of undue influence, but as it was her acquiescence rendered her claim barred by laches. (But see *Morley v Loughman*.)

Allen v Rescous (1676) 2 Lev 174   [17]

The plaintiff gave the defendant £1 in return for his promise to beat a third person but if he failed to carry out the assault the defendant was to pay the plaintiff £2. The defendant failed to fulfil his mission and the plaintiff sued to recover £2. *Held*, the action must fail as the consideration for the whole contract was illegal and void. (See also *Fores v Johnes*.)

Alliance Bank Ltd v Broom (1865) 34 LJ Ch 256   [18]

A bank required security from a customer in respect of an overdrawn account. The customer promised to give certain security but later refused to carry out his promise. *Held*, the court would assume that there was some forbearance to sue on the part of the bank and this was sufficient consideration for the customer's promise to give security. (See also *Horton v Horton*.)

Alpenstow Ltd v Regalian Properties plc [1985] 2 All ER 545   **[19]**

Following negotiations, the plaintiffs wrote to the defendants agreeing that if, following the grant of planning permission, they wished to sell any part of their interest in the property (a) they would give notice to the defendants of their willingness to sell to the defendants at a stated price, (b) within 28 days of the notice the defendants would inform them of their acceptance of the notice, subject to contract, and within seven days thereafter the plaintiffs would submit a draft contract for approval by the defendants and (c) within 28 days of receipt of the draft contract the defendants would approve the contract and exchange contracts within seven days thereafter. The letter concluded by stating that the plaintiffs were awaiting confirmation of acceptance of the agreement set out in the letter. The defendants duly accepted the agreement. Subsequently planning permission was granted and the plaintiffs gave notice of their willingness to sell part of their interest to the defendants. The defendants accepted the contract but, on request for a draft contract as agreed, the plaintiffs contended that the letter setting out the agreement was 'subject to contract' and accordingly was not a binding contract. The defendants sought specific performance of the agreement and registered cautions against the land concerned in order to protect their position. The plaintiffs moved to have the cautions removed, and the question arose as to the effect of the words 'subject to contract' in the circumstances. *Held*, the motion would be dismissed. Although the words 'subject to contract' have a clear prima facie meaning, being in themselves merely conditional, here there was a very strong and exceptional context which would induce the court not to give them that meaning. (But see *A-G of Hong Kong v Humphreys Estate (Queen's Gardens) Ltd.*)

Amar Singh v Kulubya. See **Mistry Amar Sigh v Kulubya**

Amoco Australia Pty v Rocci Bros Motor Engineering   **[20]**
Co Pty [1975] 1 All ER 968 (Privy Council)

The plaintiffs were refiners and distributors of petrol, and the defendants operated petrol stations. They entered into an agreement whereby the defendants would build a service station on their own land and at their own expense, the plaintiffs to provide the necessary plant and equipment. In return, the defendants granted a lease to the plaintiffs for 15 years at £1 a year, plus 3p a gallon for all petrol delivered by the plaintiffs, who in turn granted an underlease to the defendants at £1 a year for 15 years less one day. Both deeds were executed together, but the lease provided that it was not dependent on any other agreement. In the underlease, the defendants covenanted not to cease carrying on the business of a petrol station during its term, and that they would buy all petrol from the plaintiffs, with a stipulated minimum. Some five years later, the defendants began to remove the plaintiffs' pumps and replace them with others. *Held*, the contract was not severable and, despite the provisions of the lease, the two documents were part of the same transaction. The covenant was in unreasonable restraint of trade. (See also *Esso Petroleum Co Ltd v Harper's Garage (Stourport) Ltd.*)

Anderson Ltd v Daniel [1924] 1 KB 138   **[21]**

The parties contracted for the sale and purchase of 10 tons of artificial manure. The plaintiff sued to recover the purchase price and the defendant maintained that he should not succeed as certain statutory requirements as to an invoice stating the contents of the manure had not been complied with. The statute provided that where fertiliser was sold and the seller failed to give an invoice, he should be liable to a penalty. *Held*, the fact that no invoice had been given entitled the defendant to refuse to pay the purchase price as non-compliance with the statutory provision rendered the contract illegal. The object of the statute was not merely to impose a penalty but also to protect the purchasers of fertilisers. (But see *Marles v Philip Trant & Sons Ltd.*)

Andrews v Hopkinson [1956] 3 All ER 422 [22]

The defendant was a dealer in second-hand cars and his sales manager assured the plaintiff that a 1934 Standard saloon was a 'good little bus' and added: 'I would stake my life on it. You will have no trouble with it.' The plaintiff decided to buy the vehicle and entered into a hire-purchase agreement with a finance company to whom the defendant sold the car. The plaintiff acknowledged in a delivery note that he was satisfied as to the car's condition, but a week later the steering mechanism failed and, as a result, the plaintiff was seriously injured in a collision with a lorry. The defective condition of the steering was of long standing and could have been easily discovered by a competent mechanic. *Held*, the plaintiff was entitled to damages for breach of warranty, including damages for personal injuries, as the words of the defendant's sales manager amounted to a warranty that the car was in good condition and reasonably safe for use on the highway. (See also *Shanklin Pier Ltd v Detel Products Ltd.*)

Anglia Television Ltd v Reed [23]
[1971] 3 All ER 690 (Court of Appeal)

The plaintiffs decided to make a film for television and engaged Reed as leading actor. Before doing this, the plaintiffs had incurred expenses in employing a director, a designer and others, amounting to £2,750. Later Reed found that he could not take the part and repudiated the contract. Unable to find a substitute, the plaintiffs accepted the repudiation and abandoned the film. They then sued Reed for breach of contract (for which he admitted liability) claiming as part of the damages the wasted expenditure incurred before the contract was made with Reed. *Held*, the plaintiffs were entitled to succeed. 'If the plaintiff claims the wasted expenditure, he is not limited to the expenditure incurred *after* the contract was concluded. He can claim also the expenditure incurred *before* the contract, provided that it was such as would reasonably be in the contemplation of the parties as likely to be wasted if the contract was broken' (*per* Lord DENNING MR). (Distinguished in *C&P Haulage v Middleton*; see also *CCC Films (London) Ltd v Impact Quadrant Films Ltd.*)

Anglo-Auto Finance Co Ltd v James [24]
[1963] 3 All ER 566 (Court of Appeal)

A hire-purchase agreement in respect of a Vauxhall motor car did not contain a clause purporting to deal with depreciation or deterioration of the vehicle but provided that in the event of the hiring being determined by the plaintiff finance company there should become due and payable by the defendant hirer 'a sum equal to the amount (if any) by which the hire-purchase price (less the deposit plus monthly instalments already paid) exceeds the net amount realised by the sale of the said vehicle'. In other words, under this clause the plaintiffs were entitled to recover one hundred per cent of the total hire-purchase price whether determination took place in the first or the forty-seventh month of the contract (the agreement provided for the payment of forty-eight monthly instalments). *Held*, 'bearing in mind . . . the way in which this clause [operates]—viz, to produce precisely the same result whatever the situation in which it is put into effect—it seems to me . . . I cannot do other than conclude, as I do, that this . . . is a penalty clause, and as such unenforceable' (*per* WILLMER LJ). (See also *EP Finance Co Ltd v Dooley.*)

Appleby v Myers (1867) LR 2 CP 651 [25]

The plaintiffs contracted to erect certain machinery on the defendant's premises. When the work was nearly completed the premises and the machinery were destroyed by an accidental fire. The plaintiffs claimed payment in respect of that part of the work which had been carried out. *Held*, their claim would fail as they were not entitled to recover anything until the whole of the work was finished. (See also *Cutter v Powell*; but see s. 1(3) of the Law Reform (Frustrated Contracts) Act 1943.)

7

Appleson v H. Littlewood Ltd [1939] 1 All ER 464 **[26]**
(Court of Appeal)

The plaintiff sued to recover money which he alleged he had won on the defendants' football pool, a basic condition of which was that no legal relationship should arise from the transaction. *Held*, the action must fail and it was not contrary to public policy to include a clause providing that the transaction should be 'binding in honour only'. (See also *Rose and Frank Co v J.R. Crompton & Brothers Ltd.*)

Archbolds (Freightage) Ltd v S. Spanglett Ltd **[27]**
[1961] 1 All ER 417 (Court of Appeal)

The defendants were furniture manufacturers and they had five vans which had 'C' licences, which entitled them to carry only their own goods. However, the defendants contracted with the plaintiffs to transport a consignment of whisky from Leeds to London and, due to the defendants' negligence, the whisky was stolen in transit. The plaintiffs sought to recover damages and it was shown that at all material times they did not know and should not have known that the defendants had only 'C' licences and were therefore not entitled to carry the whisky on their behalf, although this fact was known to the defendants. *Held*, the plaintiffs should succeed. The contract for the carriage of whisky was 'collateral' and not as such prohibited by statute, expressly or by implication, as the statute merely regulated the means by which carriers should carry goods. Further, it was not a rule of law that 'where a contract is on the face of it legal and is not forbidden by statute, but must in fact produce illegality by reason of a circumstance known to one party only, it should be held illegal so as to debar the innocent party from relief' (*per* PEARCE LJ). (But see *Allan (J.M.) (Merchandising) Ltd v Cloke* and *Bedford Insurance Co Ltd v Instituto de Resseguros do Brasil.*)

Archer v Brown [1984] 2 All ER 267 **[28]**

Having already sold the share capital in a company several times over to other unsuspecting victims, the defendant sold the shares to the plaintiff for £30,000, the plaintiff borrowing the money from a bank. The plaintiff also entered into a service agreement with the company whereby he was to be joint managing director, with the defendant, at a salary of £16,750 per annum. On discovering the fraud, the plaintiff claimed the return of the £30,000, damages resulting from the defendant's deceit (including bank interest), damages for deceit or breach of contract and exemplary damages. The defendant (who had been convicted and imprisoned) conceded that the plaintiff was entitled to rescission and the return of the £30,000. *Held*, the defendant's concession as to rescission could not deprive the plaintiff of damages in deceit. Even if the plaintiff was restricted to claiming relief for misrepresentation, he was entitled to damages as well as rescission because the misrepresentation was fraudulent; even if it had been innocent, the plaintiff would have been entitled to damages under s. 2 of the Misrepresentation Act 1967. The plaintiff was also entitled to bank interest (the defendant being aware of the loan and that the plaintiff could not repay it immediately), damages for loss of employment (£2,500) and expenses incurred in seeking new employment (£1,000) and moderate aggravated damages for injured feelings (£500). However, the plaintiff was not entitled to exemplary damages, even if they could be awarded in deceit, because the defendant had already been punished (imprisoned) for his fraud. (See also *Redgrave v Hurd.*)

Ardennes (Cargo Owners) v Ardennes (Owners) **[29]**
[1950] 2 All ER 517

The defendants orally promised that their ship would proceed direct to London and in reliance upon this promise the plaintiffs agreed to the shipment of 3,000 cases of their mandarines for sale in the London market. The bill of lading provided that the defendants were able to carry the goods to London 'proceeding by any route, and whether directly or indirectly to such port' and were permitted 'to carry the goods beyond their port of destination'. The ship did not sail straight to London but went first to Antwerp and as a result the cargo was delivered later than could have reasonably been expected. The plaintiffs obtained a lower price for their fruit, had to pay a higher import duty and claimed damages for breach of contract in respect of this loss. *Held*, they were entitled to succeed as the bill of lading was not, in itself, the contract between the parties but merely evidence of its terms. The promise to proceed direct to London was part of the contract and the plaintiffs were awarded damages for breach of this provision. (See also *De Lassalle v Guildford*; but see *Pilkington v Wood*.)

Ashbury Railway Carriage and Iron Co v Riche (1875)   [30]
LR 7 HL 653 (House of Lords)

The memorandum of association of the appellant company stated that its objects were 'to make, and sell, or lend on hire, railway carriages and waggons, and all kinds of railway plant, fittings, machinery, and rolling-stock; to carry on the business of mechanical engineers and general contractors; to purchase, lease, work, and sell mines, minerals, land, and buildings; to purchase and sell, as merchants, timber, coal, metals, or other materials, and to buy and sell any such materials on commission or as agents'. The directors of the appellant company agreed to purchase a concession for making a railway in Belgium and afterwards contracted to assign the concession to a company formed in that country. *Held*, such an agreement was ultra vires and void as it was of a nature not included in the memorandum of association and as such could not be ratified even by the whole body of shareholders.

Ashmore, Benson, Pease & Co v Dawson [1973]   [31]
2 All ER 856 (Court of Appeal)

The defendants agreed to carry a load for the plaintiffs. As the plaintiffs' transport manager watched, the defendants overloaded their lorries in breach of statutory regulations. One of the lorries toppled over, and the vehicle and its load were damaged. The plaintiffs claimed damages. *Held*, although the contract was lawful in its inception, it was illegal in its execution to the knowledge of the plaintiffs. Damages were not, therefore, recoverable. (See also *Allan (J.M.) Merchandising Ltd v Cloke*.)

Associated Distributors Ltd v Hall and Hall [1938]   [32]
1 All ER 511 (Court of Appeal)

A hire-purchase agreement in respect of a tandem bicycle made provision for its determination by the hirer and, in the event of the hirer's default, by the owner. Clause 7 of the agreement stipulated that in the event of its determination for any cause whatsoever there would be payable by the hirer 'by way of compensation for depreciation . . . such sums as with the amount previously paid for rent shall make up a sum equivalent to not less than one-half of the total amount'. The hirer elected to terminate the hiring and the court was asked to decide whether the sum which the owners claimed under clause 7 was liquidated damages or a penalty. *Held*, the hirer had exercised an option on the terms of clause 7 and the question whether sums payable under that clause constituted liquidated damages or a penalty did not arise. It followed that the hirer had to pay the amount which he had made himself liable to pay under that clause. (But see *Cooden Engineering Co Ltd v Stanford*.)

Aswan Engineering Establishment Co v Lupdine Ltd   [33]
[1987] 1 All ER 135 (Court of Appeal)

The plaintiff construction company bought liquid waterproofing compound from the first defendants for shipment to Kuwait: it was packed in plastic pails manufactured and supplied by the second defendants. On arrival, the pails were stacked, and left in the sun, on the quayside; they collapsed and the entire consignment of the compound was lost. The pails could only have withstood the extremely high temperatures if they had been packed in their containers in a particular way. The first defendants alleged that the pails were not of merchantable quality and that there was an implied term that the pails would be fit for the particular purpose. The first defendants having gone into liquidation, the plaintiffs claimed against the second defendants in negligence, alleging that they owed them a duty of care to provide suitable pails on that particular journey. *Held*, the first defendants' and the plaintiffs' claims could not succeed. The pails were of merchantable quality within s. 14(6) of the Sale of Goods Act 1979 (they were not required by this provision to be suitable for *every* purpose for which they might be used) and there was no evidence that the first defendants had relied on the second defendants' skill and judgment in providing the pails so as to imply a condition as to fitness for the particular purpose under s. 14(3) of the 1979 Act. The damage suffered by the plaintiffs was not of a type which the second defendants could reasonably have been expected to foresee.

Atlantic Baron, The. See **North Ocean Shipping Co Ltd v Hyundi**

A-G of Hong Kong v Humphreys Estate (Queen's Gardens)   [34]
Ltd [1987] 2 All ER 387 (Privy Council)

The appellants and a group including the respondents agreed in principle but subject to contract that the government would grant the group a Crown lease for development in exchange for 83 of the group's flats. The government took possession of the flats and fitted them out; senior civil servants moved in and the government disposed of their previous residences. For its part, the group paid the government the agreed difference in value between the flats and the Crown property, but before the contract was executed the group purported to withdraw and terminate the government's right to occupy the flats. The appellants maintained that the respondents were estopped from withdrawing from the transaction. *Held*, this was not the case. In order to succeed, the appellants had to show not only that they had acted to their detriment, but also that the group had created and encouraged a belief or expectation that they would not withdraw and that the government had relied on that belief or expectation: on the facts, the group had not encouraged or allowed such a belief or expectation. '. . . the government acted in the hope that a voluntary agreement in principle expressly made "subject to contract" and therefore not binding would eventually be followed by the achievement of legal relationships in the form of grants and transfers of property. It is possible but unlikely that in circumstances at present unforeseeable a party to negotiations set out in a document expressed to be "subject to contract" would be able to satisfy the court that the parties had subsequently agreed to convert the document into a contract or that some form of estoppel had arisen to prevent both parties from refusing to proceed with the transactions envisaged by the document. But in the present case the government chose to begin and elected to continue on terms that either party might suffer a change of mind and withdraw' (*per* Lord TEMPLEMAN). (See also *Cohen v Nessdale Ltd*.)

Attwood v Lamont [1920] 3 KB 571 (Court of Appeal)   [35]

The plaintiff, who was a draper, tailor and general outfitter at Kidderminster, employed the defendant as a cutter and head of the tailoring department. The defendant's contract of employment contained a covenant that he would not engage in 'the trade or business of a tailor, dressmaker, general draper, milliner, hatter, haberdasher, gentlemen's, ladies' or children's outfitter at any place within a radius of 10 miles of the [plaintiff's] place of business' at Kidderminster. This restraint referred to business carried on in other departments of the plaintiff's business with which the defendant was not concerned. The defendant subsequently set up business as a tailor at Worcester, which is more than 10 miles from Kidderminster, but he did business with several of the plaintiff's customers and took orders in Kidderminster. The plaintiff sought an injunction to restrain this activity and the defendant maintained that the agreement upon which the plaintiff relied was invalid as it was in restraint of trade and too wide in its terms to be reasonable. The plaintiff argued that the covenant relating to business as a tailor should be severed from the rest and enforced because it was reasonable. *Held*, the provisions formed a single covenant for the protection of the plaintiff's entire business and not several covenants for the protection of his several businesses and therefore could not be severed. The plaintiff was not entitled to an injunction. (But see *Putsman v Taylor*; see also *Petrofina (Great Britain) Ltd v Martin*.)

Attwood v Small (1838) 6 Cl & Fin 232 (House of Lords)   [36]

The appellant negotiated with the respondents for the sale of certain mines and iron works. The respondents asked questions as to the capabilities of the property and the appellant's answers were verified on inspection by persons appointed by the respondents. Six months after the sale was completed the respondents discovered that the statements had been inaccurate and sought to rescind the contract on the grounds of misrepresentation. *Held*, their action must fail as the respondents had not relied upon the appellant's statements, but tested their accuracy, and after having knowledge, or the means of knowledge, declared that they were satisfied that the statements were correct. (See also *Jennings v Broughton*.)

Australian Hardwoods Pty Ltd v Commissioner for   [37]
Railways [1961] 1 All ER 737 (Privy Council)

The appellant company was engaged in the timber business and the respondents held an occupation permit which entitled them to occupy certain lands and to operate a sawmill. The parties entered into an agreement under which, inter alia, the appellants were to take over the sawmill and sell sleepers to the respondents at a fixed price. The agreement was to run for ten years, subject to determination on three months' notice by either side if there had been a breach on the other side of 'any clause or provision of this agreement'. The appellants defaulted and the respondents gave notice of termination, but the appellants sought specific performance of certain terms of the agreement containing an option to purchase which they had purported to exercise after the giving of notice of termination by the respondents. *Held*, their claim would fail. 'A plaintiff who asks the courts to enforce by mandatory order in his favour some stipulations of an agreement which itself consists of interdependent undertakings between the plaintiff and the defendant cannot succeed in obtaining such relief if he is at the time in breach of his own obligations . . . Secondly, where the agreement is one which involves continuing or future acts to be performed by the plaintiff, he must fail unless he can show that he is ready and willing on his part to carry out those obligations, which are in fact part of the consideration for the undertaking of the defendant that the plaintiff seeks to have enforced. Here, the appellant could never show that it was ready and willing to perform its share of the agreement . . . ; for its breaches had brought on it the notice of determination which precluded it for good from doing anything more in furtherance of that agreement' (*per* Lord RADCLIFFE).

Avon Finance Co Ltd v Bridger [1985] 2 All ER 281   [38]
(Court of Appeal)

An elderly couple purchased a house for their retirement, the arrangements being undertaken by their son. Part of the money was to be provided by the son and, in order to raise it and without telling his parents, he obtained a loan from the plaintiff finance company on the security of the house, the son undertaking to procure the execution by his parents of the legal charge. This he did by telling his parents that the documents they were signing were connected with a building society mortgage which was the principal means of financing the purchase. The son's payments fell into arrears and the plaintiffs sought possession of the house. *Held*, their action could not succeed. Although the parents could not rely on non est factum as they had not exercised reasonable care in signing the charge (applied: *Saunders v Anglia Building Society*), the transaction was voidable in equity as the plaintiffs had appointed the son to procure the security, they should have been aware that the son would exercise influence over his parents and they (the parents) had not received independent legal advice (applied: *Lloyds Bank Ltd v Bundy*). (Distinguished in *Bank of Baroda v Shah*.)

Baily v De Crespigny (1869) LR 4 QB 180   [39]

The lessor covenanted that he would not permit any buildings to be erected on certain land opposite the demised premises but a railway company compulsorily acquired the land under powers given by Act of Parliament and built a station. The lessee claimed to be entitled to damages. *Held*, the claim would fail as the statute had discharged the lessor from his covenant. (See also *Metropolitan Water Board v Dick, Kerr and Co Ltd*.)

Bain v Fothergill (1874) LR 7 HL 158 (House of Lords)   [40]

The defendants contracted to assign a certain mining royalty to the plaintiffs but the defendants' lessors refused to give their consent to the transfer, thus rendering the contract incapable of completion. The plaintiffs claimed damages for loss of bargain. *Held*, their action would fail although the plaintiffs were entitled to recover the expenses which they had incurred. (See also *Wallington v Townsend* and *Ray v Druce*; but see *Watts v Spence*.)

Bainbridge v Firmstone (1838) 8 Ad & El 743   [41]

The plaintiff gave the defendant permission to weigh two of his boilers and the defendant promised that 'he would, within a reasonable time . . . leave and give up the boilers in as perfect and complete a condition' as when he borrowed them. The defendant broke his promise and when sued for breach of contract maintained that there was no consideration to support it. *Held*, he was liable, as the consideration could be found in the benefit which the defendant derived and the detriment which the plaintiff suffered in parting with possession of the boilers. (See also *Coggs v Bernard*.)

Baldry v Marshall [1925] 1 KB 260 (Court of Appeal)   [42]

The plaintiff asked the defendant motor dealers for a car 'suitable for touring purposes'. The defendants recommended a 'Bugatti', which the plaintiff ordered. The car was unsuitable for touring, and the plaintiff claimed to reject it and recover the price. The written contract contained a clause excluding 'guarantees or warranties, statutory or otherwise'. *Held*, the stipulation as to suitability was a condition, not a guarantee or warranty, and was not therefore excluded. (See also s.14 of the Sale of Goods Act 1979.)

Balfour v Balfour [1919] 2 KB 571 (Court of Appeal)   [43]

The defendant, who was about to go abroad, promised to pay his wife £30 per month in consideration of her agreeing to support herself without calling on him for any further maintenance. The wife contended that the defendant was bound by this promise. *Held*, there was no legally binding contract between the parties as it was an ordinary domestic arrangement which was not intended to create legal relations. (See also *Spellman v Spellman*.)

Ballett v Mingay [1943] 1 All ER 143 (Court of Appeal)   [44]

The appellant, a minor, borrowed an amplifier and microphone from the respondent but failed to return the goods as he himself had parted with possession of them. The respondent brought an action in detinue. *Held*, the respondent should succeed as the parting with possession of the goods by the appellant was outside the purview or contemplation of the bailment. (But see *Johnson v Pye*.)

Bank Line Ltd v Arthur Capel & Co [1919] AC 435   [45]
(House of Lords)

The parties entered into an agreement by which the defendants agreed to let a steamer to the plaintiffs for a period of 12 months. The ship was requisitioned by the Government before it was delivered and the plaintiffs claimed damages for non-delivery. *Held*, the plaintiffs would not succeed as the requisitioning had destroyed the character of the chartered service, the charter had therefore been frustrated and the letting was at an end. (But see *Maritime National Fish Ltd v Ocean Trawlers Ltd* and *Finelvet AG v Vinava Shipping Co Ltd, The Chrysalis.*)

Bank of Baroda v Shah [1988] 3 All ER 24 (Court of Appeal)   [46]

By a legal charge in favour of the plaintiff bank the defendants charged their property with the payment to the plaintiffs of all moneys at any time owed to the plaintiffs by Seasonworth Ltd. The defendants took this step as the result of misrepresentation and undue influence exerted by the second defendant's brother, a director of Seasonworth, whose solicitors acted for the defendants in connection with the charge although they (the defendants) had not instructed them to do so. Seasonworth having defaulted, the bank sought possession of the defendants' property. *Held*, they were entitled to succeed. There was no legal obligation on the bank to ensure that the defendants received entirely independant advice before executing the charge and the bank was not infected with the brother's conduct or the solicitors' misrepresentation to the bank that they had authority to act for the defendants. (Followed: *Coldunell Ltd v Gallon*; distinguished: *Avon Finance Co Ltd v Bridger.*)

Bannerman v White (1861) 10 CB (NS) 844   [47]

The parties negotiated for the sale of hops and previously to this the defendants had made it known that they did not wish to buy hops to which sulphur had been applied. When samples were produced the defendants inquired as to whether any sulphur had been used and they were assured that it had not. It appeared that five acres of the crop out of a total of 300 acres had been sulphured and the defendants repudiated the contract. *Held*, the plaintiff's statement that the hops had not been treated with sulphur entitled the defendants to repudiate the contract. (But see *Heilbut, Symons & Co v Buckleton.*)

Barton v Armstrong [1975] 2 All ER 465 (Privy Council)   [48]

A and B were major shareholders in a company. B signed a deed agreeing to buy A's shares on terms set out. B later claimed that the agreement was void on the grounds that he had been coerced into signing by threats made by A. It was found as a fact that the threats were made, but that the main reason for the contract was commercial necessity. *Held*, B's action should succeed. It was for A to show that the threats made to B contributed nothing to his decision to sign. In the circumstances the proper inference was that duress had played a part.

Basildon District Council v J.E. Lesser (Properties) Ltd   [49]
[1985] 1 All ER 20

The first defendants, system builders, submitted a tender, including design drawings, to complete site works and sub-structures of some dwellings for the plaintiffs, subject, amongst other things, to the completion of a formal contract; the standard-term contract was concluded after further exchanges between the parties. Subsequently, defects developed in some of the buildings, necessitating repairs, and the plaintiffs sued, inter alia, for damages. *Held*, they were entitled to succeed. It was an implied term that the buildings would be fit for habitation, not least because the plaintiffs had relied on the expertise of the first defendants, as system builders, to produce habitable dwellings. Even if this term had not been implied, there would have been implied the lesser term that the first defendants were to design the buildings with the skill and care to be expected of system builders. (Distinguished: *Lynch v Thorne*.)

Batty v Metropolitan Property Realisations Ltd   [50]
[1978] 2 All ER 445 (Court of Appeal)

The plaintiffs purchased a newly built leasehold house from the first defendants, a development company. The house had been built by the second defendants. The house was built on a steep hillside which subsequently proved wholly unsuitable for building. The plaintiffs claimed against the development company in tort for negligence and for breach of contract and against the builders for negligence. They also claimed against the local authority for negligence or breach of statutory duty in respect of the council's duty to inspect the foundations. *Held*, the defects lay not in the construction of the house, but in the nature of the land on which it was built. The fault could have been detected by experts and the development company was therefore liable for breach of the contractual warranty that the house was fit for habitation. Additionally, they were liable in tort for failing properly to inspect the site before taking the decision to build. The builders were also held liable in tort, but the local authority was not liable. (See also *Esso Petroleum Co Ltd v Mardon*.)

Beale v Taylor [1967] 3 All ER 253 (Court of Appeal)   [51]

The defendant advertised a car for sale as a 'Herald convertible, white, 1961, twin carbs.' The plaintiff answered the advertisement, went to the defendant's home, and having inspected the car there, bought it. In fact, though neither realised it at the time, the rear half of the car was from a 1961 Herald convertible, and the front half from an earlier model, the two halves having been welded together. No one could see from an ordinary examination of the car that it was anything other than the defendant had advertised it as being. On discovering the true position, the plaintiff brought an action against the defendant for damages under s.13 of the Sale of Goods Act 1893 for breach of condition. The defendant contended that the plaintiff had seen the car before buying it and had then bought it on his own assessment of its value. *Held*, the plaintiff was entitled to damages because, although the description of the car was not false to the knowledge of either party, yet fundamentally the seller was selling a car of the description advertised. (See also *Nicholson and Venn v Smith Marriott*.)

Beaumont v Reeve (1846) 8 QB 483   [52]

The defendant seduced the plaintiff and induced her to live with him for five years as his mistress. The plaintiff alleged that she had suffered great injury to her character and reputation and had been deprived of the means of earning an honest living and in consideration of this and by way of compensation the defendant promised to pay the plaintiff an annuity of £60. The plaintiff did not receive any money and she sued for breach of contract. *Held*, the defendant's promise could not be enforced as the consideration was moral and not legal and it was also past. (See also *Benyon v Nettlefold*.)

Bedford Insurance Co Ltd v Instituto de Resseguros do   [53]
Brasil [1984] 3 All ER 766

The plaintiffs, a Hong Kong insurance company, authorised London brokers to act as their agents up to a specified limit and neither the plaintiffs nor the brokers were authorised, as required by statute, to carry on business in marine insurance. It was an offence to carry on insurance business in contravention of the relevant Act of Parliament. Contracts of marine insurance were written by the brokers on the plaintiffs' behalf and reinsured with the defendants. Claims having been settled by the plaintiffs, they sought an indemnity from the defendants. *Held*, their action could not succeed. The contracts written by the brokers were illegal and void ab initio and they could not therefore form the basis of a reinsurance contract with the defendants. (But see *Archbolds (Freightage) Ltd v S. Spanglett Ltd.*)

Behn v Burness (1863) 3 B & S 751   **[54]**

It was agreed that the plaintiff's ship, 'then in the port of Amsterdam, and being tight, staunch, strong and every way fitted and ready for the voyage, should, with all possible dispatch proceed to Newport, Monmouthshire, and the defendant should there load her with a full cargo of coals, which she should carry to Hong Kong'. In fact the ship concerned was not in Amsterdam at the date of the contract but was four days' sail away. The defendant refused to load the cargo of coals. *Held*, he was entitled to do so as the words 'now in the port of Amsterdam' amounted to a condition precedent, the breach of which entitled the defendant to repudiate the contract. (See also *Bentsen v Taylor, Sons & Co*; but see *Harrison v Knowles and Foster*.)

Bell v Lever Brothers Ltd [1932] AC 161 (House of Lords)   **[55]**

The appellant was employed for a fixed term as chairman of a company in which the respondents had a controlling interest. When this contract of employment still had a substantial time to run, owing to the amalgamation of the company of which the appellant was chairman, which meant that the appellant's services were no longer required, the respondents agreed to the payment of a certain sum to the appellant by way of compensation and this amount was actually paid. It afterwards appeared that during the course of his employment the appellant had made certain speculative deals in cocoa on his own account which would have entitled the respondents to dismiss him summarily without the payment of compensation, although at the time that the settlement was negotiated neither of the parties applied their minds to this possibility. The respondents contended that they had paid the compensation on the mistaken belief that they were legally bound to do so and sought to recover the amount which the appellant had actually received. *Held*, the mistake in question was not one which would entitle the respondents to recover the amount of compensation paid to the appellant. (But see *Strickland v Turner* and *Sybron Corpn v Rochem Ltd.*)

Belvoir Finance Co Ltd v Stapleton [1970]   **[56]**
3 All ER 664 (Court of Appeal)

The plaintiffs bought cars from dealers and, by a separate contract, let them on hire-purchase to X Ltd who took delivery direct from the dealers. The hire-purchase contracts were illegal because they contravened statutory regulations. The contracts with the dealers were also tainted with illegality because the dealers knew of the illegal arrangement. Stapleton, as agent of X Ltd, sold the cars to third parties without the plaintiffs' consent. X Ltd went into liquidation and the plaintiffs sued Stapleton for conversion. *Held*, property transferred by one person to another, in pursuance of a conspiracy to effect an illegal purpose, remains vested in the transferee, despite its illegal origin. Therefore, although the plaintiffs had obtained the cars under illegal contracts, as the contracts had been executed and the property in the cars had passed to the plaintiffs, they were able to claim against the defendant who, as X Ltd's agent, was liable to them in conversion. (See also *Bowmakers Ltd v Barnet Instruments Ltd* and *Sajan Singh v Sardara Ali.*)

Bentley (Dick) Productions Ltd v Harold Smith [57]
(Motors) Ltd [1965] 2 All ER 65 (Court of Appeal)

The plaintiff told the defendant dealer that he was on the look-out for a well vetted Bentley car and the defendant truthfully assured the plaintiff that he (the defendant) was in a position to find out the history of cars. Later, the defendant informed the plaintiff that he had just purchased 'one of the nicest cars we have had in for quite a long time', that it had been fitted with a replacement engine and gearbox and (falsely but not fraudulently) that it had done twenty thousand miles only since it had been so fitted (the speedometer read twenty thousand miles). The plaintiff purchased the car for £1,850 but it was a considerable disappointment to him and he brought an action for breach of warranty. *Held*, he was entitled to succeed as the inference that the representation was intended as a warranty had not been rebutted. 'If a representation is made in the course of dealings for a contract for the very purpose of inducing the other party to act on it, and it actually induces him to act on it by entering into the contract, that is prima facie ground for inferring that the representation was intended as a warranty . . . But the maker of the representation can rebut this inference if he can show that it really was an innocent misrepresentation, in that he was in fact innocent of fault in making it, and that it would not be reasonable in the circumstances for him to be bound by it' (*per* Lord DENNING MR). (See also *Esso Petroleum Co Ltd v Mardon*; but see *Hopkins v Tanqueray*.)

Bentsen v Taylor, Sons & Co [1893] 2 QB 274 [58]
(Court of Appeal)

A charterparty described a certain ship as 'now sailed or about to sail from a pitch pine port to the United Kingdom'. In fact the ship did not sail until nearly one month after the date of the charterparty. *Held*, the description of the ship as 'now sailed or about to sail' was of substance to the contract. It was a condition precedent and not a mere warranty and the charterers would have been entitled to repudiate the contract. (See also *Behn v Burness*.)

Benyon v Nettlefold (1850) 3 Mac & G 94 [59]

A man covenanted to pay Miss Caroline Nettlefold an annuity of £200 pa. On the face of it, the deed was valid but it afterwards appeared that the real consideration for the promise was an agreement between the man and Miss Nettlefold that they should thereafter live together as man and wife. Miss Nettlefold sued to enforce payment of the annuity. *Held*, she would not succeed as the contract upon which she based her claim was founded upon an immoral consideration. (But see *Nye v Moseley*.)

Berg v Sadler and Moore [1937] 1 All ER 637 [60]
(Court of Appeal)

The parties had entered into a price-maintenance agreement with the Tobacco Trade Association. The plaintiff was found to have broken the terms of the agreement and as a 'cut-price retailer' was placed on the stop list which meant that he would not be supplied with goods by members of the Association. The plaintiff persuaded another member of the Association to obtain goods on his behalf from the defendants. The plaintiff paid the defendants £72 19s for 39,500 cigarettes through the good offices of the third member but the defendants became suspicious and refused to supply the goods or refund the amount paid. The plaintiff claimed the return of the money. *Held*, the plaintiff's claim would fail as he had attempted to obtain the cigarettes by false pretences, an illegal act. (See also *Bigos v Bousted* and *St John Shipping Corpn v Joseph Rank Ltd*.)

Bernstein v Pamson Motors (Golders Green) Ltd [61]
[1987] 2 All ER 220

The plaintiff bought a new Nissan Laurel from the defendants: three weeks and 140 miles later its camshaft seized up on a motorway. Next day the plaintiff purported to reject the car on the ground that it was not of merchantable quality within s. 14 of the Sale of Goods Act 1979. The car was repaired under warranty at no cost to the plaintiff, but he refused to have it back. He argued that he was entitled to recover damages and to rescind the contract of sale. *Held*, the car had not been of merchantable quality within s. 14(6) of the 1979 Act but, on the facts and in the light of s. 35(1) of the 1979 Act, he had lost the right to reject it. Consequently, he was entitled only to damages for, inter alia, five days' loss of use of the car. (But see *Rogers v Parish (Scarborough) Ltd.*)

Berry v Berry [1929] 2 KB 316   [62]

By a deed of separation a husband agreed to pay his wife a certain allowance. The parties purported to vary the terms of the deed by an agreement in writing. *Held*, the written variation would be enforced. (But see *Goss v Lord Nugent.*)

Bessler, Waechter, Glover & Co v South Derwent Coal   [63]
Co Ltd [1937] 4 All ER 552

There was a written agreement for the delivery of 70,000 tons of coal over a certain period. At that time statute required such a contract to be in writing but the parties orally agreed that the date on which the coal was to be delivered should be put forward. *Held*, this oral provision was binding as it did not constitute a variation of the contract but a mere voluntary forbearance to insist on delivery or acceptance and as such did not need to be in writing. (But see *Morris v Baron & Co.*)

Beswick v Beswick [1967] 2 All ER 1197 (House of Lords)   [64]

By a written agreement P.B. assigned his business as a coal merchant to his nephew, J.B. In consideration, J.B. agreed to employ P.B. as a consultant at £6 10s 0d a week for the rest of his life, and further to pay P.B.'s wife an annuity of £5 a week for her life, after P.B.'s death. P.B.'s wife was not a party to the contract. After P.B.'s death, J.B. paid one sum of £5 to the widow, but refused to pay any more. The widow sought an order for specific performance of the agreement in her capacity as administratrix of her husband's estate and in her personal capacity. *Held*, the widow as administratrix was entitled to enforce the agreement by an order for specific performance in her own personal favour. However, the House of Lords rejected the argument that s. 56 of the Law of Property Act 1925 applied to such an agreement, and hence the widow would be unable to enforce the agreement in her personal capacity. (See also *Smith and Snipes Hall Farm Ltd v River Douglas Catchment Board.*)

Bettini v Gye (1876) 1 QBD 183   [65]

The plaintiff entered into a contract to sing for the defendant for a certain period and at a fixed salary and agreed to be in London six days before the commencement of his engagement for the purpose of rehearsal. In fact, due to illness, he arrived four days later than he had promised and the defendant refused to proceed with the engagement. *Held*, the provision as to rehearsal was not a condition precedent as it did not go to the root of the matter and for this reason the defendant was not entitled to avoid the contract. (But see *Poussard v Spiers & Pond.*)

Bigg v Boyd Gibbins Ltd [1971] 2 All ER 183   [66]
(Court of Appeal)

The parties were negotiating for the sale of some freehold property belonging to the plaintiffs. The plaintiffs wrote to the defendants stating: 'As you are aware that I paid £25,000 for this property, your offer of £20,000 would appear to be at least a little optimistic. For a quick sale I would accept £26,000 . . .' The defendants replied: I accept your offer' and asked the plaintiffs to contact the defendants' solicitors. In their final letter the plaintiffs said: 'I am putting the matter in the hands of my solicitors . . . My wife and I are both pleased that you are purchasing the property.' The plaintiffs alleged that this exchange of correspondence constituted an agreement for the sale of the property and sought specific performance. *Held*, although an agreement on price did not necessarily mean an agreement for sale and purchase, nor did the use of the word 'offer' always amount to an offer in law, on the facts it was clear from the terms of the correspondence that the plaintiffs' first letter constituted an offer the acceptance of which by the defendants constituted a binding agreement. Specific performance was granted. (But see *Harvey v Facey* and *Clifton v Palumbo*, both of which were distinguished.)

Bigos v Bousted [1951] 1 All ER 92   **[67]**

Bousted's young daughter suffered from pleurisy and he was advised to send her abroad before the winter. Owing to currency restrictions his daughter's allowance was restricted to £40, which was quite inadequate, and he entered into an oral agreement with Mrs Bigos whereby she would make available £150 in Italian money for the use of Bousted's daughter and Bousted agreed to repay this amount in English currency in England. Bousted deposited a share certificate with Mrs Bigos as security for the repayment of the £150. Both parties knew that the agreement was unlawful. Mrs Bigos failed to make the promised £150 available in Italy and Bousted claimed the return of the share certificate. *Held*, the claim would fail as the agreement providing for the deposit of the share certificate was tainted with illegality. This was not a case where the agreement had not been performed because of the repentance of the party seeking to enforce it. (See also *Boissevain v Weil* and *Miller v Karlinski*; but see *Taylor v Bowers*.)

Bisset v Wilkinson [1927] AC 177 (Privy Council)   **[68]**

The appellant sought to recover the purchase money under an agreement for the sale of certain land but the respondents claimed to be entitled to rescind the contract on the ground of misrepresentation. It was shown that the appellant had stated that it was his belief that the land in question would carry 2,000 sheep if properly worked but in fact it had never been able to support that number. *Held*, the contract would not be rescinded on the ground of misrepresentation as the statement as to the carrying capacity of the land was merely an opinion which the appellant honestly entertained. (But see *Smith v Land and House Property Corporation*.)

Blay v Pollard and Morris [1930] 1 KB 628 (Court of Appeal)   **[69]**

Pollard and Morris, who had carried on business as garage proprietors in partnership, decided to end this relationship with effect from a certain date. Pollard's father, a solicitor, prepared the necessary agreement but it contained a term which, contrary to their oral agreement, made Morris liable for rent which fell due before the date of dissolution. When asked to read the agreement Morris had said that he could not understand it but signed it nevertheless. *Held*, in the absence of fraud or misrepresentation, Morris was bound by its terms. (But see *Thoroughgood's Case*.)

Boast v Firth (1868) LR 4 CP 1   **[70]**

An apprentice chemist and druggist was bound to his master by the terms of the apprenticeship-deed for a period of five years. Before his apprenticeship was completed the apprentice contracted a permanent illness which prevented him from doing his work and his master claimed damages to compensate him for the loss of his services. *Held*, the master's action would fail as the illness, an act of God, was a sufficient excuse for the non-performance of the contract. (See also *Poussard v Spiers & Pond*.)

Boissevain v Weil [1950] 1 All ER 728 (House of Lords)   **[71]**

A Dutchman lent an Englishwoman a sum of money in French currency while both were resident in enemy occupied Monaco. The Englishwoman gave a cheque and certain other security for the money but the whole transaction was prohibited by statute. The Dutchman sought to recover the amount of the loan. *Held*, his action would fail as in these circumstances the contract of loan was illegal. (See also *Bigos v Bousted*.)

Bolton v Madden (1873) LR 9 QB 55   [72]

The parties were subscribers to a charity the objects of which were determined by members who had votes according to the amount of their subscription. It was agreed that if the plaintiff would give 28 votes for an object favoured by the defendant, at the next election the defendant would use 28 votes in accordance with the wishes of the plaintiff. The defendant refused to vote as requested by the plaintiff. *Held*, the plaintiff was able to recover the amount which he had subscribed in order to obtain 28 additional votes to be used in lieu of those promised by the defendant; the fact that the consideration for the defendant's promise may not have been adequate was the concern of the parties and not of the court.

Bolton v Mahadeva [1972] 2 All ER 1322 (Court of Appeal)   [73]

The plaintiff agreed to instal central heating and do other work in the defendant's house. The contract price for the central heating was a lump sum of £560. On completion, the defendant complained that the work was defective and refused to pay. The trial judge found that there were serious defects, the cost of remedying which was £174.50, and gave judgment for the balance, i.e., £431.50. The defendant appealed. *Held*, a plaintiff was only entitled to recover on a lump sum contract, subject to set-off in respect of defects, where the contract had been substantially performed. In considering this, it was relevant to take into account the nature of the defects and the proportion between the cost of rectifying them and the contract price. As installed, the central heating system failed to heat the house adequately, and taking into account the cost of repairs, it was impossible to say that the contract had been substantially performed. (Distinguished: *Dakin (H) & Co Ltd v Lee*.)

Bowler v Lovegrove [1921] 1 Ch 642   [74]

Bowler and Blake, the plaintiffs, were in partnership as auctioneers and estate agents at Portsmouth and Gosport and employed the defendant as an outside canvassing and negotiating clerk. The defendant promised that he would not for one year after the termination of his employment 'carry on or be interested in carrying on the business of auctioneers and estate agents . . . within the borough of Portsmouth or in the town of Gosport'. The defendant left the plaintiffs' employment and immediately commenced business on his own account as an estate agent within the prohibited area. *Held*, the plaintiffs could not enforce this agreement as it was against public policy. The restrictive provision was wider than was reasonably necessary for the protection of the plaintiffs' business as in the great majority of cases customers were customers for one transaction only. (But see *Fitch v Dewes*.)

Bowmakers Ltd v Barnet Instruments Ltd [1944]   [75]
2 All ER 579 (Court of Appeal)

The appellants hired some machine tools from the respondents under certain hire-purchase agreements. The respondents had bought the tools from one Smith, but this sale was illegal as it was made in contravention of a statutory instrument. The appellants sold the tools, thus converting them to their own use, and the respondents claimed damages for conversion. The appellants maintained that as the sale by Smith to the respondents was illegal, the hire-purchase agreements were affected by that illegality and should not, on the ground of public policy, be enforced. *Held*, the respondents could recover as their right to the tools and their cause of action was unaffected by and wholly

19

independent of the previous illegal sale. (See also *Mistry Amar Singh v Kulubya* and *Sajan Singh v Sardara Ali*; but see *Taylor v Chester*.)

Branca v Cobarro [1947] 2 All ER 101 (Court of Appeal)   **[76]**

The parties negotiated for the sale of a mushroom farm and signed a document containing the terms of their agreement which concluded: 'This is a provisional agreement until a fully legalised agreement drawn up by a solicitor and embodying all the conditions herewith stated is signed'. The purchaser sued for the return of his deposit and the vendor contended that their 'provisional agreement' was a binding contract. *Held*, there was an immediately binding contract 'until' the document was replaced by one expressed in more precise and formal language. If the parties had used the word 'tentative' instead of 'provisional' it would probably have been held otherwise, but each case depends on the intention of the parties as found by the court. (But see *Chillingworth v Esche*.)

Bridge v Campbell Discount Co Ltd [1962]   **[77]**
1 All ER 385 (House of Lords)

By a hire-purchase agreement the respondent finance company agreed to let and the appellant agreed to hire a used Bedford Dormobile. Clause 6 of the agreement provided that the appellant could terminate the hiring by giving the respondents written notice of termination and that thereupon the provisions of clause 9 should apply. Clause 9 provided, inter alia, that in the event of such termination the appellant should pay to the respondents 'all arrears of hire rent due and unpaid at the date of termination . . . with interest thereon . . . and by way of agreed compensation for depreciation of the vehicle such further sum as may be necessary to make the rentals paid and payable hereunder equal to two-thirds of the hire-purchase price'. Within two months of the date of the agreement and after paying only the initial and the first monthly rentals the appellant wrote to the respondents: 'Owing to unforeseen personal circumstances I am very sorry but I will not be able to pay any more payments on the Bedford Dormobile. Will you please let me know when and where I will have to return the car.' The appellant returned the vehicle to the dealers concerned in the transaction within the following two weeks and the respondents sought to recover the sum payable under clause 9 of the hire-purchase agreement. *Held*, by a majority, the appellant had not exercised his option under clause 6, but had simply declared his inability to go on with the contract. The respondents' claim would fail as the sum stipulated in clause 9 was a penalty and not a genuine pre-estimate of the loss which would be suffered by the respondents in the event of the termination of the hiring. The respondents' remedy was to claim from the appellant any damage that they could show themselves to have actually suffered by reason of his breach of contract. (But see *Lombank Ltd v Cook*.)

Bridge v Savage (1885) 15 QBD 363   **[78]**

The plaintiff employed the defendant on a commission basis to make bets on horses on his behalf. The defendant carried out his instructions and made the bets but refused to pay the winnings to the plaintiff. In an action for money had and received the defendant relied up s.18 of the Gaming Act 1845. *Held*, the plaintiff could recover as s.18, although rendering void all wagering transactions, did not prevent the plaintiff recovering the amount of the winnings from the defendant. (But see *Cohen v Kittell*.)

Brinkibon Ltd v Stahag Stahl und   **[79]**
Stahlwarenhandelsgesellschaft mbH [1982] 1 All ER 293
(House of Lords)

Following negotiations regarding the sale of steel bars to be delivered to Egypt, the buyers, an English company, accepted by telex sent from London to Vienna the terms of sale offered by the sellers, an Austrian company. The contract was never performed and the buyers claimed damages for breach of contract. Had the contract been made within the court's jurisdiction? *Held*, it had not – it had been made where (and when) acceptance of the offer was received by the offeror, that is, in Austria. (Approved: *Entores Ltd v Miles Far East Corporation*.)

British Bank for Foreign Trade Ltd v Novinex Ltd   [80]
[1949] 1 KB 623 (Court of Appeal)

The defendants contracted to pay the plaintiffs 'an agreed commission on any other business transacted with your friends'. The plaintiffs introduced some of their friends to the defendants and the plaintiffs claimed commission on two sales of oilskin suits which were transacted as a result. The defendants argued that they were not bound to pay commission as the amount of commission had not been agreed. *Held*, a contract to pay a reasonable sum by way of commission would be implied from the conduct of the parties. (See also *Powell v Braun*.)

British Crane Hire Corporation v Ipswich Plant Hire Ltd   [81]
[1974] 1 All ER 1059 (Court of Appeal)

A crane was hired under an oral agreement between two large companies who were both engaged in the plant hire business. The owner's usual printed conditions of hire, which were standard in the trade, were sent on later. *Held*, the conditions of hire were part of the contract notwithstanding that there had been no 'course of dealing'. The standard conditions were fair and reasonable and the hirers knew that conditions were always applied.

British Movietonews Ltd v London and District Cinemas   [82]
Ltd [1951] 2 All ER 617 (House of Lords)

There was a contract for the supply of newsreels determinable by four weeks' notice but in view of a certain Order restricting the supply of film made under the Defence Regulations the parties entered into a supplemental agreement dated May 1943; this modified some of the terms of the original agreement but provided that the original agreement was in all other respects to 'remain in full force and effect until such time as the Order is cancelled'. In 1948, when film was again in plentiful supply, but the Order was still in force, the defendants gave four weeks' notice to determine the agreement and the plaintiffs sued for breach of contract. *Held*, the plaintiffs were entitled to recover as the supplemental agreement had expressly provided that the original contract was to remain in force 'until such time as the Order is cancelled' and as the Order was still in force the original agreement could not be validly determined. (See also *Davis Contractors Ltd v Fareham Urban District Council*.)

British Reinforced Concrete Engineering Co Ltd v   [83]
Schelff [1921] 2 Ch 563

The plaintiffs engaged in the manufacture and sale of BRC road reinforcements and the defendants, who had a much smaller business, sold loop reinforcements. The defendants covenanted to sell their business to the plaintiffs and agreed that they would not, for a certain period, be concerned in the manufacture or sale of road reinforcements. One of the defendants entered employment in breach of this agreement and the plaintiffs sued upon the covenant. *Held*, their action must fail as the covenant was wider than that reasonably necessary for the protection of the plaintiffs in respect of the particular business sold, i.e., the restraint would only be justifiable and valid if it had been confined to the restriction of the sale of loop road reinforcements. (See also *Vancouver Malt and Sake Brewing Co Ltd v Vancouver Breweries Ltd*.)

British Russian Gazette and Trade Outlook Ltd v   **[84]**
Associated Newspapers Ltd [1933] 2 KB 616 (Court of Appeal)

One Talbot, a director of the plaintiff company, sued the defendants in respect of an alleged libel. A representative of the defendants met Talbot and terms of a settlement were arranged whereby Talbot agreed to accept 1,000 guineas in full discharge and settlement of his claims and of that of the plaintiff company and undertook to discontinue the action against the defendants. Before the agreed amount was paid Talbot proceeded with the action in breach of the agreement. *Held*, he was not entitled to do so as he was bound by the terms of the settlement, consideration for which was to be found in executory promises by the defendants. (But see *Foakes v Beer*.)

Brodie v Brodie [1971] P 271   **[85]**

Immediately before their marriage the parties entered into an agreement in writing which provided that they would live apart and this agreement was confirmed by an indorsement immediately after the marriage ceremony. *Held*, the agreement was void as it was contrary to public policy to contract with a view to a future separation. (But see *Wilson v Wilson*.)

Brogden v Metropolitan Railway Co (1877) 2 App Cas 666   **[86]**
(House of Lords)

The appellant supplied the respondents with coal and after a number of years suggested that they should enter into a formal contract. A draft of the contract was submitted to the appellant who completed certain details, introduced a new term by adding the name of an arbitrator, wrote 'approved' at the end of the paper, signed his name and returned the draft to the respondents. The contract was never executed but for some time coal was supplied and payment made in accordance with the terms contained in the draft agreement. *Held*, while mere mental assent to the terms of the draft would not be sufficient, because the parties had acted upon the draft, there was, from the time when the respondents first ordered coal after the return of the draft or at latest when the appellant completed delivery of the order, a valid contract between them. (See also *Stevenson, Jaques & Co v McLean*.)

Brooke (Lord) v Rounthwaite (1846) 5 Hare 298   **[87]**

Particulars of sale described an estate as containing 'upwards of sixty-five acres of fine oak timber trees, the average size of which approached fifty feet'. There was a conflict of evidence as to whether the average size of the trees was thirty-five or twenty-two feet but both parties agreed that fifty feet was an over-statement. *Held*, the representation in the particulars of sale having been proved to be incorrect, the contract for the purchase of the estate would not be specifically enforced. (But see *Scott v Hanson*.)

Broughton v Snook [1938] 1 Ch 505   **[88]**

The plaintiff orally agreed to purchase the Bridge Inn and with the consent of the owner went into possession and made alterations and improvements to the value of nearly £200. *Held*, these actions were necessarily referable to the contract as the existence of the agreement was the only reasonable explanation for them: they constituted acts of part performance and the plaintiff was entitled to a decree of specific performance. (See also *Kingswood Estate Co Ltd v Anderson*.)

Brown and Davis Ltd v Galbraith [1972] 3 All ER 31   **[89]**
(Court of Appeal)

The defendant's car was damaged in a collision and he arranged with the plaintiffs to tow it in. He told them that he had a comprehensive insurance policy and was later given an estimate of the cost of repairs. The insurance company's assessors agreed the cost of repairs direct with the plaintiffs and, in giving written confirmation to them, it was stated that they should recover from the defendant direct the £25 excess for which the defendant was liable under the insurance policy. The insurance company authorised the repairs to proceed. The car was repaired and the defendant collected it, but he refused to sign a satisfaction note as he was dissatisfied with the repairs. The insurance company failed before any payment was made by them to the plaintiffs, who sued the defendant for the full cost of repairs. *Held*, the claim must fail. The defendant was not liable for more than the £25 excess for repairs (and a small towing charge). Two contracts had been entered into, but it did not follow that a term was to be implied into the one between the plaintiffs and the defendant that the defendant would pay the whole cost of repairs and towing. It was necessary to show that such a term was so obvious that it ought to be implied to give business efficacy to the contract. The circumstances of the case showed that this was not so and there was no basis on which to found an implication that the defendant had accepted any liability for the main account. (See also *Charnock v Liverpool Corporation* and *Trollope and Colls Ltd v North West Metropolitan Hospital Board*.)

Bunge Corpn v Tradax SA [1981] 2 All ER 513   [90]
(House of Lords)

A contract for the sale and purchase of soya bean meal provided that one shipment was to be in June and that the buyers, who were to provide the vessel, should give at least 15 days' notice of its probable readiness. They did not give such notice until 17 June and the sellers maintained that the late notice was a breach of contract amounting to a repudiation and they claimed damages. *Held*, the sellers should succeed. '. . . the statement . . . appears to me to be correct, in particular in asserting (1) that the court will require precise compliance with stipulations as to time wherever the circumstances of the case indicate that this would fulfil the intention of the parties, and (2) that broadly speaking time will be considered of the essence in "mercantile" contracts . . . The relevant clause falls squarely within these principles, and such authority as there is supports its status as a condition' (*per* Lord W<small>ILBERFORCE</small>). (Distinguished: *Hong Kong Fir Shipping Co Ltd v Kawasaki Kisen Kaisha Ltd*.)

Burnard v Haggis (1863) 14 CB (NS) 45   [91]

The defendant, who was under age, went to the stables of the plaintiff and hired a horse to ride on the road. The plaintiff stipulated that the horse was not to be ridden by anyone but the defendant and was not to be used for jumping. The defendant let his friend ride the horse and the friend forced the animal to attempt a fence but the jump was unsuccessful, the horse falling and being transfixed by a hedge-stake. *Held*, the plaintiff was entitled to damages in tort as such conduct was not contemplated by the contract and had in fact been specifically forbidden. (See also *Walley v Holt*; but see *Jennings v Rundall*.)

Bushwall Properties Ltd v Vortex Properties Ltd   [92]
[1976] 2 All ER 283 (Court of Appeal)

A contract for the sale of land provided that the purchase price of £500,000 was 'to be phased as to £250,000 upon first completion, as to £125,000 twelve months thereafter and as to the balance of £125,000 a further twelve months thereafter' and 'on the occasion of each completion a proportionate part of the land shall be released forthwith to' the plaintiffs. In breach of the agreement, the defendants conveyed the land to X, who offered to sell it to the plaintiffs for £500,000 payable immediately. The plaintiffs accepted the offer and completed the sale on those terms. They then sued the defendants for breach of the original contract of sale. The defendants argued that there was no binding contract since the reference to 'a proportionate part of the land' was too uncertain in that the agreement did not provide whether the plaintiffs or the defendants were to have the power to select 'a proportionate part' of the land. *Held*, the contract was void for uncertainty in the absence of any express term as to how the land to be included in each phase was selected.

Butler Machine Tool Co Ltd v Ex-Cell-O Corporation Ltd   [93]
[1979] 1 All ER 965 (Court of Appeal)

The plaintiffs offered to sell machine tools to the defendants subject to their own terms and conditions which included a price variation clause. The defendants replied purporting to accept the offer on their own terms, which did not include a price variation clause. The plaintiffs acknowledged the order by returning to the defendants a tear-off slip. After delivery, the plaintiffs claimed increased costs, which the defendants refused to pay. *Held*, the transaction must be analysed in terms of offer and acceptance. The defendants' order was not an acceptance of the plaintiffs' offer but was a counter-offer which was tantamount to a rejection. The contract had been concluded on the defendants' terms and conditions by the plaintiffs' acknowledgment of the order.

Byrne & Co v Leon Van Tienhoven & Co (1880)   [94]
5 CPD 344

The defendants, who carried on business in Cardiff, wrote to the plaintiffs, whose office was in New York, offering to sell certain goods at a fixed price. On the day on which they received the offer the plaintiffs telegraphed their acceptance, but three days previously the defendants had sent a letter withdrawing the offer; this did not arrive until after the acceptance had been confirmed by post. The plaintiffs sought damages for breach of contract. *Held*, the plaintiffs were entitled to damages as there was a binding contract from the moment the offer was accepted and the withdrawal was of no effect as it was not received by the plaintiffs until after acceptance. (See also *Henthorn v Fraser*.)

C & P Haulage v Middleton [1983] 3 All ER 94   [95]
(Court of Appeal)

The appellant self-employed motor engineer was granted by the respondents a contractual licence to occupy a yard on a renewable six-monthly basis. He spent money on the premises even though the licence provided 'Any fixtures you put in are left'. Ten weeks before the end of the initial six months the appellant was unlawfully ejected and, as a temporary measure, the local authority allowed him to use his home for the purpose of his business. He claimed the cost of the improvements effected by him to the yard. *Held*, his claim could not succeed as he was no worse off than if the contract had been fully performed. He was, however, awarded nominal damages of £10. (Distinguished: *Anglia Television Ltd v Reed*.)

CHT Ltd v Ward [1963] 3 All ER 226   [96]
The defendant was a member of Crockfords, a club owned by the plaintiffs, and her account was debited with the total face value of the chips handed to her. The chips were used in playing poker under conditions in which it was lawful gaming and also for the purchase of food, liquor and cigarettes. An account was sent to the defendant on a weekly basis and if at any time her account was in credit (i.e., she had paid in more chips in any week than she had received) the plaintiffs paid her the credit balance by cheque. In common with other members, when she won she had the choice of having her account credited with her winnings or drawing cash for any credit balance standing on her account. The plaintiffs sued to recover the amount of a debit balance. *Held*, the plaintiffs had in fact paid the defendant's gaming losses and it followed that under the provisions of s. 1 of the Gaming Act 1892 the action was brought on a promise made by the defendant to the plaintiffs to pay them sums paid by them in respect of contracts

rendered null and void by the Gaming Act 1845 and that the plaintiffs could not recover the sums so paid. (See also *M'Kinnell v Robinson*.)

Callisher v Bischoffsheim (1870) LR 5 QB 449   [97]

The plaintiff alleged that certain moneys were due to him from the Government of Honduras and was about to institute proceedings to enforce payment. The defendant promised to deliver certain debentures to the plaintiff and the consideration for this promise was the plaintiff's forbearance to sue the Honduras Government. In fact the plaintiff did not have a claim which he could prosecute successfully and the defendant argued that there was therefore no consideration for his promise to deliver the debentures. *Held*, the defendant was bound as the fact that the plaintiff could not have maintained a successful action against the Honduras Government did not vitiate the contract and destroy the validity of the consideration. The plaintiff entertained a bona fide belief that he could bring a successful action but if he had known his claim to be unfounded there would have been no contract between the parties. (But see *Wade v Simeon*.)

Car and Universal Finance Co Ltd v Caldwell [1964]   [98]
1 All ER 290 (Court of Appeal)

Caldwell, the vendor of a car, was induced to part with possession of it on payment by cheque. The cheque was not met, and the fraudulent purchaser avoided communication with Caldwell, who informed both the police and a national motoring organization. Some time later, the purchaser sold the car to X, from whom Caldwell sought possession. *Held*, as Caldwell had, by overt conduct, effectively rescinded the contract, the fraudulent buyer could not pass a good title, and Caldwell was entitled to succeed. (See also *Reese River Silver Mining Co Ltd v Smith*.)

Carlill v Carbolic Smoke Ball Co [1893] 1 QB 256   [99]
(Court of Appeal)

The plaintiff bought a medical preparation called 'The Carbolic Smoke Ball' on the faith of an advertisement issued by the defendants in which they offered to pay £100 to any person who contracted influenza after using one of their smoke balls in a specific manner and for a specified period. 'To show their sincerity' the defendants deposited £1,000 with their bankers. The plaintiff bought one of the smoke balls and used it as prescribed but never the less contracted influenza and sued for £100. The defendants contended that there was no binding agreement. *Held*, (i) an offer may be made to the world at large and the advertisement was such an offer which was accepted by any person who bought the smoke ball and complied with the conditions as to manner and period of use (see also *Shipton v Cardiff Corporation*); (ii) there was no need for the plaintiff to communicate acceptance of the offer as the defendants had made no mention of the necessity for communication in the advertisement and had impliedly intimated that it would be sufficient acceptance to act upon the offer, that is, to use the smoke ball as prescribed (but see *Powell v Lee*); (iii) the offer was not 'mere puff' as the fact that they had deposited £1,000 was sufficient evidence of their intention to create legal relations with users of the smoke ball (but see *Balfour v Balfour*.)

Carlton Hall Club Ltd v Laurence [1929] 2 KB 153   [100]

The plaintiffs were proprietors of a club which met for social purposes and for the playing of cards, billiards and other games. Members taking part in games for money were supplied with 'chips' upon which were marked their value and the members paid for their 'chips' by cheque. The defendant borrowed £26 7s 3d in 'chips' for the purpose of playing snooker and poker and paid for them by cheques which were not met. The plaintiffs did not sue upon these cheques as securities for money knowingly lent for gaming are rendered void by the Gaming Acts, but sought to recover by suing on the agreement for the loan. *Held*, their action must fail as the combined effect of s. 1 of the Gaming Act 1710 and s. 1 of the Gaming Act 1835, is to render void not only a security for money knowingly lent for gambling but by implication the consideration for a contract for the loan of money for this purpose, whether the gaming was legal or illegal. (See also *MacDonald v Green* and *William Hill (Park Lane) Ltd v Hofman*.)

Carney v Herbert [1985] 1 All ER 438 (Privy Council)   **[101]**

The appellant and the three respondents between them owned the shares of Airfoil Ltd and were the directors of that company and of its subsidiary, Newbridge Ltd. The respondents agreed to sell their shares in Airfoil to Ilerain Ltd, a company controlled by the appellant, and the appellant and Newbridge guaranteed the payment of the purchase price, Newbridge's guarantee being secured by mortgages on its land. The appellant contended that he was not liable on the guarantee since the sale agreement was illegal and unenforceable because the mortgages amounted to the provision of security by a subsidiary of the company whose shares were being purchased, contrary to the provisions of a local statute. *Held*, this was not the case. The illegal mortgages could not be said to go to the heart of the transaction and they could therefore be severed from the remainder of the contract. There was no public policy arising from the nature of the illegality which prevented the enforcement of the severed contract. (See also *Nicolene Ltd v Simmonds*.)

Carpenters Estates Ltd v Davies [1940] 1 All ER 13   **[102]**

The plaintiffs bought some land from the defendant for building purposes and the defendant covenanted that he would construct certain roads and sewers. The defendant made the roads but neglected to make the sewers. The plaintiffs claimed specific performance of the defendant's promise. *Held*, an order for specific performance would be made as an award of damages would not be a sufficient remedy.

Cartwright v Hoogstoel (1911) 105 LT 628   **[103]**

The defendant offered the plaintiff the lease of some premises and said that his offer would remain open for seven days. The plaintiff purported to exercise this option within the period specified but before acceptance he was informed of conduct on the part of the defendant which was quite inconsistent with the offer and consistent only with an absolute withdrawal of the offer. *Held*, the plaintiff was not entitled to specific performance as the conduct of the defendant which had come to the notice of the plaintiff was a sufficient retraction of the offer. (See also *Dickinson v Dodds*.)

Casey's Patents, Re [1892] 1 Ch 104 (Court of Appeal)   **[104]**

The joint owners of certain patents informed C that in consideration of services rendered they would give him a one-third share of the patents. The defendants contended that this promise was not binding as the consideration was past. *Held*, the plaintiff would succeed in his action on the defendants' promise as there was an implication at the time of rendering the services that they would be paid for and the share in the patents would be regarded as such payment. (See also *Lampleigh v Brathwait* and *Pao On v Lau Yiu*.)

Caton v Caton (1967) LR 2 HL 127 (House of Lords)   **[105]**

C, who had made a proposal of marriage to the plaintiff, wrote out terms which were meant to represent the basis of a marriage settlement. The names of both parties appeared on this paper but the settlement was never executed because the plaintiff, who duly married C, agreed to forgo the execution of the deed of settlement on the condition that C would leave her certain property by his will. C did not honour his promise and the plaintiff sought specific performance of the original agreement for a marriage settlement on the terms which had been committed to writing. *Held*, her action must fail because there was not a sufficient note or memorandum of the agreement for a marriage settlement as it had not been signed by C. The mere fact that his name had been written in the draft did not constitute a sufficient signature as it had not been introduced with a view to governing or authenticating the document. (But see *Leeman v Stocks*.)

### CCC Films (London) Ltd v Impact Quadrant Films Ltd	[106]
[1984] 3 All ER 298

The defendants granted the plaintiffs a licence to distribute three films in 26 countries and the plaintiffs asked the defendants to insure and send by recorded delivery video tapes of the films to be used for marketing purposes. In breach of this agreement the defendants sent the tapes uninsured by ordinary post in the course of which they were lost. The defendants also failed to perform subsequent agreements to send replacement tapes. The plaintiffs were unable to produce evidence of loss of profits so they sued to recover $12,000 as wasted expenditure. *Held*, they were entitled to succeed as they had an unfettered choice whether to claim for loss of profits or for wasted expenditure. The onus of proving that the plaintiffs would not have recouped their outlay of $12,000 if they had received the tapes and exploited the films lay on the defendants and they had not discharged that burden. (See also *Anglia Television Ltd v Reed*.)

### Central London Property Trust Ltd v High Trees	[107]
House Ltd [1947] KB 130, [1956] 1 All ER 256

In 1937 the plaintiffs let a block of flats to the defendants for a term of 99 years at a ground rent of £2,500 pa. In 1940, as few of the flats were occupied because of the war, the plaintiffs agreed to reduce the rent to £1,250 as from the beginning of the term. The defendants continued to pay the reduced rent until 1945 when all the flats were let and the plaintiffs claimed that the full rent was again payable. *Held*, the plaintiffs were entitled to recover the full rent from the time when the flats were again occupied; had they sued for the full rent between 1940 and 1945 they would have been estopped from asserting their strict legal right to demand payment in full, as when parties enter into an arrangement which is intended to create legal relations and in pursuance of such arrangement one party makes a promise to the other which he knows will be acted on and which is in fact acted on by the promisee, the promise is binding on the promisor to the extent that it will not allow him to act inconsistently with it, although the promise may not be supported by consideration in the strict sense. 'I . . . apply the principle that the promise, intended to be binding, intended to be acted on and in fact acted on, is binding so far as its terms properly apply. It is binding as covering the period down to 1945, and from that time full rent is payable' (*per* DENNING J). (But see *Combe v Combe*.)

### Central Railway Company of Venezuela v Kisch (1867)	[108]
LR 2 HL 99 (House of Lords)

The appellants issued a prospectus which contained representations which were untrue and deceptive but the respondent was given the opportunity of inspecting certain reports and plans which would have supplied the correct information, the lack of which he afterwards alleged entitled him to rescind the contract. *Held*, no mis-statement or concealment of any material fact or circumstances would be permitted in a prospectus and as there had been such a misrepresentation in reliance upon which the respondent had agreed to buy the shares he was entitled to be relieved from the contract. It was no answer to his claim that he could have discovered the true position if he had carried out the inspections open to him. (See also *Redgrave v Hurd*.)

27

Chapelton v Barry Urban District Council [1940]   **[109]**
1 All ER 356 (Court of Appeal)

Deck chairs were stacked up on the beach and beside them was a notice which said 'Barry Urban District Council. Cold Knap. Hire of chairs, 2*d* per session of 3 hours . . .' The appellant paid for the hire of two chairs and was given two tickets on the back of which was a condition which purported to exclude the respondents' liability for any injury which the hirer should sustain. The appellant did not read this condition. The canvas on one of the chairs was defective and the appellant claimed damages in respect of the injuries which resulted. *Held*, damages would be awarded as the appellant was entitled to assume that the conditions of hire were to be found in the notice near the stack of chairs. The ticket was a mere voucher or receipt to prove payment or the time of commencement of hire. (See also *Olley v Marlborough Court Ltd.*)

Chaplin v Hicks [1911] 2 KB 786 (Court of Appeal)   **[110]**

The plaintiff accepted the defendant's offer to apply for selection for employment by him as an actress for a term of three years. Twelve such engagements were offered and the plaintiff was one of the fifty applicants from whom the twelve were to be selected. The plaintiff was given insufficient notice of the interview at which the final choice was to be made and thereby lost her chance of selection. The plaintiff claimed damages for breach of contract. *Held*, she was entitled to succeed as the damage which she had suffered (i.e. loss of opportunity) was within the contemplation of the parties as the possible direct outcome of the defendant's breach of contract and therefore not too remote. Although it was difficult, if not impossible, to arrive at an accurate assessment of the amount of damages which should be awarded, the question had rightly been left to the jury who had concluded that the plaintiff had been deprived of something which had a monetary value and decided that the plaintiff should receive £100. 'I . . . wish to deny with emphasis that, because precision cannot be arrived at, the jury has no function in the assessment of damages' (*per* VAUGHAN WILLIAMS LJ).

Chaplin v Leslie Frewin (Publishers) Ltd [1965] 3 All   **[111]**
ER 764 (Court of Appeal)

C, the son of the famous film actor, was a minor, and in need of money. He and his wife, who was of full age, entered into two contracts, to have his life story written by two ghost writers, and published by the defendants. The copyright in the book was to vest in C and his wife, who warranted that the book contained nothing defamatory or objectionable, and agreed to indemnify the publishers against claims in consequence of any breach of the warranty. Although told by the defendants to get independent legal advice, neither C nor his wife did so. A few months later, C and his wife passed the proofs, having made certain amendments to passages that might be defamatory. Later, C consulted solicitors, who on his behalf repudiated the agreement on grounds of his minority. C now objected to the book on grounds that included its unpleasantness and that there were libellous passages in it. He sought an injunction restraining the defendants from printing and publishing the book. *Held*, his claim must fail. The question whether the contract was for C's benefit must be judged at the date when it was made and, so considered, it was prima facie for C's benefit, since the publishers alleged that the allegedly defamatory passages were justifiable and since C benefited financially. (See also *Doyle v White City Stadium Ltd.*)

Chappell & Co Ltd v Nestlé Co Ltd [1960] 2 All ER   **[112]**
701 (House of Lords)

The plaintiffs owned the copyright in a dance tune. X made records of the tune which they sold to the defendants for 4*d* each. The defendants advertised these records to the public for 1*s* 6*d* each but required, in addition, three wrappers from Nestlé products.

The plaintiffs sued the defendants for breach of copyright. The defendants pleaded s. 8 of the Copyright Act 1956 which provided that recordings of musical work may be made for retail sale providing the copyright owner is paid a royalty of $6\frac{1}{4}$ per cent of 'the ordinary retail selling price'. The question was whether this statutory royalty was to be based on the 1s 6d a record, or whether the wrappers (which were thrown away) were part of the consideration. *Held*, the plaintiffs' claim should succeed. 'A contracting party can stipulate for what consideration he chooses. A peppercorn does not cease to be good consideration if it is established that the promisee does not like pepper and will throw away the corn': *per* Lord SOMERVELL. (See also *Haigh v Brooks*.)

Chapple v Cooper (1844) 13 M & W 252   [113]

Anne Cooper's husband died and she placed an order with an undertaker for the conduct of his funeral. When the undertaker sued to recover his charges Anne relied on the fact that she was a minor and the undertaker contended that she was liable as the contract into which she had entered was one for 'necessaries'. *Held*, the undertaker would succeed as the decent Christian burial of his wife and lawful children is a personal advantage and reasonably necessary to a husband and there was no reason why the decent burial of her husband should not likewise be regarded as of advantage and necessary to Anne. (See also *Helps v Clayton*.)

Charnock v Liverpool Corporation [1968] 3 All ER   [114]
473 (Court of Appeal)

The plaintiff took his car to X's garage for repair. At a meeting at the garage between the plaintiff, X's manager, and an assessor employed by the plaintiff's insurers, it was agreed that the insurance company would pay the cost of repairs, this being confirmed by them in writing. The garage took eight weeks to repair the car. The plaintiff was awarded damages against X for the failure to repair the car within a reasonable time. X appealed against this judgment on the ground that there was no contract between them and the plaintiff, and that their only contract was with the insurance company. *Held*, although there was a contract by the insurers with the repairers, there was also a contract between X and the plaintiff to carry out the repairs. It was an implied term of that contract that the repairs would be carried out within a reasonable time, and as this had not been done, X was liable in damages. (See also s. 14 of the Supply of Goods and Services Act 1982; but see *Brown and Davis Ltd v Galbraith*.)

Chichester and Wife v Cobb (1866) 14 LT 433   [115]

The two plaintiffs had agreed to marry one another and the defendant wrote to the female plaintiff and promised to give her £300 when all the arrangements for the marriage were completed. The plaintiffs married but the £300 was never paid. *Held*, there was a binding contract founded on a sufficient consideration. (See also *Shadwell v Shadwell*.)

Chillingworth v Esche [1924] 1 Ch 97   [116]

The plaintiffs agreed to purchase the defendant's nursery for £4,800 'subject to a proper contract to be prepared by the vendor's solicitors'. The purchasers refused to sign a contract which had been approved by their solicitors and executed by the vendor and did not complete the transaction. *Held*, the consent was conditional upon a 'proper contract' being signed and the plaintiffs were entitled to recover their deposit. (But see *Branca v Cobarro*.)

Clarke v Dunraven, The Satanita [1897] AC 59   [117]
(House of Lords)

Two yachts were entered by their respective owners for a club race and each owner had undertaken to be bound by the club rules, one of which provided that an owner was to be liable for any damage which arose from a breach of the rules. In breach of a rule one yacht ran into and sank the other and the offended owner brought an action for damages. *Held*, there was a contract between the owners on which the owner of the damaged yacht could bring a successful action because by entering for the race and agreeing to be bound by the rules there was created by inference a contractual obligation to make good any damage caused in breach of the rules. (But see *Gibson v Manchester City Council*.)

Clay v Yates (1856) 1 H & N 73   [118]

The plaintiff, a printer, orally agreed to print for the defendant 500 copies of a book entitled 'Military Tactics', to which a dedication, which had not at that time been written, was to be prefixed. After printing had begun the plaintiff saw the dedication, which contained libellous matter, for the first time and refused to complete the work. The plaintiff sought to recover for work, labour and materials. *Held*, the plaintiff was justified in refusing to complete the printing of the book and was entitled to be paid for that part of the work which he had carried out. (See also *Cowan v Milbourn*.)

Clements v London and North Western Railway Co   [119]
[1894] 2 QB 482 (Court of Appeal)

The plaintiff, who was a minor, entered the service of the defendants as a porter and agreed to become a member of the defendants' insurance scheme, to the funds of which the defendants contributed, and to forfeit his right to sue the defendants under the Employers' Liability Acts. The insurance scheme did not restrict the payment of compensation to those cases for which the employers would otherwise be liable, but the amount of benefit payable under the scheme was rather less than that which could be recovered under the Employers' Liability Acts. The scheme also provided that claims should be forfeited in certain circumstances and that all disputes should be settled by arbitration. The plaintiff was injured in the course of his employment and sued to recover damages from the defendants. *Held*, the action must fail as the plaintiff's contract of service, which contained a clause prohibiting the institution of proceedings of this kind, was binding upon him as it was, taken as a whole, advantageous to him. (See also *Doyle v White City Stadium Ltd*.)

Cleveland Petroleum Co Ltd v Dartstone Ltd [1969]   [120]
1 All ER 201 (Court of Appeal)

S, the fee simple owner of a garage, leased the premises to the plaintiffs for 25 years. The plaintiffs granted an underlease to X Ltd, who covenanted, inter alia, not to sell or distribute motor fuels other than those supplied by the plaintiffs. Subsequently, the underlease was assigned to the defendants, who undertook to perform the covenants. The defendants challenged the validity of the tie. *Held*, the tie was valid and not an unreasonable restraint of trade because the defendants, not having been in possession previously, took possession under a lease and knowingly accepted the covenant. They thereby bound themselves to it. (See also *Esso Petroleum Co Ltd v Harper's Garage (Stourport) Ltd*.)

Clifford Davis Management Ltd v WEA Records Ltd   [121]
[1975] 1 All ER 237 (Court of Appeal)

The plaintiff was manager of a 'pop group', two of whose members were talented composers who wanted to get their songs published. He persuaded them to sign publishing agreements with him. Although they were experienced performers and were of full age, they were not experienced in business. The agreements were professionally drafted in standard form and neither of the young men took independent advice before signing. The terms of the agreements were somewhat one-sided, and bound the defendants to assign copyrights to the plaintiff for a nominal sum, subject to a royalty payment if the plaintiff chose to exploit the songs. Subsequently the plaintiff and the group split up, and the two young men wrote new songs for the group which were recorded. The plaintiff brought an action for an injunction to restrain the defendant distributors from infringing his copyright in the songs. *Held*, the defendants had established a prima facie case that the agreements were unenforceable in that they had been made in circumstances where there was inequality of bargaining power. The plaintiff's application was refused. (See also *Schroeder v Macaulay* and *Lloyds Bank Ltd v Bundy*.)

Clifton v Palumbo [1944] 2 All ER 497 (Court of Appeal)   [122]

The defendant was negotiating for the purchase of a large estate owned by the plaintiff who wrote 'I am prepared to offer you . . . my . . . estate for £600,000 . . . I also agree that a reasonable and sufficient time shall be granted to you for the examination and consideration of all the data and details necessary for the preparation of the Schedule of Completion'. *Held*, in the circumstances of the case, this letter did not amount to an offer to sell but was a preliminary statement as to price to enable negotiations to proceed. (See also *Harvey v Facey* and *Bigg v Boyd Gibbins Ltd.*)

Clubb v Hutson (1865) 18 CB (NS) 414   [123]

The plaintiff sought to enforce payment of a promissory note and the defendant contended that he should not succeed as, before making the note, the plaintiff had preferred a charge of obtaining by false pretences against the defendant and the note was given in consideration of the plaintiff consenting to withdraw the charge. *Held*, the plaintiff would fail as it was in the interest of the public that the suppression of a prosecution should not be made a matter of private bargain. (But see *Fisher & Co v Apollinaris Co.*)

Clyde Cycle Co v Hargreaves (1898) 78 LT 296   [124]

An apprentice, who was a minor, earned 21s per week and lived with his parents, bought a racing bicycle for £12 10s. The plaintiff, from whom the machine was purchased, brought an action against the apprentice to recover the balance of the price. There was evidence that the defendant had used the bicycle for racing (for which he had won several prizes) and occasionally on the road. *Held*, in the circumstances of the case and remembering that it was a common practice for persons in the defendant's position to use bicycles, the plaintiff would succeed as the machine was necessary to the defendant. (See also s. 2 of the Sale of Goods Act 1979; but see *Peters v Fleming*.)

Coggs v Bernard (1703) 2 Ld Raym 909   [125]

The defendant undertook to carry several hogsheads of brandy from one cellar to another but through neglect many gallons of brandy were spilt. It was not alleged that the defendant was a common carrier or suggested that he had been paid anything for his pains. *Held*, although no one could have compelled the defendant to remove the hogsheads, the plaintiff's trusting him with the goods was sufficient consideration to make him liable for any damage that they might sustain. (See also *Bainbridge v Firmstone*.)

Cohen v Kittell (1889) 22 QBD 680   [126]

The plaintiff employed the defendant to bet on commission. The defendant failed to carry out the plaintiff's instructions to make certain bets and the plaintiff claimed damages for breach of contract by the defendant as the plaintiff's agent. The plaintiff claimed as damages the excess of gains over losses which would have been received by the defendant if the bets had been made, less the amount of his agreed commission. *Held*, the action must fail as the bets themselves, the subject-matter of the agency, would not have been recoverable by reason of s. 18 of the Gaming Act 1845. (But see *De Mattos v Benjamin.*)

Cohen v Nessdale Ltd [1982] 2 All ER 97 (Court of Appeal)   **[127]**

The defendant landlord offered, 'subject to contract', to sell his plaintiff statutory tenant a long lease of his flat for £20,000. Negotiations continued for two months, but the tenant then broke them off as the landlord had applied to increase the rent. Six months later the parties orally agreed the sale and purchase of a 99-year lease for £17,000; later that day the landlords confirmed the agreement in writing 'subject to contract'. The plaintiff sought specific performance of the oral contract claiming that his making of the first payment of rent under the new lease was part performance. *Held*, his claim could not succeed as a 'subject to contract' qualification, once introduced into negotiations, can only cease to apply to the negotiations if the parties expressly or by necessary implication agree that it should be expunged and this was not the case here. (See also *Tiverton Estates Ltd v Wearwell*; but see *Alpenstow Ltd v Regalian Properties plc.*)

Coldunell Ltd v Gallon [1986] 1 All ER 429 (Court of Appeal)   **[128]**

A son in his fifties needed money for his business and his father offered to help him; the son arranged for the plaintiff moneylenders to lend his father £20,000 who, as the plaintiffs knew, would then give the money to the son. The loan was secured by a charge on the father's house with the son a surety. In completing the transaction, the plaintiffs' solicitors dealt solely with and through the son. They sent the parents a letter advising them to seek independent legal advice but they never received it. The parents' signatures were procured by the son in the presence of his own solicitor but he (the solicitor) did not advise them as to the nature and effect of the transaction. The son forged his father's signature on the cheque and kept the money. Neither the loan nor the interest was repaid and the plaintiffs sought to enforce the charge on the house. *Held*, they were entitled to succeed. Although the son had exercised undue influence, he had not been the plaintiffs' agent. The plaintiffs' only duty was to point out the desirability of taking independent legal advice. (Distinguished: *Kingsnorth Trust Ltd v Bell*; followed in *Bank of Baroda v Shah.*)

Collins v Godefroy (1831) 1 B & Ad 950   **[129]**

An attorney had attended a trial of a civil action for six days on the defendant's subpoena and the defendant afterwards promised to pay him a fee of six guineas. *Held*, the promise could not be enforced as the plaintiff, having been subpoenaed, was under a duty to attend and there was no consideration for the defendant's promise to pay him a fee. (But see *England v Davidson.*)

Collins v Howard [1949] 2 All ER 324 (Court of Appeal)   **[130]**

The plaintiff promised the defendant that he would provide the capital to enable them to form a limited company and, unknown to the defendant, he sold certain shares to provide the money. The defendant subsequently refused to proceed with the matter and the plaintiff bought an equal number of the same shares at an extra cost, due to fluctuation, of £245. The plaintiff sought to recover this sum by way of damages. *Held*, he could not succeed as the loss did not arise naturally from the defendant's breach of contract and there were no special circumstances by which knowledge of the dealing with the shares should be imputed to the defendant. (But see *Compania Naviera Maropan SA v Bowaters Lloyd Pulp & Paper Mills Ltd.*)

Combe v Combe [1951] 1 All ER 767 (Court of Appeal)   **[131]**

A wife had obtained a decree nisi and her solicitors wrote to the husband's solicitors to ask them to confirm that he would allow her £100 pa and they confirmed that this was the case. The wife did not apply to the court for maintenance and the husband did not observe his promise to pay her £100 pa. *Held*, as the husband had not requested the wife to refrain from making an application to the court there was no consideration for his promise; even if he had made such a request there would have been no consideration, as the wife's promise not to apply for an order would not be binding on her so as to preclude her from applying for an order for permanent maintenance. The principle stated in *Central London Property Trust Ltd v High Trees House Ltd* must be 'used as a shield and not as a sword' (*per* BIRKETT LJ). (But see *Tool Metal Manufacturing Co Ltd v Tungsten Electric Co Ltd.*)

Commercial Plastics Ltd v Vincent [1964] 3 All ER 546   [132]
(Court of Appeal)

The plaintiffs manufactured thin PVC calendered sheeting and one of the many ways in which this was used was in the manufacture of adhesive tape. In this field the plaintiffs had about twenty per cent of the United Kingdom market and they had five principal rivals, although they (the plaintiffs) manufactured about eighty per cent of the market for plastic sheeting used to make adhesive tape and this represented about twenty per cent of the plaintiffs' total production. The defendant was employed by the plaintiffs to co-ordinate research and development work in connection with adhesive tape production and his contract of service provided that he would not 'seek employment with any of our competitors in the PVC calendering field, for at least one year after leaving our employ'. The defendant gave one month's notice in accordance with the terms of his contract of service and entered the employment of one of the plaintiffs' competitors in the PVC calendering field. The plaintiffs sought to enforce the restrictive provision contained in the defendant's contract of service with them. *Held*, they would fail because the restriction was void as it was wider than was reasonably necessary for the protection of the plaintiffs' trade secrets. There was no evidence to prove that the plaintiffs needed for their protection a restriction that was potentially world-wide and the plaintiffs had failed to show that it was necessary for the restrctive provision to apply to the whole of the PVC calendering field, as opposed to the production of sheeting for adhesive tape. (See also *Strange* (SW) *Ltd v Mann.*)

Compagnie de Commerce et Commission SARL v   [133]
Parkinson Stove Co Ltd [1953] 2 Lloyd's Rep 487 (Court of Appeal)

The appellants negotiated with the respondents for the purchase of steel sheets and the respondents stipulated that the appellants should accept their offer on a certain form and that no other method of acceptance, verbal or written, would be valid. The appellants tendered their acceptance by letter but subsequently purported to cancel the order. *Held*, there had been no valid acceptance of the respondents' offer and there was no binding contract but in such cases it would be possible to hold that the respondents had waived the condition as to mode of acceptance, expressly or by conduct. (See also *Eliason v Henshaw.*)

Compania Naviera Maropan SA v Bowaters Lloyd   [134]
Pulp and Paper Mills Ltd [1955] 2 All ER 241
(Court of Appeal)

A charterparty in respect of the steamship *Stork* provided that: 'Charterers have the right to order the ship to load at two safe berths or loading places'. The charterers directed the ship to load at a place on the east coast of Newfoundland but during a heavy gale she dragged her anchors and was severely damaged. *Held*, the owners were entitled to damages for breach of contract as the charterers had ordered the vessel to load at an unsafe place. The damages flowed naturally from the charterers' breach of contract. (But see *Hadley v Baxendale.*)

Constantine (Joseph) Steamship Line Ltd v Imperial [135]
Smelting Corporation Ltd [1941] 2 All ER 165 (House of Lords)

The respondents chartered a steamship from the appellants but on the day before she was due to load her cargo an explosion occurred in the neighbourhood of her auxiliary boiler which made it impossible for the ship to undertake the voyage. The respondents claimed damages for failure to load the cargo and the appellants maintained that they were not liable as performance of the contract had been frustrated. *Held*, the case would be decided in favour of the appellants as the party denying frustration had to prove negligence on the part of the party relying on that defence and this the respondents had been unable to do. (See also *Jackson v Union Marine Insurance Co Ltd*.)

Cooden Engineering Co Ltd v Stanford [1952] [136]
2 All ER 915 (Court of Appeal)

A hire-purchase agreement in respect of a motor car provided that upon the determination of the agreement by the owners the car should be returned and the hirer should pay the instalments which were outstanding at the date of such determination and, by way of compensation for depreciation, 40 per cent of the instalments which had not yet fallen due. *Held*, this sum was a penalty and could not therefore be recovered. (But see *Stockloser v Johnson*.)

Cook v Swinfen [1967] 1 All ER 299 (Court of Appeal) [137]

The defendant solicitor was negligent in his handling of the plaintiff's divorce proceedings which, as a result, were not defended. A decree nisi was awarded against her and, because of the defendant's negligence, no maintenance was sought for her or her child. The plaintiff suffered a nervous breakdown, partly as a result of this, and also loss of earnings. She sued for damages. *Held*, the nervous breakdown was not a reasonably foreseeable consequence of the defendant's negligence, and the damage so suffered was too remote. However, Lord DENNING MR, with whom the rest of the court concurred, said 'just as in tort, so also in the law of contract, damages can be recovered for nervous shock or anxiety state if it is a reasonably foreseeable consequence.' But for 'injured feelings, mental distress, anger and annoyance' no damages can be recovered. (See also *Addis v Gramophone Co Ltd*.)

Cooper v Phibbs (1867) LR 2 HL 149 (House of Lords) [138]

The appellant sought to be relieved from an agreement whereby he contracted to take from the respondent a three-year lease of a salmon fishery. At the time of making the agreement the appellant believed that the fishery belonged to the respondent but it afterwards appeared that the fishery was the property of the appellant himself. *Held*, the appellant was entitled to have the agreement for the lease set aside subject to the respondent having a lien on the property in respect of money spent on purchasing certain fishing rights and improving the fishery. (See also *Huddersfield Banking Co Ltd v Henry Lister & Son Ltd*.)

Cooper v Willis (1906) 22 TLR 582 [139]

The parties entered into a settlement in respect of certain racing debts. The debtor, the defendant, agreed to give the plaintiff two cheques payable at a future date and not to set up a defence under the Gaming Acts if the plaintiff should need to sue upon the cheques. One cheque was dishonoured and the defendant, in breach of the terms of the settlement, relied upon the Gaming Acts by way of defence. *Held*, his defence would succeed; the agreement whereby the defendant purported to prevent himself from taking advantage of the statutory defence under the Gaming Acts was illegal and void as it prejudiced the administration of justice. (See also *Keir v Leeman*.)

Coral v Kleyman [1951] 1 All ER 518   [140]

The plaintiff was a bookmaker to whom the defendant's son had lost, but not paid, £355 15s. The defendant signed an undertaking to the effect that he would pay the amount due in consideration of the plaintiff not reporting his son to the Committee of Tattersalls. The plaintiff sued to enforce payment under the agreement. *Held*, the action would fail. The undertaking was merely a device to contravene s.18 of the Gaming Act 1845 under which the debt could not be recovered from the son. The plaintiff knew that he could not succeed against the son so his forbearance to report him to Tattersalls was not a consideration sufficient to support the contract. (See also *Hill v Hill (William) (Park Lane) Ltd.*)

Cornish v Midland Bank plc [1985] 3 All ER 513   [141]
(Court of Appeal)

The plaintiff bank customer signed a second mortgage in favour of the bank without being aware that it secured not only a loan of £2,000 for renovations to a farmhouse jointly owned with her husband, but also unlimited further advances made to the husband. *Held*, inter alia, the bank had assumed a duty to give the plaintiff proper advice as to the effect of the mortgage; it had been negligent in the way it had discharged that duty and the plaintiff was therefore entitled to damages against it. However, the mortgage itself would not be set aside; the only relationship existing between the plaintiff and the bank was that of banker and customer and no unfair advantage had been taken of her and no presumption of undue influence had arisen. (Followed: *National Westminster Bank plc v Morgan*.)

Couchman v Hill [1947] 1 All ER 103 (Court of Appeal)   [142]

The plaintiff bought a heifer at an auction and the catalogue described it as 'unserved'. The conditions of sale provided that the auctioneers gave no warranty in respect of the condition or description of any of the animals but before the sale and when the heifer was in the ring, the plaintiff asked the defendant and the auctioneer to confirm that it was 'unserved'. This confirmation was given but within eight weeks of the sale the heifer died as a result of carrying a calf at too young an age for breeding. *Held*, the statements that the heifer was 'unserved' constituted a warranty which over-rode the conditions of sale and the plaintiff was able to recover damages for breach of this warranty. (But see *Routledge v McKay*.)

Couturier v Hastie (1852) 8 Exch 40   [143]

The plaintiffs, who were merchants, shipped 1,180 quarters of Indian corn and the defendants, their del credere agents, successfully negotiated a sale. The corn had to be sold before the voyage was completed because tempestuous weather had made it heated and fermented but the plaintiffs nevertheless sought to recover the price of the cargo. The implied guarantee on the part of the defendants as to the due performance of the contract which arose from the special relationship of the parties had not been reduced to writing and the defendants maintained that they were protected under the provisions of s. 4 of the Statute of Frauds. *Held*, the defendants were liable by reason of the payment of del credere commission and not solely because of their implied guarantee and for this reason their liability was not one to pay the debt of another within the meaning of the section. (See also *Sutton & Co v Gray*.) On appeal to the House of Lords (1856) 5 HL Cas 673. *Held*, the contract contemplated that there was an existing something to be sold and bought and capable of transfer but as the corn had been sold at the time of the sale by the defendants this was not the case and the defendants were not liable. (See also *Scott v Coulson*; but see *McRae v Commonwealth Disposals Commission*.)

Cowan v Milbourn (1867) LR 2 Exch 230 [144]

The defendant agreed to let certain assembly rooms to the plaintiff, but on discovering that it was intended to use the rooms for the purpose of delivering lectures which were to be blasphemous in content the defendant withdraw his consent to the letting. The plaintiff claimed damages for breach of contract. *Held*, the plaintiff could not recover. The purpose for which the rooms were let was illegal and for this reason the contract between the parties could not be enforced at law. (See also *Clay v Yates*.)

Cowan v O'Connor (1888) 20 QBD 640 [145]

An order to make certain bets was telegraphed from Regent Street to Ludgate Circus and a reply by telegram from Ludgate Circus said 'You are on'. *Held*, the contract was made at Ludgate Circus and consequently the action for breach of such contract was within the jurisdiction of the Lord Mayor's Court. (But see *Entores Ltd v Miles Far East Corporation*.)

Cowern v Nield [1912] 2 KB 419 [146]

The defendant was a minor who carried on business as a hay and straw merchant. The plaintiff ordered some clover and hay and sent his cheque in settlement. The goods were never delivered and the plaintiff brought an action to recover the amount which he had paid. *Held*, the plaintiff's claim must fail as the transaction in question was a trading contract and whether or not it was for the benefit of the defendant, in the absence of fraud, he could not be liable under such an agreement.

Cox v Philips Industries Ltd [1976] 3 All ER 161 [147]

The plaintiff claimed damages from his employers for breach of contract as they had removed him to a position of less responsibility where the duties were very vague. As a result he had become frustrated, depressed and ill. When he complained about the situation, he was made redundant and was given five months' salary in lieu of notice. He claimed damages for the vexation and frustration caused by the breach. The employers claimed that damages for emotional distress were limited to contracts for pleasure and enjoyment. *Held*, it was within the contemplation of the employers when they had originally given the plaintiff a position of responsibility that a breach of the contract would lead to frustration and distress. Consequently he was entitled to compensation for the emotional distress caused by the breach. Damages for emotional distress arising from a breach of contract were not limited to contracts for giving pleasure and enjoyment. (See also *Jarvis v Swans Tours Ltd* and *Addis v Gramophone Co Ltd*.)

Cricklewood Property and Investment Trust Ltd v [148]
Leightons Investment Trust Ltd
[1945] 1 All ER 252 (House of Lords)

A building lease was entered into in 1936 for a term of 99 years whereby the tenants were to erect a number of shops to form a shopping centre. War came before the work was completed and the tenants refused to pay the rent reserved by the lease on the ground that the lease had been frustrated by restrictions imposed by the Government on building and the supply of materials. *Held*, the tenants' view would not be supported as the interruption of building did not destroy the identity of the arrangement or make it unreasonable to carry out the work as soon as the restrictions were lifted. (See also *Eyre v Johnson* and *National Carriers Ltd v Panalpina (Northern) Ltd*.)

Crow v Rogers (1724) 1 Stra 592   [149]

John Hardy owed the plaintiff £70 and it was agreed between Hardy and the defendant that the defendant would pay the plaintiff £70 in return for a promise by Hardy that he would convey his house to the defendant. The plaintiff sought to recover £70 from the defendant. *Held*, the action must fail as the plaintiff was a stranger to the consideration. (See also *Price v Easton*.)

Cumber v Wane (1721) 1 Stra 426   [150]

The defendant gave the plaintiff a promissory note for £5 in satisfaction of a debt of £15. *Held*, the plaintiff could recover the balance. (See also *D & C Builders Ltd v Rees*.)

Cundy v Lindsay (1878) 3 App Cas 459 (House of Lords)   [151]

Messrs Lindsay & Co were linen manufacturers in Belfast and Alfred Blenkarn, who occupied a room in a house looking into Wood Street, Cheapside, wrote to them and proposed buying a quantity of their goods. Blenkarn used the address '37, Wood Street' Cheapside' and signed the letters, without using an initial or Christian name, in such a way that his signature appeared to be 'Blenkiron & Co'. There was a highly respectable firm of W. Blenkiron & Son carrying on business at 123, Wood Street and Messrs Lindsay & Co, who knew of this firm's reputation but not the number of the premises where they carried on business, supplied the goods ordered by Blenkarn and addressed them to Messrs Blenkiron & Co, 37, Wood Street, Cheapside. Blenkarn did not pay for the goods but disposed of them to the defendants who were sued by Messrs Lindsay & Co for unlawful conversion. *Held*, no contract had been concluded with Blenkarn, who therefore had no property in the goods to transfer to the defendants; consequently the defendants were liable to the extent of their value. (But see *Henderson & Co v Williams*.)

Curtis v Chemical Cleaning and Dyeing Co Ltd   [152]
[1951] 1 All ER 631 (Court of Appeal)

The plaintiff took a white satin wedding dress to the defendants for cleaning. She was asked to sign a document which contained a clause that the dress 'is accepted on condition that the company is not liable for any damage howsoever arising' but, before she signed, she was told that the effect of the document which she was about to sign was to exclude liability fo damage to beads or sequins. Without reading all the terms of the document the plaintiff then signed as she was asked. The dress was stained due to the negligence of the defendants. *Held*, the defendants were liable as the innocent misrepresentation as to the extent of the exception clause had the effect of excluding the clause from the contract between the parties. (See also s.13 of the Supply of Goods and Services Act 1982; but see *L'Estrange v F. Graucob Ltd*.)

Cutter v Powell (1795) 6 Term Rep 320   [153]

The defendant agreed to pay Cutter 30 guineas 'provided he proceeds, continues and does his duty as second mate' on a voyage from Kingston, Jamaica, to Liverpool. Cutter began the journey but died when the ship was about one week's sail from Liverpool. His administratrix sought to recover a proportion of the agreed wage in respect of that part of the journey for which Cutter had acted as a second mate. *Held*, she was unable to succeed as Cutter had not performed his part of the contract. (See also *Appleby v Myers*.)

D & C Builders Ltd v Rees [1965] 3 All ER 837   [154]
(Court of Appeal)

The plaintiffs had carried out work for the defendant to the value of £482 13s 1d. For months they pressed for payment. Finally, the defendant's wife, who knew that the plaintiffs were in financial difficulties, offered £300 in settlement of the debt, saying that if the offer were not accepted, nothing would be paid. The plaintiffs accepted a cheque for £300 and gave a receipt 'in completion of the account'. Later, they sued for the balance, and the question arose whether the action was barred by accord and satisfaction. *Held*, the plaintiffs were not barred from recovering the balance. There was no true accord because the plaintiffs' consent had been obtained under pressure, nor was there any equitable ground disentitling them to recover. (See also *Pinnel's Case* and *Foakes v Beer*.)

Dakin (H.) & Co Ltd v Lee [1916] 1 KB 566 (Court of Appeal)   **[155]**

The plaintiffs, who were builders, sought to recover the balance of the price of certain repairs carried out at the defendant's house. The defendant resisted their claim as concrete underpinning a wall was 2 ft thick instead of 4 ft as specified in the contract, columns of solid iron 4 in in diameter had been used instead of hollow iron 5 in in diameter and certain joists over the bay window had not been bolted as stipulated. *Held*, the plaintiffs were entitled to recover the balance of their charges, less an amount in respect of that part of the work which had been carried out contrary to the specification, as the defendant could only withhold payment if he could show that the total work carried out by the plaintiffs was of no benefit to him, that it was entirely different to that which they contracted to do or that they had abandoned the work and left it unfinished. (Distinguished in *Bolton v Mahadera*; but see *Sumpter v Hedges*.)

Daly v General Steam Navigation Co Ltd, The Dragon   **[156]**
[1979] 1 Lloyd's Rep 257

The plaintiff was injured when a mooring cable on a cross-Channel ferry lashed her shoulder when the vessel was casting off. The defendants claimed that they were protected by an exclusion clause in the ticket. The plaintiff argued that the contract ran from the date of booking the ticket and that as the booking had been accepted with no mention of any conditions of carriage, none could apply. The ticket containing the conditions of carriage had subsequently arrived by post. *Held*, the contract was effective from the date the plaintiff's booking was accepted, at which time no conditions had been brought to the plaintiff's attention. Conditions could not be incorporated subsequently and thus the defendants were not able to rely on the exemption clause. (See also *Interfoto Picture Library Ltd v Stiletto Visual Programmes Ltd*.)

Daniels v Trefusis [1914] 1 Ch 788   **[157]**

There was an oral agreement for the purchase of certain land and the vendor, at the request of the purchaser, assented to give notice to two tenants who gave up possession in consequence. *Held*, the vendor was entitled to specific performance as the giving of notice constituted an act of part performance which was unequivocally referable to the contract which he alleged had been concluded between the parties. (See also *Rawlinson v Ames*.)

Davies v Collins [1945] 1 All ER 247 (Court of Appeal)   **[158]**

The respondent took his uniform to the appellants for cleaning and repair. He was handed a docket which stipulated that 'Whilst every care is exercised cleaning and dyeing garments, all orders are accepted at owner's risk entirely and we are unable to hold ourselves responsible for damage, shrinkage, colour or defects developed in necessary handling. The proprietors' liability for loss is limited to an amount not exceeding 10 times the cost of cleaning.' The uniform was sent to a sub-contractor but was never returned and the respondent claimed the full value of the uniform. *Held*, he was entitled to recover the amount for which he claimed as the mere presence of a limitation clause in this form was sufficient to exclude the appellants' right to send the uniform to another contractor and therefore when they did allow another to perform the work they were in breach of their contract and denied such protection as it may have otherwise afforded. (See also *Woolmer v Delmer Price Ltd.*)

Davies v London and Provincial Marine Insurance Co   [159]
(1878) 8 Ch D 469

In the belief that the retention of money by one of their agents amounted to a felony, the company ordered his arrest. Friends of the suspected person offered to deposit a sum of money by way of security for his defaults but while the offer was being considered the company was advised that the agent had not committed a felony and the directions for his arrest were withdrawn. At a second interview on the same day, the friends agreed to deposit the money as a security for any deficiency but they were not told that the directions for the arrest of their friend had been withdrawn. *Held*, this agreement should be rescinded as the agent's friends ought to have been told of the change of circumstances. (See also *Williams v Bayley.*)

Davies v Sweet [1962] 1 All ER 91 (Court of Appeal)   [160]

The plaintiff offered to a partner in X & Co, a firm of estate agents, £75 for certain land. A deposit of £5 was paid and a receipt was written on the firm's notepaper headed 'chartered auctioneer and estate agent', which read, so far as is material, 'Received from D a deposit of £5 for land on which Evans Row houses previously stood . . . sold at £75 . . . X & Co'. It was found by the court that the estate agents had authority to enter into a contract on behalf of the vendor. The plaintiff sought specific performance. *Held*, there was a sufficient memorandum in writing to satisfy s. 40(1) of the Law of Property Act 1925, the vendor being sufficiently described, since the receipt contained nothing to show that the firm signed as agents for a principal, and since an agent who contracted in his own name did not cease to be contractually bound because the other party knew, when the contract was made, that he was acting as agent. (See also *Hawkins v Price.*)

Davis Contractors Ltd v Fareham Urban District   [161]
Council [1956] 2 All ER 145 (House of Lords)

The plaintiffs contracted to build the defendants 78 council houses within eight months for a fixed price. Through no fault on the part of the plaintiffs there was a scarcity of skilled labour and the work took 22 months to complete. The plaintiffs maintained that by reason of the scarcity of labour the contract had been brought to an end and that they were entitled to recover a sum in excess of the contract price on the basis of a quantum meruit. *Held*, their claim should fail, as the scarcity of labour had not frustrated the contract and the plaintiffs had not been released from its terms as regards price. (See also *Tsakiroglou & Co Ltd v Noblee & Thorl GmbH.*)

Deacons v Bridge [1984] 2 All ER 19 (Privy Council)   [162]

The plaintiffs were a large firm of solicitors in Hong Kong and, before he resigned to set up his own practice there, the defendant was the partner in charge of the intellectual property and trade marks department which, like the other departments, was largely self-contained. The partnership agreement provided, inter alia, that if a partner ceased to be a partner he was not to act as a solicitor in Hong Kong for a period of five years for any client of the firm or any person who had been a client in the preceding three years. *Held*, the plaintiffs were entitled to an injunction to enforce the restrictive covenant the terms of which, in all the circumstances, were not unreasonable. It was reasonable, as between the parties, for the firm to protect itself against the appropriation by the defendant of any part of the firm's goodwill, notwithstanding the division of the firm's practice into self-contained departments (See also *Kerr v Morris.*)

De Francesco v Barnum (1890) 45 Ch D 430   **[163]**

A minor and her mother executed a deed whereby the infant, who was to be apprenticed to the plaintiff for seven years with a view to being taught stage dancing, agreed that she would not marry or accept any professional engagements during the period of her apprenticeship without the consent of the plaintiff. The contract also contained terms whereby the young woman was to be paid a certain small sum for such engagements as she should fulfil, but there was no stipulation that the plaintiff should provide engagements for the infant or maintain her while she was unemployed. In breach of this agreement she signed a contract to dance for the defendant and the plaintiff sought to enforce the provisions of the deed and claimed damages for breach of contract. *Held*, the claim must fail as the provisions of the deed were unreasonable and could not be enforced against the minor or her mother and no action would lie against the defendant for enticing her away from the plaintiff's employment. (But see *Clements v London & North Western Railway Co.*)

De La Bere v Pearson Ltd [1908] 1 KB 280   **[164]**

The defendants advertised in their newspaper that their city editor would advise readers on financial matters. The plaintiff wrote to ask for the name of a 'good stockbroker'. The editor recommended a broker whose honesty he had no reason to doubt but who was, in fact, an undischarged bankrupt. The plaintiff sent £1,400 to the broker who immediately misappropriated the money and the plaintiff sued the defendants for breach of contract. *Held*, the defendants were liable for breach of their contract (the defendants' advertisement was the offer and the plaintiff accepted it when he wrote to them) to use reasonable care that the person recommended should answer the description of a 'good stockbroker'. 'There was a contract as between the plaintiff and the defendants . . . to take reasonable care in the nomination of a broker, and I think there was a clear breach of this contract . . . the measure of damages would include all damage which would be sustained by the plaintiff through consequences arising in strict course of business with a stockbroker' (*per* VAUGHAN WILLIAMS LJ).

De Lassalle v Guildford [1901] 2 KB 215 (Court of Appeal)   **[165]**

The parties agreed terms for the lease of a house but the plaintiff refused to hand over the counterpart of the lease until he had received a verbal assurance that the drains were in order. The drains were not in good order and the plaintiff sought to recover damages for breach of warranty. *Held*, the plaintiff would succeed as the verbal assurance constituted a warranty which was collateral to the lease and for the breach of which an action could be maintained. (See also *Otto (M) and E Otto v Bolton and Norris.*)

De Mattos v Benjamin (1894) 63 LJQB 248   **[166]**

The plaintiff employed the defendant to make bets for him as his agent but the defendant failed to pay him the winnings. When sued for money had and received the defendant relied on s. 1 of the Gaming Act 1892. *Held*, the plaintiff could recover as the Act would not be allowed to enable a person who had received money on behalf of another to retain it for his own use. (See also *Bridger v Savage.*)

Denman v Brise [1948] 2 All ER 141 (Court of Appeal)   **[167]**

A house let on a monthly tenancy and subject to the Rent Acts was destroyed by enemy action and when the landlord erected a new building the former tenant claimed to be entitled to possession. *Held*, judgment would be given in favour of the tenant as the contractual relationship of landlord and tenant was not destroyed under the doctrine of frustration since this has no application to a demise of real property. (See also *Hillingdon Estates Co v Stonefield Estates Ltd*; but see *National Carriers Ltd v Panalpina (Northern) Ltd.*)

Dennant v Skinner [1948] 2 All ER 29   [168]

A van had been knocked down to the highest bidder and the auctioneer asked him his name. The bidder said that his name was King and that he was the son of the proprietor of King's Motors of Oxford, a firm of high repute, which he was representing. These representations were repeated and certain evidence as to his identity produced when the man offered to pay by cheque but it transpired, after his cheque had been dishonoured, that although his name was King he had no connection with the well-known firm of King's Motors. The plaintiff, the seller of the car, sued to recover the car or its value from the person to whom King had sold it. *Held*, the contract was made when the hammer fell and at that moment there was no mistake as to the identity of the bidder and the property in the car passed to him. He was therefore able to give the defendant a good title to the car and for this reason the action would fail. (But see *Hardman v Booth*.)

Denton v Great Northern Railway Co (1856) 5 E & B 860   [169]

The defendants issued a time-table and the plaintiff presented himself at a station to catch a train which was advertised therein, but which did not run. *Held*, the circulation of the time-table was an offer by the defendants which was accepted by the plaintiff when he tendered the price of his ticket. (But see *Spencer v Harding*.)

Derry v Peek (1889) 14 App Cas 337 (House of Lords)   [170]

The Plymouth, Devonport and District Tramways Co was authorised to make certain tramways by special Act of Parliament which provided that the carriages might be moved by animal power and, with the consent of the Board of Trade, by steam or any mechanical power for fixed periods and subject to the regulations of the Board. The company issued a prospectus stating that 'one great feature of this undertaking, to which considerable importance should be attached, is, that by special Act of Parliament obtained, the company has the right to use steam or mechanical motive power, instead of horses'. The plaintiff bought shares on the faith of this statement but the Board of Trade afterwards refused their consent to the use of steam power and the company was wound up. At the time of issuing the prospectus the company honestly believed that consent would be granted as a matter of course. *Held*, the plaintiff's action in deceit must fail, as the statement contained in the prospectus was not a fraudulent misrepresentation as the company entertained an honest belief that it was true. (See also *Akerhielm v De Mare*.)

Diamond v Campbell-Jones [1960] 1 All ER 583   [171]

The defendants wrongly repudiated an agreement for the sale by the defendants to the plaintiff of a leasehold property in Mayfair and the question arose as to the amount of damages that the plaintiff was entitled to recover. The agreement was subject to and with the benefit of a contract for the grant of a new lease and this contract required the premises to be converted by the lessee into ground floor office accommodation and residential maisonettes. The plaintiff was a dealer in real property but it was not shown that the defendants were aware of this or that he intended to carry out a conversion of the premises. *Held*, the amount of damages should be limited to the difference between the purchase price and the market value at the date of the breach of contract as there were no special circumstances sufficient to impute to the defendants knowledge that the plaintiff intended to convert the property for profit. (See also *Ardennes (Cargo Owners) v Ardennes (Owners)*.)

Dickinson v Dodds (1876) 2 Ch D 463 (Court of Appeal)   [172]

The defendant signed a document which took the form of an agreement to sell certain property to the plaintiff but added a postscript 'This offer to be left over until Friday . . .' The plaintiff decided to buy the property on the day before the offer (it was found that the document constituted an offer and not an agreement) expired but on the Thursday afternoon he heard from another person that the defendant had contracted to sell the property to a third party. On the Thursday evening the plaintiff delivered a formal acceptance at the house where the defendant was staying, and at about seven o'clock on the following morning a duplicate of this acceptance was handed to the defendant. The plaintiff sought a decree of specific performance. *Held*, the decree would not be awarded as retraction of an offer need not be express and in this case was implied by the sale of the property to the third party. 'If a man who makes an offer dies, the offer cannot be accepted after he is dead' (*per* MELLISH LJ). (See also *Cartwright v Hoogstoel*.)

Dies v British and International Mining and Finance Corporation Ltd [1939] 1 KB 724   [173]

The purchaser ordered rifles and cartridges to the value of £270,000 and paid £100,000 by way of prepayment of part of the purchase price. The purchaser afterwards refused to take delivery of the goods and to pay the balance of the purchase price and the vendors elected to treat the contract as at an end. The purchaser sought to recover the amount of his prepayment. *Held*, he was entitled to succeed, subject to the payment of damages to the vendors in respect of his breach of contract. (See also *O'Neil v Armstrong, Mitchell & Co.*)

Diggle v Higgs (1877) 2 Ex D 422 (Court of Appeal)   [174]

Two men agreed to walk a match for £200 a side, the money to be deposited with a stakeholder, the defendant, and paid to the winner. The plaintiff lost the match but before the defendant had paid over the stakes to the winner gave notice to the defendant that he was not to pay the winner and demanded the £200 which he, the plaintiff, had deposited with the defendant. The defendant nevertheless paid £400 to the winner and the plaintiff sued to recover £200. *Held*, he was entitled to succeed. The proviso to s.18 of the Gaming Act 1845, rendered the contract void but this did not prevent the plaintiff from recovering the amount of his own deposit from the stakeholder although the winner would not have been able to recover that of the plaintiff if the defendant had withheld payment. (See also *Varney v Hickman*.)

Doyle v White City Stadium Ltd [1935] 1 KB 110 (Court of Appeal)   [175]

The plaintiff, a minor, was a boxer and a term of the contract with the British Boxing Board of Control by which he was granted a licence to box provided that payment of the money due to a boxer might be withheld if he was disqualified for one of various reasons. The plaintiff took part in a contest for the heavyweight championship of Great Britain but was disqualified in the second round. The plaintiff sought to recover the amount due to him in respect of the fight and contended that he was not bound by the terms of the contract with the British Boxing Board of Control as he was an infant. *Held*, the plaintiff's action must fail as he was bound by the agreement, which was closely analogous to a contract of employment, because it was, on the whole, for his benefit. (See also *Slade v Metrodent Ltd* and *Chaplin v Leslie Frewin (Publishers) Ltd*.)

Dunlop Pneumatic Tyre Co Ltd v New Garage and Motor Co Ltd [1915] AC 79 (House of Lords)   [176]

The appellants, manufacturers of motor tyres, supplied goods to the respondents under a contract which provided that the respondents would not sell tyres at less than the appellants' list price. It was further provided that if the respondents sold a tyre in breach of this agreement they would pay the appellants £5. *Held*, this sum would be regarded as liquidated damages and not as a penalty. (But see *Ford Motor Co (England) Ltd v Armstrong*.)

Dunlop Pneumatic Tyre Co Ltd v Selfridge & Co   [177]
Ltd [1915] AC 847 (House of Lords)

The defendants, who were large storekeepers and sold tyres retail to the public, ordered tyres made by the plaintiffs from Messrs. A. J. Dew & Co, who were motor accessory factors. In accordance with the requirements of a contract between the plaintiffs and Messrs. A. J. Dew & Co, an agreement purporting to be made between the defendants and Messrs A. J. Dew & Co, provided that in consideration of Messrs A. J. Dew & Co allowing them certain discounts off the plaintiffs' list prices, the defendants would not sell or offer any tyres made by the plaintiffs at less than list prices. The plaintiffs sued the defendants for breach of this agreement. *Held*, their action could not succeed as 'only a person who is a party to a contract can sue on it' (*per* Viscount HALDANE LC). (See also *Scruttons Ltd v Midland Silicones Ltd*; but see *Gregory and Parker v Williams*.)

Dutton v Poole (1678) Freem 471   [178]

The defendant's father intended to cut down some oak trees to make provision for his children, including the plaintiff, but the defendant promised his father that if he spared the trees he (the defendant) would give his sister (the plaintiff) £1,000. The plaintiff sought to enforce this promise. *Held*, she was entitled to do so. (But see *Crow v Rogers*.)

EP Finance Co Ltd v Dooley [1964] 1 All ER 527   [179]

Under the terms of a hire-purchase agreement in respect of a second-hand Bentley motor car, in the event of the termination of the agreement by the return of the vehicle the defendant hirer was liable to pay to the plaintiff hire-purchase company all arrears of rent calculated on a daily basis, the cost of repairs and replacement and 'by way of agreed depreciation . . . a sum equal to fifty per cent of the total hire-purchase price . . . plus a further five per cent of such total hire-purchase price for each month which has elapsed between the receipt of the [car] by the owners up to seventy-five per cent of the said total price less . . . the total of the sum already paid and the moneys due to the owners for hire rentals at the date of the receipt of the [car] by them'. The defendant contended that this clause constituted a penalty and therefore could not be relied upon by the plaintiffs. *Held*, the formula used was not a genuine pre-estimate of the damage in this particular case and it followed that the clause was a penalty. However, the plaintiffs were entitled to recover damages for breach of the agreement as opposed to a sum under the terms of the agreement, in this case one month's arrears, with interest, and the cost of repairs. (But see *Dunlop Pneumatic Tyre Co Ltd v New Garage and Motor Co Ltd*.)

Eastes v Russ [1914] 1 Ch 468 (Court of Appeal)   [180]

The plaintiff, a pathologist, carried on the business of 'The Laboratories of Pathology and Public Health' in Queen Ann Street and there were only two or three similar institutions in London. At that time this work involved a new method of medical research. The defendant was engaged by the plaintiff as an assistant microscopist and a term of his contract of employment stipulated that he would not engage in any similar work within ten miles of the plaintiff's laboratory. The defendant left the plaintiff's employment and shortly afterwards established a pathological laboratory within half a mile of that of the plaintiff. The plaintiff sought to restrain him. *Held*, the restriction, which, in the absence of any provision to the contrary, lasted during the whole of the defendant's life, was wider than was reasonably necessary for the protection of the plaintiff and was therefore void. (But see *Fitch v Dewes*.)

Eastham v Newcastle United Football Club Ltd   [181]
[1963] 3 All ER 139

The plaintiff entered into a contract of employment with Newcastle United but later sought a transfer to another club. Newcastle United were unwilling to release him and placed him on their list of retained players, although his yearly contract with them had not been renewed. Under the rules of the Football Association and the regulations of the Football League while so retained the plaintiff was unable to play for another club in England, Scotland, Northern Ireland, Eire and most other countries where association football is played, provided Newcastle United offered him a 'reasonable' wage. *Held*, the plaintiff was entitled to declarations that his retention was not binding upon his as it was an unlawful restraint of trade. 'There may be players who have shown quite plainly that they are not going to continue with a particular club or to re-sign with it, and in their case, placing them on the retain list does substantially interfere with their right to seek other employment and—I emphasise this—does so at a time when they are not the employees of the retaining club. That seems to me to operate substantially in restraint of trade' (*per* WILBERFORCE J).

Eastwood v Kenyon (1840) 11 Ad & El 438   [182]

The plaintiff incurred expense in the maintenance and education of a child to whom he was guardian and in the management and improvement of her property. The plaintiff borrowed money to enable him to make this provision for the child and when she became of age she promised to repay this loan and the defendant, who became the girl's husband, made a similar promise. *Held*, the plaintiff could not recover as there was no consideration to support the defendant's promise to pay and mere moral obligation was not sufficient. (See also *Thomas v Thomas*.)

Edgington v Fitzmaurice (1885) 29 Ch D 459   [183]
(Court of Appeal)

The directors of a company issued a prospectus inviting subscriptions for debentures and stating that their purpose in issuing debentures was to complete alterations to the company's premises, purchase horses and vans and develop trade. The plaintiff advanced money on certain of these debentures in reliance upon the statements in the prospectus and in the erroneous belief that the debenture holders would have a charge upon the property, but it turned out that the real object of the loan was to enable the directors to pay off pressing liabilities. *Held*, the mis-statement of the objects for which the debentures were issued was a material mis-statement of fact which rendered the directors liable in deceit although the plaintiff was influenced by his own mistake as to the effect of the transaction. (See also *Wells v Smith*.)

Edwards v Carter [1893] AC 360 (House of Lords)   [184]

The father of an intended husband, who was nearly of age, made a marriage settlement whereby the father promised to pay an annuity and the son agreed to vest in the trustees of the settlement upon certain trusts all property to which he should become entitled under the father's will. The father died nearly four years after the execution of the settlement and left certain property to his son. More than a year after the death of his father the son purported to repudiate the settlement. *Held*, he would have been able to do so within a reasonable time of his coming of age as the settlement as regards the son was voidable, not void, but as he had not repudiated the settlement within a reasonable time he was bound by its terms.

Edwards v Skyways Ltd [1964] 1 All ER 494   [185]

The plaintiff was told that it was necessary for the defendants, his employers, to declare a redundancy of approximately fifteen per cent of their pilot strength and, in accordance with the terms of his contract of service, he was given three months' notice of termination. In discussions between the defendants and the British Air Line Pilots Association (duly authorized agents of the plaintiff) it was agreed that pilots declared redundant would receive from the defendants an ex gratia payment approximating to the amount contributed by the defendants for each member of a pension fund. The plaintiff, a member of the pension fund, sought to recover a sum equal to the contributions made by the defendants to the pension fund on his behalf. *Held*, the plaintiff was entitled to succeed. The use of the words 'ex gratia' did not by itself warrant the conclusion that the promise was not intended by the parties to be enforceable in law, i.e., that there was no intention to enter into legal relations, and the fact that the agreed payment was to be of an amount 'approximating to' the amount of the defendants' contributions did not make the agreement unenforceable on the ground that its terms were too vague. 'In a case of this nature the onus is on the party who asserts that no legal effect was intended, and the onus is a heavy one' (*per* MEGAW J). (But see in *Kleinwort Benson Ltd v Malaysia Mining Corpn Bhd*; see also *Parker v Clark*.)

Egerton v Earl Brownlow (1835) 4 HL Cas 1   **[186]**
(House of Lords)

A testator provided that if Lord Alford should die without having acquired the title of Duke or Marquis of Bridgwater certain gifts to him and his issue should fail. *Held*, this condition was void as it was contrary to public policy and the gifts in the will were not to be affected by it.

Elias v George Sahely & Co (Barbados) Ltd [1982]   **[187]**
3 All ER 801 (Privy Council)

By telephone, the parties agreed the sale and purchase of certain premises and, later that day, the purchaser's lawyer wrote to the vendor's lawyer confirming the contract and enclosing a cheque as a deposit, adding that the deposit was 'to be held by you as stakeholder pending completion of the contract for sale'. The vendor's lawyer sent a receipt for the deposit but did not acknowledge the letter. The purchaser sought specific performance. *Held*, he was entitled to succeed. On the facts, an oral contract had been concluded and it would be enforced because the letter (setting out the terms of the concluded bargain) and the receipt together constituted a sufficient memorandum of the sale for the purposes of the Barbados Statute of Frauds. Although the vendor's lawyer had received the deposit as stakeholder it did not follow that he could not sign (the receipt) on behalf of the vendor. (See also *Steadman v Steadman*.)

Eliason v Henshaw (1819) 4 Wheaton 225 (Supreme   **[188]**
Court of the United States)

A offered to purchase flour from B and the letter which contained this offer stipulated the price to be paid and mode of transport and in a postscript A added: 'Please write by return of wagon whether you accept our offer'. B accepted the offer but in a letter sent by the first regular mail and A contended that it was not a valid acceptance as it was not sent 'by return of wagon'. *Held*, there was no contract as an offer creates no obligation unless it is accepted according to the terms on which the offer was made. Any departure from these terms invalidates the offer unless the different mode of acceptance is agreed by the person who made the offer. (See also *Tinn v Hoffmann & Co.*)

Ellen v Topp (1851) 6 Exch 424   **[189]**

Richard Topp, a minor, was an apprentice to an 'auctioneer, appraiser, and corn-factor'. Before Richard's apprenticeship was completed the master gave up the trade of corn-factor and Richard maintained that because of this he was no longer bound by the apprenticeship deed. *Held*, this argument would be upheld as the master had by his own choice disabled himself from acting as master in all three trades. (But see *Laws v London Chronicle (Indicator Newspapers) Ltd*.)

Ellesmere (Earl) v Wallace [1929] 2 Ch 1 (Court of Appeal)   **[190]**

The defendant nominated his horse 'Master Michael' for two races at Newmarket. The horse did not run and the plaintiffs, the Jockey Club, sued to recover the entrance fee. The defendant maintained that these sums could not be recovered as they were payable under a wagering contract. *Held*, the plaintiffs were entitled to succeed as they, one of the parties to the contract, did not stand to win or lose anything by the entry of the defendant's horse for these two races. The contract was not, therefore, a wagering contract. (See also *Thacker v Hardy*.)

Empire Meat Co Ltd v Patrick [1939] 2 All ER 85   **[191]**
(Court of Appeal)

The respondents were the owners of a butcher's business carried on in Mill Road, Cambridge, and the appellant was their manager. The appellant had contracted that he would not establish a rival business of butcher or meat seller within a distance of five miles of the respondents' shop, but he left their employment and shortly afterwards opened a butcher's shop a few doors away. There was evidence that the vast majority of the trade of the respondents' shop was done within a mile or even a half-mile of their premises. *Held*, the appellant's covenant could not be enforced as the area of restriction was, in the circumstances of the case, unnecessarily wide. (See also *M & S Drapers v Reynolds*.)

England v Davidson (1840) 11 Ad & El 856   **[192]**

The defendant offered a reward of £50 to anyone who gave information which led to the conviction of a certain felon and the plaintiff, a police constable, supplied the information. The defendant argued that the promise was of no effect as the plaintiff was bound to supply such information as part of his duty as a policeman. *Held*, the giving of the information was consideration for the defendant's promise to pay the reward and the plaintiff would succeed in his action to recover it. (See also *Glasbrook Brothers Ltd v Glamorgan County Council*.)

English Hop Growers Ltd v Dering [1928] 2 KB 174   **[193]**
(Court of Appeal)

The plaintiff society, English Hop Growers Ltd, was formed to organise the marketing and sale of home-grown hops. The defendant was a member and undertook to deliver to the society all hops grown or produced by him during 1926 on certain land consisting of 63 acres. It was provided that if any of his hops should not be delivered in accordance with the provisions of this agreement the defendant would pay to the society liquidated damages of £100 per acre. The defendant failed to deliver any hops and the plaintiff society sued to recover £6,300. *Held*, they were entitled to succeed as the agreement was not unreasonable as being in restraint of trade. The contract had been entered into from equal positions of bargaining and to their mutual advantage as it sought to avoid undue competition and excessive fluctuations of price. (See also *Hitchcock v Coker*; but see *McEllistrim v Ballymacelligott Co-operative etc, Society Ltd*.)

Entores Ltd v Miles Far East Corporation [1955]   **[194]**
2 All ER 493 (Court of Appeal)

The parties entered into an agreement by means of telex whereby each company had in its office (the plaintiffs were in London and the defendants in Amsterdam) a teleprinter which was connected by the Post Office to a teleprinter in the other office so that a message typed on one would be automatically typed out by the other. The contract was broken and the question arose as to where the contract had been concluded. *Held*, in cases where there was instantaneous communication, the contract was made when and where the acceptance was received; in this case, in London. (Approved in *Brinkibon Ltd v Stahag Stahl und Stahlwarenhandelsgesellschaft mbH*; but see *Cowan v O'Connor*.)

Ertel Bieber & Co v Rio Tinto Co Ltd [1918] AC 260   [195]
(House of Lords)

An English company contracted to supply three German companies with cuperous sulphur ore. The agreement contained a provision that the contract was to be suspended in the event of war. War came and the English company sought declarations that the contracts were abrogated by that event. *Held*, notwithstanding the suspensory clause, the contracts had become illegal and void and the declarations asked for would be made.

Esso Petroleum Co Ltd v Harper's Garage   [196]
(Stourport) Ltd [1967] 1 All ER 699 (House of Lords)

The respondents, owners of Corner Garage, charged the same by way of legal mortgage to the appellants to secure the repayment of a principal sum of £7,000 and covenanted to repay that sum with interest by quarterly instalments over twenty-one years, and during the continuance of the mortgage to purchase exclusively from the appellants all motor fuels which they might require at Corner Garage. The mortgage further provided that the respondents were not entitled to redeem the security otherwise than in accordance with the covenant as to repayment. *Held*, the mortgage stipulation relating to the purchase of fuel was within the ambit of the legal doctrine relating to covenants in restraint of trade, and it was unenforceable as being in unreasonable restraint of trade, and the respondents were entitled to redeem the mortgage. (Applied in *Alec Lobb (Garages) Ltd v Total Oil (GB) Ltd*; but see *Cleveland Petroleum Co Ltd v Dartstone Ltd*.)

Esso Petroleum Co Ltd v Mardon   [197]
[1976] 2 All ER 5 (Court of Appeal)

The plaintiffs granted a tenancy of a new filling-station to the defendant. Before the tenancy was granted, the plaintiffs' representative told the defendant that they estimated an annual throughput of petrol of 200,000 gallons a year by a third year, although the defendant thought that a lower figure was more realistic. The defendant took the tenancy in reliance on the estimate. After three years the throughput was less than 100,000 gallons a year, largely because of the physical characteristics and lay-out of the site. The defendant was unable to make a profit, could not pay for the petrol, and the plaintiffs resumed possession. The issue was whether the defendant could recover on a counterclaim against the plaintiffs for breach of warranty and/or negligence in respect of the plaintiffs' estimate. *Held*, the counterclaim should succeed, and the plaintiffs were liable to the defendant for breach of warranty and also for negligence. The measure of damages was the loss the defendant has suffered by reason of having been induced to enter into the disastrous contract. (See also *Bentley (Dick) Productions Ltd v Harold Smith*.)

Euro-Diam Ltd v Bathurst [1988] 2 All ER 23   [198]
(Court of Appeal)

The plaintiffs, an English company, supplied diamonds to wholesalers in England and abroad. In a sale or return transaction, they sent diamonds worth over US$223,000 to West Germany together with an invoice stating the value of the diamonds to be US$131,411; the intention was to enable the customer to avoid German customs duty. Some of the diamonds were stolen in Germany; their value was agreed as being US$142,173.90 and the plaintiffs sued the insurers to recover that sum. *Held*, they would succeed as, inter alia, the principle that, on grounds of public policy, the courts would not assist a party who had been guilty of illegal conduct of which the courts should take notice did not apply where – as here – there was no direct, proximate connection between the plaintiffs' claim and the illegality (the understated invoice). (Applied: *St John Shipping Corporation v Joseph Rank Ltd.*)

Evans (J.) & Son (Portsmouth) Ltd v Andrea [199]
Merzario Ltd [1976] 2 All ER 930 (Court of Appeal)

The plaintiffs imported machines from Italy and, for many years, had contracted with the defendant forwarding agents to make their transport arrangements. The course of dealing between the parties was on the standard conditions of trade. After some years, the defendants gave the plaintiffs an oral assurance that in future shipments the machines would be transported in containers under deck. On faith of this assurance, the plaintiffs agreed to change over to container transport. Due to the defendant's oversight, a container was shipped on deck and the machine was lost overboard. The standard conditions gave the defendants complete freedom over the means and procedure to be followed in transportation of goods subject to express written instructions. The plaintiffs claimed damages from the defendants, alleging that the carriage of the container on deck had been a breach of the contract for carriage. *Held*, the plaintiffs were entitled to damages. The defendants' oral assurance amounted to an enforceable contractual promise and the defendants were liable for breach of it unless they could rely on the standard printed conditions. They could not do this so as to exempt them from liability for breach of the oral promise, which was to be treated as overriding the printed conditions. (See also *Mendelssohn v Normand Ltd.*)

Eyre v Johnson [1946] 1 All ER 719 [200]

Johnson had taken a lease of certain premises and, under the terms of the lease, covenanted to keep them in repair. He applied for a licence (which at that time was required) to enable him to carry out necessary repairs to the premises but his application was refused. *Held*, although it would have been illegal, in these circumstances, for Johnson to do the repairs, his covenant was not frustrated and he was liable to pay damages. (See also *Denman v Brise.*)

Eyre v Measday [1986] 1 All ER 488 (Court of Appeal) [201]

The plaintiff consulted the defendant gynaecologist regarding a sterilisation operation. He told her that it 'must be regarded as a permanent procedure', but he did not say that there was a small risk (less than 1%) of a subsequent pregnancy. After the operation, the plaintiff gave birth to a child and she sought damages for breach of contract. *Held*, her action could not succeed. On the facts, the defendant's representations meant no more than that the operative procedure was incapable of being reversed and a term or unqualified collateral warranty that the expected result (the plaintiff's sterility) would actually be achieved would not be implied. (But see *Thake v Maurice.*)

Faccenda Chicken Ltd v Fowler [1986] 1 All ER 617 [202]
(Court of Appeal)

The plaintiffs sold fresh chickens from refrigerated vans and the defendant was their sales manager. Having left the plaintiffs' employment, he set up his own similar business in the same area and eight of the plaintiffs' other employees joined him. The plaintiffs sought, inter alia, damages for breach of their contracts of employment in using the plaintiffs' sales information to the plaintiffs' disadvantage or detriment. *Held*, the plaintiffs would fail as the duty of fidelity owed by an employee to a former employer is not as great as the duty implied in a current contract of employment whereby use or disclosure of confidential information, even though not amounting to a trade secret, would be a breach of the duty of good faith. A former employer would only be protected if the confidential information could be classed as a trade secret (or was so confidential as to require such protection); here it could not. Furthermore, use or disclosure of confidential information could not be restricted by a covenant in a contract of employment unless the information was a trade secret or its equivalent. (See also *Herbert Morris Ltd v Saxelby*.)

Fairline Shipping Co v Adamson [1974] 2 All ER 967   [203]

The plaintiff's agent orally arranged to store some perishable goods in a cold store. The defendant was managing director of the cold storage company and, when writing to confirm the arrangements, used his private letterheading. Inter alia, the question arose as to whether the contract was between the plaintiff and the company or the plaintiff and the defendant. *Held*, in order to constitute a contract the acceptance of an offer had to be communicated to the offeror and the uncommunicated acceptance of the offer could not have the effect of binding the offeror. If the defendant's letter constituted an offer by him to take over the company's contract, the absence of any response from the plaintiff's agent could not be construed as an acceptance capable of binding the defendant. The claim in contract failed. (See also *Felthouse v Bindley*.)

Farr, Smith & Co v Messers Ltd [1928] 1 KB 397   [204]

In an action for breach of an oral contract the defendants contended that damages should not be awarded as the contract had not been evidenced by a sufficient note or memorandum in writing. In their original defence (new plaintiffs had been substituted and this step was accepted as marking the commencement of a new action), which had been signed by counsel, the defendants had set out the terms of the agreement. *Held*, damages would be awarded as this defence constituted a sufficient note or memorandum. (See also *Parker v Clark*.)

Fawcett v Smethurst (1914) 84 LJKB 473   [205]

The defendant, who was a minor, hired the plaintiff's car in order to drive to a place six miles away to fetch his luggage and the plaintiff alleged that he had stipulated that the defendant was to be absolutely liable for such damage as was sustained by the car during the period of hire. The defendant drove to the place where his luggage was, but then drove a friend to a place twelve miles further on. In the course of this journey, without any negligence on the part of the defendant, the car caught fire and was damaged beyond repair. The plaintiff sought to recover damages in respect of his loss. *Held*, the action must fail. The defendant was not liable in tort as the extended journey was of the same nature as the original one. Although it might have been necessary for the defendant to hire the car to fetch his bags, it was not a necessary for him to enter into a contract of hire containing an onerous term, such as that which the plaintiff alleged was embodied in the contract in question, whereby the defendant was to be liable for all loss or damage to the car irrespective of negligence on his part. (But see *Burnard v Haggis*.)

Felthouse v Bindley (1862) 11 CB (NS) 869   [206]

The defendant was an auctioneer who had been instructed to sell the farming stock of John Felthouse. John's uncle was interested in one of the horses which was to be sold and after some verbal negotiations in which a misunderstanding arose as to whether the price was £30 or 30 guineas the uncle wrote to John, admitting that there might have been a mistake and offered to split the difference and pay £30 15s. He concluded: 'If I hear no more about him, I consider the horse mine at £30 15s.' John did not reply to this letter but instructed the defendant to withdraw the horse from the sale. By mistake it was put up with the rest of the stock and sold. *Held*, the uncle's action against the auctioneer for conversion must fail as the plaintiff had no property in the horse as the silence of John did not amount to acceptance of the plaintiff's offer to buy for £30 15s. (See also *Harvey v Facey*; but also *Carlill v Carbolic Smoke Ball Co.*)

Fenwick v Macdonald, Fraser & Co Ltd (1904) 6 F   **[207]**
(Ct of Sess) 850 (Scottish Court of Session)

At a sale by auction a bull was 'offered for unreserved sale'. The auctioneer withdrew the lot before the fall of the hammer and the person who had made the highest bid brought an action for delivery of the bull or for damages. *Held*, as the bidder is not bound until the fall of the hammer neither is the auctioneer and it makes no difference that the sale was said to be without reserve. (But see *Warlow v Harrison*.)

Fercometal SARL v Mediterranean Shipping Co SA, The   **[208]**
Simona [1988] 2 All ER 742 (House of Lords)

In June 1982 the charterers entered into a charterparty with shipowners for the carriage of steel coils from Durban to Bilbao on the owners' vessel: the charterers were entitled to cancel if the ship was not ready to load on or before 9 July. On 2 July the owners requested an extension to enable them to load other cargo first; in this case the vessel would not be able to load the steel coils until 13 July. The charterers cancelled the contract forthwith and engaged another vessel, but the owners did not accept this repudiation and on 5 July they told the charterers that the vessel would start loading on 8 July. The vessel arrived in Durban on 8 July and, although the owners tendered notice of readiness, they were not in fact ready to load the steel coils. The owners brought a claim for deadfreight for the charterers' wrongful repudiation. *Held*, they could not succeed. The owners, having affirmed the contract when they refused to accept the charterers' premature repudiation, could only avoid the cancellation provision by tendering the vessel ready to load on time (which they had not) or by establishing (which they could not) that their failure so to tender the vessel was the result of their acting on a representation by the charterers that they had given up their option to cancel. (See also *Startup v Macdonald.*)

Fibrosa Spolka Akcyjna v Fairbairn Lawson   **[209]**
Combe Barbour Ltd [1942] 2 All ER 122 (House of Lords)

In July 1939 the parties contracted for the delivery of certain machinery to Gdynia, in Poland. The appellants paid £1,000 on the signing of the contract and after it had been frustrated by the occupation of Gdynia by the Germans they argued that they were entitled to the return of this advance payment. *Held*, this view would prevail as the money had been paid upon a consideration (in these circumstances meaning the performance of a promise) which had wholly failed. (See also s. 1(2) of the Law Reform (Frustrated Contracts) Act 1943.)

Fielding and Platt Ltd v Najjar [1969] 2 All ER 150   **[210]**
(Court of Appeal)

The plaintiffs agreed to manufacture and sell an aluminium extrusion press to a foreign company of which the defendant was a director. Delivery was to be made in 10½ months and payment was to be made by two promissory notes. The defendant asked the plaintiffs to describe the goods misleadingly on the invoice so as to mislead the foreign customs authorities. The first promissory note was not paid on the due date, and subsequently the plaintiffs suspended work and obtained summary judgment against the defendant who, inter alia, pleaded illegality as a defence. *Held*, the defence of illegality could not succeed because the request to describe the goods misleadingly was not a term of the contract. Even had it been a term it would have been severable. The defendant had also failed to show that the plaintiffs knew of the illegal purpose of the false invoice and had agreed to participate in that purpose. (But see *Foster v Driscoll*.)

Financings Ltd v Baldock [1963] 1 All ER 443   [211]
(Court of Appeal)

The defendant entered into a hire-purchase agreement with the plaintiffs in respect of a Bedford truck. The cash price of the truck was £675, the interest charge £97 16s, and the defendant paid £100 as the first instalment of rent, the balance being payable over two years by twenty-four monthly instalments of £22 0s 8d 'unless determined by the hirer or the owner', and the agreement also provided for interest at ten per cent on all overdue instalments. The agreement could be determined by the plaintiffs for failure to pay any instalment or by the defendant by returning the truck. In either event, under clause 11 of the agreement there became payable to the plaintiffs such further sum as with the total amount of instalments previously paid would equal two-thirds of the total hiring cost as agreed compensation for depreciation or the amount of instalments and other moneys already due, whichever was the greater. The defendant defaulted in paying two instalments and the plaintiffs 'put an end to the hiring' and retook possession of the truck at the same time telling the defendant that they would allow him seven days to pay the arrears. Nothing was heard from the defendant, so the truck was again offered for sale and some eighteen months later was sold for £140. The plaintiffs sued to recover £538 1s but recovered judgment for damages to be assessed. *Held*, 'when an agreement of hiring is terminated by virtue of a power contained in it and the owner retakes the vehicle, he can recover damages for any breach up to the date of termination, but not for any breach thereafter, for the simple reason that there are no breaches thereafter' (*per* Lord DENNING MR). Clause 11 was a penalty clause and therefore unenforceable and it followed that the plaintiffs were entitled to recover only two months' instalments plus interest at ten per cent. In this case there had been no repudiation by the defendant of the obligation to pay future instalments, but only non-payment, and the plaintiffs, under an express stipulation in that behalf, had terminated the agreement. In these circumstances they could recover only unpaid instalments with interest by way of damages for breach of the agreement prior to its termination. (But see *Lombard North Central plc v Butterworth*.)

Financings Ltd v Stimson [1962] 3 All ER 386   [212]
(Court of Appeal)

The defendant saw an Austin motor car which he wished to buy on the premises of the Stanmore Motor Co and on 16 March 1961 he signed a hire-purchase agreement form produced to him by the dealer. This form was not in itself an agreement, but only an offer by the defendant to enter into a hire-purchase agreement with the plaintiff finance company. The plaintiffs signed an acceptance on 25 March 1961. On 18 March the defendant paid the first instalment of £70 and drove the car away but, because he was not satisfied with its condition and performance, returned it two days later and told the dealer that he no longer wished to purchase it. During the night of 24/25 March the car was stolen from the dealer's premises and was later recovered, badly scratched and damaged. The plaintiffs sold the car and sought damages from the defendant and the defendant counterclaimed for the return of the deposit of £70. *Held*, the defendant's counterclaim would succeed and the plaintiffs would fail as by returning the car to the dealer (the plaintiffs' agent, a person authorised to receive a revocation) the defendant had revoked his offer and there was no concluded contract between the parties. Further, on the facts of the case, the offer made by the defendant was conditional upon the car remaining in substantially the same condition until the moment of acceptance and, in view of the damage which occurred before the plaintiffs' acceptance was given, the plaintiffs were not in a position to accept the offer because the condition on which it was made had not been fulfilled. On this ground also there was no contract.

Finelvet AG v Vinava Shipping Co Ltd, The Chrysalis [1983] 2 All ER 658 [213]

A vessel under charter docked at Basrah on 14 September 1980: eight days later war broke out between Iraq and Iran and the ship became trapped on the Shatt-al-Arab. The Iraqis prevented the ship leaving because of the risk of damage and injury and on 14 November the charterers purported to cancel the charterparty. By 24 November, most informed people in shipping circles believed that trapped vessels would be unable to leave safely for several months, probably much longer. *Held*, the contract had not been frustrated until 24 November: it had not been automatically frustrated by the outbreak of war as its performance remained legally possible. (But see *Bank Line Ltd v Arthur Capel & Co.*)

Fisher v Bell [1960] 3 All ER 731 [214]

A shopkeeper displayed in his shop window a knife behind which was a ticket 'Ejector knife — 4s'. He was charged with offering for sale a flick knife, contrary to a now repealed statute. *Held*, no offence had been committed as the exhibition of goods in a shop window is not in itself an offer for sale. 'According to the ordinary law of contract, the display of an article with a price on it in a shop window is merely an invitation to treat. It is in no sense an offer for sale the acceptance of which constitutes a contract' (*per* Lord PARKER CJ). (See also *Payne v Cave.*)

Fisher & Co v Apollinaris Co (1875) 10 Ch App 297 [215]

The prosecutors in a trade-mark case offered no evidence against the offender when the matter was brought for trial. The accused was accordingly acquitted and it was agreed that he should write a letter of apology which the prosecutors were authorised to publish. The offender sought to avoid this agreement on the ground of duress. *Held*, this plea would fail and the agreement would be upheld as in the case of an offence of this nature where the offender may be proceeded against either civilly or criminally, there is nothing illegal or improper in a compromise of the criminal proceedings. (But see *Kearley v Thomson.*)

Fitch v Dewes [1921] 2 AC 158 (House of Lords) [216]

A Tamworth solicitor entered into an agreement with his managing clerk whereby the managing clerk undertook to serve for three years and that he would not, on the expiration or sooner determination of his term of employment, 'be engaged or manage or concerned in the office, profession, or business of a solicitor, within a radius of seven miles of the Town Hall of Tamworth'. *Held*, although the covenant was unlimited in point of time, it would be enforced as it did not in the circumstances exceed what was reasonably required for the solicitor's protection and was not against the public interest. (See also *Deacons v Bridge*; but see *Routh v Jones* and *Wyatt v Kreglinger and Fernau.*)

Fitch v Snedaker (1868) 38 NY 248 (Court of Appeals of the State of New York) [217]

A sheriff offered a reward of $200 to any person 'who will give such information as shall lead to the apprehension and conviction of the person or persons guilty of the murder' of an unknown woman. The plaintiff contended that as he had given the required information he was entitled to recover the amount of the reward although at the time of giving the information he did not know that the reward had been offered. *Held*, his action must fail as the plaintiff could not be said to have assented to the defendant's offer since he did not know of its existence, and unless the offer was accepted there was no contract between the parties. (But see *Gibbons v Proctor.*)

Fitzgerald v Dressler (1859) 7 CB (NS) 374   [218]

A parcel of linseed was sold by A to B who sold it to C. C orally promised to pay A (in the normal course of events he would have paid B, the person from whom he bought the goods) for the linseed if A would deliver the goods to C who at the time had a property in the seed subject to A's lien for the price. *Held*, A was entitled to enforce this promise, consideration for which could be found in A's surrender of his lien over the goods when delivery was made and it could not be maintained that C's promise was merely a guarantee to make payment if B should default so that the promise was brought within the protection afforded by s. 4 of the Statute of Frauds. (But see *Harburg India Rubber Comb Co v Martin*.)

Flavell, Re, Murray v Flavell (1883) 25 Ch D 89   [219]
(Court of Appeal)

A partnership agreement between two solicitors provided that the personal representatives of a deceased partner should be entitled to receive out of the net profits of the partnership business a yearly sum to be paid to his widow for her own benefit. *Held*, the partnership agreement had created a trust, of which the personal representatives were trustees, in favour of the widow and she was entitled to receive the amount specified in the agreement. (But see *Gandy v Gandy*.)

Flureau v Thornhill (1776) 96 ER 635   [220]

The plaintiff bought a house at an auction. The defendant, the vendor, was unable to make a good title to the land and the plaintiff claimed damages for loss of bargain. *Held*, the plaintiff's claim would not succeed as he was only entitled to recover his deposit, with interest and costs. (See also *Bain v Fothergill*).

Foakes v Beer (1884) 9 App Cas 605 (House of Lords)   [221]

There was an agreement between a judgment debtor and creditor whereby, in consideration of the debtor paying part of the judgment debt and costs and the balance by instalments, the creditor would not proceed on the judgment. The debtor eventually paid the amount of the debt and costs and the creditor sought to recover interest on the original judgment debt. *Held*, she was entitled to recover such interest as payment of a smaller sum (i.e. the debt and costs) was not consideration for the promise to accept this amount in satisfaction of the judgment debt, costs and interest. (But see *British Russian Gazette, etc, Ltd v Associated Newspapers Ltd*; see also *Vanbergen v St Edmund's Properties Ltd* and *D & C Builders Ltd v Rees*.)

Foley v Classique Coaches Ltd [1934] 2 KB 1   [222]
(Court of Appeal)

The plaintiff, who was a retail dealer in petrol, contracted to supply the defendants, who were the owners of motor coaches, with all the petrol which they required for the purposes of their business 'at a price to be agreed by the parties in writing and from time to time'. No agreement in writing as to the price was ever concluded and after three years the defendants purported to repudiate the contract. *Held*, they were not entitled to do so as in the absence of an express agreement a term would be implied that the petrol supplied by the plaintiff should be of reasonable quality and sold at a reasonable price.

Ford Motor Co (England) Ltd v Armstrong (1915)   [223]
31 TLR 267 (Court of Appeal)

A dealer, the defendant, agreed to sell the plaintiffs' motor-cars and, in the event of his selling any car or parts below list price, to pay £250 for every breach of such undertaking 'such sum being the agreed damages which the manufacturers will sustain'. *Held*, the sum of £250 was a penalty and not liquidated damages. (But see *Associated Distributors Ltd v Hall and Hall.*)

Fores v Johnes (1802) 4 Esp 97 [224]

The defendant placed an order 'for all the caricature prints that had ever been published' with the plaintiff, a printseller in Piccadilly, but refused to accept delivery as several were obscene and immoral. The plaintiff sued to recover the price of the prints. *Held*, the action must fail as the contract was illegal and void by reason of the fact that some of the prints were immoral and obscene. (See also *Berg v Sadler & Moore.*)

Forsikringsaktieselskapet Vesta v Butcher [1988] [225]
2 All ER 43 (Court of Appeal); affd [1989] 1 All ER 402

The plaintiffs were awarded damages for breach of a reinsurance contract, but it was found that they had been guilty of contributory negligence. They contended, inter alia, that the Law Reform (Contributory Negligence) Act 1945 did not apply to a claim for breach of contract. *Held*, where—as here—liability in contract was the same as liability in the tort of negligence independently of the existence of any contract, blame could be apportioned under the 1945 Act, even though the claim was made in contract.

Foster v Driscoll [1929] 1 KB 470 (Court of Appeal) [226]

Agreements were entered into the real object of which was to smuggle whiskey into the United States of America contrary to the prohibition laws of that country. *Held*, the object of the transaction constituted a breach of international comity and the agreements were therefore contrary to public policy and void. (See also *Regazzoni v K. C. Sethia* (1944) *Ltd* and *Fielding and Platt Ltd v Najjar.*)

Foster v Mackinnon (1869) LR 4 CP 704 [227]

The defendant, an old man of feeble sight, was induced to sign his name on the back of a bill of exchange by a fraudulent misrepresentation that he was signing a guarantee. *Held*, if the defendant signed without knowing that it was a bill of exchange under the belief that it was a guarantee, and if he had not been guilty of negligence in so signing, he was entitled to be released from liability under the bill. (See also *Lewis v Clay* and *Saunders v Anglia Building Society.*)

Francis v Municipal Councillors of Kuala Lumpur [228]
[1962] 3 All ER 633 (Privy Council)

The appellant clerk was dismissed and he sought, inter alia, a declaration that the termination of his employment was wrongful and void and that he had the right to continue his employment with the respondents. *Held*, because of the general principle of law that the courts will not grant specific performance of contracts of service such a declaratory judgment would only be made in special circumstances. In this case there were no circumstances which would make it either just or proper to make such a declaration. (See also *London Theatre of Varieties Ltd v Evans.*)

Freeth v Burr (1874) LR 9 CP 208 [229]

The plaintiffs contracted to buy 250 tons of pig iron from the defendants, half of this amount to be delivered in two weeks, the remainder in four. None of the iron was delivered in accordance with the terms of the contract but when the first 125 tons had been received the plaintiffs at first refused to pay the full amount of the contract price and purported to set off damages in respect of the failure by the defendants to deliver the goods within the time specified. The defendants thereupon refused to supply the remaining 125 tons and the plaintiffs sued them for breach of contract. *Held*, the mere non-payment for the first portion of the goods did not put an end to the contract so as to defeat the plaintiffs' claim. (See also *Mersey Steel and Iron Co v Naylor, Benzon & Co.*)

Freevale Ltd v Metrostore (Holdings) Ltd [1984]   [230]
1 All ER 495

In writing, the defendants agreed to sell and the plaintiffs to buy certain pieces of land. Subsequently, a receiver was appointed in respect of the defendants' affairs, appointed out of court by a debenture holder. Specific performance would have been appropriate, but could this order be made in view of the receivership? *Held*, it could as the appointment of the receiver had not destroyed the plaintiffs' equitable interest in the land under the contract. (See also *Wakeham v Mackenzie.*)

Frost v Knight (1872) LR 7 Exch 111   [231]

The defendant promised to marry the plaintiff when his father died. Before his father passed away the defendant made it known that he no longer intended to marry the plaintiff who thereupon and in the lifetime of the defendant's father claimed damages for breach of promise of marriage. *Held*, the plaintiff would succeed as a breach of contract had been committed on which she could found her claim. She was entitled to proceed as if the death of the defendant's father had actually occurred. (NB—breach of promise is no longer actionable.)

Galloway v Galloway (1914) 30 TLR 531   [232]

The parties, who believed that they were lawfully married, entered into a deed of separation. It afterwards appeared that their marriage was void as the defendant's first wife was alive at the time of his marriage to the plaintiff. *Held*, there had been a mutual mistake of fact as to the relationship of the parties and in these circumstances the separation agreement was void. (But see *Bell v Lever Brothers Ltd.*)

Gandy v Gandy (1885) 30 Ch D 57 (Court of Appeal)   [233]

By a deed of separation the husband covenanted with the trustees to pay to them an annuity for the use of his wife and two eldest daughters and also, in some respects at the discretion of the trustees, all the expenses in connection with the maintenance and education of his two youngest daughters. When one of the two youngest daughters was 16 the husband refused to maintain her and she brought an action as beneficiary against the husband and the trustees to enforce the husband's covenant so far as she was concerned. *Held*, because the trustees were given a certain discretion, it was not possible to hold that the deed had created a trust in favour of the youngest daughters and for this reason the action failed. (But see *Affréteurs Réunis Société Anonyme v Leopold Walford (London) Ltd.*)

Gardner v Coutts & Co [1967] 3 All ER 1064   [234]

In July 1948, J, a vendor of land who retained an adjoining smaller property, entered into a written agreement, on the day after the conveyance of the land he had sold, that the purchaser and her successors should have an option of purchasing the adjoining property should he, at any time during his life, wish to sell it. In 1958 the plaintiff became entitled to the land with the benefit of this right of pre-emption. In 1963 J conveyed the adjoining property by way of gift to F, without making offer of the first refusal. J having died, the plaintiff sued his executors for damages. *Held*, it was implicit in the grant of the first refusal that the person who had to offer the first refusal should not give the property away without offering it, and so defeat the right of pre-emption. Accordingly, the plaintiff was entitled to damages. (See also *Moorcock, The.*)

Garnham, Harris & Elton Ltd v Alfred W. Ellis [235]
(Transport) Ltd [1967] 2 All ER 940

The plaintiffs made an oral contract with the defendants for the carriage of some copper wire from London to Glasgow. The contract was subject to a trade association's standard terms, one of which excluded liability for 'non-delivery (howsoever arising)', unless non-delivery was reported to the carrier within 28 days of the receipt of the goods by him. The defendants decided to sub-contract the work, though no express power to do so was given, and they employed a rogue, without checking his identity or character. The load of wire disappeared and its loss was not discovered until the expiry of the time limit. *Held*, the defendants were not protected by the clause because the right to sub-contract could not be implied, because of the valuable nature of the goods, and as carried out the sub-contracting amounted to the tort of conversion. (But see *Suisse Atlantique, etc v Rotterdamsche etc.*)

General Billposting Co Ltd v Atkinson [1909] AC 118 [236]
(House of Lords)

The respondent was employed as the company's manager. His contract of service provided that the engagement should be subject to 12 months' notice by either side and also contained a covenant in restraint of trade. The appellants wrongfully dismissed the respondent without notice. *Held*, this action constituted a repudiation of the contract by the appellants and the respondent was not bound by the clause which restricted his right to engage in similar work. (But see *Konsksi v Peet.*)

Gibbons v Proctor (1891) 64 LT 594 [237]

The defendant gave instructions for the printing of handbills to announce that a reward of £25 would be given to any person who gave information to the superintendent of police which led to the conviction of a certain criminal. The plaintiff, a police constable, communicated the information required to a fellow police officer some nine hours before the instructions for the printing of the handbills were given but the information reached the superintendent after the handbills had been printed and distributed. The plaintiff sought to recover the reward of £25. *Held*, he was entitled to do so as the condition (the communication of the information to the superintendent) was fulfilled after the publication of the handbills. (But see *Bloom v American Swiss Watch Co.*)

Gibbons v Westminster Bank Ltd [1939] 3 All ER 577 [238]

The defendant bank wrongfully dishonoured the plaintiff's cheque. *Held*, the plaintiff was entitled to recover only nominal damages unless special or actual damage could be proved, but this proof is not required where the plaintiff in a similar case is a trader.

Gibson v Manchester City Council [1979] 1 All ER 972 [239]
(House of Lords)

A council tenant who wished to purchase the freehold interest in his house filled in an application form supplied by the council. The council wrote him a letter which informed him that it might be prepared to sell the house to him on terms stated and invited him to make a formal application on an attached form. He filled in the form and returned it with a letter stating that he wished to continue with the purchase. The council subsequently reversed its policy of selling houses to tenants. *Held*, the language of the council's letter stating that it might be prepared to sell the house was such that it could not be converted into a firm offer capable of acceptance. There was no legally enforceable contract of sale. (But see *Clarke v Dunraven, The Satanita.*)

Gilchester Properties Ltd v Gomm [1948] 1 All ER 493 [240]

During negotiations for the purchase of certain premises the defendants, the vendors, stated in answer to inquiries by the purchasers, the plaintiffs, that the rents payable by the tenants were £449 10s which was an innocent misrepresentation as they actually amounted to £398 10s. The plaintiffs sought specific performance of the contract and abatement of purchase price. *Held*, their claim would fail as to award specific performance with a deduction in purchase price would be the equivalent of an award of damages in respect of an innocent misrepresentation. The appropriate remedy was rescission. (See also *Reese River Silver Mining Co Ltd v Smith*.)

Glasbrook Brothers Ltd v Glamorgan County Council [241]
[1925] AC 270 (House of Lords)

During a strike a colliery manager applied for police protection for his colliery and insisted that it could only be efficiently protected by the stationing of a police force on the colliery premises. The police superintendent thought that a mobile force would give sufficient protection and would only billet police officers at the colliery when the manager agreed to pay the force at a specified rate. *Held*, there was consideration for the manager's promise as the police superintendent was only under a duty to provide what protection he thought was reasonable and sufficient. As he had provided more than this the manager was bound by his promise to pay the amount agreed. (But see *Collins v Godefroy*.)

Goldsoll v Goldman [1915] 1 Ch 292 (Court of Appeal) [242]

Both parties were dealers in imitation jewellery, one in Old Bond Street and the other in New Bond Street. In order to avoid competition the defendant sold his business to the plaintiff and covenanted that he would not for a period of two years carry on or be engaged, concerned or interested in the sale of real or imitation jewellery in any part of the United Kingdom, France, United States, Russia or Spain or within 25 miles of Berlin or Vienna. The defendant committed breaches of this covenant and the plaintiff sought an injunction. *Held*, unless the terms of the covenant could be severed it would be void as it was wider than was reasonably necessary for the plaintiff's protection. However, the injunction would be granted as the covenant not to carry on business in the United Kingdom, which was reasonable in the circumstances of the case, was severable from the rest as was the covenant which prevented the defendant from dealing in real jewellery, the provision restraining him from dealing in imitation jewellery being also reasonably necessary for the plaintiff's protection. (But see *Attwood v Lamont* and *British Reinforced Concrete Engineering Co Ltd v Schelff*.)

Goldsworthy v Brickell [1987] 1 All ER 853 (Court of Appeal) [243]

The plaintiff owned a large (and valuable) farm, but it was run down and losing money. From November 1976 the defendant, a neighbouring farmer, began to give the plaintiff advice and help: the plaintiff came to trust him implicitly and by early 1977 the defendant was effectively managing the farm. In April the 85 year old plaintiff granted the defendant a tenancy of the farm at an annual rent of £500 with an option to purchase at the 'prevailing value' on the plaintiff's death. The agreement provided that the plaintiff could remain in the farm house, prohibited rent increases and permitted (but did not oblige) the defendant to make improvements; the plaintiff did not receive independent advice. In 1983 the plaintiff sought rescission of the tenancy agreement on the ground of undue influence. *Held*, his action would be successful. On the facts, undue influence would be presumed and, as it could not be said that the plaintiff had affirmed the agreement, it was just and equitable that it be set aside. (But see *National Westminster Bank plc v Morgan*.)

Goodinson v Goodinson [1954] 2 All ER 255   **[244]**
(Court of Appeal)

A husband and wife entered into an agreement whereby the husband would pay to the wife a weekly sum for the support and maintenance of the wife and their child. The wife covenanted that so long as the husband made these weekly payments she would not 'commence or prosecute any matrimonial proceedings against the husband', that she 'would maintain herself and the child and indemnify the husband against all debts incurred by her' and would not 'in any way at any time hereafter pledge the husband's credit'. The wife claimed payment of arrears of maintenance under this agreement and the husband maintained that she should not succeed as the clause prohibiting the taking of matrimonial proceedings was illegal and for this reason that the agreement itself was void. *Held*, the wife was entitled to recover as the clause which purported to restrain the institution of matrimonial proceedings would be eliminated from the agreement. (Distinguished in *Sutton v Sutton*; see also *Ronbar Enterprises Ltd v Green*.)

Goodman v Chase (1818) 1 B & Ald 297   **[245]**

The defendant's son, having failed to satisfy a judgment of £686, had been arrested by the sheriff and was about to be taken to prison when the defendant obtained his release by orally promising to pay the amount of the judgment debt. *Held*, the defendant was not protected by s. 4 of the Statute of Frauds. The release of his son had discharged the son's debt and the promise by the defendant was an original promise and not one to answer for the debt, default or miscarriage of another which, to be enforceable, needed to be in writing.

Gore v Gibson (1845) 13 M & W 623   **[246]**

The defendant indorsed a bill of exchange when in a state of intoxication. *Held*, the defendant was not bound by this indorsement as no contract made by a person in this condition, when he does not know what he is doing, is binding upon him. (But see *Molton v Camroux*.)

Core v Van der Lann (Liverpool Corpn intervening)   **[247]**
[1967] 1 All ER 360 (Court of Appeal)

The plaintiff was injured when boarding a Liverpool Corporation 'bus, and claimed damages against its conductor on grounds of his alleged negligence in failing to take proper precautions for her safety. She was travelling on an elderly person's free pass, issued on the following condition: 'In consideration of my being granted a free pass . . . I undertake and agree that the use of such pass by me shall be subject to the conditions overleaf, which have been read to or by me before signing.' The conditions exempted the corporation and its servants and agents from liability to the holder for loss of life, injury or other loss or damage to property, however caused, and stated that the pass was a 'licence' only. The corporation sought to stay the proceedings on grounds that they constituted a fraud on them. *Held*, they were not entitled to a stay of proceedings because, (i) on the facts the issue and acceptance of the pass constituted a contract and not merely a licence, and the condition relied on by the corporation was made void by statute; and, (ii) even if this were not so, the corporation had no interest entitling them to relief as they were under no obligation to indemnify the conductor. (See s. 29 of the Public Passenger Vehicles Act 1981; but see *Wilkie v LPTB*.)

Goss v Lord Nugent (1833) 5 B & Ad 58   **[248]**

The defendant agreed in writing to purchase 14 lots of freehold land from the plaintiff. As the plaintiff could not make a good title to one of the lots, the defendant orally agreed to waive the title to that lot. The defendant afterwards refused to pay the balance of the purchase money in view of the plaintiff's defective title to this one piece of land. *Held*, the plaintiff could not recover the purchase price as the original contract would not be enforced because of the bad title to one lot and it was not possible to vary a contract which was required to be evidenced in writing by means of an oral agreement. (But see *Morris v Baron & Co.*)

Gould v Gould [1969] 3 All ER 728 (Court of Appeal)   [249]

The husband left the wife in May 1966 and then orally agreed to pay her £15 a week 'as long as I can manage it'. He kept the agreement until October 1967 when he fell behind with the payments. In February 1968 he informed the wife that he could not pay the full amount in future, and the wife then sued for arrears of maintenance under the terms of the agreement. *Held*, the wife's claim must fail. It had not been within the contemplation of the parties to make a legally binding agreement. The uncertainty of the terms and the absence of any quid pro quo from the wife precluded that result. (See also *Jones v Padavatton*; and *Balfour v Balfour*.)

Grainger & Son v Gough [1896] AC 325 (House of Lords)   [250]

The appellants were agents for a French wine merchant and canvassed for orders and distributed price-lists on his behalf. *Held*, the canvassing by the agents was not an offer to sell the goods. The orders they received were offers to buy, made by the prospective customers, and no contract was created until something which amounted to acceptance of the customer's offer was done by the merchant or his agents. (See also *Pharmaceutical Society of Great Britain v Boots Cash Chemists (Southern) Ltd.*)

Grant v Maddox (1946) 15 M & W 737   [251]

The plaintiff agreed to perform at the defendant's theatre for a term of three years at a certain weekly salary. The defendant paid the plaintiff's salary only during the theatrical season. *Held*, parol evidence was admissible to show that, according to the usage of the theatrical profession, an engagement for three years meant that the actress was to be paid only during those weeks when the theatre was open in those years.

Great Northern Railway Co v Witham (1873) LR 9 CP 16   [252]

The plaintiffs invited tenders for the supply of goods, including iron, for a period of 12 months. The defendant submitted a tender to supply the goods over the period at a fixed price and in 'such quantities . . . as the company's store-keeper may order from time to time'. The plaintiffs accepted this tender and the defendant made several deliveries of iron, but before the period of 12 months expired he refused to supply any more. The plaintiffs sued for breach of contract. *Held*, although there was no binding contract on the part of the plaintiffs to order any goods during the year in question, the defendant was bound to supply such as were ordered. The defendant had made a standing offer which was accepted by the plaintiffs whenever they ordered goods.

Gregory v Ford [1951] 1 All ER 121   [253]

An employee drove his employer's lorry negligently and caused injury to the plaintiff. At the time of the accident the lorry was not covered by a policy of insurance against third-party risks and driving the lorry without such a policy was a breach of a statutory duty. *Held*, there was an implied term in the contract of service that the employee should not be required to do an unlawful act and for this reason he was able to recover from his employer the amount of damages and costs which he was liable to pay to the plaintiff. (See also *Moorcock, The.*)

Gregory and Parker v Williams (1817) 3 Mer 582   [254]

Parker was indebted to Williams, his landlord, and also to Gregory. Williams promised Parker that if he would surrender his lease and assign all his property to him he (Williams) would first pay off the debt to Gregory, then to himself and pay the balance (if any) to Parker. Parker acted in accordance with this suggestion but Williams failed to pay Gregory. *Held*, Gregory and Parker were able to compel the performance of this promise in equity as Parker was a trustee for Gregory. (See also *Flavell, Re.*)

Greig v Insole [1978] 1 WLR 302   [255]

Some English professional cricket players contracted with a promoter to play a series of winter matches in Australia. The International Cricket Conference and the Test and County Cricket Board made or proposed to make new rules which effectively banned the players from test and county cricket if they played for the promoter. It was claimed on the cricketers' behalf that the new rules were void as being in unreasonable restraint of trade. *Held*, the new rules were so void. The cricketing authorities had not shown that the ban was reasonable or justified. The new rules would substantially restrict the areas in which the cricketers could earn a living. As Australia was the only test playing country whose finances were threatened by the proposed series of matches, the new rules went further than was reasonably necessary for the protection of the game. The International Cricket Conference was found to have induced the players to breach their contract with the promoters.

Grist v Bailey [1966] 2 All ER 875   [256]

B agreed to sell a freehold house to G at a price of £850, in the belief that the house was subject to an existing statutory tenancy. In fact the house was not subject to a statutory tenancy, and on a vacant possession basis was worth £2,250. G sought specific performance of the agreement, and B pleaded the existence of a common mistake of fact, and counterclaimed for rescission of the sale agreement. *Held*, the sale agreement would be set aside for a fundamental common mistake of fact, on terms which gave G the option to buy the house at vacant possession price. (See also *Solle v Butcher*; but see *Bell v Lever Bros Ltd.*)

Guild & Co v Conrad [1894] 2 QB 885 (Court of Appeal)   [257]

The defendant orally promised the plaintiff that if he, the plaintiff, would accept certain bills for a firm in which the defendant's son was a partner he, the defendant, would provide the plaintiff with funds to meet the bills. *Held*, to be enforceable this promise need not be in writing as it was an indemnity and not a guarantee and therefore not within the provisions of s. 4 of the Statute of Frauds. (See also *Yeoman Credit Ltd v Latter.*)

Guthing v Lynn (1831) 2 B & Ad 232   [258]

The plaintiff purchased a horse for £63 and promised to give the defendant an additional £5, or the buying of another horse, 'if the horse was lucky'. *Held*, this promise was too vague to be legally enforced. (See also *Scammell and Nephew Ltd v Ouston.*)

Hadley v Baxendale (1854) 9 Exch 341   [259]

The plaintiffs were millers and mealmen in Gloucester. The crankshaft of the steam engine which worked their mill was fractured and they ordered another from a firm in Greenwich who asked that the old shaft should be sent to them for use as a pattern. The plaintiffs gave the shaft to the defendants, who were common carriers, and the defendants promised to deliver the shaft on the following day. In fact they took a week to deliver it and because their mill was out of action for longer than would otherwise have been the case the plaintiffs claimed damages for loss of profit. *Held*, the plaintiffs would not succeed as the loss of profit could not reasonably be considered a consequence of the breach of contract which could have been fairly and reasonably contemplated by both parties when they entered into the contract of carriage. 'Where two parties have made a contract which one of them has broken, the damages which the other party ought to receive in respect of such breach of contract should be such as may fairly and reasonably be considered either arising naturally, i.e., according to the usual course of things, from such breach of contract itself, or such as may reasonably be supposed to have been in the contemplation of both parties, at the time they made the contract, as the probable result of the breach of it. Now, if the special circumstances under which the contract was actually made were communicated by the plaintiffs to the defendants, and thus known to both parties, the damages resulting from the breach of such a contract, which they would reasonably contemplate, would be the amount of injury which would ordinarily follow from a breach of the contract under the special circumstances so known and communicated. But, on the other hand, if these special circumstances were wholly unknown to the party breaking the contract, he, at the most, could only be supposed to have had in his contemplation the amount of injury which would arise generally, and in the great multitude of cases not affected by any special circumstances, from such a breach of contract. For, had the special circumstances been known the parties might have specially provided for the breach of contract by special terms as to damages in that case; and of this advantage it would be very unjust to deprive them' (*per* ALDERSON B). (But see *British Columbia, etc, Saw-Mill Co Ltd v Nettleship*; see also *Koufos v C. Czarnikow Ltd*, *Victoria Laundry (Windsor) Ltd v Newman Industries Ltd* and *Parsons (H) (Livestock) Ltd v Uttley Ingham & Co Ltd*.)

Hamlyn & Co v Wood & Co [1891] 2 QB 488   [260]
(Court of Appeal)

The plaintiffs agreed to buy all the grains made by the defendants, who were brewers, at an ascertainable price and for a period of ten years. After five years the defendants sold their business and in consequence ceased to supply grains to the plaintiffs who claimed damages for breach of contract. *Held*, their claim must fail as a term would not be implied to the effect that the defendants would not by any voluntary act make it impossible for them to supply grains to the plaintiffs. A term will only be implied to give a transaction such efficacy as both parties intended it to have and each case must be decided on its merits. (But see *Robb v Green*.)

Hancock v B. W. Brazier (Anerley) Ltd [1966]   [261]
2 All ER 901 (Court of Appeal)

A builder sold a house, which was in the course of erection, it being an express term of the contract that the house would be completed in a proper manner. Before the contract was made, the foundations had been laid and, unknown to the builder, the hard-core used as a base contained soluble sulphates, which made it totally unsuitable. More than two years after the sale had been completed, the sulphates caused the concrete to expand and crack, causing substantial damage to the house. The plaintiff claimed damages for breach by the builder of implied warranty of fitness of materials. *Held*, the claim would succeed, for the express term of the contract dealt only with workmanship and not with fitness of materials. Where a purchaser buys a house from a builder who contracts to build it, a threefold warranty is implied: (a) that the builder will do the work in a good and workmanlike manner; (b) supplying good and proper materials; and, (c) that the house would be reasonably fit for human habitation. (But see *Lynch v Thorne*; see also *Gregory v Ford* and *Independent Broadcasting Authority v EMI Electronics Ltd*.)

Harburg India Rubber Comb Co v Martin [1902]   **[262]**
1 KB 778 (Court of Appeal)

The plaintiffs were judgment creditors of a company of which the defendant was a director and in which he held a large number of shares. The plaintiffs agreed to withdraw a writ of execution against the company in consideration of an oral promise by the defendant to indorse two bills of exchange for the amount of the debt. The plaintiffs claimed damages for breach of this promise. *Held*, their action must fail as the defendant's promise was made to a person to whom another was already indebted which brought the promise within s. 4 of the Statute of Frauds. In these circumstances the defendant's oral promise constituted a guarantee and not an indemnity and for this reason it could not be enforced. (But see *Fitzgerald v Dressler*.)

Hardman v Booth (1863) 1 H & C 803   **[263]**

An agent for the plaintiffs, who were worsted manufacturers, called at the place of business of 'Gandell & Co' with a view to obtaining orders for goods. At that time the firm consisted of Thomas Gandell only and the business was managed by Edward Gandell who was his son and also his clerk. The agent had asked to be directed to the offices of 'Messrs Gandell' where he found Edward who led the agent to believe that he was a member of the firm of Gandell & Co. Business was transacted and when the goods, which were invoiced to 'Edward Gandell & Co', were delivered, Edward pledged them with the defendant who afterwards sold them under his power of sale. *Held*, the defendant was liable in conversion as there was no contract of sale between the plaintiffs and Edward as they had believed, to Edward's knowledge, that they were dealing with Gandell & Co and not Edward personally. In consequence Edward had no property in the goods to pledge to the defendant. (See also *Cundy v Lindsay*.)

Hare v Murphy Brothers Ltd [1974] 3 All ER 940   **[264]**
(Court of Appeal)

The claimant was a foreman of previous good character. He was sentenced to 12 months' imprisonment for an assault unconnected with his employment. The question arose as to whether the prison sentence automatically terminated his contract of employment. *Held*, the passing of the sentence automatically terminated the contract of employment as from the date of the sentence since it had rendered it impossible for the claimant to perform his part of the contract. (But see *Davis Contractors Ltd v Fareham Urban District Council*.)

Hare v Nicoll [1966] 1 All ER 285 (Court of Appeal)   **[265]**

The plaintiff had an option to purchase 25,000 shares in a private company, so long as he gave notice of his intention to do so by 1 May 1963, and paid for them by 1 June 1963. He failed to pay for them by that date, and so the defendant sold the shares to a third party. The plaintiff sued for breach of contract. The defendant maintained that she was not liable because the time of payment was of the essence of the contract, that payment had not been made by the specified date, and that therefore the option had lapsed. *Held*, time was of the essence of the contract and strict compliance was required both as to the time for the giving of the notice to exercise the option and as to the time of payment. (Distinguished in *Millichamp v Jones*; see also *Rickards (Charles) Ltd v Oppenheim*.)

Harnor v Groves (1855) 15 CB 667   **[266]**

The plaintiff agreed to buy and the defendant duly delivered 25 sacks of flour of the same quality as that which had recently been sold to one Mackness. When the plaintiff had used half a sack of the flour he realised that it was of an inferior quality and the defendant admitted that that which he had supplied to Mackness had been better. The plaintiff used two more sacks and sold another. *Held*, because he had used two sacks and sold another he was precluded from rescinding the contract and recovering the purchase price. (But see *Keen v Holland.*)

Harris v Nickerson (1873) LR 8 QB 286   [267]

An auctioneer advertised that certain goods, including office furniture, would be sold at a certain place on certain days. The plaintiff went to the sale but all the lots of office furniture, in which he was interested, were withdrawn and he sued the auctioneer to recover damages for his loss of time and expenses. *Held*, the plaintiff's claim must fail as the advertising of the sale was a mere declaration of intention to hold a sale and not an offer which could be accepted to form a binding contract. If the sale was not held the auctioneer was not bound to indemnify those who attended. (But see *Warlow v Harrison.*)

Harris v Wyre Forest District Council [1988] 1 All ER 691   [268]
(Court of Appeal)

The plaintiffs applied to the defendants for a mortgage and signed an application form containing a disclaimer by the defendants of responsibility for their surveyor's inspection and report. The surveyor carried out his work negligently, overlooking a serious fault, and, after completing the purchase in reliance on the report, the plaintiffs sued for damages. *Held*, they could not succeed. The disclaimer prevented a duty of care arising and it was not subject to the requirement of reasonableness under s. 2(2) of the Unfair Contract Terms Act 1977 since that Act only applied if a duty of care already existed. (But see *Phillips Products Ltd v Hyland.*)

Harrison v Battye [1974] 3 All ER 830 (Court of Appeal)   [269]

An agreement to purchase the defendant's house was to come into being only on the exchange of contracts. The plaintiff's solicitors sent their part of the contract signed to the defendant's solicitors. The defendant signed his part of the contract, but his solicitors, in error, returned the plaintiff's part of the contract to the plaintiff. The defendant then refused to proceed with the transaction. The plaintiff sought specific performance of the contract, and an order that the defendant's solicitors deliver up the defendant's part, claiming that an attempt to exchange contracts was equivalent to an exchange. *Held*, the plaintiff's claim must fail as no exchange had taken place which had been the only means contemplated of concluding the contract. The sale of a house which was 'subject to contract' was not complete until two identical parts were exchanged. If the parts differed in any material respect there was no contract. (See also *Eccles v Bryant.*)

Harrison v Knowles and Foster [1917] 2 KB 606   [270]

The defendants gave the plaintiffs particulars in writing of two steamships which they hoped to sell and stated that the dead-weight capacity of each ship was 460 tons. The particulars also contained the words 'not accountable for errors in description'. The plaintiffs bought the ships and subsequently discovered that their dead-weight capacity was only 360 tons. *Held*, the difference between the stated and actual dead-weight of the ships was a matter of degree and not of kind and the statement was, therefore, a warranty and not a condition but the defendants had excluded liability for breach of warranty by using the words 'not accountable for errors in description'. (But see *Behn v Burness.*)

Harrison and Jones Ltd v Bunten and Lancaster   [271]
Ltd [1953] 1 All ER 903

The appellants, who were manufacturers of articles made of kapok, and the respondents, who were importers of kapok, contracted for the sale of 300 bales of Calcutta kapok, Sree brand, which was to be equal to a standard sample in the respondents' possession. After the goods had been delivered it appeared that the kapok contained an admixture of cotton which rendered it unsuitable for use in the appellants' machines. At the date of the contract both parties believed that the agreement was in respect of pure kapok. *Held*, such a mutual mistake of fact would not render the contract a nullity although, from the point of view of the buyer, the mistake was of fundamental importance. (See also *Rose (Frederick E.) (London) Ltd v William H. Pim Jnr & Co Ltd*.)

Hart v O'Connor [1985] 2 All ER 880 (Privy Council)   [272]

The appellant agreed to buy farmland in New Zealand from a sole trustee who, unknown to the appellant, was of unsound mind when he signed the agreement. The present trustees and beneficiaries sought to have the sale set aside. *Held*, they would not succeed. In cases such as this, where the affliction was not apparent and the consequent incapacity unknown to the other party, the validity of the contract would be judged by the same standards as a contract made by a person of sound mind and here there had been no unfairness amounting to equitable fraud. (See also *Molton v Camroux*.)

Hartley v Ponsonby (1857) 7 E & B 872   [273]

Some members of the crew deserted and a vessel was left short of hands. In order to induce the remainder of the crew to complete the voyage the master promised to pay each seaman an additional £40. It was found that it was dangerous and unreasonable for the ship to go to sea with the smaller crew. *Held*, the crew's original agreement did not require them to sail a ship which was unseaworthy due to lack of hands and their undertaking to continue the voyage with the reduced crew was consideration for the master's promise. (See also *Ward v Byham*.)

Hartog v Colin and Shields [1939] 3 All ER 566   [274]

The defendants offered to sell the plaintiff 30,000 Argentine hare skins at certain prices per pound but after the plaintiff had accepted this offer the defendants failed to deliver the skins, as they had intended, as was the usual practice, that they should be sold at the specified prices per piece. *Held*, the plaintiff's action for damages would not succeed as he must have realised that the offer made by the defendants contained a mistake. (But see *Scott v Littledale*.)

Harvela Investments Ltd v Royal Trust Co of Canada (CI) [275]
Ltd [1985] 2 All ER 966 (House of Lords)

The plaintiffs and the second defendants were rival offerors for a parcel of shares held by the first defendants who bound themselves to accept the highest offer. The plaintiffs offered $2,175,000 and the second defendants '$2,100,000 or . . . $101,000 in excess of any other offer'. The second defendants' bid was accepted and the plaintiffs contended that the second defendants' bid had been invalid. *Held*, this was the case as a referential bid (such as the second defendants') was inconsistent with the purpose of a sale, such as that here, by fixed bidding. As to whether it was a fixed bidding sale or an auction sale depended on the presumed intention of the vendor as deduced from the express provisions of the invitation to bid. No fresh contract had been created by the acceptance of the second defendants' referential bid because, at the time, the first defendants had been acting under the misapprehension that the second defendants were entitled to the shares.

Harvey v Facey [1893] AC 552 (Privy Council)   [276]

The appellants telegraphed 'Will you sell us Bumper Hall Pen? Telegraph lowest cash price' and the respondents replied 'Lowest price for Bumper Hall Pen £900'. The appellants then telegraphed 'We agree to buy Bumper Hall Pen for £900 asked by you. Please send us your title-deed in order that we may get early possession', to which they received no reply and thereupon brought an action for specific performance. *Held*, the action must fail as the respondents' telegram was not an offer to sell but a statement of the minimum price required for the property if they eventually decided to sell. The appellants' final telegram was itself an offer to buy the property for £900, acceptance of which could not be implied by the silence of the respondents. (See also *Clifton v Palumbo* and *Bigg v Boyd Gibbins Ltd*.)

Hawkins v Price [1947] 1 All ER 689 [277]

A vendor and purchaser reached agreement for the sale of a bungalow and the vendor gave the following receipt in respect of the payment by the purchaser of £100 deposit: 'Received of [the purchaser] the sum of £100 being deposit on bungalow and ground named "Oakdene", Station Road, Stoke Mandeville, Bucks., sold for £1,000'. The receipt made no mention of the fact that vacant possession was to be given by a certain date. The purchaser sought a decree of specific performance. *Held*, a decree would not be awarded as the contract was not evidenced by a sufficient note or memorandum as required by s. 40 of the Law of Property Act 1925 in that the receipt made no mention of the agreement as to vacant possession. This agreement was a material term of the contract of benefit to both parties, so that it could not be waived by the purchaser to enable him to proceed on those terms of the agreement evidenced by the receipt. (See also *Timmins v Moreland Street Property Co Ltd*.)

Head v Tattersall (1871) LR 7 Exch 7 [278]

The plaintiff bought a horse from the defendant who said the horse had hunted with the Bicester hounds and promised that if the horse did not answer this description it was to be returned by the following Wednesday 'otherwise the purchaser shall be obliged to keep the lot with all faults'. The horse had not hunted with the Bicester hounds and the plaintiff returned the horse within the period specified and sued to recover the purchase price. *Held*, he would succeed as the option to return the horse was a condition subsequent and it made no difference that the horse had been injured, through no fault of the plaintiff, while in the plaintiff's possession.

Heilbut, Symons & Co v Buckleton [1913] AC 30 [279]
(House of Lords)

The appellants' manager had been instructed to obtain applications for shares in a rubber company. The respondent telephoned the appellants' manager and said 'I understand you are bringing out a rubber company' and the manager replied 'We are.' The respondent asked 'if it was all right' and was told 'We are bringing it out' to which the respondent rejoined 'That is good enough for me'. As a result of this conversation 6,000 shares were allotted to the respondent but they quickly fell in value. The respondent contended that as the company could not be properly described as a rubber company there was a breach of warranty that it was a rubber company whose main object was to produce rubber. *Held*, the words of the appellants' manager constituted a mere representation and not a warranty. (But see *Couchman v Hill* and *IBA Ltd v EMI Construction Ltd*.)

Henderson v Stevenson (1875) 32 LT 709 [280]
(House of Lords)

A steam packet company sought to exclude their liability for loss or injury to the passenger or his luggage by means of a condition printed on the back of its passenger tickets. One of their ships was wrecked and a passenger sought to recover damages for loss of his luggage. *Held*, the passenger would succeed as the liability of the owners of the ship would not be excluded without very clear evidence that the condition had been brought to the notice of the passenger and that he had assented to it. (But see *Parker v South Eastern Railway Co.*)

Henderson & Co v Williams [1895] 1 QB 521   [281]
(Court of Appeal)

The plaintiffs were sugar merchants and the defendant a warehouseman. The owner of goods lying in the warehouse was induced by the fraud of one Fletcher to instruct the defendant to transfer the goods to the order of Fletcher and the goods were accordingly placed at his disposal. Fletcher sold the goods to innocent purchasers, the plaintiffs, but when Fletcher's fraud was discovered the defendant refused to deliver the goods to the plaintiffs. *Held*, the plaintiffs' action for damages would succeed. The original owners had enabled Fletcher to hold himself out as owner of the goods in such a way as to induce the plaintiffs to enter into a contract and the defendant was estopped from afterwards denying Fletcher's title to the goods. (See also *King's Norton Metal Co Ltd v Edridge, Merrett & Co Ltd.*)

Henthorn v Fraser [1892] 2 Ch 27 (Court of Appeal)   [282]

The defendants handed the plaintiff an option to purchase some houses for £750, but on the following day between 12 and 1 o'clock posted a letter of withdrawal which did not reach the plaintiff until 5 pm on the same day. At 3.50 pm on that day the plaintiff posted a letter of acceptance which was delivered after the defendants' office had closed. The defendants refused to complete and the plaintiff brought an action for specific performance. *Held*, the decree would be made as where it is reasonably to be expected that the post might be used as a means of communicating the acceptance, although the offer was not sent by post, the acceptance is complete as soon as it is posted. A revocation of an offer is of no effect until brought to the notice of the person to whom the offer was made so that in the case of a withdrawal by post it takes effect when the letter of withdrawal is received and not when it is posted. (But see *Re London and Northern Bank.*)

Herbert Morris Ltd v Saxelby [1916] 1 AC 688   [283]
(House of Lords)

The appellants carried on business as engineers and were the leading manufacturers of hoisting machinery in the United Kingdom. The respondent had been employed by them for several years as a draughtsman and in various other capacities and had entered into a contract to serve for two years certain, and thereafter subject to four weeks' notice on either side, at a salary of £3 17s 6d per week. The respondent covenanted that he would 'not at any time during a period of seven years from the date of his ceasing to be employed by the company whether under this agreement or otherwise howsoever either in the United Kingdom of Great Britain or Ireland carry on either as principal, agent, servant or otherwise alone or jointly or in connection with any person firm or company' work similar to that undertaken by the appellants. In breach of this agreement the respondent became employed by competitors of the appellants, a company in Manchester engaged in the manufacture of lifting machinery. The appellants claimed to be entitled to an injunction to restrain the respondent from committing breaches of his contract. *Held*, the appellants would not succeed as the covenant was wider than that required for their protection. In circumstances such as this an injunction will only be granted to restrain a former servant from competing with his former master if the former employer has an exceptional proprietary right which requires protection, such as a trade connection or secret. (See also *Faccenda Chicken Ltd v Fowler.*)

Hermann v Charlesworth [1905] 2 KB 123 (Court of Appeal)   [284]

The defendant was proprietor of *The Matrimonial Post and Fashionable Marriage Advertiser*. In consequence of an advertisement in this paper the plaintiff, who was seeking a husband, signed an agreement whereby she would pay the defendant £250 if a marriage took place as a result of an introduction made by the defendant. The plaintiff also paid a 'special client's fee' of £52, £47 of which was to be returned if the plaintiff had not become engaged or married within nine months. The defendant did not succeed in arranging a marriage for the plaintiff within nine months and the plaintiff sued to recover £52. *Held*, she was entitled to recover as the money was paid by her as the consideration for an illegal contract and the fact that the defendant had brought about introductions and incurred expense did nothing to defeat the plaintiff's claim.

Herne Bay Steam Boat Co v Hutton [1903] 2 KB 683   [285]
(Court of Appeal)

The parties entered into an agreement whereby the plaintiffs' ship was to be 'at the disposal' of the defendant on a certain date 'for the purpose of viewing the naval review and for a day's cruise round the fleet'. The Royal review was afterwards cancelled but the fleet was still at Spithead on the day in question. In view of the cancellation of the review the defendant did not use the ship and declined to pay the balance of the hire. The plaintiffs claimed damages for breach of contract. *Held*, the plaintiffs should succeed. The naval review was not the sole foundation of the contract as the object of the voyage was also to cruise round the fleet. (But see *Krell v Henry*.)

Heron II, The. *See* Koufos v C. Czarnikow Ltd

Heyman v Darwins Ltd [1942] 1 All ER 337 (House of Lords)   [286]

A contract between the parties contained a clause to the effect that all disputes which should arise under the contract should be referred for arbitration. A dispute arose and, in view of the repudiation of the contract by the respondents, the appellants maintained that they could not afterwards rely on the arbitration clause. *Held*, this view would not be upheld as the repudiation of the contract, although accepted by the appellants, did nothing to impair the validity of the arbitration clause. (See also *Woolf v Collis Removal Service*.)

Heywood v Wellers [1976] 1 All ER 300 (Court of Appeal)   [287]

The appellant went to the defendant solicitors as she wished to recover a £40 debt and to prevent the debtor from molesting her. She was given the wrong advice regarding the cost and length of proceedings. High Court proceedings were started instead of magistrates' court proceedings and finally, when an injunction was obtained ordering the debtor not to molest the appellant, he was not taken to court when he did molest her again. The appellant claimed £170 of the costs actually paid and £150 for 'damages and expenses'. *Held*, the solicitors were not entitled to recover any costs as they had failed completely to fulfil their part of the contract as their work had been useless. They were in breach of their duty to take reasonable care as they had not prevented the appellant from being molested. Consequently, the appellant was entitled to damages for the disappointment, upset and mental distress she had suffered as a result of their breach of contract. (See also *Jackson v Horizon Holidays Ltd.*; and *Jarvis v Swan's Tours Ltd.*)

Hill v Hill (William) (Park Lane) Ltd [1949] 2 All ER 452   [288]
(House of Lords)

The appellant, a race horse owner, was indebted to the respondents, who were bookmakers, in the sum of £3,635 12s 6d and was unable to pay this amount. The Committee of Tattersalls decided that the appellant should pay £635 12s 6d within 14 days and the balance by monthly instalments of £100. The respondents brought an action to recover the amount of the debt under this agreement although it was conceded that the original contracts, which resulted in the appellant's indebtedness, were wagers and therefore void. *Held*, the payments under the instalment agreement were payments of a 'sum of money . . . alleged to have been won upon any wager' within s. 18 of the Gaming Act 1845, and could not therefore be recovered. (See also *Coral v Kleyman*.)

Hillas & Co v Arcos Ltd (1932) 38 Com Cas 23   [289]
(House of Lords)

There was an agreement in writing for the supply of wood during 1930 and it contained an option to buy more wood during the following year but the option clause did not specify the precise kind or size of timber to be supplied, the ports to which it was to be shipped or the manner of shipment. The suppliers argued that the option clause was not binding as it was intended merely to form the basis of a future agreement. *Held*, the agreement in respect of the supply of timber during 1930 was couched in similar terms and had been duly observed. The option clause showed a sufficient intention to be bound and could create a valid contract, as those points which were not specifically resolved in the option clause could be determined by reference to the previous dealings between the parties and normal business practice in the timber trade. (See also *Foley v Classique Coaches Ltd*; but see *Scammell and Nephew Ltd v Ouston*.)

Hillingdon Estates Co v Stonefield Estates Ltd   [290]
[1952] 1 All ER 853

In 1938 the purchasers contracted in writing to buy certain land at South Ruislip for building purposes. The contract was not completed, partly because of the war, and in 1948 the Middlesex County Council made a compulsory purchase order in respect of the whole of the land. The purchasers contended that the basis of the agreement had thus been destroyed and that they were therefore discharged from their contract. The vendors counterclaimed for specific performance. *Held*, the vendors would succeed. The contract had not been frustrated as the making of the compulsory purchase order did nothing to preclude the performance of the contract, i.e., the conveyance of the legal estate from the vendors to the purchasers. (See also *Paradine v Jane*.)

Hirachand Punamchand v Temple [1911] 2 KB 330   [291]
(Court of Appeal)

The debtor's father offered to pay Rs 1,500 'in full settlement' of the debt and enclosed a draft for that amount. The creditor cashed the draft and afterwards brought an action against the debtor to recover the balance of the debt. *Held*, the action could not be maintained as the creditor must be taken to have accepted the draft on the terms on which it was sent, that is, 'in full settlement' of the debt. (See also *Welby v Drake*.)

Hitchcock v Coker (1837) 6 Ad & El 438   [292]

The plaintiff was a chemist in Taunton and employed the defendant as an assistant. The defendant promised that if he should at any time thereafter exercise this particular trade of business in Taunton or within three miles thereof he would pay the plaintiff £500 as liquidated damages. The defendant subsequently carried on business in breach of this clause. *Held*, although the restriction was of an indefinite duration, the restraint was not, in the circumstances, unreasonable or oppressive and the plaintiff was entitled to recover the amount specified in the agreement. (See also *Dunlop Pneumatic Tyre Co Ltd v New Garage and Motor Co Ltd*; but see *Eastes v Russ*.)

Hivac Ltd v Park Royal Scientific Instruments Ltd   [293]
[1946] 1 All ER 350 (Court of Appeal)

The plaintiff company, which engaged in the highly skilled work of the manufacture of midget valves for deaf aids, discovered that a number of their employees were doing spare time work for a competitor, the defendants. The plaintiffs sought an injunction to restrain the employment of their staff by the defendants and this relief would be given if it could be shown that by working for the defendants the employees were breaking their contracts of service. *Held*, an injunction would be granted as the employees were in breach of their obligation to render faithful service to the plaintiffs which was an implied term of their contract of service. (See also *Winter Garden Theatre (London) Ltd v Millenium Productions Ltd.*)

Hoare v Rennie (1859) 5 H & N 19   [294]

There was a contract by which the plaintiffs agreed to supply the defendants with 667 tons of iron in June, July, August and September, about one quarter of the total quantity to be delivered in each month. The plaintiffs shipped 2 tons in June and thus broke their contract but nevertheless contended that the defendants were bound to accept and pay for this smaller amount. *Held*, judgment would be entered in favour of the defendants as they had the right to say that the plaintiffs had not performed their contract and on this ground to refuse delivery. (See also *White & Carter (Councils) Ltd v McGregor.*)

Hollier v Rambler Motors (AMC) Ltd [1972]   [295]
1 All ER 399 (Court of Appeal)

The plaintiff's car needed some repair work done to it. He telephoned the defendants' garage and asked if and when they could do the work. The defendants' manager replied that they could not do the work immediately but if the plaintiff could have the car brought to the garage they would attend to the defects in due course. The plaintiff agreed, and these were the only express terms agreed. On three or four occasions during the preceding five years the defendants had carried out work for the plaintiff and on each occasion he had signed an 'invoice' describing the work to be done and the price. Underneath the space for signature was a clause stating that 'The company is not responsible for damage caused by fire to customers' cars on the premises'. A fire occurred owing to the defendants' negligence and the defendants pleaded that, although on this occasion the plaintiff had not signed an 'invoice', the exemption clause had been incorporated in the oral contract by a course of dealing and its effect was to bar the plaintiff's claim. *Held*, the plaintiff's claim should succeed. There was insufficient previous course of dealing to justify the incorporation into the contract of the exemption clause. In any case, the clause could be read as being a mere warning that liability did not exist for loss caused by fire started without negligence. Ambiguous clauses are construed contra proferentem. (See also *McCutcheon v David MacBrayne Ltd.*)

Hollins v J. Davy Ltd [1963] 1 All ER 370   [296]

The plaintiff garaged his Sunbeam Rapier with the defendants and terms of the contract excluded the defendants' liability for (a) loss or damage however caused, and (b) loss or misdelivery of any vehicle arising from any cause including negligence. The defendants' servant negligently allowed a stranger to drive away the plaintiff's car honestly but mistakenly believing that the plaintiff had sent him to collect it. The stranger stole the car and the plaintiff sought to recover, inter alia, damages for breach of contract. *Held*, his action would fail: the defendants' servant had acted honestly and it followed that there had not been such a deliberate disregard of contractual obligations as would disentitle the defendants from relying on the exemption clauses. (See also *Suisse Atlantique, etc v Rotterdamsche, etc.*)

Holwell Securities Ltd v Hughes   [297]
[1974] 1 All ER 161 (Court of Appeal)

The defendant granted the plaintiffs an option to purchase a dwelling-house, the option to be exercised within six months by notice in writing to the defendant. The plaintiffs posted a letter exercising the option and sent it by ordinary post. The letter was not delivered. *Held*, the option was not validly exercised since it could only be so exercised in the prescribed way. The rule that an acceptance of an offer could be effected, so as to constitute a binding contract, merely by posting a letter of acceptance, did not apply when the express terms of the offer stipulated that the acceptance had to reach the offeror. (But see *Henthorn v Fraser* and *Household Fire Insurance Co v Grant*.)

Hong Kong Fir Shipping Co Ltd v Kawasaki [298]
Kisen Kaisha Ltd [1962] 1 All ER 474 (Court of Appeal)

On 26 December 1956, the defendants chartered the *Hong Kong Fir* from the plaintiffs, its owners, for a period of twenty-four months from the time at which it arrived at Liverpool. The charter period began on 13 February 1957 but it was necessary for the vessel to undergo repairs for about twenty of the first twenty-four weeks of the charter and in June 1957 the defendants repudiated it. It was found that the delays were attributable to breaches of the charter by the plaintiffs in failing to maintain the vessel in an efficient state and also that in June 1957 the defendants had no reasonable grounds for thinking that the plaintiffs would be unable to make the vessel seaworthy at the latest by mid-September. *Held*, the defendants were not entitled to repudiate the charter as the plaintiffs' obligation to maintain the vessel was a warranty (for the breach of which the remedy was damages) and not so fundamental a matter as to amount to a condition of the contract, the breach of which would have entitled the defendants to accept it as a repudiation and to withdraw from the charter. Further, the delays, serious though they were, were not such as to amount to a frustration of the contract, i.e. to make further commercial performance of the contract impossible. (Distinguished in *Bunge Corpn v Tradax SA*.)

Hood v West End Motor Car Packing Co [1917] 2 KB 38 [299]

The plaintiff wished to ship a motor car from London to Messina and insured it against marine risks. He did not give notice of the fact that it was to be carried on deck and there was evidence that if such notice had been given many underwriters would have refused to insure altogether and that others would have charged a very high premium. The car was damaged by sea and rendered valueless. *Held*, the risk was not covered by the policy as the fact that the car was to be carried on deck had not been disclosed. (See *Seaman v Fonereau*; and see also s. 18 of the Marine Insurance Act 1906.)

Hopkins v Tanqueray (1854) 15 CB 130 [300]

The defendant sent his horse to Tattersall's for sale by auction and when he saw the plaintiff examining the horse's legs he said 'You need not examine his legs; you have nothing to look for; I assure you he is perfectly sound in every respect' and the plaintiff replied 'If you say so, I am perfectly satisfied'. The plaintiff attended the auction sale on the following day and bought the horse which was subsequently found to be unsound. *Held*, the plaintiff could not recover his loss as the defendant's assurance was a mere representation and not a warranty which formed part of the contract. (But see *Bannerman v White*.)

Horne v Midland Railway Co (1873) LR 8 CP 131 [301]

The plaintiffs, who were shoe manufacturers in Kettering, obtained a contract for the supply of a quantity of shoes to a London firm at 4*s* per pair, an exceptionally good price, and the shoes were to be delivered by a certain date. The plaintiffs delivered the shoes to the defendants, a railway company, for carriage to London, in time, in the normal course of events, for delivery in accordance with the terms of the contract, and told the station master that they, the plaintiffs, had undertaken to deliver the shoes by the date specified in the contract. The shoes arrived in London a day late and the purchasers of the shoes refused to accept delivery. The plaintiffs were forced to sell them at 2s 9d a pair and contended that the defendants were liable in damages for the difference between this price and that fixed by the contract. *Held*, the plaintiffs' claim must fail as this loss was not such as might reasonably be considered to have arisen naturally from the defendants' breach of contract and could not reasonably be supposed to have been contemplated by both parties when the contract of carriage was made. (But see *Simpson v London and North Western Railway Co.*)

Horsfall v Thomas (1862) 1 H & C 90   [302]

The defendant employed the plaintiff to make a steel gun. When the plaintiff delivered the gun it was defective in such a way as would have justified the defendant in refusing to accept delivery and this defect might have been apparent if the gun had been examined. The gun was fired by the defendant and after several shots it burst and became worthless. There was some evidence that the plaintiff had concealed the defect and when he sued to recover the cost of the gun the defendant maintained that he was entitled to rescind the contract as the plaintiff had induced him to accept delivery by fraud and misrepresentation. *Held*, the plaintiff would succeed as the defendant's contention as to fraud and misrepresentation was defeated by the fact that the defendant had not examined the gun so that the concealment of the defect had not influenced his acceptance. (See also *Smith v Chadwick*.)

Horton v Horton [1960] 3 All ER 649 (Court of Appeal)   [303]

The defendant husband executed a separation agreement under seal whereby he undertook to pay the plaintiff wife 'the monthly sum of £30'. Such payments continued for about ten months and they were made without deduction of tax, although tax should have been deducted by the husband who should have accounted for the tax to the Inland Revenue. The husband then executed a supplemental agreement not under seal and without any expressed consideration by which he undertook to pay a monthly amount 'which after deduction of tax shall amount to the clear sum of £30'. The parties originally intended that the husband should pay the monthly sums free of tax and they entered into the supplemental agreement to clarify the position. Was the supplemental agreement enforceable by the plaintiff or was she merely entitled to £30 a month less tax? *Held*, she was entitled to £30 a month free of tax. The original deed did not carry out the parties' intention and the wife could have made some claim to rectification and had some prospect of success. It followed that the supplemental agreement was made for consideration, viz, that the wife refrained from taking rectification proceedings. (See also *Collisher v Bischoffsheim*.)

Houghton Main Colliery Co Ltd, Re [1956] 3 All ER 300   [304]

A limited company went into voluntary liquidation at a time when it was under an obligation to pay pensions to two men. *Held*, in assessing the amount which should be paid to the two men by way of compensation for breach of contract, their income tax liability should be taken into account and the sums payable to them reduced accordingly. (See also *Parsons v BNM Laboratories Ltd.*)

Household Fire and Carriage Accident Insurance   [305]
Co Ltd v Grant (1879) 4 Ex D 216 (Court of Appeal)

The defendant applied for shares in the plaintiffs' company. The shares were allotted to the defendant and notice of the allotment was posted to him but never arrived. The question arose as to whether the defendant was a shareholder. *Held*, he was, as the contract was completed at the time of posting the letter of acceptance and this was the case although the letter was delayed or never delivered. (See also *Byrne & Co v Leon Van Tienhoven & Co.*)

Howard Marine & Dredging Co Ltd v   [306]
A. Ogden & Sons (Excavations) Ltd [1978]
2 All ER 1134 (Court of Appeal)

An excavation and dredging company hired barges from the owners. During pre-contract negotiations, the owners substantially overstated the dead-weight capacity of the barges. They did so having consulted Lloyd's Register, but not the correct information which was contained in the barges' documents. On discovering the overstatement, the dredging company refused to pay the hire charges and claimed damages for misrepresentation under s. 2(1) of the Misrepresentation Act 1967. This provides that where a misrepresentation would have been actionable if fraudulent, the person making it is liable even though the misrepresentation is not fraudulent, unless he proves that he believed, on reasonable grounds, that the misrepresentation was true. *Held*, that as the misrepresentation would have been actionable if fraudulent, the onus was on the owners to prove their reasonable belief in its truth. The evidence did not establish that the owners had objectively reasonable grounds for disregarding the correct figures in the barges' documents and preferring the incorrect information in Lloyd's Register. Accordingly, the owners had not discharged the onus placed on them by s. 2(1) of the 1967 Act and were therefore liable.

Howatson v Webb [1908] 1 Ch 1 (Court of Appeal)   [307]

A solicitor was asked to execute a deed and did so on being told that it was a conveyance relating to property in which he had an interest. In fact it was a transfer by way of mortgage. *Held*, the solicitor was bound by the terms of the mortgage as the misrepresentation related to the contents and not to the character of the deed. (See also *Saunders v Anglia Building Society*.)

Howes v Bishop [1909] 2 KB 390 (Court of Appeal)   [308]

A wife was induced by her husband to sign a promissory note in respect of the debt of another. The wife had not received independent advice. *Held*, the wife was nevertheless liable on the promissory note as there was no general rule which, in such circumstances, required undue influence to be disproved. (But see *Zamet v Hyman*.)

Hoyle, Re, Hoyle v Hoyle [1893] 1 Ch 84 (Court of Appeal)   [309]

A testator orally promised his partners in a firm of solicitors that he would guarantee them against loss from a certain debt due from the testator's son. In his will the testator stated that 'he had guaranteed' the firm in this respect and in a codicil he 'confirmed the guarantee mentioned in his will'. *Held*, these references in the will and codicil were a sufficient note or memorandum in writing for the purposes of s. 4 of the Statute of Frauds. (See also *Farr, Smith & Co v Messers Ltd*.)

Huddersfield Banking Co Ltd v Henry Lister & Son   [310]
Ltd [1895] 2 Ch 273 (Court of Appeal)

The defendant company mortgaged their leasehold mills and all the fixed plant and machinery therein to the plaintiffs. An order was made for the winding-up of the defendant company and the plaintiffs, after inspecting the premises, agreed that certain looms were not affixed to the premises within the provisions of the mortgage and therefore consented to an order being made for the sale of certain machinery and plant, including these looms. The plaintiffs, who afterwards ascertained that the looms in question were originally affixed to the mills and had been wrongfully loosened and severed after the winding-up order had been made, claimed a declaration that the consent order should be set aside and that the looms were their property as mortgagees. *Held*, they were entitled to succeed as they had given their consent to the order while they were under a common mistake as to a material fact as to whether the looms were attached to the property so as to form part of it. (See also *Solle v Butcher.*)

Hughes v Metropolitan Railway Co (1877) 2 App Cas 439   [311]
(House of Lords)

The appellant gave the respondents six months' notice to repair but before the notice expired opened negotiations for the purchase of their lease. These negotiations were broken off and when six months had passed from the service of the notice the appellant brought an action of ejection. *Held*, the respondents were entitled to relief in equity as the negotiations had the effect of suspending the notice, which would not expire until six months had passed from the time when the negotiations were discontinued. (See also *Central London Property Trust Ltd v High Trees House Ltd*; but see *Ajayi v Briscoe.*)

Hunt and Winterbotham (West of England) Ltd   [312]
v BRS (Parcels) Ltd [1962] 1 All ER 111 (Court of Appeal)

The plaintiffs contracted with the defendants for the carriage of fifteen parcels of woollen goods to Manchester. Only twelve parcels arrived and the defendants relied upon a term of the special contract of carriage by which their liability was limited. If there had been a fundamental breach of the contract the defendants would not have been so protected. *Held*, on the facts of this particular case the defendants were not obliged to prove the absence of such a breach and as the plaintiffs had not alleged that a fundamental breach of the contract was the cause of the loss their claim to the full value of the goods could not succeed. (See also *Hong Kong Fir Shipping Co Ltd v Kawasaki Kisen Kaisha Ltd.*)

Hutton v Warren (1836) 2 Gale 71   [313]

The lease of a farm was determined and the lessee claimed to be entitled to a reasonable sum in respect of tillage, sowing and cultivation. The lessee, as an off-going tenant, relied upon the custom of the country as the foundation of his claim, the lease itself making no provision for any such payment. *Held*, the lessee was entitled to recover as custom required a tenant to plough and to sow and a landlord to pay for this work. (But see *Affréteurs Réunis Société Anonyme v Leopold Walford (London) Ltd.*)

Hyde v Wrench (1840) 3 Beav 334   [314]

The defendant offered to sell his farm for £1,000. The plaintiff at first made a counter-offer of £950 but two days later agreed to pay £1,000 and when the defendant refused to complete the sale brought an action for specific performance. *Held*, there was no binding contract between them as the counter-offer had destroyed that previously made and the original offer was not revived when the plaintiff purported to tender acceptance. (But see *Brogden v Metropolitan Railway Co.*)

Independent Broadcasting Authority v   [315]
EMI Electronics Ltd and BICC Construction Ltd
(1980) 14 BLR 1 (House of Lords)

At the request of the appellants, IBA, BICC designed three cylindrical televisions masts. Thereafter, IBA engaged EMI as sub-contractors for the design, supply and erection of the masts and, on IBA's instructions, EMI engaged BICC as sub-contractors for the design, supply and erection of the masts. Faults appeared in the first mast erected and IBA wrote directly to BICC who gave a written assurance that they were 'well satisfied that the structures will not oscillate dangerously'. A mast erected subsequently collapsed and IBA brought proceedings against EMI claiming damages for breach of contract and negligence and also against BICC claiming damages for negligence, breach of warranty and negligent misstatement. As a result of the claims made against them, EMI claimed over against BICC. *Held*, (i) Although EMI took no part in the design of the mast, in light of the express terms of their accepted tender, EMI contractually accepted responsibility for the design of the mast. (ii) The written assurance by BICC was not a contractual warranty because there was no evidence that, at the time it was given, either party intended the creation of a contractual undertaking: see *Heilbrut, Symons & Co v Buckleton*. (iii) BICC were negligent in the design of the mast and owed a duty of care to IBA in relation to the written assurance. Since the assurance had been given negligently and IBA had relied on it BICC were liable in damages. 'One who in the course of his business contracts to design, supply and erect a televison aerial mast is under an obligation to ensure that it is reasonably fit for the purpose for which he knows it is intended to be used' (*per* Lord SCARMAN). (See also *Hancock v B. W. Brazier (Anerley) Ltd*.)

Interfoto Picture Library Ltd v Stiletto Visual   [316]
Programmes Ltd [1988] 1 All ER 348

In response to the defendant advertising agency's enquiry, on 5 March the plaintiff library of photographic transparencies, with whom the defendants had not dealt before, sent them 47 transparencies packed in a bag with a delivery note which clearly specified that the transparencies were to be returned by 19 March. Under the heading 'Conditions', which was printed prominently in capitals, the delivery note set out nine printed conditions, one of which said that a holding fee of £5 plus VAT per day would be charged for each transparency retained longer than 14 days. It was unlikely that the defendants read these conditions and, having forgotten about the transparencies, they did not return them until 2 April. The plaintiffs sent the defendants an invoice for £3,783.50 and, when the defendants refused to pay, they sued to recover the amount of the invoice. *Held*, their claim would fail as the condition, an unreasonable and extortionate clause, had not been fairly and reasonably brought to the defendants' attention. However, the defendants were ordered to pay on a quantum meruit (£3.50 per week per transparency) for their retention beyond a reasonable period. (Applied: *Parker v South-Eastern Railway Co* and *Thornton v Shoe Lane Parking Ltd*; see also *Daly v General Steam Navigation Co Ltd, The Dragon*.)

Interoffice Telephones Ltd v Robert Freeman Co Ltd   [317]
[1957] 3 All ER 479 (Court of Appeal)

There was an agreement for the hiring of a telephone installation for a period of twelve years but, six years before the expiration of this term, the hirers repudiated the contract and the owners regained possession of the apparatus. The owners claimed damages for breach of contract. *Held*, as the owners had enough plant to satisfy all demands which might have been made upon them without recourse to the apparatus hired under the agreement in question and the owners' loss would not therefore be diminished by a re-hiring of such apparatus, they would be entitled to recover by way of damages the loss of rental for the unexpired term, less appropriate deductions, so that the owners should be placed so far as possible in the same position as if the contract had been performed by the hirers. (But see *Payzu Ltd v Saunders*.)

Jackson v Horizon Holidays Ltd [1975] 3 All ER 92   [318]
(Court of Appeal)

The plaintiff booked a holiday for himself and his family with the defendants. The defendants' brochure described the hotel as 'of the highest standard' and listed numerous facilities. None of these materialised and the plaintiff's holiday was spoilt. *Held*, the plaintiff was entitled to damages not only for his disappointment, but also for that of his family. Although he was not a trustee for his wife and children, he had entered into the contract for their benefit. (See *Beswick v Beswick* and *Jarvis v Swans Tours Ltd*.)

Jackson v Union Marine Insurance Co Ltd (1874)   [319]
LR 10 CP 125

The *Spirit of the Dawn* was chartered to sail from Liverpool to Newport with a view to taking a cargo of iron rails to San Francisco. The ship struck rocks in Carnarvon Bay and was forced to return to Liverpool for repairs which took about eight months to carry out. *Held*, the original adventure had been frustrated and both parties were discharged from the contract. (But see *Tamplin (FA) Steamship Co Ltd v Anglo-Mexican Petroleum Products Co Ltd.*)

Jarvis v Swan's Tours Ltd   [320]
[1973] 1 All ER 71 (Court of Appeal)

The defendants' winter sports holidays brochure represented various facilities available at a ski-resort. On faith of these representations, the plaintiff booked a holiday. The advertised facilities were not available and the plaintiff was very disappointed. The plaintiff claimed damages for breach of contract to provide the holiday promised. *Held*, the plaintiff was entitled to compensation for loss of entertainment and enjoyment. Damages for mental distress can be recovered in an action for breach of contract in a proper case. This was such a case, since the parties contemplated that on breach there might be mental inconveniences, e.g., frustration, annoyance and disappointment. (See also *Heywood v Wellers* and *Jackson v Horizon Holidays Ltd.*)

Jennings v Broughton (1854) 5 De GM & G 126   [321]

The directors of a mining company sought and obtained expert advice as to the value of a certain mine and issued a prospectus and advertised 'in glowing and exaggerated colours' to invite applications for shares. The plaintiff purchased some shares but only after he had examined the mine itself and the reports of the experts upon which the prospectus and advertisements were founded. *Held*, the plaintiff's claim for rescission on the ground of misrepresentation in the prospectus and advertisements must fail as in making his application for shares he had not relied upon them but on his own observations and reading of the reports. (See also *Northumberland and Durham District Banking Co, Re.*)

Jennings v Rundall (1799) 8 Term Rep 335   [322]

The defendant, a minor, hired a mare from the plaintiff on the understanding that the animal was to be ridden with moderation. The defendant 'wrongfully and injuriously rode, used, and worked the said mare in so immoderate, excessive and improper a manner . . . that . . . the said mare became, and was greatly strained, damaged, etc' and the plaintiff claimed damages in tort. *Held*, the plaintiff could not succeed in tort as his action was founded on the contract of hire. (See also *Leslie (R) Ltd v Sheill*; but see *Burnard v Haggis.*)

Johnson v Pye (1665) 1 Sid 258   [323]

By telling lies, the defendant, who was a minor, induced the plaintiff to lend him £300. *Held*, an action in tort for deceit could not succeed. (See also *Jennings v Rundall.*)

Jones v Padavatton [1969] 2 All ER 616 (Court of Appeal)   [324]

The plaintiff, who lived in Trinidad, made an offer to the defendant (her daughter) to maintain her if she began to study for the Bar. The agreement was an informal one, and there was uncertainty as to its exact terms. The daughter came to London and began to read for the Bar, her fees and maintenance being paid by the plaintiff. Two years later the plaintiff offered to buy a large house in London, to be occupied partly by the defendant and partly by tenants, the rental income to go to the daughter in lieu of the maintenance previously paid to her. The house was bought in the mother's name. Three years later the plaintiff claimed possession of the house, and the daughter counter-claimed some £2,000, said to have been paid in respect of it. The daughter had not completed her studies at the time of the hearing. *Held*, the mother was entitled to possession, and the daughter had no legal interest in the property. The agreement was a family arrangement, not intended to be legally enforceable; and in any event it was too vague and uncertain to be enforceable as a contract. (See also *Balfour v Balfour* and *Parker v Clark*.)

Jones v Vernon's Pools Ltd [1938] 2 All ER 626 [325]

The plaintiff alleged that he had completed and posted a coupon by way of entry for the defendants' football pool but the defendants said that they had never received it. One of the conditions governing the competition provided that all arrangements relating to the pool and to the coupons and to 'any agreement or transaction entered into or payment made by or under it shall not be attended by or give rise to any legal relationships, rights, duties or consequences whatsoever or be legally enforceable ... but all such arrangements, agreements and transactions are binding in honour only'. *Held*, the plaintiff could not enforce payment as the parties had denied, by the conditions, that it was their intention to create legal relations. (See also *Appleson v H. Littlewood Ltd*.)

Joscelyne v Nissen [1970] 1 All ER 1213 [326]
(Court of Appeal)

The plaintiff sought rectification of a written contract whereby he made over his car-hire business to the defendant, his daughter. It had been expressly agreed that, in return, she should pay certain coal, gas and electricity bills. This agreement was not incorporated into the written contract. The defendant failed to pay the bills and the plaintiff sought a declaration that she should so pay them and, alternatively, that the agreement should be rectified to that effect. *Held*, the agreement should be rectified. The rectification was based on antecedent expressed accord on a point adhered to in intention by the daughter and father as parties to the subsequent written contract and since both parties were in agreement up to the moment when they executed the written contract that the daughter should pay the bills, and the written contract did not conform to that agreement, the court had jurisdiction to rectify the written contract, although there may have been no concluded and binding contract between the parties until the written contract was executed.

Kaufman v Gerson [1904] 1 KB 591 (Court of Appeal) [327]

The defendant, a married woman, was induced by the plaintiff to sign an agreement which provided that, in consideration of the plaintiff forbearing to prosecute the defendant's husband, which would have meant ruin for him and disgrace to his wife and children, the defendant would repay within three years the amount of the plaintiff's money which her husband had appropriated to his own use. *Held*, this contract would not be enforced. (See also *Lemenda Trading Co Ltd v African Middle East Petroleum Co Ltd*.)

Kearley v Thomson (1890) 24 QBD 742 (Court of Appeal) [328]

A firm of solicitors acted for the petitioning creditor in certain bankruptcy proceedings and incurred costs which were to be paid out of the estate. One of the bankrupt's friends, the plaintiff, offered to pay the solicitors, the defendants, a certain sum of money in settlement of these costs if they would undertake not to appear at the public examination of the bankrupt or to oppose his discharge. The defendants agreed to this and were paid the agreed amount and observed the conditions imposed by the plaintiff in so far as they did not appear at the public examination, but before an application was made for the discharge of the bankrupt the plaintiff sued to recover the money he had paid. *Held*, the plaintiff's claim must fail. There had been a partial carrying into effect of an illegal purpose in a substantial manner and this prevented the plaintiff from recovering the money which he had paid under the illegal agreement. (See also *Cooper v Willis*.)

Keen v Holland [1984] 1 All ER 75 (Court of Appeal)   [329]

Although the defendant knew that the plaintiff landowners had not been willing to grant him a tenancy which would be protected by the Agricultural Holdings Act 1948 and both parties believed that the tenancies granted did not attract such protection, the defendant relied on that Act when the plaintiffs sued for possession. *Held*, he was entitled to do so as the provisions of the Act could not be overridden by estoppel (even if the conditions for an estoppel existed) and it was not unconscionable for the defendant to rely on the Act's protection. (See also *Peyman v Lanjani*.)

Keir v Leeman (1846) 9 QB 371   [330]

The plaintiff prosecuted several persons for riot and assault upon a constable who was engaged in levying execution upon the property of another on the plaintiff's behalf. The plaintiff said that he would not proceed with the indictment if the defendants would promise to pay the amount of the debt in respect of which the writ of execution had been issued together with the costs of the prosecution. The defendants accepted this offer and by leave of the court no evidence was given against them and they were therefore acquitted. The defendants did not honour their promise and the plaintiff sued to enforce it. *Held*, judgment would be entered for the defendants as the contract to withdraw the prosecution was void as it was founded upon an illegal consideration. The fact that the judge had consented to the arrangement did not render the compromise lawful. (See also *Clubb v Hutson*.)

Kelly v Solari (1841) 9 M & W 54   [331]

An insurance company, the plaintiffs, effected a policy on the life of the defendant's late husband. The policy was allowed to lapse, but the plaintiffs forgot this fact, and when the defendant's husband died the defendant applied for and received a large payment. *Held*, the plaintiffs were entitled to recover the amount which they paid. (See also *Norwich Union Fire Insurance Society Ltd v Wm H. Price Ltd*.)

Kenyon, Son and Craven Ltd v Baxter Hoare &   [332]
Co Ltd [1971] 2 All ER 708

The plaintiffs stored 250 tons of groundnuts in the defendants' warehouse, and when received there the nuts were apparently in good condition. The warehouse was structurally sound and suitable for storing nuts, but it was not rat-proof. The contract provided that the defendants should 'not be liable for loss of or damage to goods unless (it) occurs whilst the goods are in the actual custody of the company and under its actual control and unless such loss or damage is due to the wilful neglect or default of the company or its servants', and a further clause limited any liability to a specified amount. Rats badly damaged the groundnuts, and when sued the defendants pleaded the exemption clause. *Held*, the plaintiffs' claim must fail and the exemption clause was effective on its true construction. (See also *Photo Production Ltd v Securicor Transport Ltd*.)

Kerr v Morris [1986] 3 All ER 217 (Court of Appeal)   [333]

A partnership agreement between doctors within the national health service provided that, if one of them was expelled from the partnership, he would not for two years practise within a radius of two miles. The defendant was so expelled and he proposed to set up in practice a few doors away. *Held*, an interlocutory injunction would be granted as the restrictive covenant was not contrary to public policy or the public interest. The remaining partners were entitled to protect the practice's goodwill by a reasonable restraint of trade even though, by statute, it was unsaleable. (See also *Michael (John) Design plc v Cooke.*)

Kingsnorth Trust Ltd v Bell [1986] 1 All ER 423 [334]
(Court of Appeal)

A husband wished to expand by buying another business and he arranged to borrow £18,000 from the plaintiffs, security for the loan to include a second charge on the matrimonial home in which his wife had a beneficial interest. Unknown to the plaintiffs, it was arranged that the husband would obtain his wife's signature to the mortgage deed and the wife duly signed, induced by the husband's fraudulent misrepresentation that the loan was for the benefit of his existing business. The wife did not receive any independent advice. Following the husband's default, the plaintiffs obtained an order for possession. *Held*, the order would be set aside. The husband had been the plaintiffs' agent in obtaining the wife's execution of the deed and they were bound by his fraudulent misrepresentation made to her. (Distinguished in *Coldunell Ltd v Gallon*.)

King's Norton Metal Co Ltd v Edridge, Merrett [335]
& Co Ltd (1897) 14 TLR 98 (Court of Appeal)

Both parties were metal manufacturers and the plaintiffs had received a letter ordering certain goods which purported to come from Hallam & Co, Soho Hackle Pin and Wire Works, Sheffield. At the head of the paper on which the letter was written there was a representation of a large factory with a number of chimneys and a statement that the firm had depots and agencies in Belfast, Lille and Ghent. The plaintiffs supplied the goods but it afterwards appeared that they had been ordered by a man called Wallis who in turn had sold them to the defendants. The firm Hallam & Co did not exist but the plaintiffs had received payment in respect of previous orders made in the name of that firm. On the occasion in question Wallis did not pay for the goods and the plaintiffs brought an action for damages for conversion. *Held*, their action must fail as they were found to have contracted with the writer of the letter. The property in the goods had therefore passed to Wallis who was able to give the defendants a good title to the goods when they purchased them. (See also *Phillips v Brooks Ltd*.)

Kingswood Estate Co Ltd v Anderson [1962] [336]
3 All ER 593 (Court of Appeal)

Certain landlords owned a house in which a widow resided with her invalid son: the property was within the limits of the Rent Restriction Acts and the widow was a statutory tenant. As they wished to develop the property it was necessary for the landlords to find the widow suitable alternative accommodation and to this end they purchased another house. Before the widow agreed to move it was orally agreed that there would be a tenancy of the new premises during the joint lives of the widow and her son and the life of the survivor. The landlords sought possession of the new premises and the widow relied upon the oral agreement by way of defence. *Held*, the widow's defence would succeed as moving into the new accommodation constituted a sufficient act of part performance which entitled her to rely on the bare oral contract and prevented the landlords from relying upon the lack of a written memorandum to satisfy s. 40(1) of the Law of Property Act 1925. (But see *Maddison v Alderson*; see also *Wakeham v Mackenzie*.)

Kiriri Cotton Co Ltd v Dewani [1960] 1 All ER 117 [337]
(Privy Council)

In order to obtain a sub-lease of a flat in Kampala, a tenant paid a premium to the landlord. The Uganda Rent Restriction Ordinance stipulated tht any person who, in consideration of the sub-letting of a dwelling-house, asked for a premium was guilty of an offence, but neither the landlord nor the tenant thought that the payment of a premium was an illegal act. *Held*, as the duty of observing the law rested on the landlord, the parties were not in pari delicto and the tenant was entitled at common law to recover the premium.

Kleinert v Abosso Gold Mining Co (1913) 58 Sol Jo 45   [338]
(Privy Council)

The defendant mining company agreed with the plaintiff for the removal of a certain quantity of waste rock within two years and the company agreed to provide a crusher to facilitate the work. The crusher provided was inadequate for its purpose and when the rock was not removed within the time specified the plaintiff claimed damages for breach of contract. *Held*, he was entitled to recover as it would be implied that each party had agreed to do all that was necessary to enable the work to be carried out, and as the defendant company had failed to provide an adequate crusher it constituted a breach of this implied term. (See also *Foley v Classique Coaches Ltd*.)

Kleinwort Benson Ltd v Malaysia Mining Corp Bhd (1989)   [339]
Times, 8 February (Court of Appeal)

The plaintiff bank agreed with the defendants to make a loan facility of up to £10m available to the defendants' wholly-owned subsidiary. As part of this agreement, the defendants gave the plaintiffs two 'letters of comfort' stating that it was their policy to ensure that their (the defendants') subsidiary was at all times in a position to meet its liabilies under the agreement. The subsidiary went into liquidation and the plaintiffs sought payment of the amount owing from the defendants. *Held*, the plaintiffs would not succeed as there was nothing in the evidence to show that the parties intended the letters to be a contractual promise. (But see *Rose & Frank Co v J. R. Crompton & Bros Ltd* and *Edwards v Skyways Ltd*.)

Konski v Peet [1915] 1 Ch 530   [340]

The defendant was employed as a saleswoman in the plaintiff's business of a tailor and furriers subject to a week's notice on either side, and she signed an agreement which contained a provision restricting her future business activities. The plaintiff dismissed the defendant and gave her one week's wages in lieu of notice. *Held*, this did not constitute wrongful dismissal amounting to repudiation of the contract and the defendant remained bound by such of the restrictive provisions as were valid. (See also *Heyman v Darwins Ltd*.)

Kores Manufacturing Co Ltd v Kolok Manufacturing   [341]
Co Ltd [1958] 2 All ER 65 (Court of Appeal)

The parties occupied adjoining premises and engaged in the manufacture of carbon papers, typewriter ribbons and similar products. They agreed that they would not without the written consent of the other 'at any time employ any person who during the then past five years shall have been a servant' of that other. The defendants proposed to employ a chemist in breach of this agreement and the plaintiffs sought an injunction to prevent such employment. *Held*, the injunction would not be granted as the agreement between the parties was void and unenforceable because the reciprocal restraints which it contained, which did not distinguish between employees possessing trade secrets and confidential information and those who did not and were not limited to the period for which the parties' factories were in close proximity to each other, were excessive and unreasonable in the interests of parties to it. (But see *English Hop Growers Ltd v Dering*.)

Koufos v C. Czarnikow Ltd, The Heron II [1967]   **[342]**
3 All ER 686 (House of Lords)

A vessel was chartered for a voyage from Constanza to Basrah for the carriage of sugar. She deviated to Berbera to load livestock for the shipowners. If she had not deviated she would have arrived at Basrah 10 days earlier than she did in fact. The charterers claimed damages for the difference between the market value of the sugar at the due date of delivery and at the actual date of delivery. *Held*, their claim should succeed. Although the shipowners did not know what the charterers intended to do with the sugar, they knew that there was a market for sugar in Basrah. They must have realised that at least it was not unlikely that the sugar would be sold there on arrival, and that in any ordinary market, prices were apt to fluctuate daily. It was an even chance that the fluctuation would be downwards. The loss was of a kind which the shipowners, when they made the contract, ought to have realised was liable to result from a breach causing delay in delivery. (N.B. The Law Lords emphasised that the measure of damages in contract and the measure of damages in tort are not the same. In contract there is opportunity for the injured party to protect himself against risk by directing the other party's attention to it before the contract is made; in tort there is no such opportunity, and a tortfeasor cannot reasonably complain if he has to pay for unusual but foreseeable damage resulting from his wrongdoing.) (See also *Hadley v Baxendale* and *Victoria Laundry (Windsor) Ltd v Newman Industries Ltd.*)

Krell v Henry [1903] 3 KB 740 (Court of Appeal)   **[343]**

The processions in connection with the coronation of Edward VII were due to be held on 26 and 27 June 1902, and shortly before this the defendant agreed to hire from the plaintiff a flat in Pall Mall along which the processions were to pass. The contract made no mention of the purpose of the letting but when the processions were not held on the days originally appointed the defendant refused to pay the balance of the rent. *Held*, the plaintiff's claim to recover such amount would fail as, by a necessary inference drawn from the surrounding circumstances, the holding of the procession on the days planned was regarded by both parties as the foundation of the contract. (But see *Herne Bay Steam Boat Co v Hutton.*)

Lakeman v J. P. Mountstephen (1874) LR 7 HL 17   **[344]**
(House of Lords)

The appellant was chairman of a local board of health and the respondent was a builder and contractor who had often executed works for the board. A question arose in relation to the construction of certain drains and when the respondent was asked why he was not making the necessary connections he intimated that he would carry out the work if the board or the appellant would order the work and become responsible for the payment of his charges. The appellant replied 'Go on, Mountstephen, and do the work, and I will see you paid'. The respondent did the work but the board refused to pay and the respondent sued upon the appellant's promise 'I will see you paid'. The appellant contended that his promise could not be enforced as it did not satisfy the requirements of s. 4 of the Statute of Frauds as to writing. *Held*, the respondent would succeed as the appellant's promise did not constitute a promise to pay the debt of another as the local board were not indebted to the respondent; for this reason the appellant's promise would be enforced as the statutory requirement as to writing did not apply. (See also *Guild & Co v Conrad.*)

Lamare v Dixon (1873) LR 6 HL 414 (House of Lords)   **[345]**

Lamare, a wine merchant, signed an agreement for a lease in respect of some wine cellars owned by Dixon. Before Lamare took possession of the premises Dixon orally promised that they would be made dry. In fact they remained damp and, after occupying the cellars for two years and regularly paying the rent, Lamare refused to execute a lease and withdrew from the premises. Dixon sought an order for the specific performance of the agreement for a lease. *Held*, such an order would not be granted as Lamare's conduct did not prevent him from relying upon the non-performance of Dixon's oral promise, which had been an inducement to him to enter into the agreement, as a good defence to such a claim. (See also *Whittington v Seale-Hayne*.)

Lampleigh v Braithwait (1615) 80 ER 255 [346]

The defendant had feloniously slain another and, at his request, the plaintiff did all that he could to obtain the King's pardon for the defendant. This involved 'many days labour' and much 'riding and journeying at his own charges' and in consideration of this the defendant afterwards promised to pay the plaintiff £100. *Held*, there was a binding contract to make this payment as the promise to pay £100 'couples itself' with the request to obtain the King's pardon and the plaintiff's efforts on the defendant's behalf were executed in consideration for the defendant's promise. (See s. 15 of the Supply of Goods and Services Act 1982; see also *Re Casey's Patents* and *Pao On v Lau Yiu*.)

Lamson Pneumatic Tube Co v Phillips (1904) [347]
91 LT 363 (Court of Appeal)

The plaintiffs manufactured and sold pneumatic tube systems for use in shops and stores for the transmission of cash and documents from one part of the building to another. The defendant was employed as the plaintiffs' general agent and his contract of employment provided that he would not within five years of the cessation of his employment engage, in the Eastern Hemisphere, in any business similar to that of the plaintiffs. *Held*, this provision was valid and binding as it did not exceed what was reasonably necessary for the protection of the plaintiffs in their business, having regard to the nature of the business and the position held by the defendant. (But see *Leng (Sir W. C.) & Co Ltd v Andrews*.)

Lancashire Loans Ltd v Black [1934] 1 KB 380 [348]
(Court of Appeal)

A daughter married at 18 and after the marriage went to live with her husband. Some time after the daughter came of age her mother, who was very extravagant and a frequent borrower from moneylenders, requested her daughter to raise certain money to pay off her debts, sign promissory notes and give a second charge on a vested interest in remainder without which the moneylenders refused to make any further loans. The only advice which the daughter received was from a solicitor who acted for the mother and the moneylenders. The moneylenders sued to enforce a promissory note given by the daughter. *Held*, so far as the daughter was concerned, the transaction must be set aside. She had given the note under her mother's influence and as the moneylenders had notice of the fact that the mother had exercised undue influence they were in no stronger position than she was.

Lancaster v Walsh (1838) 4 M & W 16 [349]

A person was robbed of bank notes and issued handbills to the effect that he would pay a reward of £20 to the person who gave information leading to the conviction of the thief. *Held*, the offer was accepted by the first person to give the information required and such person was entitled to the reward. The second person to give the 'information' could not accept the offer or recover £20. (But see *Fitch v Snedaker*.)

Landom Trust Ltd v Hurrell [1955] 1 All ER 839 [350]

A hire-purchase agreement in respect of a motor car provided that, in the event of the termination of the agreement by the owners, the car should be returned by the hirer who would also be required to pay 75 per cent of the purchase price from which would be deducted the amount of the instalments already paid by the hirer. *Held*, such a clause did not provide a genuine pre-estimate of damage but for the payment of a penalty and for this reason it would not be enforced. (But see *Alder v Moore*.)

Lavery v Pursell (1888) 39 Ch D 508   [351]

There was a contract for the sale of 'the building materials' of a house which was to be demolished. *Held*, such a contract was for the sale of an interest in land within s. 4 of the Statute of Frauds (now s. 40 of the Law of Property Act 1925) and in this case the contract could not be enforced as there was not a sufficient memorandum or note. (See also *Webber v Lee*.)

Law v Dearnley [1950] 1 All ER 124   [352]

The plaintiff sought to recover the sum alleged to have been paid by him to a bookmaker in respect of bets which he had made on behalf of the defendant as his agent. Although s. 1 of the Gaming Act 1892 would normally defeat the plaintiff's claim, it was argued that the plaintiff could recover on an account stated as the defendant had orally admitted that he was indebted to the plaintiff and agreed the amount of the debt. *Held*, the claim would not succeed. An action to recover the amount of the bets was not maintainable under s. 1, and the provision could not be circumvented by basing a claim on an account stated.

Laws v London Chronicle (Indicator Newspapers) Ltd   [353]
[1959] 2 All ER 285 (Court of Appeal)

An advertisement representative disobeyed an order by the managing director of the company by which she was employed and she was dismissed summarily for misconduct. *Held*, she was entitled to damages for wrongful dismissal as her single act of disobedience did not show that she was repudiating the contract of service or one of its essential conditions. (But see *Ellen v Topp*.)

Lazenby Garages Ltd v Wright   [354]
[1976] 2 All ER 770 (Court of Appeal)

The plaintiffs were second-hand car dealers from whom the defendant agreed to purchase a second-hand car for £1,670, to be delivered several weeks later. The defendant repudiated the contract. The plaintiffs resold the car for £1,770. They sued the defendant for breach of contract claiming £345, this sum being calculated as representing the difference between the amount the plaintiffs paid for the vehicle and what the defendant had agreed to pay. *Held*, second-hand cars were in their nature unique and there was no basis for any proper inference as to what the effect on the plaintiffs' trade would have been if the car had in fact been sold and delivered to the defendant. There was no 'available market' for second-hand cars and the appropriate test was what could reasonably be expected to have been in the contemplation of the parties as a natural consequence of the breach. The defendant could not possibly have contemplated that, as a result of his breach, the plaintiffs would sell one car less. As the plaintiffs had sold the car for more than the price agreed with the defendant they had suffered no loss and were not entitled to damages. (See also *Hadley v Baxendale*.)

Leaf v International Galleries [1950] 1 All ER 693   [355]
(Court of Appeal)

The plaintiff bought an oil painting of Salisbury Cathedral and accepted it as a genuine Constable on the representation of the sellers, the defendants. Five years after the sale the plaintiff discovered that the painting was not by Constable and he claimed rescission on the ground of innocent misrepresentation. *Held*, his claim must fail as the action had not been commenced within a reasonable time and, further, the mistake in question was not one which would entitle the plaintiff to avoid the contract. (See also *Harrison & Jones Ltd v Bunten & Lancaster Ltd*; but see *Peco Arts Inc v Hazlitt Gallery Ltd*.)

Learoyd v Bracken [1894] 1 QB 114 (Court of Appeal)   [356]

A broker made certain dealings on the Stock Exchange for his principal and an attempt was made to recover the commission in respect of these transactions. The contract notes which the broker had sent to his principal had not been stamped in accordance with the statutory requirements and this omission on the part of the broker rendered him liable to certain penalties. *Held*, the fact that the contract notes had not been stamped did not affect the validity of the contract between the broker and his principal, who was therefore liable to pay the broker's commission. (But see *Anderson Ltd v Daniel*.)

Lee (John) & Son (Grantham) Ltd v Railway Executive   [357]
[1949] 2 All ER 581

A railway warehouse was let to the plaintiffs by the defendants and the plaintiffs sued to recover damages in respect of damage caused to their goods by a fire which resulted from the negligence of the defendants. The tenancy agreement provided that 'The tenant shall be responsible for and shall release and indemnify the [defendants] and their servants and agents from and against all liability for personal injury (whether fatal or otherwise), loss of or damage to property and any other loss, damage, costs and expenses however caused or incurred (whether by the act or neglect of the [defendants] or their servants or agents or not) *which but for the tenancy hereby created* or anything done pursuant to the provisions hereof *would not have arisen*'. *Held*, the plaintiffs could recover as the effect of the words which are here printed in italics was to confine the protection which the clause afforded to liability arising out of the relationship of landlord and tenant.

Lee-Parker v Izzet [1972] 2 All ER 800   [358]

In 1967 a contract of sale was made for the purchase of a freehold house 'subject to the purchaser obtaining a satisfactory mortgage'. X, the purchaser went into possession and under an oral arrangement paid £5 a week to the defendant, the registered proprietor, who later executed an equitable mortgage in favour of the plaintiff. The plaintiff in due course claimed possession against X, who asserted her rights as a purchaser in possession and relied on the 1967 contract. *Held*, until the condition in the contract had been fulfilled there was no binding contract of sale. The condition was, in any event, void for uncertainty, as the amount of the loan and terms of repayment had been left at large. Thus uncertainty avoided the whole contract, and so the plaintiffs were entitled to possession. (See also *Scammel v Ouston*.)

Leeman v Stocks [1951] 1 All ER 1043   [359]

The vendor's house was offered for sale by auction and the purchaser was the highest bidder. Before the sale began the auctioneer wrote 'W. E. Stocks' (the vendor's name) in the appropriate place on a printed form of agreement, entered the date for completion and particulars of the property and affixed a 6d stamp. When bidding was completed the auctioneer inserted the purchaser's name and address, a description of the premises, the purchase price and the name of the purchaser's solicitor. The purchaser signed the document over the 6d stamp but neither the auctioneer nor the vendor signed it in the usual way. *Held*, the agreement had been 'signed by the party to be charged [the vendor] or by some other person thereunto by him lawfully authorised' within s. 40 of the Law of Property Act 1925, as evidence showed that neither party intended any other signature to be added to the document and that it was their intention that the agreement should be the final written record of the contract. (But see *Caton v Caton*.)

Lemenda Trading Co Ltd v African Middle East [360]
Petroleum Co Ltd [1988] 1 All ER 513

The defendants contracted with the Qatar national oil company for the supply of crude oil, at the same time signing a 'side letter' confirming that the contract had been negotiated without the involvement of agents or brokers on a commission basis. Under the law of Qatar, a commission contract for the supply of oil by the national oil company was void and unenforceable on grounds of Qatar public policy. The defendants later entered into an agreement with the plaintiffs whereby the plaintiffs, in return for a commission on any oil shipped, agreed to assist the defendants in procuring the renewal of the supply contract by exerting influence on the chairman or managing director of the national oil company. The supply contract was renewed and the plaintiffs sued for their commission. *Held*, their claim could not succeed as such an agreement for the use of personal influence was contrary to public policy in both England and Qatar and would not be enforced in England. (See also *Kaufman v Gerson* and *Parkinson v College of Ambulance Ltd*.)

Leng (Sir W. C.) & Co Ltd v Andrews [1909] 1 Ch 763 [361]
(Court of Appeal)

The plaintiffs sought an injunction to restrain the defendant from being connected with any newspaper business carried on in Sheffield or within a radius of 20 miles of the Town Hall. The defendant was employed by the plaintiffs as a junior reporter on their paper the *Sheffield Daily Telegraph*. A term of his contract of employment provided that he would not, after leaving the plaintiffs' service, 'be connected, as proprietor, employee, or otherwise, with any newspaper business carried on' in Sheffield or within a radius of 20 miles. The defendant entered the service of the Sheffield Independent Press Ltd, who were newspaper proprietors, as a reporter. *Held*, the plaintiffs would not succeed as the restriction was wider than was reasonably necessary for the protection of their interests and therefore could not be enforced. (See also *Mason v Provident Clothing and Supply Co Ltd*.)

Leslie (R.) Ltd v Sheill [1914] 3 KB 607 (Court of Appeal) [362]

The plaintiffs were money-lenders and they sued the defendant, a minor, to whom they had advanced £400, to recover the amount of the loan plus £75 interest. The jury found that the plaintiffs had been induced to make the loan by the fraudulent misrepresentation of the defendant that he was of full age. *Held*, the plaintiffs could not recover in tort for deceit as the action was based on the contract of loan. (See also *Fawcett v Smethurst*.)

L'Estrange v F. Graucob Ltd [1934] 2 KB 394 [363]
(Court of Appeal)

The plaintiff ordered an automatic slot machine by signing a printed form supplied by the defendants for this purpose and on this form in very small print were certain special terms. One of these terms provided that 'any express or implied condition, statement or warranty . . . is hereby excluded'. The machine did not work satisfactorily and the plaintiff, who contended that she was not bound by the condition as she had not read it and knew nothing of its contents, claimed damages. *Held*, her action must fail as, having signed the contract, in the absence of misrepresentation, she was bound by its terms and the provision in the contract had successfully excluded the defendant's liability under the implied warranty that the machine was fit for the purpose for which it was sold. (But see *Curtis v Chemical Cleaning and Dyeing Co Ltd*.)

Levison v Patent Steam Cleaning Co [1977] 3 All ER 498 [364]
(Court of Appeal)

When cleaners collected a carpet for cleaning from the plaintiff's house, the plaintiff signed a printed form which provided that goods were accepted at owner's risk and limited the maximum value of the carpet to £40 for the purposes of any claim. In fact, the carpet was worth £400. The carpet was never returned to the defendants. *Held*, there was inequality of bargaining power between the parties. Where this was so, in relation to a standard form contract, the party with superior bargaining power could not rely on an exclusion clause contained in the contract if it had been guilty of a breach going to the root of the contract. The contract in this case was one for bailment and the onus of proof was on the bailee (the defendants) to show what happened to the goods while they were in his possession. As the defendants could not explain what had happened to the carpet, they could not rely on the exclusion clause. Accordingly, the defendants were liable for the full value of the carpet. (See also *Alderslade v Hendon Laundry Ltd.*)

Lewis v Averay [1971] 3 All ER 907   [365]
(Court of Appeal)

The plaintiff advertised a car for sale. A man telephoned for an appointment to view the car, but did not give his name. He came along and tested the car and the plaintiff took him to a flat to discuss the details. At the flat the potential buyer stated that he was 'Richard Green', the well-known actor, and he agreed to buy the car at £450. He tendered a cheque in payment, signed 'R. A. Green' and on producing evidence of his identity he was allowed to take the car away. The cheque proved worthless. The buyer was a rogue, not Richard Green, and later sold the car to the defendant, who bought it in good faith. The plaintiff sued the defendant in conversion. *Held*, where a transaction takes place between people face to face there is a presumption that the offer by one person is made to the other and not to any person that other says he is, and there was nothing on the facts of the case to rebut this presumption. Thus, the plaintiff's offer was made to the rogue and not to 'Richard Green'. The rogue accordingly got a voidable title to the car, under which he sold the car to the defendant before the contract between the plaintiff and the rogue had been avoided. The plaintiff's claim therefore failed. (See also *Phillips v Brooks Ltd.*)

Lewis v Clay (1897) 67 LJQB 224   [366]

A document had been covered with blotting paper in which four holes had been cut and the defendant was asked to sign his name in these holes for the purpose, he was told, of witnessing a deed concerning a private matter. In fact the defendant signed certain promissory notes. *Held*, the notes would be cancelled so far as the defendant was concerned. He had been induced to sign them by a fraudulent representation which led him to believe that he was witnessing a deed. The defendant had no knowledge of the promissory notes and he had not been negligent and for these reasons he would not be bound by his signature in any way. (But see *Howatson v Webb*; see also *Saunders v Anglia Building Society.*)

Liverpool City Council v Irwin [1976]   [367]
2 All ER 39 (House of Lords)

The conditions in a block of high-rise flats were such that there was no lighting on the stairs, the lifts were continually in disrepair, the rubbish chutes were blocked and the cisterns overflowed. This situation was due partly to vandalism, partly to non-cooperation by the tenants and partly to neglect by the landlords, the council. When the tenants refused to pay rent, the council claimed possession. The tenants counter-claimed for damages alleging that the council was in breach of their implied obligation to keep the common parts in repair. *Held*, the contract under which the tenants took possession contained no covenant by the landlord; as the contract did not state fully all the terms the court would complete it by taking into account the actions of the parties and the circumstances. The contract implied a grant of exclusive possession with implied easements for the tenants to use the stairs, lifts and rubbish chutes. As these were essentials without which the tenants could not live, using the test of necessity, the landlords were under an obligation to maintain the common parts in good repair and accordingly such an obligation was to be implied. This also placed a responsibility on the tenants to behave reasonably. Consequently, in the circumstances, there was no breach of the landlord's obligation. (Applied in *Wettern Electric Ltd v Welsh Development Agency*.)

Lloyd v Johnson (1798) 1 Bos & P 340   **[368]**

The plaintiff's wife washed clothes for the defendant, a prostitute, and sought to recover her charges for this work. There was evidence that to the knowledge of the plaintiff and his wife the clothes in question were used for the purposes of the defendant's trade. The defendant maintained that the contract was void on the ground of immorality. *Held*, the plaintiff would succeed as the court would not take into consideration the immoral purpose for which the clothes were worn. (But see *Pearce v Brooks*.)

Lloyds Bank Ltd v Bundy [1974] 3 All ER   **[369]**
757 (Court of Appeal)

The defendant was an elderly farmer who was not well-versed in business affairs. Both he and his son were customers of the same bank. His son's company was in financial difficulties, and the defendant guaranteed the company's overdraft, by way of a charge on his house, which was his only asset. At a subsequent meeting, the bank required the defendant to give a charge for the full value of his house as a condition of continued financial support for the company. The bank failed to advise the defendant to obtain independent advice on the company's affairs. The defendant signed the necessary documents produced by the bank manager. Subsequently, the bank enforced the charge and guarantee against the defendant. *Held*, the guarantee and charge would be set aside. The relationship between the bank and the defendant was one of trust and confidence. The confidential relationship imposed a duty of fiduciary care on the bank to advise the defendant to obtain independent advice. There was a breach of that duty and a presumption of undue influence, and the transaction was set aside on that ground. (Applied in *Avon Finance Co Ltd v Bridger* and *O'Sullivan v Management Agency and Music Ltd*; distinguished in *Alec Lobb (Garages) Ltd v Total Oil (GB) Ltd*; see also *Allcard v Skinner*; but see *National Westminster Bank plc v Morgan*.)

Locker and Woolf Ltd v Western Australian   **[370]**
Insurance Co Ltd [1936] 1 KB 408 (Court of Appeal)

When proposing for fire insurance in respect of their premises the claimants failed to disclose that an insurance on their motor cars had been declined by another company on the grounds of misrepresentation and non-disclosure. *Held*, the non-disclosure of this previous refusal was a material fact in the proposal for fire insurance which entitled the respondents to avoid the policy. In all classes of insurance what constitutes a 'material fact' is decided by reference to s. 18 of the Marine Insurance Act 1906. (See also *Hood v West End Motor Packing Co*.)

Lombard North Central plc v Butterworth [1987] 1 All ER
267 (Court of Appeal)   **[371]**

The plaintiff finance company leased a computer to the defendant for a period of 5 years. Clause 2(a) of the hiring agreement made punctual payment of the quarterly instalments of the essence of the agreement; under cl. 5 failure to make due and punctual payment entitled the plaintiffs to terminate the agreement; cl. 6 provided that, on termination, the plaintiffs were entitled to all arrears and all future instalments. The defendant paid the first two instalments promptly; the next three were late and on four occasions payment made by direct debit was recalled by the bank. When the sixth instalment was 6 weeks overdue, the plaintiffs wrote to the defendant to terminate the agreement; subsequently they sold the computer for just £172.88. *Held*, cl. 6 was unenforceable as, in the absence of a repudiatory breach, it created a penalty; the defendant's conduct in failing to make payments punctually had not amounted to a repudiation by him of the agreement. However, in the light of cl. 2(a), prompt payment was a condition and, when read with cll. 5 and 6, it had the effect of making default in punctual payment a breach of the agreement going to the root of the contract. Accordingly, the plaintiffs were entitled to terminate the contract, independently of cl. 6, and to recover damages for the loss of the whole transaction. (But see *Financings Ltd v Baldock*.)

London and Northern Bank, Re [1900] 1 Ch 220 [372]

J applied for shares in a bank. On 26 October he wrote to withdraw his application and on that afternoon the directors resolved to allot shares to J and the allotment notice was handed to a postman at 7 am on the following day but was not actually posted, that is, received in a post office, until after the letter of withdrawal had been received by the bank. *Held*, the retraction was effective as the acceptance was not posted until after the receipt of the withdrawal. (But see *Adams v Lindsell*.)

London and Northern Estates Co v Schlesinger [1916] [373]
1 KB 20

The defendant, an Austrian, was lessee of a flat at Westcliffe-on-Sea. On the outbreak of war the defendant became an alien enemy and as such was prohibited from living in certain places, including Westcliffe-on-Sea. The defendant refused to pay his rent and his landlords, the plaintiffs, brought an action to recover it. *Held*, the plaintiffs were entitled to judgment as the defendant's residence in the flat was not the foundation of the contract between the parties. (See also *Matthey v Curling*.)

London Assurance v Mansel (1879) 11 ChD 363 [374]

In answer to a question contained in a proposal to the plaintiffs for an assurance on his life the defendant did not disclose the fact that he had made application to several other offices and been declined. The plaintiffs accepted his proposal but the fact that he had been declined by other insurers was afterwards discovered. *Held*, the concealment of this fact was material and they were entitled to have the contract of insurance set aside. (See also *Locker & Woolf Ltd v Western Australian Insurance Co Ltd*.)

Long v Lloyd [1958] 2 All ER 402 (Court of Appeal) [375]

The defendant advertised for sale a motor lorry which he described as being in 'exceptional condition' and told the plaintiff, who purchased it, that it was capable of 40 mph and did eleven miles to the gallon. Two days later certain defects appeared and the plaintiff accepted the defendant's offer to pay half the cost of a reconditioned dynamo. On the following day the plaintiff's brother set out to drive the lorry to Middlesbrough but it broke down on the way and an expert found that it was not in a roadworthy condition. The defendant's representations concerning the vehicle were untrue, although honestly made, and the plaintiff sought to rescind the contract on the ground of the defendant's innocent misrepresentation. *Held*, the plaintiff had finally accepted the lorry and any right of rescission which he might otherwise have had was lost. (See also *Leaf v International Galleries*.)

Long v Millar (1879) 4 CPD 450 [376]

An estate agent, the defendant, contracted to sell the land of one of his clients. The plaintiff signed an agreement and paid a deposit in return for which he was given a receipt signed by the defendant. *Held*, there was a sufficient memorandum for the purposes of what is now s. 40 of the Law of Property Act 1925, as the agreement and the receipt should be taken together. (See also *Pearce v Gardner*.)

Lord Strathcona Steamship Co Ltd v Dominion Coal   **[377]**
Co Ltd [1926] AC 108 (Privy Council)

The respondents chartered the steamship *Lord Strathcona* for use for a number of years on the St. Lawrence during the summer season. During the period of the charterparty the ship was sold to the appellants with notice of the charterparty but they refused to let the respondents use the ship in accordance with the terms of the charter. The respondents sought an injunction to restrain the appellants from using the ship in any way which was inconsistent with the charterparty. *Held*, the injunction would be granted as the appellants were in the position of constructive trustees. (See also *Sky Petroleum Ltd v VIP Petroleum Ltd*; but see *Port Line Ltd v Ben Line Steamers Ltd*.)

Lumley v Wagner (1852) 1 De GM & G 604   **[378]**

The defendant contracted to sing at the plaintiff's theatre for a certain period and promised that she would not sing elsewhere during that time without his written consent. *Held*, an injunction would be granted to restrain the defendant from singing for a third party in breach of this agreement. (See also *Warner Brothers Pictures Inc v Nelson*; but see *Whitwood Chemical Co v Hardman* and *Page One Records Ltd v Britton*.)

Lurie v Lurie [1938] 3 All ER 156   **[379]**

A husband and wife, who were living apart and concerning whose marriage divorce proceedings were pending, entered into an agreement which provided that the wife would return to the husband and that, in the event of a future separation, the husband would make certain provision for her. *Held*, in such a case, the provision providing for a future separation did not render the agreement void as being against public policy. (But see *Brodie v Brodie*.)

Lyle-Meller v A. Lewis & Co (Westminster) Ltd   **[380]**
[1956] 1 All ER 247 (Court of Appeal)

The parties entered into an agreement whereby the plaintiff, who had lodged at the Patent Office three applications for letters patent in connection with gas-filled lighters and refills, undertook that he would not himself use or exercise his inventions and that when the patents should be granted, he would grant to the defendants sole and exclusive licences under such patents. The agreement further provided that pending the grant of such licences the defendants should be entitled to use and exercise the plaintiff's inventions as if the licences under the patents had in fact been granted and that during the continuance of the agreement the defendants should pay to the plaintiff specified royalties on goods sold which embodied the inventions so long as the inventions embodied should be protected by valid letters patent in the United Kingdom. In accordance with the agreement the plaintiff discontinued the sale of lighters and refills and the defendants rendered accounts and paid what were called 'royalties' in respect of sales made by them. Letters patent were never granted and, in view of this, two years later the defendants repudiated liability for the payment of royalties to the plaintiff. They also asserted that their lighters and refills did not, on a true construction of the specifications, embody the plaintiff's inventions. *Held*, the plaintiff was entitled to recover royalties as the conduct of the defendants amounted to a clear representation that their goods embodied the plaintiff's invention and that they were liable to pay royalties. (See also *Hughes v Metropolitan Railway Co*.)

Lynch v Thorne [1956] 1 All ER 744 (Court of Appeal)   **[381]**

The plaintiff agreed to purchase from the defendant, a builder, a plot of land with a building in the course of erection. The defendant agreed to and did complete the house in accordance with the specification annexed to the contract but, because the building was in an exposed position, damp penetrated into one of the bedrooms. The plaintiff claimed damages alleging that it was an implied term of the contract of sale that the house when completed should be reasonably fit for human habitation. *Held*, his action could not succeed as, in these circumstances, no such term would be implied. (Distinguished in *Basildon District Council v J. E. Lesser (Properties) Ltd*; but see *Gregory v Ford*; see also *Hancock v B. W. Brazier (Anerley) Ltd*.)

M and S Drapers v Reynolds [1956] 3 All ER 814 [382]
(Court of Appeal)

The defendant, a collector-salesman employed by the plaintiffs, a firm of credit drapers, promised that for a period of five years following the determination of his contract of service he would not sell or canvass or solicit orders by way of the business of a credit draper from any person whose name should have been inscribed on the books of his employers as a customer during the three years immediately preceding such determination upon whom he had called in the course of his duties for his employers. The defendant left the service of the plaintiffs and sold goods in breach of this provision of his contract of service. *Held*, in all the circumstances of the case, the restraint for as long as five years for a man in the defendant's position was an unreasonable restraint of trade and would not be enforced. (See also *Eastham v Newcastle United Football Club Ltd*.)

McArdle, Re [1951] 1 All ER 905 (Court of Appeal) [383]

The occupants carried out certain improvements and decorations in a house at a cost of £488 and after the work was completed those beneficially interested in the property executed a document by which they promised, in consideration of the execution of the work, to repay £488. *Held*, the consideration for the promise was past as the work had been completed when the promise was made and the claim to recover £488 must fail. (See also *Roscorla v Thomas* but see *Nye v Moseley*.)

McCutcheon v David MacBrayne Ltd [1964] [384]
1 All ER 430 (House of Lords)

The appellant asked his brother-in-law, Mr McSporran, to have his (the appellant's) car sent by the respondents to West Loch Tarbert. Mr McSporran took the car to Port Askaig where the respondents' purser quoted the freight which he (Mr McSporran) paid and for which he was given a receipt. The ship carrying the appellant's car sank owing to negligent navigation by the respondents' servants; the car was a total loss and the appellant sought to recover its value. The respondents' liability was excluded under the terms of their printed conditions if, as they maintained, those conditions had been incorporated in the contract of carriage. Reference was made to the conditions on the receipt given to Mr McSporran and the conditions were displayed on notices in the respondents' offices, but neither the appellant nor Mr McSporran had read these notices and Mr McSporran put the receipt in his pocket without looking at it. The purser omitted to ask Mr McSporran to sign a risk note, which included the conditions, although it had been prepared for his signature. Both Mr McSporran and the appellant had signed risk notes on some other occasions, but not always; they had never read them, but they knew that they contained conditions. *Held*, the appellant was entitled to succeed. The receipt given to Mr McSporran after he had paid the freight and the notices displayed in the offices did not form part of the oral contract (the receipt was given after the contract had been concluded and the appellant and Mr McSporran had not read the notices: the respondents had not done what was reasonably sufficient in bringing them to their attention) and there had been no consistent course of dealing by which the conditions could be imported as terms of the contract of carriage. 'The course of dealing on earlier occasions is often relevant in determining contractual relations, but does not assist when, as here, there was on the part of the respondents a departure from an earlier course in that they omitted to ask the appellant's agent to sign the document by which they would have obtained protection' (*per* Lord HODSON). (See also *Henderson v Stevenson* and *Hollier v Rambler Motors (AMC) Ltd*; but see *Hillas & Co v Arcos Ltd*.)

Macdonald v Green [1950] 2 All ER 1240 (Court of Appeal)   [385]

The plaintiff was managing director of a bookmaking company to which the defendant was indebted in the sum of £4,020 in respect of betting transactions. The plaintiff agreed to lend the amount of the debt privately to the defendant who undertook to repay it to the plaintiff in weekly instalments. The plaintiff sued to recover the balance outstanding under this agreement. *Held*, the action must fail as there was a stipulation, to be inferred from the circumstances, that the loan of £4,020 was to be applied solely in payment of the defendant's betting debt to the company and the transaction therefore fell within s. 1 of the Gaming Act 1892, and was void. (See also *CHT Ltd v Ward*.)

McEllistrim v Ballymacelligot Co-operative   [386]
Agricultural and Dairy Society Ltd [1919] AC
(House of Lords)

The respondents carried on the business of manufacturing for sale cheese and butter from milk supplied by members. The society bound itself to accept all the milk produced by members' cows kept on land within a defined area and the members agreed not to sell such milk to any other creamery unless the consent of the committee of the society had first been obtained. The rules also provided that members were not allowed to withdraw from the society unless their shares had been transferred or cancelled and the consent of the committee, which could be withheld without assigning any reason, was required before such transfer or cancellation could take effect. *Held*, such an agreement imposed upon members greater restrictions than were reasonably required for the protection of the society and was therefore illegal and void as in restraint of trade. (See also *Kores Manufacturing Co Ltd v Kolok Manufacturing Co Ltd*.)

McGregor v McGregor (1888) 21 QBD 424   [387]

A husband and wife took out cross-summonses against each other for assault but agreed to withdraw the summonses and live apart if the husband, on his part, would promise to pay the wife maintenance of £1 per week. *Held*, the wife's action for arrears of maintenance would succeed. The fact that the agreement was between husband and wife was not in itself sufficient to make it unenforceable and this was a case where the parties had intended to create legal relations. (See also *Carlill v Carbolic Smoke Ball Co*.)

M'Kinnell v Robinson (1838) 3 M & W 434   [388]

The defendant borrowed £30 from the plaintiff which, to the knowledge of the plaintiff, was to be used for the purpose of playing Hazard, an illegal game. *Held*, the plaintiff could not recover this sum as it was lent for the express purpose of a violation of the law and to enable the defendant to do a prohibited act. (See also *Tatam v Reeve*.)

McManus v Cooke (1887) 35 Ch D 681   [389]

The parties, who owned adjoining houses, orally agreed that they would pull down and rebuild a party wall and that each of them would be entitled to build a lean-to resting on the new wall and inclining upwards and outwards to the respective houses. The plaintiff carried out his part of the agreement but the defendant erected a lean-to which did not comply with its provisions as to height. *Held*, the oral agreement had given each party an easement of light over the other's land and the plaintiff was entitled to have it enforced. While the agreement was one to which what is now s. 40 of the Law of Property Act 1925 applied, the doctrine of part-performance also applied and 'the defendant having obtained all the advantages which this agreement was intended to give him, it would be a fraud on his part to refuse to carry out his part of the agreement, and to resist an attempt to compel him to do so by insisting on the Statute of Frauds' (*per* KAY J). (See also *Daniels v Trefusis*.)

McRae v Commonwealth Disposals Commission [390]
(1951) 84 CLR 377 (High Court of Australia)

The defendants invited tenders 'for the purchase of an oil tanker lying on Jourmaund Reef'. The plaintiff's offer of £285 was accepted and at considerable expense he fitted out a salvage expedition. The tanker could not be found and it was established that no tanker had been in the locality of Jourmaund Reef at any material time. The plaintiff sought to recover, inter alia, damages for breach of contract. *Held*, he should succeed and recover the amount of the purchase price and the amount spent in reliance upon the promise that there was an oil tanker at the locality stated. 'The only proper construction of the contract is that it included a promise by the [defendants] that there was a tanker in the position specified. The [defendants] contracted that there was a tanker there . . . If, on the other hand, the case of *Couturier v Hastie* and this case ought to be treated as cases raising a question of "mistake", then the [defendants] cannot in this case rely on any mistake as avoiding the contract, because any mistake was induced by the serious fault of their own servants, who asserted the existence of a tanker recklessly and without any reasonable ground. There *was* a contract, and the [defendants] contracted that a tanker existed in the position specified. Since there was no such tanker, there has been a breach of contract, and the [plaintiff is] entitled to damages for that breach' (*per* DIXON and FULLAGAR JJ). (But see *Couturier v Hastie*; see also s. 2(1) of the Misrepresentation Act 1967.)

Maddison v Alderson (1883) 8 App Cas 467 [391]
(House of Lords)

Thomas Alderson induced the appellant to serve him for many years without wages as his housekeeper by making an oral promise to leave her a life estate in his land. Alderson did in fact make a will which purported to carry out his promise but it was of no effect as it was not properly attested. The appellant sought a decree of specific performance in respect of the intestate's oral promise. *Held*, her plea would be rejected as her acts in serving the intestate until his death were not unequivocally, and in their own nature, referable to some such agreement as that alleged and therefore would not constitute such part performance as to take the case beyond the provisions of s. 4 of the Statute of Frauds (now s. 40(1) of the Law of Property Act 1925). The fact that the Statute had not been complied with rendered the contract unenforceable but not void. (But see *McManus v Cooke* and *Wakeham v Mackenzie*.)

Magee v Pennine Insurance Co Ltd [1969] [392]
2 All ER 891 (Court of Appeal)

In 1961, the plaintiff, who could not drive, bought a car for his son aged 18, who at that time had a provisional licence. The proposal form for the insurance policy was wrongly filled in by the manager of the garage where the car was bought, and stated, inter alia, that the plaintiff had a provisional licence. Four years later, the car was written off as a result of an accident which occurred while the son was driving. The plaintiff had claimed £600 but accepted the defendants' offer of £385 to settle, the agreement being repudiated by the defendants after making enquiries about the statements in the proposal. The county court judge found that the defendants were entitled to repudiate the policy because of the inaccuracy of the answers in the proposal but that there was a concluded agreement to settle at £385 and no fraud. The plaintiff was given judgment for £385. The defendants appealed. *Held*, by a majority, the settlement agreement should not in all the circumstances be held binding on the insurance company in equity. Both parties were under a mutual mistake with regard to the policy: they thought it was good and binding. The mistake was fundamental, and the parties did not think the policy was avoidable. (See *Solle v Butcher* and *Bell v Lever Bros.*)

Maritime National Fish Ltd v Ocean Trawlers Ltd   [393]
[1935] AC 524 (Privy Council)

The appellants chartered the *St. Cuthbert*, a steam trawler, from the respondents to be used only for fishing. It was an offence to use an otter trawler without first obtaining a licence from the Canadian Minister of Fisheries and the *St. Cuthbert* was fitted with this equipment and could not use any other. The appellants applied for five licences but were granted only three. They stipulated the three trawlers to which they were to apply and excluded the *St. Cuthbert*. It was argued that the appellants' liability under the charterparty had been determined. *Held*, this argument would not succeed; the charterparty had not been frustrated, as the failure to obtain a licence for the *St. Cuthbert* was due to the election of the appellants. (See also *Davis Contractors Ltd v Fareham Urban District Council* and *Ocean Tramp Tankers Corporation v V/O Sovfracht*.)

Marles v Philip Trant & Sons Ltd [1953] 1 All ER 651   [394]
(Court of Appeal)

The defendants were seed merchants and the plaintiff a farmer. The plaintiff ordered 29 cwt of dressed spring wheat seed which the defendants had described as Fylgia. The greater part of the seed delivered was not Fylgia nor was it suitable for spring sowing. It was Vilmorin, a winter wheat, and the plaintiff successfully claimed damages for breach of contract and breach of warranty. The defendants claimed to be indemnified by the third party from whom they had purchased the seed under the description of Fylgia. When the defendants delivered the seed to the plaintiff they omitted to comply with certain statutory requirements and the third party argued that the defendants could not recover from them as the contract between the defendants and the plaintiff was illegal. *Held*, the defendants would succeed against the third party as their contract with the plaintiff was not illegal and void but merely unenforceable due to its illegal performance. (See also *St. John Shipping Corporation v Joseph Rank Ltd.*)

Marshall v Glanvill [1917] 2 KB 87   [395]

A representative for a firm of drapers joined the Royal Flying Corps. Four days later he would in any case have been conscripted. *Held*, the contract of service had been terminated and not merely suspended, as it had become unlawful for the representative to fulfill his part of the contract by serving his former master. (See also *Morgan v Manser, Metropolitan Water Board v Dick, Kerr and Co Ltd* and *Hare v Murphy Brothers Ltd.*)

Martin-Baker Aircraft Co Ltd v Canadian Flight   [396]
Equipment Ltd [1955] 2 All ER 722

Manufacturers of aircraft ejection seats agreed 'to permit' a Canadian company 'to manufacture, sell and exploit' all their products on the American continent. Provision was also made for the payment, every six months, of royalties, but the agreement contained no provision for determination. *Held*, bearing in mind that the relationship created was essentially a commercial relationship of confidence and trust, the agreement was determinable on reasonable notice which, in this case, was 12 months. (See also *Staffordshire Area Health Authority v South Staffordshire Waterworks Co*; but see *Lynch v Thorne.*)

Mason v Provident Clothing and Supply Co Ltd [1913]   [397]
AC 724 (House of Lords)

The defendant was employed by the plaintiffs, a clothing and supply company with branches all over England, as a canvasser and collector. His contract provided that the defendant would not within three years of the termination of his employment be employed by or assist any person, firm or company carrying on or engaged in a business similar to that of the plaintiffs 'within 25 miles of London'. The plaintiffs dismissed the defendant who thereupon entered the employment of the People's Supply Company, who carried on a similar business to that of the plaintiffs within 25 miles of London. The plaintiffs sought an injunction to restrain the defendant from violating his original contract of employment. *Held*, the plaintiffs' claim must fail as the restriction was wider than was reasonably necessary for the plaintiffs' protection. All covenants in restraint of trade are void unless it can be shown that they are reasonable and as a general rule a restraint imposed on the vendor of a business may be more severe than that imposed upon a servant by his master. (See also *Empire Meat Co Ltd v Patrick*.)

Matthews v Baxter (1873) LR 8 Exch 132   [398]

The defendant attended an auction and bought certain houses and land from the plaintiff. At the time of making his bid the defendant was so drunk as to be incapable of transacting business or knowing what he was doing but after he had become sober he ratified and confirmed his contract. The defendant refused to complete the purchase and the plaintiff claimed damages for breach of contract. *Held*, he was entitled to recover as the defendant's contract was voidable only, and not void, and therefore capable of ratification by him when he regained sobriety. (But see *Gore v Gibson*; see also s. 3 of the Sale of Goods Act 1979).

Matthey v Curling [1922] 2 AC 180 (House of Lords)   [399]

A house known as Offley Holes, which had been requisitioned by the military authorities, was destroyed by fire and the lessor claimed damages for breach of the lessee's covenant to repair and to rebuild on the occurrence of such an event. The lessee contended that the requisitioning of the house operated to determine the lease and free him from the covenants which it contained and that the lease had been frustrated by the destruction of the premises by fire. *Held*, the lessee remained bound by the terms of the lease. (See also *Cricklewood Property & Investment Trust Ltd v Leightons Investment Trust Ltd*.)

Mendelssohn v Normand Ltd [1969] 2 All ER 1215   [400]
(Court of Appeal)

The plaintiff left his car in the defendants' garage and was given a ticket which stated that the defendants 'will not accept responsibility for any loss sustained . . . no variation of these conditions will bind the (defendants) unless made in writing signed by their duly authorised manager'. The plaintiff did not read the conditions. He had used the garage before and intended to lock the car, as was his practice, because he had a case containing valuables on the back seat. A garage attendant told him that the car must not be locked. The plaintiff gave the attendant the keys, and the attendant promised to lock the car later. The suitcase was stolen, and the plaintiff sued the defendants. *Held*, the plaintiff was entitled to damages. The defendants could not rely on the exemption clause, although the conditions printed on the ticket formed part of the contract, because the attendant's statement that he would lock the car took priority over the printed conditions. It was a representation having a decisive influence on the transaction. The attendant had apparent authority to make the representation and it was an inducing clause of the contract. (See also *Curtis v Chemical Cleaning & Dyeing Co*.)

Mersey Steel and Iron Co v Naylor, Benzon & Co   [401]
(1884) 9 App Cas 434 (House of Lords)

The respondents bought 5,000 tons of steel blooms from the appellants to be delivered at the rate of 1,000 tons monthly. In the first month the appellants delivered about half of the specified amount and in the next month made another delivery. Shortly before payment for these quantities became due a petition was presented for the winding-up of the appellants and the respondents, acting in good faith and in accordance with the erroneous advice of their solicitor, withheld payment. The liquidator of the appellants sued to recover the price of the steel actually delivered and the respondents counterclaimed for damages for breach of contract. *Held*, the respondents were entitled to succeed as their refusal to pay did not, in the circumstances of the case, constitute a repudiation of the contract so as to discharge the appellants from all further liability under it. (See also *Freeth v Burr*.)

Metropolitan Water Board v Dick, Kerr & Co Ltd [402]
[1918] AC 119 (House of Lords)

In July 1914 the appellants contracted to construct extensive reservoirs near Staines within six years. The agreement contained a proviso to the effect that if the work should be 'unduly delayed or impeded' an extension of the time for the completion of the work would be granted. War broke out and in February 1916 the Minister of Munitions ordered the work to stop and the plant to be sold. This prohibition was still in force in November 1917. The appellants claimed that the order had put an end to the contract. *Held*, this plea would be upheld as the interruption caused by the prohibition was of such a character and duration as to make the contract when resumed essentially different from that the performance of which was compulsorily brought to an end. (See also *Bank Line Ltd v Arthur Capel & Co.*)

Michael (John) Design plc v Cooke [1987] 2 All ER 332 [403]
(Court of Appeal)

The defendants, an associate director and a senior designer, left the plaintiffs' high-class shopfitting company and set up in business on their own. Their contracts with the plaintiffs provided, in effect, that they would not for two years do business with any of the plaintiffs' clients. The plaintiffs learned that a client of theirs was intending to place an order with the defendants and that they were not, in any event, going to do further business with the plaintiffs. The plaintiffs sought an interlocutory injunction. *Held*, they were entitled to succeed. The covenants were prima facie enforceable and the fact that this particular customer would not do any further business with the plaintiffs was not per se a reason for excluding that customer from the scope of the injunction. (See also *Fitch v Dewes*.)

Midland Bank plc v Shephard [1988] 3 All ER 17 [404]
(Court of Appeal)

A husband made arrangements with the bank to transfer his overdraft to a new joint account with his wife and the bank subsequently agreed a further overdraft for the husband's business purposes. Although the wife knew of the husband's intention to borrow the money, she did not know and was not told that it would be a liability on the joint account. The husband became bankrupt and the bank obtained summary judgment against the wife: she appealed. *Held*, the appeal would be dismissed. The confidential relationship between husband and wife did not by itself give rise to a presumption of undue influence and in this case there was no evidence that the husband had induced the wife to sign the joint account mandate by means of fraudulent misrepresentation or by some fraudulent concealment, or that he had induced the wife to sign by exercising undue influence over her. (See also *Bank of Baroda v Shah*.)

Miller v Karlinski (1945) 62 TLR 85 (Court of Appeal) [405]

There was a contract of employment whereby the employee was to be paid a salary of £10 per week and to receive from his employer, in addition to expenses properly incurred, the amount payable out of his salary in respect of income-tax and this sum was to be included in his account for expenses. The employee sued to recover arrears of salary and expenses. *Held*, he would not succeed as the whole contract, an object of which was to defraud the revenue, was illegal and therefore void on the ground of public policy. (See also *Bigos v Bousted*.)

Miller's Agreement, Re, Uniacke v A-G [1947] 2 All ER 78   [406]

By deed Noad transferred his interest in a partnership to his fellow partners, Miller and Vos, who undertook to pay certain annuities to Noad's three daughters from the date of his death. The question arose as to whether the daughters were liable to pay estate duty and succession duty in respect of these annuities by reason of the fact that the agreement had conferred upon them 'beneficial interests'. *Held*, the daughters were not so liable as they were strangers to the covenant in the deed, under which they therefore had no rights either at common law or in equity as the deed would not be construed as having created a trust in their favour. (But see *Smith and Snipes Hall Farm Ltd v River Douglas Catchment Board*.)

Millichamp v Jones [1983] 1 All ER 267   [407]

By an agreement under seal, the defendant granted the plaintiffs an option to purchase a plot of land, the agreement providing for the serving of a notice of intention to purchase and payment of a deposit within a stated time. The plaintiffs duly served the notice but inadvertently failed to pay the deposit and they sought specific performance. *Held*, they were entitled to succeed. Although a requirement as to the payment of a deposit is a fundamental term breach of which entitles a vendor to treat the contract as at an end (and to sue for damages including the unpaid deposit), where, as here, the failure to pay the deposit was a mere oversight, the vendor should first give the purchaser an ' opportunity to pay. (Distinguished: *Hare v Nicoll*.)

Mistry Amar Singh v Kulubya [1963] 3 All ER 499   [408]
(Privy Council)

The plaintiff, an African and registered owner of certain Mailo land, purported to lease the land to the defendant, an Indian, and, as both parties were aware, the agreements contravened certain statutory enactments which prohibited the leasing of Mailo land to non-Africans. The plaintiff sought to recover possession. *Held*, he was entitled to succeed because his right to possession did not depend on the illegal agreements, but rested on his registered ownership of the land. The defendant could not rely on the illegal agreements and without doing so he could not defeat the plaintiff's claim. (See also *Bowmakers Ltd v Barnet Instruments Ltd*. But see *Shaw v Shaw*.)

Mitchell v Homfray (1881) 8 QBD 587 (Court of Appeal)   [409]

Without receiving independent advice Mrs Geldard gave her doctor, the defendant, £800 to enable him to buy a house. The jury found that the defendant had not exercised any undue influence and that after the relationship of doctor and patient had come to an end, three years before Mrs Geldard's death, she always stood by what she had done. *Held*, Mrs Geldard's executors were not entitled to recover the amount of the gift. (See also *Allcard v Skinner*; but see *Moody v Cox*.)

Mitchell (George) (Chesterhall) Ltd v Finney Lock Seeds Ltd   [410]
[1983] 2 All ER 737 (House of Lords)

Under an agreement made in December 1973 the appellant seed merchants supplied the respondent farmers with Dutch winter cabbage seed. The invoice, in standard form, limited liability for defective seed to its replacement or refund of the purchase price and further purported to exclude liability for loss or damage arising from the use of the seeds, for consequential loss or damage 'or for any other loss or damage whatsoever'. As a result of the negligence of the appellants' associate company, the seed supplied was of inferior quality and the respondents lost a year's production. The respondents sought damages for breach of contract. *Held*, they were entitled to succeed. Although the limitation clause was enforceable at common law, in the circumstances it would not have been fair or reasonable to permit the appellants to rely on it. (Applied: *Photo Production Ltd v Securicor Transport Ltd*; but see *Ailsa Craig Fishing Co Ltd v Malvern Fishing Co Ltd.*)

Molton v Camroux (1849) 18 LJ Ex 68, 356   [411]

The deceased purchased two annuities from the National Loan Fund Life Assurance Society. At the time of this transaction, unknown to the society, the deceased was a mentally disabled person. The personal representatives of the deceased sought to recover the purchase money from the society. *Held*, they were not entitled to do so as an executed contract entered into in good faith and in the normal course of business is not void by reason of the fact that at the time of making the contract one of the parties, unknown to the other, was of unsound mind. (See also *Matthews v Baxter* and *Hart v O'Connor*.)

Moody v Cox [1917] 2 Ch 71 (Court of Appeal)   [412]

Cox, a solicitor, sold property of which he was trustee, to Moody, one of his clients. Moody alleged that the property was considerably overvalued, and sought to have the contract set aside on grounds of undue influence. *Held*, rescission would be granted. 'If a man who is in the position of solicitor to a client, so that the client has presumably confidence in him and the solicitor has presumably influence over the client, desires to contract with his client, he must make a full disclosure of every material fact that he knows, and must take upon himself the burden of satisfying the court that the contract is one of full advantage to his client' (*per* SCRUTTON LJ). (But see *Mitchell v Homfray*.)

Moorcock, The (1889) 14 PD 64   [413]

The appellants made an agreement with the respondent for the use of their wharf and jetty for the purpose of loading and storing cargo from the *Moorcock*. The bed of the river adjoining the jetty was vested in a third party: it was beyond the control of the appellants and they had taken no steps to ascertain whether it was a safe place for the *Moorcock* to lie as was inevitable at low water on every tide. The vessel grounded and suffered damage because of the uneven condition of the river bed. *Held*, the appellants were liable as the jetty could not have been used without the *Moorcock* grounding and in these circumstances they would be deemed to have impliedly represented that they had taken reasonable care to ascertain that the river bed adjoining the jetty was in such a condition as not to cause injury to the vessel. (Applied in *Wettern Electric Ltd v Welsh Development Agency*; but see *Hamlyn & Co v Wood & Co.*)

Morgan v Manser [1947] 2 All ER 666   [414]

The defendant was a variety artiste (Charlie Chester) and, by an arrangement concluded in 1938, the plaintiff was to act as his manager for a period of 10 years. War came and the defendant was called-up. The plaintiff claimed damages for breach of contract. *Held*, the plaintiff's action would be unsuccessful as the contract between the parties had been frustrated by the calling-up of the defendant. (See also *Boast v Firth*; but see *Mount v Oldham Corporation*.)

Morley v Loughnan [1893] 1 Ch 736   [415]

Loughnan was a member of a religious sect whose main tenet was to give everything to the Lord; he was employed as a travelling companion to one Morley, who was an epileptic who had inherited a large fortune. Loughnan converted Morley to that sect, received him into his family and in the course of six or seven years obtained from him most of his fortune amounting to about £140,000. Morley died and his executors sued to recover the money given to Loughnan. *Held*, it ought to be refunded as Loughnan had obtained the money by undue influence under the guise of religion. (See also *Powell v Powell*.)

Morris v Baron & Co [1918] AC 1 (House of Lords)   **[416]**

By an agreement in writing the appellant contracted to sell to the respondent 500 pieces of moss blue serge. The appellant instituted proceedings to recover the value of 223 pieces of cloth which were delivered under the contract and the respondents counterclaimed in respect of their failure to deliver the remainder. The parties orally agreed terms of settlement in this action. *Held*, notwithstanding the then requirements as to writing, the original written contract had been impliedly rescinded by the conclusion of the oral settlement of the claims of both sides. The settlement itself constituted a new contract but as it did not satisfy the statutory requirements as to writing it could not be enforced.

Moschi v LEP Air Services Ltd [1972] 2 All ER 393   **[417]**
(House of Lords)

The defendants agreed to pay £40,000 to the plaintiffs, payment to be made in seven weekly instalments. The defendants' managing director personally guaranteed payment of the debt. After three weeks, the payments were in arrears, and this amounted to a repudiation of the contract by the defendants. The plaintiffs accepted the repudiation and then sued the guarantor for the recovery of the money. *Held*, the guarantor was liable. The plaintiffs' acceptance of the repudiation was not a variation of the contract so as to discharge the guarantor from his liability, and he was liable to make good in damages the whole loss which the plaintiffs had suffered.

Mount v Oldham Corporation [1973] 1 All ER 26   **[418]**
(Court of Appeal)

The plaintiff headmaster owned a special school for maladjusted children. As a result of pending criminal charges (of which he was subsequently cleared) he was away from school for six months. The running of the school was continued by the staff. The defendants withdrew children from the school without notice and, when sued for a term's fees in lieu of notice, pleaded that the contract was frustrated. *Held*, the plaintiff's claim should succeed. His temporary absence did not frustrate the contract. The claim was properly made for a term's fees rather than damages since the usage of the educational world was a term's notice or a term's fees in lieu. (But see *Morgan v Manser*.)

Mountstephen v Lakeman. *See* **Lakeman v J. P. Mountstephen**

Mullett v Mason (1866) LR 1 CP 559   **[419]**

The plaintiff bought a cow from the defendant, a cattle dealer, who had fraudulently represented that it was free from infectious disease, although he knew that it was not. The cow was placed with five others which caught the disease and died. *Held*, the plaintiff was entitled to recover damages in respect of the loss of these cows, which was the direct and natural consequence of the plaintiff acting upon the defendant's fraudulent representation that the cow which he sold to the plaintiff was free from disease.

Nash v Inman [1908] 2 KB 1 (Court of Appeal)   **[420]**

The plaintiff was a tailor in Savile Row and the defendant an undergraduate at Trinity College, Cambridge. While under age the defendant ordered certain clothes from the plaintiff, including 11 fancy waistcoats at two guineas each, and the plaintiff instituted proceedings to recover the cost of the clothes supplied. Evidence given by the defendant's father showed that the defendant already had an adequate supply of clothes suitable and necessary for his condition in life. *Held*, in view of this fact, the goods ordered from the plaintiff were not necessaries and the plaintiff's action must fail. (See also *Fawcett v Smethurst* and s. 1 of the Minors' Contracts Act 1987; but see *Chapple v Cooper*.)

National Carriers Ltd v Panalpina (Northern) Ltd [1981]   **[421]**
1 All ER 161 (House of Lords)

The appellants leased a warehouse from the respondents for a term of 10 years. In May 1979, five years into the term, the local authority closed the street giving the only access to the warehouse because of the dangerous condition of a listed building on the opposite side of the road. After holding a local inquiry, in March 1980 the Secretary of State gave his consent for the demolition of the listed building and it was envisaged by the local authority that the demolition would be completed, and the street reopened, in January 1981. The appellants maintained that the closure of the street, denying them the use of the warehouse for the purpose contemplated by the lease, had frustrated the lease. *Held*, this contention would be rejected. Although in exceedingly rare circumstances the doctrine of frustration could apply to a lease of land, the loss of use for just two out of ten years was not sufficiently grave to amount to a frustrating event. (See also *Cricklewood Property and Investment Trust Ltd v Leighton's Investment Trust Ltd* and *Universal Corporation v Five Ways Properties Ltd*.)

National Westminster Bank plc v Morgan [1985]   **[422]**
1 All ER 821 (House of Lords)

A husband was in financial difficulties and a mortgagee had commenced proceedings for possession of the house which he owned jointly with his wife. In response, the husband made a refinancing arrangement with a bank and the bank manager called to get the wife to execute a charge. During his brief visit the wife said she did not want the charge to cover her husband's business liabilities and the manager assured her in good faith—but incorrectly—that it would not do so. The wife did not receive independent legal advice before signing the charge. When the bank sought possession, the wife contended that the charge should be set aside because of the bank's undue influence. *Held*, the bank was entitled to succeed. The bank manager had not entered into a relationship with the wife in which he had a dominating influence over her, and furthermore the transaction was not unfair to the wife. The bank had not been under a duty to ensure that she received independent advice. 'It was . . . conceded by counsel for the wife that the relationship between banker and customer is not one which ordinarily gives rise to a presumption of undue influence; and that in the ordinary course of banking business a banker can explain the nature of the proposed transaction without laying himself open to a charge of undue influence. This proposition has never been in doubt, though some, it would appear, have thought that the Court of Appeal held otherwise in *Lloyds Bank Ltd v Bundy*. If any such view has gained currency, let it be destroyed now once and for all time' (*per* Lord Scarman). (Followed in *Cornish v Midland Bank plc* and *O'Sullivan v Management Agency and Music Ltd*; but see *Goldsworthy v Brickell*.)

Neuchatel Asphalte Co Ltd v Barnett [1957] 1 All ER 362   **[423]**
(Court of Appeal)

The plaintiff company carried out some work for the defendant and submitted a bill for £259, but the defendant raised some minor queries which might have reduced this sum by £15. The defendant sent a cheque for £125 'on account' and later a 'further cheque for £75 in respect of this work.' On the back of this cheque the defendant had typed: 'In full and final settlement of account' and the plaintiff company accepted this cheque, signed a receipt on the back of it and endorsed it with their rubber stamp. *Held*, the plaintiff company was entitled to be paid the balance of the account as, having regard to the correspondence between the parties and the surrounding circumstances, there was no intention on the part of the company to accept the cheque for £75 in full satisfaction of their claim. The words typed on the back of the cheque were inconsistent with the main object and intention of the transaction. (See also *Richards & Bartlet's Case*.)

Newbigging v Adam (1886) 34 ChD 582   [424]

The plaintiff was induced by certain innocent misrepresentations to enter into a contract of partnership. It afterwards appeared that the business was not what it was represented to be, in fact it was insolvent. *Held*, the plaintiff could not claim damages but was entitled to rescission of the contract, repayment of the capital which he had paid and an indemnity against all claims and demands in respect of liability created by the partnership agreement. (See also *Whittington v Seale-Hayne* and the Misrepresentation Act 1967).

New Zealand Shipping Co Ltd v   [425]
A. M. Satterthwaite & Co Ltd (The Eurymedon)
[1974] 1 All ER 1015 (Privy Council)

Cargo was shipped to the respondents as consignees in New Zealand. Carriage was subject to a bill of lading issued by the carrier's agents. The bill of lading conferred various exemptions on the carrier and extended to independent contractors employed by them. The appellants acted as stevedores for the carrier as independent contractors. After the respondents had become the holders of the bill of lading, the cargo was damaged through the stevedores' negligence during unloading. The respondents sued for damages and claimed that the appellants could not rely on the exemption clause, since they were not a party to the contract. *Held*, the exemptions were designed to cover the whole operation from loading to discharge, irrespective of the fact of who performed it. The bill of lading was a bargain between the consignor and the appellants made through the carrier as agent. The contract in fact materialised when the appellants performed services by discharging the goods, Performance was sufficient consideration for the agreement by the consignor that the appellants should have the benefit of the exemptions and immunities conferred by the bill of lading. The performance of services by the appellants in discharging the cargo was adequate consideration to constitute a contract, even though they were already under an obligation because the respondents thereby obtained the benefit of a direct obligation which they could enforce. (But see *Scruttons Ltd v Midland Silicones Ltd.*)

Nicolene Ltd v Simmonds [1953] 1 All ER 822   [426]
(Court of Appeal)

The plaintiffs offered to buy a specified quantity of reinforcing bars on certain terms and conditions and when the defendant wrote to accept the offer he said 'I assume that we are in agreement that the usual conditions of acceptance apply'. In fact there were no such usual conditions and the plaintiffs made no reference to this statement in a subsequent letter. When the defendant was sued for breach of contract for non-delivery of the bars he argued that as they had not agreed the exact form of 'the usual conditions' there was no contract between them. *Held*, this clause was meaningless and as it could be severed from the rest of the contract without impairing its sense or reasonableness it should be ignored and the correspondence between the parties had concluded a binding contract. (See also *Carney v Herbert.*)

Nicoll v Beere (1855) 53 LT 659 [427]

The defendant, who was employed by the plaintiff, a Regent Street tailor, as a cutter and fitter, agreed with the plaintiff that he would not, upon the termination of his employment, carry on business as a tailor within a radius of 10 miles of Charing Cross for the period of three years from the date of such termination. The defendant left the employment of the plaintiff and set up business in opposition about 200 yards along Regent Street from the plaintiff's premises. The plaintiff sought an injunction to restrain the defendant from continuing in business in breach of this agreement with him. *Held*, an injunction would be awarded as the agreement was valid and binding as the restraint which it imposed was not unreasonable either in point of space or time. (But see *Pearks Ltd v Cullen* and *Attwood v Lamont*.)

Nicholson and Venn v Smith Marriot (1947) 177 LT 189 [428]

The defendants auctioned some table linen, described in the sale catalogue as being seventeenth century. The plaintiffs, who were antique dealers, read the description, saw the linen, and bought it. It was in fact eighteenth century linen. *Held*, as the plaintiffs had relied upon the catalogue description, there was a breach of what is now s. 13 of the Sale of Goods Act 1979, which implies a condition that goods shall correspond with their description. (See also *Varley v Whipp*.)

Nordenfelt v Maxim Nordenfeld Guns and [429] Ammunition Co Ltd [1894] AC 535 (House of Lords)

Nordenfelt, a manufacturer of quick-firing guns and ammunition, sold his business to the respondent company and covenanted that he would not, during the period of 25 years from the incorporation of the company, engage in the manufacture of guns, gun mountings or carriages, gunpowder explosives or ammunition or in any trade or business competing or liable to compete in any way with that carried on by the respondent company. Nordenfelt was made managing director of the respondent company for which he received £2,000 pa together with commission on the net profits. Nordenfelt entered into an agreement with other manufacturers of guns and ammunition and the respondent company sought an injunction to enforce Nordenfeld's covenant. *Held*, the injunction would be granted as the covenant was valid. Although it was unrestricted as to space it was not, having regard to the nature of the business and the limited number of customers (various Governments), wider than was necessary for the protection of the company, nor injurious to the public interest. (See also *Goldsoll v Goldman*.)

North Ocean Shipping Co Ltd v Hyundai Construction Co [430] Ltd, The Atlantic Baron [1978] 3 All ER 1170

Shipbuilders and shipowners entered into a contract to build a ship, the currency of the contract being US dollars. Under the contract, the builders undertook to open a letter of credit to provide security for repayment of instalments of the price if they defaulted in performing the contract. Following the devaluation of the US dollar the builders threatened to terminate the contract unless the owners agreed to a price increase. Because they were anxious to have the ship to fulfil a charter, the owners agreed on condition that the letter of credit was correspondingly increased. The builders agreed. The increased price was paid and the ship was delivered. Subsequently the owners claimed the return of the amount paid in excess of the original price. They contended that the agreement to increase the price was void for lack of consideration or alternatively that it was voidable as it had been made under economic duress. *Held*, a promise by one party to fulfil an existing contractual obligation was not good consideration and thus the builders' original contractual liability to build the ship did not constitute good consideration. By undertaking to increase the letter of credit the builders had, however, provided consideration because this was an additional obligation.

The contract was thus not void. Although it was possible to avoid a contract on grounds of economic duress, by failing to make any protest the owners had affirmed the agreement and could not avoid it on this ground. They were not entitled to claim the return of the excess payment. (See also *Stilk v Myrick*.)

Northumberland and Durham District Banking [431] Co, Re, ex parte Bigge (1858) 28 LJ Ch 50

A shareholder objected to his name being placed on the list of contributories on the ground that he had been induced to take the shares by fraudulent reports of the affairs of the company. It was proved that he had not become a shareholder because of the statements contained in the reports and there was considerable doubt as to whether he had read or even seen them. *Held*, the shareholder could not avoid his liability on the ground of misrepresentation. (See also *Horsfall v Thomas* and *Oakes v Turquand and Harding*.)

Norwich Union Fire Insurance Society Ltd v [432] Wm H. Price Ltd [1934] AC 455 (Privy Council)

An insurance company paid the insured value of a cargo of lemons acting on the false information that they had been damaged and sold. In fact they had been sold because they ripened too quickly, a contingency for which the insurers were not liable under the terms of the policy. *Held*, the insurers were entitled to recover the amount which they paid as it had been paid under a mistake of fact. (See also *Sebel Products Ltd v Commissioners of Customs and Excise*.)

Notcutt v Universal Equipment Co (London) Ltd [1986] [433] 3 All ER 582 (Court of Appeal)

The appellant had worked for the respondents, operating a universal milling machine, for many years. He was paid at an hourly rate and, subject to statute, his employment was terminable by a week's notice. He suffered a heart attack and the medical report made it clear that he would be unable to work again. *Held*, the contract of service had been frustrated as the man's illness had rendered the performance of his contractual obligations impossible and brought about such a change in the significance of the mutual obligations that the contract, if performed, would be a different thing than that for which they had contracted. (Followed in *Shepherd (FC) & Co Ltd v Jerrom*.)

Nye v Moseley (1826) 6 B & C 133 [434]

Sophia Nye was first engaged in the household of John Moseley, a married man, in the capacity of cook but soon became her employer's mistress and bore him two children. When Moseley put an end to this relationship he promised by deed to pay her an annuity of £100 and to give the children £500 each on his death. Sophia sued to recover arrears of the annuity. *Held*, her claim would succeed as the deed was not made in contemplation of further immoral acts. If the promise had been made orally or under hand Sophia would not have succeeded as the consideration for Moseley's promise would have been past. (But see *Beaumont v Reeve* and *Roscorla v Thomas*.)

Oakes v Turquand and Harding (1867) LR 2 HL 325 [435] (House of Lords)

Relying on certain statements in a prospectus, which amounted to fraudulent misrepresentations, Oakes contracted to purchase some shares. The shares were allotted and when after nine months the company was ordered to be wound up Oakes applied to the court to have his name removed from the list of shareholders. *Held*, Oakes' name should remain on the list as he was only entitled to repudiate his liability within a reasonable time and in any case he could not do so after winding-up proceedings had been commenced. (See also *Northumberland and Durham District Banking Co, Re, ex parte Bigge.)*

Ocean Tramp Tankers Corporation v V/O Sovfracht, The Eugenia   **[436]**
[1964] 1 All ER 161 (Court of Appeal)

By a time charterparty (the voyage being the measure of the time) concluded on 9 September 1956, the *Eugenia* was chartered for a trip from Genoa 'out to India via Black Sea'. The Suez Canal had been nationalized by the Government of Egypt on 26 July 1956 and both parties to the contract realised that intervention by English and French forces might lead to the canal becoming impassable to traffic. Although the charterparty did not deal with this possibility (the matter was discussed, but no agreement was reached), it did provide that the *Eugenia* should not unless the consent of the owners be first obtained be used on any service which would bring her within a zone which was dangerous as the result of actual or threatened warlike operations; if the vessel should be brought within such a zone the owners could, inter alia, insure their interests in the vessel, the charterers to refund the premium on demand. The *Eugenia* proceeded towards the Suez Canal with a cargo of iron and steel and arrived off Port Said on 30 October to find that Egyptian anti-aircraft guns were already in action and on 31 October, after the *Eugenia* had entered the canal, bombing began and the Egyptian Government blocked the canal at both ends. The vessel was thus trapped in the canal until 8 January 1957, and on 4 January 1957, the charterers claimed that the charterparty had been frustrated by the blocking of the canal. The owners claimed hire for the period that the vessel was trapped in the canal. *Held,* the charterers were in breach of the war clause in entering the canal and could not rely upon a self-induced frustration: it followed that the owners were entitled to recover any damages they may have suffered. Their lordships also considered the hypothetical question whether, had the *Eugenia* not entered the canal, the contract would have been frustrated because the vessel's only course would have been via the Cape of Good Hope. In their lordships' view, it would not, because the blocking of the canal did not bring about a fundamentally different situation. 'The fact that it has become more onerous or more expensive for one party than he thought is not sufficient to bring about a frustration. It must be more than merely more onerous or more expensive. It must be positively unjust to hold the parties bound' (*per* Lord DENNING MR). (See also *Maritime National Fish Ltd v Ocean Trawlers Ltd*; but see *Tatem (WJ) Ltd v Gamboa.*)

Olley v Marlborough Court Ltd [1949] 1 All ER 127   **[437]**
(Court of Appeal)

The plaintiff was a guest at the defendants' hotel and during her stay some of her property was stolen. There was a notice in her room which stated that 'The proprietors will not hold themselves responsible for articles lost or stolen . . .' *Held,* this notice could not be read into the contract between the parties as the contract was concluded before the plaintiff was shown to her room and therefore before she saw the notice which purported to exclude liability. (But see *Watkins v Rymill.*)

O'Neill v Armstrong, Mitchell & Co [1895] 2 QB 418   **[438]**

The Japanese Government ordered a torpedo boat and the plaintiff contracted with the captain of the ship to serve on board for a voyage from Newcastle to Yokohama. Before the voyage was completed news was received that Japan had declared war on China and the plaintiff thereupon refused to complete the voyage. He later brought an action to recover a proportion of his agreed wage in respect of the part of the journey which he had completed. *Held,* the plaintiff was justified in leaving the ship and entitled to succeed as the Japanese Government, his ultimate employers, were responsible for exposing the plaintiff to greater risks than he had contracted to run. (See also *Dies v British, etc, Finance Corporation Ltd.*)

Oscar Chess Ltd v Williams [1957] 1 All ER 325   [439]
(Court of Appeal)

The defendant sold to the plaintiffs, who were motor dealers, a second hand Morris 10 hp saloon motor car. The defendant honestly believed that the car was a 1948 model and he showed the plaintiffs the registration book which confirmed that the vehicle was first registered in that year. Six months later the plaintiffs discovered that the vehicle was a 1939 model and they claimed damages for breach of warranty. *Held*, their action could not succeed as the true inference from all the facts was that the defendant did not intend to bind himself in contract that the car was a 1948 model, but made an innocent misrepresentation as to the date of its manufacture. (But see *Wells (Merstham) Ltd v Buckland Sand and Silica Co Ltd.*)

O'Shea, Re, ex parte Lancaster [1911] 2 KB 981   [440]
(Court of Appeal)

Lancaster lent money to O'Shea for the purpose of setting him up as a bookmaker. The business was not successful and Lancaster guaranteed an overdraft at O'Shea's bank to enable him to pay an amount which he owed to another bookmaker. *Held*, O'Shea was liable to make good to Lancaster the amount which he had to pay under this guarantee as there was no provision, express or implied, that the money was to be used for the payment of his betting losses. For this reason the money was not paid by Lancaster 'in respect of' a gaming contract within the meaning of s. 1 of the Gaming Act 1892. (But see *Carlton Hall Club Ltd v Laurence.*)

O'Sullivan v Management Agency and Music Ltd [1985]   [441]
3 All ER (Court of Appeal)

In 1970 the plaintiff, then a young unknown musician with no business experience, entered into a management contract with Mills whom he trusted implicitly. Between 1970 and 1976 the plaintiff concluded various contracts with Mills' companies; the plaintiff did not receive independent professional advice and Mills did not warn him that he ought to obtain it. The agreements, in effect, bound the plaintiff to Mills and his companies completely on terms less favourable to the plaintiff than they would have been had they been negotiated at arm's length with the benefit of independent advice. The plaintiff became enormously successful and in 1979 alleged that the agreements were void because, inter alia, they had been obtained by undue influence. *Held*, he was entitled to succeed and the contracts would be set aside even though restitutio in integrum was impossible because the contracts had been performed. However, Mills and the companies were entitled to reasonable remuneration for their significant contribution to the plaintiff's musical success. (Applied: *Lloyds Bank Ltd v Bundy* and *National Westminster Bank plc v Morgan.*)

Otto (M.) and E. Otto v Bolton and Norris [1936]   [442]
1 All ER 960

The plaintiff purchased a newly-built house from the defendants who assured her that the house was well constructed. A year later a large part of the ceiling of one of the bedrooms collapsed and caused damage. *Held*, the plaintiff was entitled to damages for breach of warranty. (See also *Hancock v B. W. Brazier (Anerley) Ltd.*)

Overbrooke Estates Ltd v Glencombe Properties Ltd   [443]
[1974] 3 All ER 511

The plaintiffs instructed auctioneers to sell a property. The auction catalogue contained a condition excluding the auctioneers' authority to make representations in relation to the property. In reply to an inquiry, the auctioneers gave the defendants information

103

about the property, and the defendants bought the property. The information was inaccurate and the defendants refused to proceed. *Held*, the plaintiffs' claim for specific performance should succeed. The condition limited the auctioneers' ostensible authority, and so the representation was not binding on the plaintiffs. The Misrepresentation Act 1967 (s. 3) only applied to a provision excluding or restricting liability for a misrepresentation made by a party or his duly authorised agent and did not qualify a principal's right publicly to limit the otherwise ostensible authority of his agent.

Paget v Marshall (1884) 28 ChD 255 [444]

The plaintiff wrote to the defendant to offer him a part of a block of three houses consisting of the first, second, third and fourth floors at a rent of £500 pa. The defendant wrote to convey his acceptance of this offer and a lease was executed whereby the floors mentioned in the exchange of letters were demised at the agreed rent. The plaintiff contended that he had always intended to keep the first floor of one of the houses as a shop. *Held*, the plaintiff was entitled to have the lease annulled on the ground of mistake or to have the lease rectified to exclude the floor which he had intended to retain for his own use. (But see *Solle v Butcher*.)

Palgrave, Brown & Son Ltd v Owners of SS [445]
Turid [1922] 1 AC 397 (House of Lords)

A charterparty provided that timber should be delivered and unloaded at a certain port 'at charterers' risk and expense as customary'. It was, in fact, the custom of the port that such work was carried out at the expense of the shipowners. *Held*, the custom could not be read into the charterparty as it was inconsistent with the express term that the expense should be borne by the charterer. (But see *Pelly v Royal Exchange Assurance Co*.)

Pao On v Lau Yiu Long [1979] 3 All ER 65 [446]
(Privy Council)

The plaintiffs controlled a private company. The defendants were majority shareholders in a public company. The plaintiffs contracted with the public company to sell the shares in the private company in return for the issue of shares in the public company. To avoid depressing the market, the plaintiffs agreed not to sell a percentage of the shares for a year. A subsidiary agreement between the parties provided for the purchase by the defendants at a fixed price at the end of a year. Later the plaintiffs refused to carry out the main agreement unless the defendants cancelled the subsidiary agreement and replaced it with a guarantee by way of indemnity. The defendants, under pressure, did so. The share price dropped and the plaintiffs sought to rely on the guarantee. The defendants refused to indemnify them. *Held*, the plaintiffs' promise, under the main agreement, not to sell a percentage of the shares for a year was made at the defendants' request and it was recognised that the plaintiffs would be compensated by some form of guarantee against a fall in price. The agreed cancellation of the subsidiary agreement left the plaintiffs unprotected. The consideration for the guarantee included the plaintiffs' promise not to sell the shares for a year and, although antecedent to the guarantee, was good consideration for the defendants' promise of indemnity. It was not merely an invalid past consideration. To secure a party's promise by threat of repudiation of a pre-existing obligation was not an abuse of dominant bargaining position. There had been commercial pressure, but no coercion. (See *Lampleigh v Braithwaite* (which was applied) and *Re Casey's Patents*.)

Paradine v Jane (1647) 82 ER 897 [447]

The defendant was lessee of certain land and when sued for arrears of rent he contended that he was not liable to pay as the land in question had been occupied by a German Prince who had 'invaded the realm with a hostile army of men' thus preventing the defendant from receiving the profits from the land. *Held*, the plaintiff was entitled to recover as the defendant had covenanted to pay the rent and if he had wished to be excused payment in circumstances such as this he should have inserted a term to that effect in the contract. (But see *Taylor v Caldwell*.)

Parker v Clark [1960] 1 All ER 93   [448]

Mr and Mrs Clark, an elderly couple, lived in a commodious house and they suggested to Mr and Mrs Parker, who had their own cottage, that they should come to live with them. Mr Clark wrote to Mr Parker and said that he and his wife would leave their house and its major contents to Mrs Parker, her sister and her daughter, 'when we both pass away', and suggested ways in which the expenses of the joint establishment could be shared. Mr Parker wrote accepting this offer and said that he would dispose of his own cottage, which he did, but less than two years after moving into Mr and Mrs Clark's home and after continued unpleasantness on the part of Mr Clark, Mr and Mrs Parker left, as an alternative, in their view, to being evicted. *Held*, Mr and Mrs Parker were entitled to damages for breach of contract as an arrangement binding in law was intended on both sides and the letter written by Mr Clark was a sufficient memorandum or note for the purposes of s. 40(1) of the Law of Property Act 1925. (See also *McGregor v McGregor* and *Re Hoyle*.)

Parker v South-Eastern Railway Co (1877) 2 CPD 416   [449]

The plaintiff deposited his bag in the defendants' cloak-room, paid 2*d* and was given a ticket on the front of which were the words 'See back': on the back there was a condition purporting to exclude the company's liability in respect of any package which was in excess of £10 in value. There was a notice in the cloak-room to the same effect. The plaintiff denied that he had seen the notice or read what was printed on the ticket. *Held*, it was a question of fact as to whether the defendants did all that was reasonably sufficient to give the plaintiff notice of the condition and in this instance the defendants had satisfied that requirement. (Applied in *Interfoto Picture Library Ltd v Stiletto Visual Programmes Ltd*; see also *Watkins v Rymill*.)

Parkinson v College of Ambulance Ltd [1925] 2 KB 1   [450]

The secretary of a charity fraudulently represented to Colonel Parkinson that he or the charity was in a position to ensure that Colonel Parkinson would receive a knighthood if he made a large donation to the funds of the charity, and undertook that the title would be conferred if the donation was made. Colonel Parkinson made a large donation as requested but as he did not receive a knighthood he sued the charity and its secretary to recover the amount of his gift. *Held*, the action must fail as a contract for the purchase of a title, however the money is to be expended, is improper and illegal, it being contrary to public policy, and as Colonel Parkinson knew that he was entering into an improper and illegal contract he could not recover the amount of his donation as damages for deceit or breach of contract nor could he repudiate the contract and recover the money on the ground that the contract was still executory. (See also *Lemenda Trading Co Ltd v African Middle East Petroleum Co Ltd*.)

Parkinson (Sir Lindsay) & Co Ltd v Commissioners   [451]
of Works and Public Buildings [1950] 1 All ER 208
(Court of Appeal)

The plaintiffs contracted with the defendants to erect an ordnance factory at a cost of £3½ millions. Under the contract the defendants could require the plaintiffs to perform additional work and at the date of the contract it was thought that this would cost a further £500,000. In order to complete the work by the date originally fixed, the parties subsequently agreed that uneconomic methods should be employed which would add

£1 million to the cost of the work and that the plaintiffs should be allowed a net profit between £150,000 and £300,000. The total cost of the work exceeded £6½ millions and the plaintiffs claimed that their net profit should not be restricted to £300,000. *Held*, their action would succeed as when the maximum profit was agreed both parties believed that the work would cost approximately £5 millions, but as the final figure was greatly in excess of this sum the additional work was not within the scope of the agreement and the plaintiffs were entitled to recover a reasonable net profit in respect of it. (But see *British Movietonews Ltd v London & District Cinemas Ltd*.)

Parsons v BNM Laboratories Ltd [1963] 2 All ER 658   [452]
(Court of Appeal)

The plaintiff chemist was employed by the defendants for a minimum period of three years at a salary of £2,000 per annum plus commission. The defendants wrongfully determined the contract of service within the three year period and the amount of damages due to him was disputed. *Held*, notwithstanding the provisions of ss. 37 and 38 of the Finance Act 1960 the common law principle applied and income tax at the standard rate should be taken into account by way of deduction from the amount of damages awarded in respect of the plaintiff's loss of annual earnings, the damages themselves being tax-free in his hands. An amount of £59 2s 6d should also be deducted in respect of the amount received by him by way of State unemployment benefit. 'The effect of the dismissal was not to deprive him of all income but to reduce his income by substituting unemployment benefit for his salary. It would be unrealistic to disregard the unemployment benefit, because to do so would confer on the plaintiff, to the extent of £59 2s 6d, a fortuitous windfall in addition to compensation' (*per* PEARSON LJ). (See also *Re Houghton Main Colliery Co Ltd*.)

Parsons (H) (Livestock) Ltd v Uttley Ingham   [453]
& Co Ltd [1978] 1 All ER 525 (Court of Appeal)

The plaintiffs were pig farmers and fed their stock on pig nuts. In 1968 they bought a bulk feed hopper from the defendants. They ordered a second one in 1971 and, when it was delivered, the ventilator on the hopper was closed. This was unnoticed because the ventilator was 28 feet above ground and the hopper was filled with nuts. A few nuts went mouldy, but they were fed to the pigs and they became ill with a serious illness called E Coli. More nuts subsequently went mouldy and the nuts were no longer fed to the pigs. It was then discovered that the hopper ventilator was closed. 254 pigs from the plaintiffs' total stock of 700 died. The defendants appealed against a decision that they were liable for all the damage of which their breach of what is now s. 14(3) of the Sale of Goods Act 1979 (fitness for purpose) was the cause. *Held*, the defendants were liable for the estimated loss directly and naturally resulting in the ordinary course of events from the breach. The unventilated hopper was a breach of a warranty that the hopper should be reasonably fit for storing pig nuts in a condition suitable for feeding to pigs. The plaintiffs' losses were caused by that breach. Although nobody could have expected E Coli to result from the mouldy nuts, it was reasonable to suppose that the parties would have contemplated at the time of the contract, in the event of the hopper being unfit for its purpose, the serious possibility of injury and even death among the pigs. Recovery was not limited because the specific consequence would not have been anticipated as long as the type of consequence was contemplated. (See also *Hadley v Baxendale*.)

Patel v Ali [1984] 1 All ER 978   [454]

The defendants contracted to sell their house to the plaintiffs: at that time (July 1979) the defendant wife, a Pakistani who spoke little English, had one child and she (the wife) was in good health. Due to the husband's bankruptcy, the wife could not have completed the sale before July 1980: by that time it had been discovered that she was suffering from bone cancer and she had a leg amputated. On 11 August the plaintiffs issued a writ seeking specific performance. At the end of that month the wife gave birth to her second child and in August 1983 she had her third. The following month the court made an order for specific performance and the wife appealed, contending that she would suffer hardship, in being deprived of daily assistance from friends and relations, if she had to move to another area. *Held*, inter alia, the order would be discharged. In view of unforeseeable changes the order would cause the wife hardship amounting to injustice and after the long delay (for which neither party was to blame) it would be just to leave the plaintiffs to their remedy in damages. (See s. 50 of the Supreme Court Act 1981; but see *Tamplin v James*.)

Payne v Cave (1789) 3 Term Rep 148 [455]

The defendant was last bidder at an auction sale but before the fall of the hammer he retracted his bid. *Held*, he was entitled to do so as it is the bid which is the offer and not the auctioneer's invitation to bid and the defendant's offer had not been accepted until the hammer fell. The defendant's offer could be revoked at any time before acceptance. (But see *Denton v Great Northern Railway Co*. See also s. 57(2) of the Sale of Goods Act 1979.)

Payzu Ltd v Saunders [1919] 2 KB 581 (Court of Appeal) [456]

The defendant agreed to sell to the plaintiffs 200 pieces of crêpe de chine. The goods were to be delivered during a period of nine months and payment was to be made for each instalment within one month of delivery. The plaintiffs did not pay for the first consignment punctually and the defendant thereupon stated that he would only deliver further supplies at the contract price if the plaintiffs would agreed to pay cash at the time of making each order. The plaintiffs did not agree to this and sued the defendant for breach of contract, claiming the difference between the contract price and the current market price. *Held*, the plaintiffs' failure to pay for the first instalment did not constitute repudiation of the contract and the defendant was therefore liable in damages for its breach. However, the plaintiffs should have mitigated their loss by accepting the defendant's subsequent offer and they were entitled to recover only the amount which they would have lost if they had done so. (But see *Pilkington v Wood*.)

Pearce v Brooks (1866) LR 1 Exch 213 [457]

The plaintiffs, who were coach-builders, supplied the defendant, who was to their knowledge a prostitute, with a brougham (a closed carriage). The jury found that the plaintiffs knew that the carriage would be used for the purposes of the defendant's trade. The plaintiffs sought to recover the amount due in respect of the hire of the brougham. *Held*, the plaintiffs' action must fail. The contract of hire was void as the plaintiffs had contributed to an immoral act by supplying the brougham with the knowledge that it was going to be used for the purposes of prostitution. (See also *Upfill v Wright*.)

Pearce v Gardner [1897] 1 QB 688 [458]

A letter signed by the defendant contained the terms of an agreement for the sale of gravel and was a sufficient memorandum in writing for the purposes of s. 4 of the Statute of Frauds except that it did not contain the name of the plaintiff, the other party to the contract. *Held*, evidence that the letter was enclosed in an envelope bearing the name of the plaintiff would be received. The letter and the envelope would be regarded as one document and together they constituted a sufficient memorandum of the contract. (But see *Timmins v Moreland Street Property Co Ltd*; see also *Long v Millar*.)

Pearks Ltd v Cullen (1912) 28 TLR 371 [459]

The defendant, who was employed by the plaintiffs as a shop assistant on the grocery counter in a branch store at Southend, agreed that for a period of two years after leaving the plaintiffs' employment he would not 'establish, carry on, or be engaged in, or interested in . . . a business of a similar character to the business of the company within the distance of two miles of any shop for the time being belonging to the company at which he has been employed within the twelve months prior to his leaving their employ'. The defendant left the plaintiffs' employment and went to work for a nearby rival in a similar capacity. The plaintiffs sought to enforce the agreement. *Held*, the plaintiffs' action must fail as the restrictive covenant was not reasonably necessary for the protection of the plaintiffs' business and could not therefore be enforced. It might have been held otherwise if the defendant had been the plaintiffs' manager, which position would have provided him with access to their trade secrets. (See also *Bowler v Lovegrove*.)

Peco Arts Inc v Hazlitt Gallery Ltd [1983] 3 All ER 193 [460]

In 1970, on the recommendation of a specialist, the plaintiffs bought from the defendants what both parties at the time believed to be an original drawing by Ingres. When, in 1981, the drawing was, for only the second time, professionally revalued for insurance purposes, it was discovered that it was a reproduction worth virtually nothing. In 1982 the plaintiffs commenced proceedings claiming on grounds of mistake of fact recovery of the purchase price and interest and rescission of the contract in equity. The defendants contended that the action was time-barred. *Held*, the plaintiffs would succeed as, on the facts, there had been no lack of diligence on their part. They were therefore protected by s. 32(1)(c) of the Limitation Act 1980. '. . . reasonable diligence means not the doing of everything possible, not necessarily the using of any means at the plaintiff's disposal, not even necessarily the doing of anything at all, but that it means the doing of that which an ordinarily prudent buyer and possessor of a valuable work of art would do having regard to all the circumstances, including the circumstances of the purchase' (*per* WEBSTER J). (Distinguished: *Leaf v International Galleries*.)

Pelly v Royal Exchange Assurance Co (1757) 1 Burr 341 [461]

The plaintiff insured his ship and its sails and furniture in respect of a return voyage to China. When the ship arrived in the River Canton for a clean and refit, according to custom, the sails and furniture were removed and placed in a storehouse. The sails and furniture were destroyed when the storehouse was burnt and the plaintiff claimed that the insurers were liable under the policy to make good his loss. *Held*, they were so liable as the custom of removing the sails and furniture would be recognised to the extent of bringing these acts within the scope of the policy. (See also *Hutton v Warren*.)

Petrofina (Great Britain) Ltd v Martin [1966] [462]
1 All ER 126 (Court of Appeal)

The plaintiffs sought to enforce a solus agreement in gross whereby the defendants had agreed to sell only the plaintiffs' fuel oil products at their garage for a period of 12 years, although this period might be extended if sales did not come up to expectation. The restriction was limited to trading at particular garage premises. *Held*, a solus agreement in gross is in restraint of trade. While not automatically bad, it is invalid unless the person seeking to enforce it can show that it is reasonable as between the parties and is not injurious to the public interest. On the facts, the plaintiffs could not show that the restraint was no more than reasonable in the circumstances because it contained a restriction on the sale of the garage unless the purchaser would enter into a similar agreement, and the period of the tie was too long. The plaintiffs' action failed. (See also *Attwood v Lamont*; but see *Esso Petroleum Co Ltd v Harper's Garage (Stourport) Ltd*.)

Peyman v Lanjani [1984] 3 All ER 703 (Court of Appeal) [463]

In October 1978 the defendant agreed with the tenants to take an assignment of the lease of a restaurant and, in order to obtain the landlord's consent, the defendant arranged for his agent to impersonate him at an interview with the landlord's agent. After the assignment had been completed, the defendant agreed to assign the lease to the plaintiff, the plaintiff's house to be taken in part exchange and the balance in cash. Contracts were exchanged (the defendant's solicitor acting for both parties) and completion was set for April 1979. The agent again impersonated the defendant in seeking the landlord's consent and, although the plaintiff and the solicitor had become aware of the impersonation, urged so to do by the solicitor the plaintiff paid the defendant £10,000 and took possession pending the landlord's formal consent. A month later, before the landlord's consent had been given, the plaintiff consulted new solicitors who advised him of his right to rescind (in view of the original impersonation) and the plaintiff purported to follow this advice. *Held*, he was entitled to do so as, at the material time, he had not known that he had the right to rescind and he could not therefore be said, by his subsequent actions, to have elected to affirm the contract. The defence of estoppel also failed because the plaintiff had not, on the facts, unequivocally represented that he was affirming the contract, his actions had not been adverse to the defendant and the defendant had not acted on them to his detriment. (But see *Harnor v Groves*.)

Pharmaceutical Society of Great Britain v Boots   **[464]** \
Cash Chemists (Southern) Ltd [1953] 1 All ER 482 \
(Court of Appeal)

Goods, which were wrapped and priced, were displayed in a 'self-service' shop. *Held*, when the customer took the goods from the shelf his action amounted to an offer to buy and this offer was accepted when the cashier received payment for the goods. The mere display of the goods did not constitute an offer by the shopkeeper to sell at the marked price. (See also *Fisher v Bell*.)

Phillips v Brooks Ltd [1919] 2 KB 243   **[465]**

A man entered the plaintiff's shop and asked to inspect some jewellery. He selected some pearls and rings to the value of £3,000 and when he was signing a cheque for that amount stated: 'You see who I am, I am Sir George Bullough', and he gave an address in St. James's Square. The plaintiff knew that there was such a man as Sir George Bullough and reference to a directory confirmed that Sir George lived at the address mentioned. The plaintiff asked the man in the shop if he would like to take the jewels with him but was told 'You had better have the cheque cleared first, but I should like to take the ring as it is my wife's birthday tomorrow'. The plaintiff let the man have the ring but his cheque was dishonoured and the man pledged the ring to the defendants from whom the plaintiff sought to recover either the ring or its value. *Held*, the plaintiff intended to contract with the man who came into the shop although he believed (mistakenly) that he was Sir George Bullough. The property in the ring had therefore passed to the actual purchaser who was able to give a good title to the defendants. For this reason the plaintiff's action failed. (See also *Lewis v Averay*.)

Phillips Products Ltd v Hyland [1987] 2 All ER 620   **[466]** \
(Court of Appeal)

The second defendants, a plant hire company, hired an excavator to the plaintiffs together with a driver, the first defendant. The contract, in standard form, provided that the driver was to be regarded as the plaintiffs' servant or agent and that they alone would be responsible for any claims. In the course of his work for them, the driver negligently damaged the plaintiffs' factory. *Held*, both defendants were liable. The relevant clause as to liability was within s. 2(2) of the Unfair Contract Terms Act 1977 and, on the facts, it was not fair and reasonable and it did not therefore afford the defendants an answer to the plaintiffs' claim. (Distinguished in *Thompson v T. Lohan (Plant Hire) Ltd*; but see *Harris v Wyre Forest District Council*.)

Photo Production Ltd v Securicor Transport Ltd   **[467]**
[1980] 1 All ER 556 (House of Lords)

An employee of the defendant security company deliberately lit a fire which set alight the plaintiffs' factory, while on night patrol duty. The defendants denied liability on the basis of exemption clauses in their contract with the plaintiffs which excluded liability for injurious acts or defaults by employees. The Court of Appeal held that the defendants could not rely thereon because they had committed a fundamental breach of contract. *Held*, allowing the defendants' appeal, there was no rule of law by which exemption clauses were deprived of effect, regardless of their terms, where there was a fundamental breach of contract. In deciding whether an exemption clause is to be applied, the question is one of construction of the contract as a whole. On its true construction, the exemption clause relied on by the defendants was clear and unambiguous and covered the deliberate acts of employees. The defendants were therefore protected by it. (Applied in *Mitchell (George) (Chesterhall) Ltd v Finney Lock Seeds Ltd*; see also *Suisse Atlantique Société d'Armement Maritime SA v NV Rotterdamsche Kolen Centrale*.)

Pilkington v Wood [1953] 2 All ER 810   **[468]**

When the plaintiff bought a house in Hampshire he employed the defendant, a solicitor, to act for him. Over a year later the plaintiff decided to sell the house and it was then that a defect in the plaintiff's title came to light. The defendant admitted that he had been guilty of negligence and the question arose as to the amount of damages which he should pay. In addition to the difference between the market value of the house with a good title and its value when the title was defective, the plaintiff claimed certain hotel, travelling and telephone expenses which he would not have incurred if he had been able to sell the house and move to Lancashire, his new place of employment, and interest on a bank overdraft which would have been paid off when the house was sold. The defendant maintained that it was the duty of the plaintiff to mitigate the damage which he had suffered by suing the vendor in respect of a breach of his implied covenant for title. *Held*, the plaintiff's duty to mitigate the damage did not go so far as to require him to undertake a difficult piece of litigation, but his claim for additional damages would fail as it arose out of facts which could not reasonably be supposed to have been in the contemplation of the parties at the time at which the plaintiff bought the house. (See also *Hadley v Baxendale* and *Interoffice Telephones Ltd v Robert Freeman Co Ltd*.)

Pinnel's Case (1602) 77 ER 237   **[469]**

The plaintiff brought an action to recover £8 10s and the defendant pleaded that he had, at the request of the plaintiff and before the amount was due, tendered £5 2s 2d which the defendant had accepted in full satisfaction of the debt. *Held*, the plaintiff would succeed on the ground of insufficient pleading, but if this had not been the case judgment would have been given in favour of the defendant as payment was made at an earlier date; this constituted satisfaction as early payment was beneficial to the plaintiff. (But see *Cumber v Wane*; see also *D & C Builders Ltd v Rees*.)

Pioneer Shipping Ltd v BTP Tioxide Ltd, The Nema [1981]   **[470]**
2 All ER 1030 (House of Lords)

A vessel was chartered for six or seven consecutive voyages from Sorel in Canada to Europe between April and December. A strike broke out at Sorel while the vessel was away on the first voyage and was still in progress when she returned, thus preventing her from being loaded for the second voyage. The parties agreed that the vessel could be used for one intermediate voyage, but when she arrived back at Sorel the port was still strike-bound. The owners claimed that the charterparty had been frustrated and the arbitrator shared this view, explaining that, at best, two further contractual voyages were likely and the performance of only three out of seven was something radically different from what had originally been agreed. *Held*, he had been justified on the facts and correct in law in arriving at this conclusion. 'I see no reason in principle why a strike should not be capable of causing frustration of an adventure by delay. It cannot be right to divide causes of delay into classes and then say that one class can and another class cannot bring about frustration of an adventure. It is not the nature of the cause of delay which matters so much as the effect of that cause on the performance of the obligations which the parties have assumed one towards the other' (*per* Lord ROSKILL). (See also *Shepherd (FC) & Co Ltd v Jerrorm.*)

Port Line Ltd v Ben Line Steamers Ltd [1958]   [471]
1 All ER 787

In November 1954, the plaintiffs entered into a time charter with the Silver Line Ltd, the owners of a certain vessel, for a period of thirty months from March 1955. In February 1956, the vessel was sold, with the plaintiffs' consent, to the defendants. The sale was subject to a bareboat charter to Silver Line Ltd, which enabled them to carry out the terms of their time charter with the plaintiffs and was for the balance of the period of the charterparty entered into in November 1954. The bareboat charter provided that 'if the ship be requisitioned, this charterparty shall thereupon expire' but there was no such clause in the charter between the plaintiffs and Silver Line Ltd. The defendants were unaware of this disparity and in August 1956, the ship was requisitioned by the Crown. The plaintiffs sued to recover the whole or part of the compensation received by the defendants from the Crown in respect of the period for which the vessel was requisitioned. *Held*, they could not succeed: '(1) Because the *Strathcona* case [*Lord Strathcona Steamship Co Ltd v Dominion Coal Co Ltd*] was wrongly decided; (2) because, even if it was rightly decided, the defendants do not come within its principles as they had no actual knowledge at the time of their purchase of the plaintiffs' rights under their charter; (3) because, even if it was rightly decided, and the defendants come within its principles (a) they were in breach of no duty to the plaintiffs since it was by no act of theirs that the vessel during the period of requisition was used inconsistently with the terms of the plaintiffs' charter . . . and (b) the plaintiffs are not entitled to any remedy against the defendants except a right to restrain the defendants from using the vessel in a manner inconsistent with the terms of the charter' (*per* DIPLOCK J). (But see *Tulk v Moxhay.*)

Posner v Scott-Lewis [1986] 3 All ER 513   [472]

Leases of flats within a block provided that the defendant landlords would employ a resident porter: the porter employed became non-resident and the plaintiff tenants sought an order for specific performance. *Held*, the order would be made. The obligation was sufficiently defined, the order would not require protracted superintendence by the court and the plaintiffs (but not the defendants) could suffer hardship if a resident porter was not in post. (Distinguished: *Ryan v Mutual Tontine Westminster Chambers Association.*)

Poussard v Spiers and Pond (1876) 1 QBD 410   [473]

The plaintiff agreed with the defendants to sing the chief female part for a period of three months in a new opera which was about to be produced at the defendants' theatre. Owing to illness the plaintiff was not able to attend the final rehearsals or the first four performances and when she offered to take her part in the fifth performance the defendants refused to accept her services and the plaintiff brought an action for wrongful dismissal. *Held*, the plaintiff could not recover as her inability to perform on the opening day and early performances was a breach of a condition precedent which went to the root of the matter and justified the rescission of the contract by the defendants. (See also *Marshall v Glanvill*; but see *Bettini v Gye.*)

Powell v Braun [1954] 1 All ER 484 (Court of Appeal)   [474]

An employer wrote to his secretary and told her that he was pleased with her past services and that he wished her to undertake added responsibility in the future. In view of this, instead of an increase in salary, he offered to pay her a yearly bonus on the net trading profits of the business. The secretary accepted this offer but the manner in which the bonus was to be assessed was never agreed. *Held*, the employer was bound to pay her a reasonable sum each year. (See also *British Bank for Foreign Trade Ltd v Novinex Ltd*.)

Powell v Lee (1908) 99 LT 284   [475]

The defendants resolved to appoint the plaintiff headmaster of a school of which they were the managers. The terms of the resolution were never communicated to the plaintiff. *Held*, there was no contract between the parties as the defendants' acceptance of the plaintiff's offer of his services had not been communicated to him. (See also *Felthouse v Bindley*.)

Powell v Powell [1900] 1 Ch 243   [476]

When Ellen was 21 she made a voluntary settlement in favour of her step-mother and she sought to have it set aside on the ground of undue influence. Ellen was advised by her step-mother's solicitor who himself prepared and became a trustee of the settlement. *Held*, the settlement would be set aside. (See also *Wright v Carter*.)

Price v Easton (1833) 4 B & Ad 433   [477]

Price owed the plaintiff £13 and agreed to work for the defendant who promised to pay the amount of Price's wages to the plaintiff in settlement of the debt. Price worked for the defendant but the defendant did not pay his wages to the plaintiff. *Held*, the plaintiff could not recover £13 from the defendant as no consideration moved from the plaintiff to the defendant. (See also *Tweddle v Atkinson*.)

Prior and Young & Marten Ltd v McManus Childs   [478]
Ltd [1968] 2 All ER 1169 (House of Lords)

A written agreement to build a dwelling-house specified that 'Somerset 13' tiles should be used for the roof. These tiles were made only by one manufacturer. The contractor sub-contracted with a supplier for the supply and fixing of the tiles. This was done, but the tiles had not been manufactured to the usual standard and were wholly unsuitable and had to be replaced. 'Somerset 13' tiles of normal manufacture would have been satisfactory. *Held*, the supplier was liable in damages to the contractor because where a person contracts to do work and supply materials for the work, he warrants, as part of the obligation to supply materials, that they will be of good quality and reasonably fit for the purpose, unless the circumstances of the contract are such as to exclude the warranty, which was not so here. (But see *Hancock v B. W. Brazier (Anerley) Ltd*.)

Prudential Assurance Company's Trust Deed, Re   [479]
[1934] Ch 338

A contributory pension scheme for the benefit of the employees of the Prudential Assurance Co contained a clause to the effect that the pension should cease if the pensioner engaged in or became connected with any business which competed with that of his former employers and in such a case the pensioner was to have the amount of his contributions returned to him, less the sum already received by him as pension. *Held*, whether or not that particular clause was invalid or unenforceable, its inclusion did not invalidate the remainder of the pension scheme. (See also *Goodinson v Goodinson*.)

Pym v Campbell (1856) 6 E & B 370   [480]

The parties negotiated for the sale of a 3/8th share in a certain invention and drew up and signed a memorandum of agreement which was not to be binding until a third party had approved the invention. *Held*, parol evidence of the fact that the agreement depended upon the approval of another for its validity was rightly admitted as it was evidence to show that no agreement had been concluded. (See also *Welch v Royal Exchange Assurance.*)

Quinn v Burch Brothers (Builders) Ltd [1966] 2 All ER 283   [481]
(Court of Appeal)

Quinn was engaged in carrying out certain building work as a sub-contractor of the defendants. It was an implied term of the contract between them that the defendants should supply any equipment reasonably necessary for the work within a reasonable time of being requested to do so. The defendants were in breach of that term in that they failed to provide a step-ladder which the plaintiff requested. To save time, Quinn used a trestle, which he knew to be unsuitable unless it was footed by another workman. The trestle was not so footed, it slipped, and Quinn suffered injury. He claimed damages in respect of this injury, framing his action in contract. *Held*, although the defendants' breach of contract provided the occasion for the plaintiff to injure himself, it was not the cause of his injury, which was his own voluntary act in using the trestle. Accordingly, the defendants were not liable to pay damages for the plaintiff's injury, for the damage he had suffered was not a natural and probable consequence of the breach of contract. (See also *Victoria Laundry (Windsor) Ltd v Newman Industries Ltd.*)

R v Clarke (1927) 40 CLR 227 (High Court of Australia)   [482]

Two police officers had been murdered and the Government of Western Australia offered a reward of £1,000 'for such information as shall lead to the arrest and conviction of the murderers'. Clarke, who knew of the reward, gave the information required, but it was found that he did so in order to clear himself of a false charge of murder and not in answer to the appeal which had been made for information. *Held*, when he gave the information, Clarke had not addressed his mind to the reward but to his release and therefore he could not be said to have accepted the offer contained in the announcement of the reward which he was unable to recover. (But see *Williams v Carwardine.*)

R & B Customs Brokers Co Ltd v United Dominions Trust Ltd [1988] 1 All ER 847 (Court of Appeal)   [483]

The plaintiffs purchased a Colt Shogun car from the defendant finance company and it was supplied to them by the third party motor dealer. A clause of the conditional sale agreement purported to exclude any implied conditions as to the car's condition or fitness in relation to business transactions. The car was the second or third vehicle which the plaintiffs had acquired on credit terms and the contract was not executed until some weeks after the plaintiffs had taken delivery. Before signing the contract the plaintiffs discovered that the car's roof leaked; two days after signing they returned it to the dealer for repair. The dealer failed to rectify the leak so the plaintiffs rejected the car and sued to recover the amount paid under the sale agreement. The defendants in turn claimed an indemnity from the dealer. *Held*, the plaintiffs were entitled to judgment. The sale of the car was subject to an implied condition as to fitness under s. 14(3) of the Sale of Goods Act 1979 and, as the transaction was only incidental to a business activity, it was a consumer as opposed to a business transaction and the exclusion clause did not provide an answer to the claim.

Raffles v Wichelhaus (1864) 33 LN (NS) 160   [484]

The defendants agreed to buy '125 bales of Surat cotton . . . to arrive ex *Peerless* from Bombay . . .' It appeared that the ship mentioned in the agreement was intended by the defendants to be the *Peerless* which sailed from Bombay in October, whereas the plaintiff offered 125 bales of Surat cotton from another ship called the *Peerless* which sailed from Bombay in December. *Held*, there was no binding contract between the parties as the defendants meant one ship and the plaintiff another. (But see *Smith v Hughes*.)

Ramsage Victoria Hotel Co Ltd v Montefiore (1866) [485]
LR 1 Exch 109

The defendant applied for shares on 8 June but no allotment was made until 23 November. *Held*, the allotment must be made within a reasonable time, the interval from June to November was not reasonable and the defendant's offer to take shares in the company had lapsed.

Rann v Hughes (1778) 7 Term Rep 350 n (House of Lords) [486]

An administratrix personally undertook and promised to pay certain moneys which were due from the estate. *Held*, there was no consideration for the promise and for this reason the undertaking would not be enforced. SKYNNER LCB said 'the law of this country supplies no means, nor affords any remedy, to compel the performance of an agreement made without sufficient consideration.' (See also *Eastwood v Kenyon*.)

Rawlinson v Ames [1925] Ch 96 [487]

The parties entered into an oral contract with regard to the lease of a flat to which it was agreed certain alterations should be made by the plaintiff. The defendant visited the flat while this work was in hand and at her suggestion and request further alterations were carried out. The defendant subsequently repudiated the contract and the plaintiff brought an action for specific performance. *Held*, the plaintiff would succeed as the work carried out by the plaintiff at the defendant's request would not have been executed if the contract alleged had not been entered into, and for this reason these acts of part performance were sufficient to take the case out of what is now s. 40(1) of the Law of Property Act 1925. (See also *Broughton v Snook*.)

Ray v Druce [1985] 2 All ER 482 [488]

The defendant granted the plaintiffs an option to purchase a building plot but, before it was exercised, the parties became aware that the land was claimed by the defendant's son and grandson. The plaintiffs exercised the option but, because of the adverse claim, the defendant was unable to give the plaintiffs a good title. *Held*, the plaintiffs were entitled to damages but, in these circumstances, they would be limited to the expenses which they had incurred. (Applied: *Bain v Fothergill*; but see *Sharneyford Supplies Ltd v Edge*.)

Reardon Smith Line Ltd v Hansen-Tangen [489]
[1976] 3 All ER 570 (House of Lords)

The appellants chartered a ship which was described in the charterparty as to be built by a named Japanese shipbuilding company and having a particular hull number. When delivered, the ship had been built by sub-contractors under the supervision of the named company, many of whose personnel had been seconded to work on the vessel. The hull number was also different. The appellants appealed against a decision that the ship in fact complied with the description having regard to Japanese custom. They contended that the words specifying the builders and the number were contractual terms forming part of the description and that because of the departure from the description they were entitled to reject the vessel. *Held*, dismissing the appeal, in reaching its decision the court had to place itself in the same factual position as that in which the parties had been when contracting. The relevant words were only intended as

114

a means of identification. The strict rule of compliance with description which applied in sale of goods cases did not apply to a contract like the present, which came under the general law of contract. Even if it did apply, the description had been complied with in the strict sense. The words fulfilled their function of providing a means of identifying the vessel. They could not be read as essential terms of the contract which must be complied with literally. (But see *Wallis, Son and Wells v Pratt and Haynes*.)

Redgrave v Hurd (1881) 20 Ch D 1 (Court of Appeal)   [490]

A solicitor inserted an advertisement in the *Law Times* stating that he had a moderate practice with extensive connections in a populous town and that he would like to take an efficient lawyer into partnership with him. Another solicitor answered the advertisement and at an interview the advertiser said that his business was worth about £300 pa. No accounts had been kept but the prospective partner inspected various papers which showed that the business produced a gross income of £200 pa and an agreement was concluded. In fact the practice was worthless. *Held*, the new partner was entitled to rescission as he had been induced to enter into a contract by representations which turned out to be untrue. It was no answer to his claim to say that if he had exercised due diligence he would have discovered the real situation. (See also *Central Railway Company of Venezuela v Kisch*, *Newbigging v Adam* and *Archer v Brown*.)

Reese River Silver Mining Co Ltd v Smith (1869)   [491]
LR 4 HL 64 (House of Lords)

The directors of a company issued a prospectus stating that they proposed to carry on the business of mining and that they had acquired a valuable mine in America. On the faith of these representations a person applied for shares but it afterwards appeared that the mine in question was valueless. *Held*, the man who applied for shares was entitled to have his contract rescinded on the ground of misrepresentation. (See also *Redgrave v Hurd* and *Car and Universal Finance Co Ltd v Caldwell*.)

Regazzoni v K. C. Sethia (1944) Ltd [1957] 3 All ER 286   [492]
(House of Lords)

In protest against the racial policy of the Government of the Union of South Africa, the Indian Government prohibited the taking out of India of goods which were either destined for or intended to be taken to the Union. The parties contracted for the sale and delivery of some jute bags cif Genoa but the court found that they contemplated and intended that the goods should be shipped from India and made available in Genoa so that the buyer might make a re-sale or fulfil a bargain of re-sale to the South African buying agency. The seller failed to deliver the jute bags and the buyer sought damages for breach of contract. *Held*, as a matter of public policy, the action would fail as the performance of the contract would have involved doing in a foreign and friendly country (India) an act which would have violated a law (which was not a revenue or penal law) of that state. (See also *Foster v Driscoll*.)

Resolute Maritime Inc v Nippon Kaiji Kyokai, The Skopas   [493]
[1983] 2 All ER 1

The plaintiffs alleged that they had been misled into making the purchase of the vessel Skopas by incorrect representations and the question arose whether an agent (one of the defendants), acting in his express or ostensible authority, could be liable under s. 2(1) of the Misrepresentation Act 1967. *Held*, he could not, nor could the person who actually made the statement for him: such liability attached to the principal alone, although the agent could be liable in fraud and negligence.

Richards and Bartlet's Case (1584) 74 ER 17 **[494]**

There was a contract for the sale of two weights of corn for £10. The corn was subsequently 'drowned by tempest' and, in view of this, the plaintiff said that he would accept 33s 4d in satisfaction of the full price of the corn. *Held*, there was no consideration for this promise as no advantage accrued to the plaintiff who was not, therefore, bound to accept the smaller amount. (But see *Pinnel's Case*.)

Richardson, Spence & Co v Rowntree [1894] AC 217 **[495]**
(House of Lords)

The respondent paid the appellants passage money for a voyage on their steamer and was handed a folded ticket which purported to exclude liability in respect of loss or injury exceeding $100. No writing was visible unless the respondent unfolded the ticket. The jury found that the respondent knew there was writing or printing on the ticket, but did not know that it related to the terms of the contract of carriage. *Held*, the appellants did not do what was reasonably sufficient to give the respondent notice of the conditions and for this reason she was not bound by them. (But see *Thompson v London, Midland and Scottish Railway Co.*)

Rickards (Charles) Ltd v Oppenheim [1950] 1 All ER 429 **[496]**
(Court of Appeal)

The defendant placed an order with the plaintiffs for the building of a new body on a Rolls Royce chassis. The work was not completed within the period specified in the contract and the defendant waived this condition, but some months later, when the work was still not completed, he said that if the car was not delivered within four weeks he would refuse to accept it. The car was not delivered within that period. *Held*, the defendant could refuse delivery and recover the chassis or its value as he was entitled to give reasonable notice again making time of the essence of the contract and in the circumstances of the case four weeks' notice was reasonable. (See also *Hare v Nicoll* and *Scandinavian Trading Tanker Co AB v Flota Petrolera Ecuatoriana, The Scaptrade*.)

Riverplate Properties Ltd v Paul **[497]**
[1974] 2 All ER 656 (Court of Appeal)

A lessor made a unilateral mistake in drafting a lease, the effect of which was that it threw the entire burden of repairing the building on the lessor. The lessor's intention was that the lessee should contribute to the cost of repairs. The lessee was unaware of the mistake. The lessor claimed rescission subject to rectification at the option of the lessee. *Held*, mere unilateral mistake in a lease is not a ground for rescission. Since the lessee had not known of the mistake which was in no way attributable to anything said or done by her, the lessor was not entitled to rescission.

Robb v Green [1895] 2 QB 315 (Court of Appeal) **[498]**

During his employment as manager of the plaintiff's business the defendant made a list of the names and addresses of the customers with a view to using it for the purpose of soliciting orders after he had left the plaintiff's service and had established a similar business on his own account. *Held*, it was an implied term of the defendant's contract of service that he would show good faith towards his master and the compilation of the list of customers was a breach of that implied term which entitled the plaintiff to damages and an injunction. (See also *Kleinert v Abosso Gold Mining Co.*)

Roberts v Gray [1913] 1 KB 520 (Court of Appeal) **[499]**

The plaintiff, who was a leading professional billiard player, agreed to take the defendant, who was a minor and also a billiard player, on a world tour during which they would compete with one another in matches. A dispute arose as to the type of billiard balls to be used and the defendant repudiated the contract. The plaintiff claimed damages for breach of contract. *Held*, he should succeed as the contract, which was in effect for the teaching and education of the defendant and was reasonable and for his benefit, was a contract for necessaries. (See also *Chaplin v Leslie Frewin (Publishers) Ltd.*)

Roberts (A.) & Co Ltd v Leicestershire County Council [1961] 2 All ER 545   [500]

The plaintiffs submitted a tender for work on a school stating that they would complete the work within seventy-eight weeks of the date of instructions to proceed. The plaintiffs' tender was accepted, but the period for completion inserted in the contract by the defendants was thirty months. The period for completion was altered for the benefit of the defendants and if the plaintiffs had tendered on this basis their price would have been higher. The defendants did not call the attention of the plaintiffs to the fact that the period for completion included in the contract differed from the period specified in the tender and the contract was executed by the plaintiffs under the belief that the period for completion stated in the contract was eighteen months. *Held*, at the time at which the contract was executed the defendants were aware of the plaintiffs' mistaken belief that the eighteen month completion period was included therein and the contract would be rectified to make provision for completion within this period. (See also *Torrance v Bolton*.)

Robertson v Minister of Pensions [1948] 2 All ER 767   [501]

The plaintiff was injured during the war and the War Office assured him that his disability had been accepted as attributable to military service. In reliance upon this statement he did not obtain independent medical opinion and took no steps to retain X-ray plates, and the question arose as to whether the assurance given by the War Office was binding on the Minister of Pensions. *Held*, the Minister was bound as the assurance was one which was intended to be binding and to be acted on by the plaintiff and which became binding when the plaintiff acted on it by forbearing to obtain medical evidence of the consequences of his injury. (But see *Combe v Combe*.)

Rogers v Parish (Scarborough) Ltd [1987] 2 All ER 232   [502]
(Court of Appeal)

The plaintiffs bought from the defendants a new Range Rover; after a few weeks' use it proved unsatisfactory and it was replaced with another. The replacement was no more satisfactory; attempts were made to repair the faults but some of them persisted. After five months and about 5,500 miles the plaintiffs purported to reject the vehicle on the ground that it was not of merchantable quality within s. 14(6) of the Sale of Goods Act 1979. *Held*, they were entitled to succeed as, on the facts and bearing in mind that the expectations of the purchaser of a new Range Rover were higher than those of a purchaser of an ordinary family car, the vehicle had not been of merchantable quality. (Applied in *Shine v General Guarantee Corp Ltd*; but see *Bernstein v Pamson Motors (Golders Green) Ltd*.)

Ronbar Enterprises Ltd v Green [1954] 2 All ER 266   [503]
(Court of Appeal)

The plaintiff company and the defendant entered into partnership to publish the *Weekly Sporting Review and Show Business*. The partnership agreement conferred on both partners the right to determine the partnership and the agreement stipulated that the outgoing partner should not 'for five years . . . directly or indirectly carry on or be engaged or interested in any business similar to or competing with the business of the partnership'. The plaintiff company determined the partnership under the terms of the agreement and the defendant entered into the employment of another company to write articles for

Sport and Show News, a similar periodical which was also published in London. The plaintiff company sought an injunction to restrain this activity. *Held*, the injunction would be granted. As it stood, the covenant, being unlimited in point of area, was unreasonably wide, but the words 'similar to or' would be struck out and the covenant was not then wider than was reasonably necessary for the protection of the plaintiff company. (See also *Goldsoll v Goldman*.)

Rooke v Dawson [1895] 1 Ch 480   [504]

A trust deed provided for the award of a scholarship and the trustees duly announced and held an examination in which the plaintiff obtained the highest marks. *Held*, the announcement was nothing more than a proclamation that the examination would be held and the trustees were not bound to award the scholarship to the candidate who gained the highest marks in the examination. (See also *Grainger & Son v Gough*.)

Roscorla v Thomas (1842) 3 QB 234   [505]

The plaintiff bought the defendant's horse and after the sale the defendant promised that the horse was sound and free from vice whereas it proved to be 'very vicious, restive, ungovernable and ferocious'. *Held*, the consideration for this promise was past and the plaintiff had no remedy. (See also *Re McArdle*.)

Rose and Frank Co v J. R. Crompton & Brothers Ltd   [506]
[1925] AC 445 (House of Lords)

The appellants carried on business in New York as dealers in carbon paper and contracted to buy certain quantities from the respondents who manufactured that commodity in England. The contract stated that 'This arrangement is not entered into . . . as a formal or legal agreement, and shall not be subject to legal jurisdiction in the Law Courts . . . but it is only a definite expression and record of the purpose and intention of the . . . parties concerned, to which they each honourably pledge themselves, with the fullest confidence . . . that it will be carried through . . . with mutual loyalty and friendly co-operation.' The appellants sued for breach of contract and non-delivery of goods. *Held*, their action must fail as legal relations had been expressly excluded, but this did not apply to instances where orders had been given and accepted as separate contracts of sale had been constituted in every case. (But see *Kleinwort Benson Ltd v Malaysia Mining Corpn Bhd*; see also *Jones v Vernon's Pools Ltd*.)

Rose (Frederick E.) (London) Ltd v William H. Pim   [507]
Jnr & Co Ltd [1953] 2 All ER 739 (Court of Appeal)

The parties contracted for the sale of a quantity of horsebeans known in Egypt as 'feveroles'. At the time of making the contract both parties believed that 'feveroles' was simply another word for horsebeans but in fact they were another type of bean altogether. *Held*, the contract was not a nullity although both parties were under a fundamental mistake as to the nature of the subject matter, and the contract would not be rectified as it accurately expressed their erroneous intention to deal in 'feveroles'. (See also *Long v Lloyd*.)

Routh v Jones [1947] 1 All ER 758 (Court of Appeal)   [508]

Two general medical practitioners in Okehampton engaged an assistant who covenanted that he would not for five years after leaving their practice engage in 'practice in any department of medicine, surgery or midwifery nor accept . . . any professional appointment' within 10 miles of that town. *Held*, in so far as this restraint forbade the assistant from becoming, for example, a consultant or medical officer of health, it was wider than was necessary for the protection of his employers' practice and amounted to an illegal restraint of trade. (See also *Schroeder Music Publishing Co Ltd v Macaulay.*)

Routledge v Grant (1828) 4 Bing 653   [509]

The defendant offered to purchase the plaintiff's house and gave him six weeks to decide whether to accept the offer. The defendant purported to withdraw his offer before the six weeks had passed. *Held*, he was entitled to do so at any time before the offer was accepted.

Routledge v McKay [1954] 1 All ER 855 (Court of Appeal)   [510]

A Douglas motor cycle combination was first registered in 1930, but when a new registration book was issued the date of original registration was given as '9.9.41'. In October 1949 the seller, who was not responsible for the incorrect entry in the registration book, in answer to a question by the buyer as to the date of the machine, said that it was a late 1941 or 1942 model and seven days later the buyer and seller entered into a contract of sale. The memorandum of agreement made no mention of the date of the machine. The buyer claimed damages for breach of warranty. *Held*, the incorrect statement in the registration book was a false representation and not a warranty and, in the absence of fraud, the buyer could not succeed. (See also *Oscar Chess Ltd v Williams.*)

Rowland v Divall [1923] 2 KB 500 (Court of Appeal)   [511]

The plaintiff bought a car from the defendant. The car was delivered to him, and he used it for four months. He then discovered that the defendant had no title to the car, which belonged to a third party, to whom he returned it. The plaintiff then sued the defendant to recover the price. *Held*, the plaintiff was entitled to treat the contract as discharged; there had been a total failure of consideration, and he did not need to rest his case on the condition as to title implied by what is now s. 12 of the Sale of Goods Act 1979. 'There has been a total failure of consideration, that is to say the buyer has not got any part of that for which he paid the purchase money. He paid the money in order that he might get the property and he has not got it' (*per* ATKIN LJ).

Royal Exchange Assurance v Hope [1928] Ch 179   [512]
(Court of Appeal)

By an insurance policy an assurance company, the plaintiffs, agreed to pay the assured, his executors, administrators or assigns the sum of £1,000 if he died before 31 July 1926. The assured assigned the benefit of the policy to the defendant and subsequently arranged to extend the period of insurance to 31 October 1926. The benefit of this extension was never assigned and the assured died on 1 October 1926. *Held*, the extension of the policy was not a new contract of insurance but a variation of the original policy, the benefit of which had been vested in the defendant who was therefore entitled to recover £1,000 by virtue of the assignment. The defendant was also entitled to the money as the assured would be regarded as having contracted for the extension of the policy for the benefit of and as trustee for the defendant. (But see *Vandepitte v Preferred Accident Insurance Corporation of New York.*)

Ryan v Mutual Tontine Westminster Chambers   [513]
Association [1893] 1 Ch 116 (Court of Appeal)

By the terms of a lease of a residential flat the landlords covenanted to provide a porter, who was to be constantly in attendance, or, during his temporary absence, a trustworthy assistant. The landlords appointed one Benton to be porter but, while he spent much of his time acting as chef at a neighbouring club, boys and charwomen performed his duties as porter. *Held*, the landlords were in breach of their covenant but the court would not grant an injunction to restrain the continuance of the breach or order the covenant to be specifically enforced. (Distinguished in *Posner v Scott-Lewis*.)

Said v Butt [1920] 3 KB 497   [514]

The proprietors of a theatre, the defendants, had good reason for excluding the plaintiff from their theatre and refused to sell him a ticket for the first performance of a play. The plaintiff asked a friend to buy a ticket in his own name on the plaintiff's behalf, which he did, but when the plaintiff attempted to gain admission his way was barred. The plaintiff claimed damages. *Held*, the identity of the plaintiff was a material factor in the formation of a contract as a result of the sale of the ticket; as the plaintiff's identity had not been disclosed, no contract had come into existence and his claim would not be successful. (See also *Sowler v Potter*.)

St. John Shipping Corporation v Joseph Rank Ltd   [515]
[1956] 3 All ER 683

A ship was overloaded and the master was prosecuted for a statutory criminal offence. The holders of a bill of lading in respect of part of the cargo carried by the ship paid most of the freight due, but withheld a sum equivalent to the overall additional cargo by which it was found that the ship was overloaded. *Held*, they were not entitled to do so as the consideration and the matter to be performed were both legal and the right to claim freight had not been brought into existence by a crime. (Applied in *Euro-Diam Ltd v Bathurst*; see also *Archbolds (Freightage) Ltd v S. Spanglett Ltd*; but see *Allen v Rescous*.)

Sajan Singh v Sardara Ali [1960] 1 All ER 269 (Privy Council)   [516]

A, who wanted to acquire a lorry but to whom a haulier's permit would not be granted, entered into an arrangement whereby the lorry would be bought by and registered in the name of S, who would obtain the permit. This was done, and the lorry was used and operated by A, to whom it was ultimately sold, he having paid for it. These transactions were contrary to Malayan statutory ordinances. After some time, S took possession of the lorry without A's consent and refused to return it to A, denying that it had been sold to him. A sought a declaration that the lorry was his and for the return of the vehicle or its value, the action being framed in detinue. *Held*, although the transaction whereby A obtained the lorry was illegal, yet A acquired title to the lorry notwithstanding that it was not registered in his name. Accordingly, A was entitled to the relief he claimed. (See also *Bowmakers Ltd v Barnet Instruments Ltd* and *Belvoir Finance Co Ltd v Stapleton*.)

Satanita, The. *See* **Clarke v Dunraven**

Saunders v Anglia Building Society [1970] 3 All ER 961   [517]
(House of Lords)

An elderly widow signed without reading a document which X told her was a deed of gift of her house in favour of her nephew. In fact, it was a purported assignment of the leasehold to X, and the old lady would not have signed had she known the facts. X mortgaged the house to the building society, and on his defaulting on the repayments due under the mortgage, they sought possession. *Held*, the plaintiff could not rely on a plea of non est factum as against the building society, because on the facts the transaction she intended and what she actually carried out were the same character, and she was bound by what she had signed. (Applied in *Avon Finance Co Ltd v Bridger*.)

Scammell and Nephew Ltd v Ouston [1941] 1 All   [518]
ER 14 (House of Lords)

The respondents agreed to purchase a motor van from the appellants but their order was given on the understanding 'that the balance of the purchase price can be had on hire-purchase terms over a period of two years'. *Held*, no precise meaning could be attributed to this clause as hire-purchase agreements varied widely and consequently there was no enforceable contract. There were no previous dealings between the parties or an accepted trade practice to which the court could refer to determine the hire-purchase terms and, in any case, their lordships found that the matter had not passed the stage of negotiation. (See also *McCutcheon v David MacBrayne Ltd*; but see *Nicolene Ltd v Simmonds*.)

Scandinavian Trading Tanker Co AB v Flota Petrolera Ecuatoriana, The Scaptrade [1983] 2 All ER 763   [519]
(House of Lords)

Payments of hire under a charterparty were to be made monthly in advance and the charter also provided that if the charterers defaulted in paying by the due date the owners could withdraw the vessel from hire. As a payment due on 8 July had not been made, on 12 July, the sum due still being unpaid, the owners gave notice to the charterers withdrawing the vessel. Tender of the overdue hire was made on the following day, but it was refused. *Held*, time had been made of the essence of the contract, there had been a breach of that condition and the owners had been entitled to elect to treat the breach as putting an end to all primary obligations under the contract which had not already been performed. The court had no discretion in such a case to grant an injunction to restrain the owners from exercising their right of withdrawal as it was juristically indistinguishable from a decree for specific performance of a contract to render services. (See also *Whitwood Chemical Co v Hardman* and *Rickards (Charles) Ltd v Oppenheim*.)

Schebsman, Re, Ex parte Official Receiver [1943]   [520]
2 All ER 768 (Court of Appeal)

Schebsman was for many years employed by a Swiss company and its English subsidiary. His employment was terminated and an agreement entered into whereby the English company would pay him £2,000 immediately and a further sum of £5,500 by instalments or, if he should die, such amount was to be paid to his widow and daughter. Schebsman was adjudicated bankrupt on 5 March 1942 and died a week later; his trustee in bankruptcy claimed the sums payable under the agreement to Schebsman's widow and daughter. *Held*, the trustee's claim would fail as the contract did not create a trust in favour of the widow and daughter. 'It appears to me that the provisions for the widow and daughter are the result of the mutual agreement and that the debtor had, in conjunction with the English company and the Swiss company, done all that was necessary to complete the title of the widow and daughter to whatever might be payable to them or either of them under the agreement. On payment to the widow or daughter the legal title to each payment was complete and I can see no equity to support the contention that there is any resulting trust in favour of the trustee in bankruptcy, for the payments result from the mutual agreement and not from a purchase or quasi-purchase by the debtor' (*per* Luxmoore LJ). (See also *Re Miller's Agreement*.)

Schroeder Music Publishing Co Ltd v Macaulay   [521]
[1974] 3 All ER 616 (House of Lords)

The plaintiff, an unknown song-writer, entered into an exclusive services agreement with the defendants in their standard form. Under it, he assigned copyright in existing works and works to be composed for a five year period. The defendants were under no obligation to publish the plaintiff's works. The plaintiff was entitled to £50 advance on royalties and further advances of £50 on recoupment of previous advances from royalties received. Only the defendants could terminate the agreement by notice. *Held*, the restraints in the agreement were not fair and reasonable. The contract was in unreasonable restraint of trade. (See also *M & S Drapers v Reynolds*.)

Scotson v Pegg (1861) 6 H & N 295   [522]

The plaintiffs entered into a contract to deliver a cargo of coal to another or to his order. That other directed the plaintiffs to deliver it to the defendant, who promised to discharge it at the rate of 49 tons per day, but this undertaking was not observed. *Held,* although the plaintiffs were already bound to deliver the coal in accordance with the order of another, there was sufficient consideration for the defendant's promise to unload the coal at the specified rate in that he received the benefit of the delivery of the coal. (See also *Chichester and Wife v Cobb.*)

Scott v Avery (1856) 5 HL Cas 811 (House of Lords)   [523]

An insurance policy in respect of a ship *Alexander* provided that the amount to be paid in respect of any loss was, in the first instance, to be ascertained by a certain committee but if the finding of that committee was unacceptable the matter was to be referred to arbitration. It was provided that the insurer was not entitled to maintain an action at law in respect of the policy until the arbitrators had given their decision. *Held,* this provision was lawful. It did not oust the jurisdiction of the court but imposed a valid condition that no action was maintainable until the arbitrators had made their award.

Scott v Coulson [1903] 2 Ch 249 (Court of Appeal)   [524]

The parties entered into a contract for the sale of a life policy in the belief that the assured was alive and the contract was completed by assignment. The assured was dead at the date on which the contract was made. *Held,* there had been a common mistake and the purchaser was entitled to have the assignment set aside. (See also *Galloway v Galloway.*)

Scott v Hanson (1829) 1 Russ & M 128   [525]

The defendant agreed to purchase land which was described in the particulars of sale as 'uncommonly rich water meadow'. In fact the land was very imperfectly watered. *Held,* this misrepresentation was not such as would enable the defendant to avoid performance of his contract. (But see *Brooke (Lord) v Rounthwaite.*)

Scott v Littledale (1858) 8 E & B 815   [526]

The parties contracted for the sale of 100 chests of Congou tea then lying in bond 'ex the ship *Star of the East*'. The sale was by sample which the defendants, the sellers, believed to be a sample of the tea referred to in the agreement but in fact and by mistake the sample was of a totally different tea. *Held,* this mistake did not entitle the defendants to avoid the contract. (But see *Raffles v Wichelhaus.*)

Scriven Brothers & Co v Hindley & Co [1913]   [527]
3 KB 564

An auctioneer, acting on the instructions of the plaintiffs, offered for sale a number of bales of hemp and tow, samples of which were on view before the sale. The catalogue did not disclose the difference in the nature of the commodities and although the samples were marked with the number of the lots it was not specified which was hemp and which was tow. When the tow was offered for sale the goods were knocked down to the defendants who thought they had been bidding for hemp. The auctioneer realised that the defendants had made a mistake, but he thought that they were mistaken only as to the value of tow. The plaintiffs sued to recover the amount of the defendants' bid. *Held,* their action must fail as there was no binding contract of sale. The parties had never been ad idem as the plaintiffs had intended to sell tow while the defendants thought they were buying hemp. (See also *Hartog v Colin & Shields.*)

Scruttons Ltd v Midland Silicones Ltd [1962] 1 All ER 1   [528]
(House of Lords)

The respondents were the consignees and owners of a drum of chemicals shipped in New York for carriage to London on the terms of the shipowners' standard bill of lading one clause of which had the effect of limiting the carrier's (i.e., the shipowners') liability for damage to the drum to 500 dollars. For some years the shipowners had engaged the appellant stevedores to discharge their vessels at the Port of London and the agreement between them provided that the appellants should have 'such protection as is afforded by the terms . . . of . . . bills of lading'. While lowering the drum into a lorry the appellants negligently dropped it causing damage to it amounting to £593. The act of lowering the drum into the lorry was one which, by the terms of their agreement with the shipowners, the appellants had contracted with the shipowners to do and which, by the terms of the bill of lading, the shipowners had contracted with the respondents to do. The appellants admitted negligence but contended that they were entitled to rely on the provisions in the bill of lading limiting liability to 500 dollars (£179). *Held*, they were not so entitled as they were strangers to the bill of lading and it is a general principle (to which this case was not an exception) that a stranger cannot rely for his protection on provisions in a contract (i.e., the bill of lading) to which he is not a party. (See also *Adler v Dickson*.)

Seaman v Fonereau (1743) 2 Stra 1183   [529]

The plaintiff insured his ship with the defendant in respect of a journey from Carolina to Holland and it afterwards appeared that at the time of making the contract he knew that his ship was leaky but this fact had not been disclosed to the defendant. The ship overcame these difficulties but was later taken by the Spaniards. *Held*, the defendant was not liable for this loss as a material circumstance had been concealed. It mattered not that the loss did not occur as a result of a weakness which had not been disclosed. (See also *London Assurance v Mansel*.)

Sebel Products Ltd v Commissioners of Customs and   [530]
Excise [1949] 1 All ER 729

The plaintiffs claimed that their 'Mobo Rocker Swing' was not liable to purchase tax and commenced proceedings to obtain a declaration to this effect. While these proceedings were pending, however, they paid to the defendants the tax which would be payable if they lost their case. The plaintiffs were successful, and sought the return of the amount paid. *Held*, while the defendants could normally refuse to refund money paid voluntarily under a mistake of law, in this case both parties intended that it should be refunded if the earlier proceedings were decided in the plaintiffs' favour and an order for repayment would be made. (See also *Kelly v Solari*.)

Sethia (K. C.) (1944) Ltd v Partabmull Rameshwar   [531]
[1950] 1 All ER 51 (Court of Appeal)

The sellers contracted to ship certain quantities of jute to Genoa but, because of export restrictions imposed by the Indian Government, less than one-third of the amount ordered was actually delivered. When sued for breach of contract the sellers contended that, in order to give the contract business efficacy, a term should be implied that delivery was 'subject to quota'. *Held*, such a term would not be read into the contract as the buyers could not have known whether the quota system would prevent the sellers, who had some choice in determining the extent of their quota, from supplying the jute and as similar contracts had been entered into 'subject to quota' it would not be implied that the parties had intended such a provision to be included on this occasion. (But see *Martin-Baker Aircraft Co Ltd v Canadian Flight Equipment Ltd*.)

Shadwell v Shadwell (1860) 9 CBNS 159 [532]

The plaintiff's uncle wrote to offer him congratulations on his engagement and promised to pay him £150 pa until such time as he was earning £600 pa as a Chancery barrister. The plaintiff married, and sued his uncle's executors upon this promise. *Held*, although the plaintiff was already bound by his promise to marry, consideration for the uncle's promise could be found in the fact that the plaintiff had incurred financial liabilities in reliance upon the uncle's promise, which would therefore be enforced. (See also *Scotson v Pegg*.)

Shanklin Pier Ltd v Detel Products Ltd [1951] 2 All ER 471 [533]

The plaintiffs entered into a contract with a certain company for the repair of their pier and, in accordance with the terms of the contract, specified that the defendants' paint should be used for the work. The defendants had told the plaintiffs that their paint had a life of from seven to ten years but in fact it had a very short life and the plaintiffs were put to much extra expense. The plaintiffs claimed damages for breach of warranty. *Held*, they were entitled to succeed. (See also *Wells (Merstham) Ltd v Buckland Sand and Silica Co Ltd*.)

Sharneyford Supplies Ltd v Edge [1987] 1 All ER 588 [534]
(Court of Appeal)

The defendant permitted two business tenants to occupy his maggot farm in return for supplying him with maggots for his anglers' business. He contracted to sell the farm to the plaintiffs and vacant possession was to be given on completion; prior to completion, though, the defendant did not secure the removal of his tenants. After completion, the tenants offered to go for £12,000, an offer that the defendant declined. The plaintiffs claimed damages for breach of contract. *Held*, they were entitled to succeed and to recover damages for loss of profits. As the defendant had not used his best endeavours to remove the defect in his title (the tenancy) the rule limiting damages to expenses did not apply. (But see *Bain v Fothergill*.)

Shaw v Shaw [1965] 1 All ER 638 (Court of Appeal) [535]

The plaintiff alleged that by an oral agreement made in London he had agreed to pay the defendant £4,000 for a flat in Majorca and had in fact paid him that sum. He also alleged that in the agreement there was an implied term that the agreement was made subject to the giving of Treasury consent to the payment under statute, and that such consent had not been received. The plaintiff sought the recovery of £4,000. *Held*, his claim would fail. 'There was an agreement; there was an implied term; that was not fulfilled, and therefore under the [statute] the payment was an illegal payment, and it follows, under the ordinary principles of law, that, in the absence of any exemption being established, the unlawful payment cannot be recovered back by the person who made it and thereby committed an unlawful act' (*per* PEARSON LJ). (See also *Bostel Brothers Ltd v Hurlock*.)

Shepherd (F. C.) & Co Ltd v Jerrom [1986] 3 All ER 589 [536]
(Court of Appeal)

Engaged as an apprentice plumber under a four-year training service agreement, with more than half of that term to run a young man was convicted of affray and conspiracy to assault and sentenced to borstal training for between six months and two years. *Held*, the agreement had been frustrated as the sentence rendered its performance radically different from that which the parties contemplated when they entered into it. (See also *Notcutt v Universal Equipment Co (London) Ltd*; but see *Tsakiroglou & Co Ltd v Noblee and Thorl*.)

Shine v General Guarantee Corp Ltd [1988] 1 All ER 911   [537]
(Court of Appeal)

The defendant finance company purchased an enthusiast's Fiat X19 from the third party which it then let to the plaintiff under a hire-purchase agreement, having described the car as being in good condition. The plaintiff subsequently discovered that the car had been written off by an insurance company after having been submerged in water for 24 hours. The plaintiff sued the defendants alleging breach of condition of merchantable quality implied by s. 14(2) of the Sale of Goods Act 1979. *Held*, he was entitled to succeed: he had thought he was buying a secondhand enthusiast's car in good condition at a fair price when in fact he was buying, at the same price, a car which no one, knowing its history, would have bought at other than a substantially reduced price. (Applied: *Rogers v Parish (Scarborough) Ltd.*)

Shipton v Cardiff Corporation (1917) 87 LJKB 51   [538]

The Cardiff corporation passed a resolution to the effect that any officer or servant of the corporation who volunteered for military service would have his pay made up to the amount of salary or wages he was receiving while in their employment. The plaintiff enlisted contrary to the wishes and without the consent of the managers of his department and he sued to recover the difference between his past and present income. *Held*, he was entitled to succeed as the resolution was an offer which was accepted by the plaintiff when he volunteered. (See also *Carlill v Carbolic Smoke Ball Co.*)

Shove v Downs Surgical plc [1984] 1 All ER 7   [539]

The plaintiff's contract of employment was wrongfully terminated and questions arose as to the assessment of damages, particularly in relation to taxation. *Held*, the plaintiff's tax liability was not too remote to be taken into account when determining his actual loss. Accordingly, the court would estimate the net amount which would have been received by the plaintiff after deduction of tax and add an amount equivalent to his estimated tax liability so that the net amount represents as realistically as possible his actual loss. However, damages could not be awarded for the plaintiff's distress. (See also *Addis v Gramophone Co Ltd.*)

Simpkins v Pays [1955] 3 All ER 10   [540]

The defendant, her grand-daughter and the plaintiff, a lodger, submitted forecasts in a fashion competition organised by a Sunday newspaper but all the entries were made out in the defendant's name. The grand-daughter's entry was successful and the prize of £750 was paid to the defendant. The plaintiff attempted to enforce the defendant's promise that they would share the prize if one of their entries should succeed. *Held*, he was entitled to recover £250 as a sufficient intention to create legal relations could be found in this mutual arrangement. (See also *Edwards v Skyways Ltd.*)

Simpson v London and North Western Railway Co   [541]
(1876) 1 QBD 274

The plaintiff was in the habit of sending cattle spice, which he manufactured, for exhibition at cattle-shows in the hope of attracting customers. The defendants, a railway company, collected some of his samples from a show ground in Bedford for carriage to another show ground in Newcastle and the plaintiff told the defendants that the goods 'must be at Newcastle on Monday certain'. The samples were not delivered until the show was over. The plaintiff, who had journeyed to Newcastle to display the goods at the show, claimed damages for loss of profit and loss of time. *Held*, the plaintiff was entitled to succeed as it would be inferred, from the circumstances of the case, that the object of the contract of carriage was within the contemplation of the parties and the plaintiff's loss flowed naturally and probably from the failure of the object. 'The principle is now settled that, whenever either the object of the sender is specially brought to the notice of the carrier, or circumstances are known to the carrier from which the object ought in reason to be inferred, so that the object may be taken to have been within the contemplation of both parties, damages may be recovered for the natural consequences of the failure of that object' (*per* COCKBURN CJ). (But see *Horne v Midland Railway Co.*)

Sky Petroleum Ltd v VIP Petroleum Ltd [1974]   [542]
1 All ER 954

The plaintiffs agreed with the defendants that, for a minimum period of ten years, they would buy all petrol for their filling stations from the defendants. Some three years later the defendants purported to terminate the agreement for an alleged breach of its terms by the plaintiffs, who brought an action and sought an interlocutory injunction to restrain the defendants from withholding petrol supplies from them. There was evidence that the plaintiffs had little prospect of finding alternative sources of supply at that time. *Held*, the injunction would be granted because the court could order specific performance of a contract to sell and purchase chattels which were not specific or ascertained in cases where damages would not provide a sufficient remedy, as was the case here. (See also *Lord Strathcona Steamship Co Ltd v Dominion Coal Co Ltd.*)

Slade v Metrodent Ltd [1953] 2 All ER 336   [543]

The plaintiff, a minor, was bound to the defendant as an apprentice dental mechanic. The agreement contained a clause to the effect that such disputes as should arise between the parties should be referred to arbitration. The plaintiff issued a writ claiming damages in respect of the alleged failure of the defendant to teach him the craft in question in accordance with the provisions of the apprenticeship deed. *Held*, assuming that the clause providing for arbitration was not for the plaintiff's benefit, the proceedings would nevertheless be stayed as the plaintiff was bound by the terms of the deed which, taken as a whole, was beneficial to him. (But see *De Francesco v Barnum.*)

Smith v Bush (Eric S.) [1987] 3 All ER 179 (Court of Appeal)   [544]

Having found a terraced property at the lower end of the housing market, the plaintiff applied to the Abbey National for a mortgage to enable her to buy it. The application form stated that she would be given a copy of the survey report and mortgage valuation obtained by the society; it also disclaimed responsibility for the contents of the report and valuation. The defendant surveyors inspected the property and their report contained a disclaimer in similar terms. On the strength of the report the plaintiff purchased the property, but after 18 months flues collapsed because chimney breasts had been removed, a fact the defendants had failed to notice. The plaintiff sought damages for negligence and the defendants relied on their disclaimer. *Held*, she was entitled to succeed. In the circumstances, it would not be 'fair and reasonable', within ss. 2(2) and 11(3) of the Unfair Contract Terms Act 1977, for the defendants to rely on the disclaimer because they knew that the report would be sent to the plaintiff and that she was likely to rely on it.

Smith v Chadwick (1884) 9 App Cas 187   [545]
(House of Lords)

A prospectus contained a statement that 'the present value of the turnover or output of the entire works is over £1,000,000 sterling per annum'. This statement was ambiguous in that it could mean that in one year the works produced goods worth £1,000,000, in which case it was untrue, or that the works were capable of this output, in which case it was correct. *Held*, in order to succeed in an action of deceit for fraudulent misrepresentation, the plaintiff had to prove that he had interpreted the statement in the sense in which it was false and that he had in fact been influenced by it in making his decision to take shares. The plaintiff failed to satisfy the court on these points. (But see *Edgington v Fitzmaurice.*)

Smith v Hughes (1871) LR 6 QB 597 [546]

The plaintiff, who was a farmer, offered to sell oats to the defendant, who was an owner and trainer of race-horses. The defendant's manager, who had taken a sample of the oats, wrote to the plaintiff on the following day to say that the defendant would buy them at a certain price but afterwards refused to accept delivery on the ground that the oats were new whereas he thought he was buying old oats. It was found that the plaintiff had not asserted that the oats were 'old' but that the defendant's manager believed that they were and the plaintiff knew that he entertained this mistaken belief. *Held*, the passive acquiescence of the plaintiff in the self-deception of the defendant's manager would not entitle the defendant to avoid the contract. 'It . . . was pressed upon us that the defendant . . . intended to buy old oats, and the plaintiff to sell new, so the two minds were not ad idem; and that consequently there was no contract. This argument proceeds on the fallacy of confounding what was merely a motive operating on the buyer to induce him to buy with one of the essential conditions of the contract . . . All that can be said is, that the two minds were not ad idem as to the age of the oats; they certainly were ad idem as to the sale and purchase of them' (*per* COCKBURN CJ). (But see *Scriven Brothers & Co v Hindley & Co.*)

Smith v Land and House Property Corporation (1884) [547]
38 Ch D 7 (Court of Appeal)

In the particulars of sale the plaintiffs said that their hotel was 'now held by a very desirable tenant . . . for an unexpired term of twenty-eight years, at a rent of £400 pa.' The defendants resisted the plaintiffs' claim for specific performance on the ground of misdescription in that it afterwards appeared that the rent was in arrear at the time of the sale and the tenant shortly afterwards filed his petition for liquidation. *Held*, the contract should be rescinded as the description of the tenant as 'very desirable' was not an expression of opinion but a misrepresentation on the faith of which the defendants contracted to purchase the hotel. (But see *Bisset v Wilkinson.*)

Smith v South Wales Switchgear Ltd [548]
[1978] 1 All ER 18 (House of Lords)

The respondents employed the appellants to carry out the annual overhaul of the electrical equipment in their factory. The contract stated that it was 'subject to our General Conditions of Contract 24001 obtainable on request'. The appellants did not ask for a copy but a copy of the second version of the conditions was sent to them. There was also an earlier and a later version, all with the number 24001. Each version contained an indemnity clause providing that the appellants would keep the respondents indemnified against any liability, loss, claim or proceedings whatsoever in respect of personal injury arising out of or in the course of execution of the work. While the work was being done, one of the appellants' electrical fitters was injured and was successful in his claim for damages against the respondents, whose negligence and/or breach of statutory duty caused the accident. It was further held that the respondents were entitled to be indemnified by the appellants under the indemnity clause. The appellants appealed arguing, amongst other things, that it was uncertain which of the three versions of the conditions applied. *Held*, the reference to the general conditions must be taken to refer to the edition current at the date of contract, i.e., the last edition. Therefore that edition must be taken to have been incorporated. However, on its wording the indemnity clause was not wide enough to cover negligence and the appeal was allowed. (But see *Alderslade v Hendon Laundry Ltd.*)

127

Smith and Snipes Hall Farm Ltd v River Douglas   **[549]**
Catchment Board [1949] 2 All ER 179 (Court of Appeal)

In 1938 a catchment board, the defendants, covenanted with a Mrs Smith and ten other owners of land through which a river ran that they, the defendants, would 'widen and deepen and make good the banks of the river . . . and maintain for all time the work when completed'. In 1940 the first plaintiff, one Smith, took a conveyance of Mrs Smith's land with the benefit of the agreement of 1938 and in 1944 Smith let the land to the second plaintiffs, Snipes Hill Farm Ltd. Two years later, owing to faulty work by the board, the banks burst and flooded the plaintiffs' land. The plaintiffs claimed damages for breach of contract and the defendants maintained that, if there was a breach, there was no privity of contract between the parties. *Held*, the defendants were liable as the covenant affected the use and value of the land and the benefit of the covenant was obviously intended to attach to the land and extend to any subsequent owners. (See also *Gregory and Parker v Williams* and s. 56(1) of the Law of Property Act 1925; but see *Beswick v Beswick*.)

Snell v Unity Finance Ltd [1963] 3 All ER 50   **[550]**
(Court of Appeal)

The plaintiff as hirer sued the defendants, a finance company, in respect of the hire-purchase of a Hillman motor car. Although the point was not taken in the county court, in the course of evidence it became clear that there had been a contravention of the terms of the relevant statutory instrument, because a deposit of twenty per cent of the cash price had not been paid before entering into the hire-purchase agreement. *Held*, it was the court's duty, as it had been the duty of the county court judge, once the facts which made the hire-purchase agreement illegal had been brought to the court's attention, to refuse to lend the plaintiff the court's aid in enforcing the contract. (See also *Anderson Ltd v Daniel*.)

Snelling v John G. Snelling Ltd [1972] 1 All ER 79   **[551]**

Three brothers were directors of the defendant company, which was financed by loans from them. In order to borrow money from a finance house, the three of them made a contract not to demand repayment of their loans to the company while the finance house loan was current. The company was not a party to the contract. It was a further term of the contract that if any of the brothers resigned his directorship, the money owed to him on loan would be forfeited. The plaintiff resigned his directorship and then sued the company for repayment of the loan. *Held*, although the company was not entitled to rely directly on the contract since it was not a party to it, the co-defendant brothers were entitled to a stay of proceedings and, since all the parties were before the court, the reality of the situation was that the plaintiff's claim had failed, and his action was dismissed. The co-defendant brothers, having proved a breach of the contract by the plaintiff, or an intention on his part to repudiate it, were entitled to a declaration that its provisions were binding on him. (See also *Beswick v Beswick*.)

Solle v Butcher [1949] 2 All ER 1107 (Court of Appeal)   **[552]**

The parties negotiated for the lease of a flat and, on the mistaken assumption that the rent was unaffected by the provisions of the Rent Acts, it was agreed that the rent should be £250 pa. It later appeared that the controlled rent was £140 pa, and the plaintiff sued to recover the rent which he alleged had been overpaid. *Held*, the plaintiff's claim to recover the amount of the rent overpaid should be dismissed but the lease would be set aside on the ground of a common mistake of fact and the plaintiff would have the option of surrendering the lease or remaining in possession and paying the full controlled rent. (See also *Cooper v Phibbs*; but see *Paget v Marshall*.)

Sowler v Potter [1939] 4 All ER 478   [553]

The defendant, whose name at the time was Ann Robinson, had been convicted for permitting disorderly conduct in a tea-room. Nearly two months after this conviction she changed her name to Ann Potter by deed poll but before this date she made an offer in the name which she was later to assume to take a lease of certain of the plaintiff's premises. The lease, which provided that the premises should be used for a restaurant or tea-room, was entered into after the defendant had legally changed her name. *Held*, the plaintiff was entitled to a declaration that the lease was void ab initio as she had granted the lease under the mistaken impression that the lessee was someone other than Ann Robinson whom she would have regarded as an undesirable tenant. (But see *Dennant v Skinner*.)

Spellman v Spellman [1961] 2 All ER 498   [554]
(Court of Appeal)

The parties were husband and wife, and when the relationship between them became less happy, it was thought that the purchase of a motor car might bring them together. To this end the husband entered into a hire-purchase agreement in respect of an Austin Healy Sprite and he told his wife that he had bought it for her. The wife's name was entered in the registration book, but shortly afterwards the husband left his wife and took the car with him. The wife claimed the car as a gift from her husband. *Held*, the wife should deliver up to her husband the registration book: she had no rights or ownership in respect of the car because, inter alia, 'there was not any intention to create legal situations, but merely an informal dealing with the matter between the husband and wife which is common in daily life and which does not result in some legal transaction, but is merely a matter of convenience' (*per* DANCKWERTS LJ). (See also *Simpkins v Pays*.)

Spencer v Harding (1870) LR 5 CP 561   [555]

The defendants issued a circular offering for sale certain stock-in-trade for which they invited tenders and the tender which the plaintiffs submitted turned out to be the highest. *Held*, there was no contract as the circular was a mere attempt to ascertain whether an offer could be obtained and was not a promise to sell to the person who made the highest tender. (See also *Rooke v Dawson*.)

Spurling (J.) Ltd v Bradshaw [1956] 2 All ER 121   [556]
(Court of Appeal)

The defendant, who had had previous business dealings with the plaintiffs, who were warehousemen, delivered to them eight barrels of orange juice for storage. A few days later he received a 'landing account' on which was printed a condition which exempted the plaintiffs from liability for any loss, damage or detention in respect of goods entrusted to them occasioned by the negligence, wrongful act or default of themselves, their servants or agents. When collected, the barrels were found to be either empty or so damaged as to be useless. The plaintiffs sought to recover their charges for storage and the defendant counter-claimed for damages for the alleged breach of an implied term of the contract of bailment to take reasonable care of the barrels. *Held*, assuming that the plaintiffs had been negligent, the defendant's counter-claim should fail as the plaintiffs were protected by the exemption clause. (But see *Woolmer v Delmer Price Ltd*.)

Staffordshire Area Health Authority v   [557]
South Staffordshire Water Works [1978]
3 All ER 769 (Court of Appeal)

Under a 1929 agreement between a water company and a health authority, the company agreed to supply a specified number of gallons of water a day free of cost to a hospital 'at all times hereafter'. The cost of supplying water rose sharply over the years. The Water Act 1973 placed a statutory duty on the company to ensure that by 1981 its charges would not show preference to or discriminate against any class of persons. Because of this, and the increased costs of supplying water, the company sought to terminate the 1929 agreement. There was no express provision in the agreement for its termination by notice. *Held*, in the absence of any express provision, the agreement was impliedly terminable on reasonable notice. (See also *Martin-Baker Aircraft Co Ltd v Canadian Flight Equipment Ltd.*)

Startup v Macdonald (1843) 6 Man & G 593   **[558]**

The parties contracted for the sale of 10 tons of linseed oil to be delivered 'within the last fourteen days of March'. The plaintiffs delivered the oil at 8.30 pm on 31 March, a Saturday, and the defendant refused to accept delivery because of the lateness of the hour. *Held*, the plaintiffs were entitled to recover damages in respect of the defendant's non-acceptance of the oil. (See also *Fercometal SARL v Mediterranean Shipping Co SA, The Simona.*)

Steadman v Steadman [1974] 2 All ER 977   **[559]**
(House of Lords)

The parties, separated since 1968, agreed in a compromise of pending litigation that the wife would surrender her interest in the matrimonial home to the husband for £1,500. They further agreed that arrears of maintenance payable by the husband would be remitted except for £100. Magistrates made consent orders embodying the agreed maintenance provisions. The husband duly paid the £100. However, the wife refused to transfer her interest in the house on the ground that the compromise agreement was unenforceable for the lack of written note or memorandum as required by the Law of Property Act 1925, s. 40. *Held*, the agreement was enforceable. It was for the plaintiff to establish facts amounting to part performance. He had to show that he acted to his detriment. These acts indicated that they were performed in reliance on a contract with the defendant as alleged. In the circumstances, the payment by the husband, taken in conjunction with the announcement to the magistrates and the delivery of a form of transfer to the wife for signature, were acts which indicated that they were carried out by him in reliance on a contract. It would therefore be inequitable to allow the wife to rely on s. 40 of the 1925 Act. (Applied in *Sutton v Sutton* and *Elias v George Sahely & Co (Barbados) Ltd*; see also *Kingswood Estate Co Ltd v Anderson* and *Maddison v Alderson*.)

Steinberg v Scala (Leeds) Ltd [1923] 2 Ch 452   **[560]**
(Court of Appeal)

An infant applied for and was allotted certain shares. She paid the amount due on allotment and also the first call. Eighteen months later, while still an infant, she purported to repudiate the contract and sought repayment of the money she had paid. *Held*, her claim must fail as there had not been a total failure of consideration, the only ground on which she could have succeeded.

Stenhouse Australia Ltd v Phillips [1974] 1 All ER 117   **[561]**
(Privy Council)

The defendant's contract of employment contained a clause whereby he undertook not, for a period of five years after determination of the contract, to engage in the business of insurance broking or solicit the clients of his employers. This restraint was to extend over a geographical area of 25 miles from Sydney. *Held*, the clause was valid, being reasonable and necessary for the protection of the plaintiff's business. The prohibition on soliciting was a narrow restraint which left open a wide field of unrestrained competitive activity by the employee, and the covenant extended only to a small number of clients, who were narrowly defined. (See also *Attwood v Lamont*.)

Stevenson, Jaques & Co v McLean (1880) 5 QBD 346   [562]

The defendant offered to sell iron to the plaintiffs at 40s per ton. The plaintiffs telegraphed to the defendant: 'Please wire whether you would accept forty for delivery over two months, or if not, longest limit you could give'. Later in the day a further telegram was sent to the defendant in which the plaintiffs accepted the original offer and when the plaintiffs sought to recover damages for breach of contract the defendant maintained that the first telegram was a counter-offer which had destroyed the offer which he originally made. *Held*, the plaintiffs' first telegram was not a rejection of the defendant's offer but an inquiry as to whether he would be prepared to modify its terms. (But see *Hyde v Wrench.*)

Stilk v Myrick (1809) 2 Camp 317   [563]

In the course of a voyage two seamen deserted and the captain, having tried in vain to replace them, entered into an agreement with the rest of the crew whereby, if they completed the voyage, they would have divided equally amongst them the wages of the deserters, in addition to their own wages. *Held*, the captain's promise was not binding. There was no consideration for the agreement as by their original contract the crew were bound to do all they could to complete the voyage. (But see *Hartley v Ponsonby*.)

Stockloser v Johnson [1954] 1 All ER 630 (Court of Appeal)   [564]

The defendant agreed to sell to the plaintiff certain plant and machinery in two quarries and the agreement provided that payment was to be made by instalments. The agreement further provided that if the plaintiff made default in payment of an instalment for a period exceeding twenty-eight days the defendant was entitled to re-take possession of the plant and machinery and that in such event all instalments paid should be forfeited to the defendant. Two years later the plaintiff failed to pay the instalments due from him and the defendant rescinded the agreement. *Held*, the plaintiff was not entitled to recover the instalments which he had paid as the forfeiture clause did not operate to exact a penalty and it was not unconscionable for the defendant to retain them. 'In my judgment, there is no sufficient ground for interfering with the contractual rights of a vendor under forfeiture clauses of the nature which are now under consideration, while the contract is still subsisting, beyond giving a purchaser who is in default, but who is able and willing to proceed with the contract, a further opportunity of doing so; and no relief of any other nature can properly be given, in the absence of some special circumstances such as fraud, sharp practice, or other unconscionable conduct of the vendor, to a purchaser after the vendor has rescinded the contract' (*per* ROMER LJ). (See also *Hitchcock v Coker, English Hop Growers Ltd v Dering*, but see *Landom Trust Ltd v Hurrell.*)

Stocks v Wilson [1913] 2 KB 235   [565]

By fraudulently representing that he was of full age, the defendant induced the plaintiff to sell and deliver to him certain of her furniture and effects for £300. The defendant sold some of the goods for £30 and gave a bill of sale of the residue by way of security for an advance of £100. The defendant failed to pay the purchase money and the plaintiff claimed the reasonable value of the goods by way of equitable relief. *Held*, the defendant was liable to pay the plaintiff the £130 which he had actually received. (But see *Leslie (R.) Ltd v Sheill.*)

Strange (SW) Ltd v Mann [1965] 1 All ER 1069   [566]

The defendant was appointed manager of the plaintiff bookmakers in Cheltenham. His contract provided that he would not for a period of three years after the cessation of his employment 'be in any way directly or indirectly engaged or interested in the business of commission agents either on his own account or in partnership with any person or persons or as manager agent or director of any other person or persons' firm or company in the town of Cheltenham or at any place within twelve miles thereof'. Although nearly three times as many of the plaintiffs' customers lived within twelve miles of Cheltenham as outside that area, some ninety-three percent of bets placed with the plaintiffs were placed over the telephone, and the rest by telegram or letter. When the defendant was dismissed from the plaintiffs' service he set up as a bookmaker in Gloucester (which is nine miles from Cheltenham). The plaintiffs sought to enforce the agreement. *Held*, they would fail because the service agreement was in unlawful restraint of trade and therefore void. There was nothing to show that the defendant has established such a personal relationship or confidence with customers living outside Cheltenham as would make it likely that such customers would seek him out after he had left the plaintiffs' employment and for this reason the relevant term of the agreement was not reasonably necessary in order to protect the plaintiffs' trade connexion' (*per* STAMP J). (But see *Fitch v Dewes*.)

Street v Blay (1831) 2 B & Ad 456   [567]

The plaintiff sold a horse to the defendant, a horse-dealer, and its soundness was a condition of the sale. On the same day the defendant sold the horse to another and after it had changed hands once more it was again sold to the defendant. It appeared that the horse was unsound at the time of the first sale but the plaintiff refused to take it back, and sued to recover the purchase money, which the defendant had never paid. *Held*, the defendant lost his right to rescind the contract and return the horse when he re-sold it, but he was entitled to reduce the damages payable to the plaintiff as he had a right of action against the plaintiff for breach of warranty. (See also *Long v Lloyd*.)

Strickland v Turner (1852) 7 Exch 208   [568]

The plaintiff purchased an annuity in ignorance of the fact that the annuitant was already dead. *Held*, the plaintiff was entitled to recover the purchase money as it had been paid wholly without consideration, i.e., he had 'purchased' something which no longer existed. (See also *Couturier v Hastie*.)

Strongman (1945) Ltd v Sincock [1955] 3 All ER 90   [569]

An architect contracted with builders to supply materials and carry out work at his premises and, in accordance with the universal practice, promised orally that he would obtain all the necessary licences. Work considerably in excess of the licence granted was carried out. *Held*, the builders were entitled to damages for breach of the warranty or collateral contract to obtain the licences. (See also *Townsend (Builders) Ltd v Cinema News & Property Management Ltd*.)

Sudbrook Trading Estate Ltd v Eggleton [1982] 3 All ER 1
(House of Lords)   [570]

A clause in a lease gave the lessees an option to purchase the reversion at a price to be agreed by two valuers, one to be nominated by the lessors and the other by the lessees and, in default of agreement, by an umpire appointed by the valuers. The lessees sought to exercise the option, but the lessors refused to appoint a valuer, claiming that the option clause was void for uncertainty. *Held*, the option would be ordered to be specifically performed. The machinery by which the value of the property was to be ascertained was subsidiary and non-essential to the main part of the agreement and, the lessors having been in breach of contract in refusing to appoint a valuer, there was no reason why the court should not substitute its own machinery and this it would do by ordering an inquiry into the reversion's fair value.

Sugar v London Midland & Scottish Railway Co   [571]
[1941] 1 All ER 172

The plaintiff had purchased a ticket from the defendants in respect of a journey on their railway and received injuries as a result of their negligence. On the front of the ticket were the words 'For conditions see back. Day Excursion' and on the back the passenger was referred to conditions contained in railway time-tables and bills which protected the defendants against claims for damages for negligence. On the plaintiff's ticket the words 'For conditions see back' had been obliterated by the date stamp. *Held*, the plaintiff could recover damages in respect of her injuries as the defendants had not taken reasonable steps to bring the conditions excluding liability to her notice. (See also *McCutcheon v David MacBrayne Ltd.*)

Suisse Atlantique Société d'Armement Maritime SA   [572]
v NV Rotterdamsche Kolen Centrale [1966] 2 All ER 61
(House of Lords)

The parties entered into a consecutive voyage charterparty, which was to remain in force for two years, for the carriage of coal from the United Kingdom to Europe. It was agreed that if the vessel was delayed beyond her lay days, demurrage would be payable at the rate of $1,000 a day. Over the two year period the vessel only performed eight voyages. The shipowners maintained that she ought to have performed a further six voyages at least if the charterers had loaded and discharged the cargo more rapidly. They alleged that they were not limited to claiming the sum payable under the demurrage clause, but were entitled to recover the full loss of freight which they would have obtained had these other voyages been performed. *Held*, only demurrage was payable. No term could be implied into the contract that there was no obligation to pay for the greatest number of voyages which could have been made if no delays had been experienced. The charterparty might have provided for this, but had not done so. Moreover, although the shipowners might have been able to treat the delays occurring during the period of the charterparty as a repudiation of the contract, they had not done so, and had elected to treat all its provisions as still binding. N.B. The House of Lords laid down that there is no rule of law that an exemption clause is nullified by a 'fundamental breach of contract' or breach of a 'fundamental term'; in each case the question is one of construction of the contract. (See also *Photo Production Ltd v Securicor Transport Ltd.*)

Sumpter v Hedges [1898] 1 QB 673 (Court of Appeal)   [573]

The plaintiff, a builder, contracted to build two houses and stables upon the defendant's land for the sum of £565. The plaintiff did part of the work, amounting in value to about £333, and then abandoned the contract. The defendant completed the buildings and the plaintiff claimed payment in respect of that part of the work which he had carried out. *Held*, the defendant was not liable to pay on a quantum meruit as there was no inference of a fresh contract to do so. (But see *Dakin (H.) & Co Ltd v Lee.*)

Sutton v Sutton [1984] 1 All ER 168   [574]

A husband and wife bought the matrimonial home with the aid of a mortgage for which the husband alone was responsible: the wife contributed to the purchase but the house was conveyed into the husband's name alone. Some years later they separated, the husband sought a divorce and they orally agreed (i) that the wife would consent to a divorce, take over responsibility for the mortgage and not apply for maintenance and (ii) that the husband would let the wife keep her savings and transfer the house to her. This agreement was not made subject to the court's approval. The wife consented to the petition, paid off the mortgage and did not apply for maintenance: after the decree absolute, the husband refused to transfer the house and the wife sought an order for specific performance. *Held*, she could not succeed. Although, inter alia, there had been a sufficient act of part performance to overcome the lack of a memorandum or note of the agreement as required by s. 40 of the Law of Property Act 1925 (applied: *Steadman v Steadman*), the court's jurisdiction under the Matrimonial Causes Act 1973 to order maintenance and property adjustment could not be ousted by a private agreement between the parties and, accordingly, it would be contrary to public policy to enforce the contract (distinguished: *Goodison v Goodison* and *Williams v Williams*).

Sutton & Co v Grey [1894] 1 QB 285 (Court of Appeal) [575]

The plaintiffs, who were stockbrokers, entered into an oral agreement with the defendant that he should introduce clients to them on the understanding that he would be paid half of the commission resulting from such transactions as proved to be profitable and pay half of any loss which might be incurred. The plaintiffs claimed payment in respect of a transaction which had been unprofitable and the defendant relied on s. 4 of the Statute of Frauds. *Held*, the plaintiffs could recover as the defendant had an interest in the transaction independently of his promise by way of guarantee to pay half the loss on business which he introduced. The contract was entered into to regulate the terms of the defendant's employment by the plaintiffs and was not merely a promise to answer for the debt or default of another within the meaning of the statute. (See also *Couturier v Hastie*.)

Swan v North British Australasian Co Ltd (1863) [576]
2 H & C 175

The plaintiff was the registered owner of 1,000 shares in a company in which the shares could only be transferred by deed executed by the transferor and transferee, and he employed a broker to sell some of his shares in another company which could only be transferred in a similar way. The broker asked the plaintiff to execute ten blank forms of transfer and the plaintiff did as he was requested. The broker used only eight of the forms for the purpose intended by the plaintiff and used the other two for the purpose of transferring some of the plaintiff's shares in the other company. *Held*, the transfers were void as there was no negligence on the part of the plaintiff to estop him from insisting that the property in the shares did not pass under the two transfers. In order to operate as an estoppel the negligence would have to be the proximate cause of the loss. (See also *Foster v Mackinnon*.)

Sybron Corp v Rochem Ltd [1983] 2 All ER 707 [577]
(Court of Appeal)

Opting for early retirement, the appellant employee, a manager, was entitled, at the respondent employers' discretion, to certain benefits under the company's pension scheme. The company exercised its discretion in the appellant's favour, but subsequently discovered that, during his employment, the appellant had been a party to fraudulent misconduct with subordinates. Accordingly, the respondents sought to recover the discretionary benefits. *Held*, they should succeed as payment of the benefits had been made under a mistake of fact induced by the appellant's breach of duty to disclose the fraudulent misconduct of the subordinate employees with whom he had acted. (But see *Bell v Lever Brothers Ltd*.)

Taddy & Co v Sterious & Co [1904] 1 Ch 354 [578]

The plaintiffs, Taddy & Co, were manufacturers of 'Myrtle Grove' tobacco and they stipulated that this tobacco should not be sold under a fixed minimum price. Taddy & Co sold some of this tobacco to a wholesaler and a term of this contract was that: 'Acceptance of the goods will be deemed a contract between the purchaser and Taddy & Co that he will observe these stipulations. In the case of a purchase by a retail dealer through a wholesale dealer, the latter shall be deemed to be the agent of Taddy & Co.'

The wholesaler re-sold the tobacco to the defendants, Sterious & Co, who had notice of this condition but nevertheless sold to the public below the prescribed minimum price. *Held*, there was no contract between the parties which the plaintiffs could enforce as conditions cannot be attached to goods so as to bind all subsequent purchasers, even if they have notice of those conditions. (But see *Lord Strathcona Steamship Co Ltd v Dominion Coal Co Ltd.*)

Tamplin v James (1880) 15 Ch D 215 **[579]**

'The Ship Inn' and a saddler's shop adjoining were put up for sale by auction and the extent of the property to be sold was clearly marked on plans which were on view in the auction room. At the back of the property were two pieces of garden which originally belonged to the vendors, the plaintiffs, but which were now let to them by the present owners. The tenants of the inn and shop used and enjoyed these gardens and the defendant, who purchased the inn and shop at the auction, refused to complete his purchase on the ground that he believed that he was buying the freehold of all that was in the occupation of the plaintiffs' tenants. The defendant said that he had not seen the plans which correctly delineated the property to be sold. *Held*, the plaintiffs were entitled to specific performance as the fact that the purchaser had made this mistake without any excuse ought not to enable him to escape from his bargain. (But see *Paget v Marshall* and *Patel v Ali.*)

Tamplin (FA) Steamship Co Ltd v Anglo-Mexican **[580]**
Petroleum Products Co Ltd [1916] 2 AC 397
(House of Lords)

The respondents chartered a ship for five years from December 1912 for the purpose of carrying oil. The ship was requisitioned by the Government in December 1914 and the appellants maintained that this had the effect of determining the charterparty. The respondents were willing to continue to pay the agreed freight and, of course, to receive the larger sum paid by the Government by way of compensation which would be payable to the appellants if it could be shown that the contract had been frustrated. *Held*, the requisitioning of the ship did not have the effect of determining or suspending the charterparty. (But see *Marshall v Glanvill.*)

Tapp v Lee (1803) 3 Bos & P 367 **[581]**

The defendant was asked for a reference in respect of one Brunell who was desirous of purchasing goods from the plaintiffs. The defendant stated that Brunell was an honest man, that he had trusted him and would trust him again: he did not say that Brunell had been a bankrupt or that he would now allow him only limited credit. The plaintiff claimed damages in respect of this false representation. *Held*, fraud was necessary to support the action and fraud may consist in the suppression of what is true as well as in the representation of that which is false. (But see *Turner v Green.*)

Tatam v Reeve [1893] 1 QB 44 **[582]**

The plaintiff received a letter from the defendant asking him to settle four accounts on his behalf. The plaintiff paid the money to the persons named in the letter and sued to recover £148 as money paid to the use of the defendant at the defendant's request. It afterwards appeared that the money was due from the defendant in respect of losing bets on horse-races but this fact was not known to the plaintiff at the time of complying with the defendant's request. *Held*, the plaintiff's action would be unsuccessful as its purpose was to recover money paid 'in respect of' a gaming contract within s. 1 of the Gaming Act 1892. (But see *Re O'Shea.*)

Tatem (W. J.) Ltd v Gamboa [1938] 3 All ER 135   **[583]**
(Court of Appeal)

The defendants hired a ship from the plaintiffs during the Spanish Civil War for the purpose of evacuating refugees. The ship was seized by a nationalist cruiser and the plaintiffs sued to recover the amount of hire which they alleged was due in respect of the period for which the ship was in nationalist hands. *Held*, the plaintiffs' claim must fail as the seizure of the ship had destroyed the foundation of the contract which would therefore be regarded as having been frustrated. (See also *Constantine (Joseph) Steamship Line Ltd v Imperial Smelting Corporation Ltd.*)

Taylor v Bowers (1876) 1 QBD 291 (Court of Appeal)   **[584]**

The plaintiff, who was financially embarrassed, made over all his stock-in-trade, including a portable steam engine and threshing machine, to one Alcock, and fictitious bills of exchange were given in the plaintiff's favour as the pretended consideration for the assignment. The stock was removed by Alcock and later charged to the defendant, who knew of the unlawful assignment, without the knowledge of the plaintiff. The plaintiff sued to recover the goods. *Held*, he was entitled to succeed. Nothing had been done to carry out the fraudulent or illegal object of the transaction beyond the delivery of the goods to Alcock. The charge would be set aside and as the plaintiff had repudiated the whole transaction he could recover his property from the defendant. (But see *Bigos v Bousted.*)

Taylor v Caldwell (1863) 3 B & S 826   **[585]**

The plaintiffs entered into an agreement with the defendants for the hire of a certain music hall for the purpose of giving a series of concerts. Before the series was due to begin the hall was destroyed by accidental fire. *Held*, the plaintiffs could not recover damages as the destruction of the hall excused both parties from the performance of their promises. (But see *London and Northern Estates Co v Schlesinger.*)

Taylor v Chester (1869) LR 4 QB 309   **[586]**

The plaintiff, at the request of the defendant, delivered to the defendant half a promissory note for £50 as a pledge or security for the payment of £20. The money was due in respect of wine and suppers supplied to the plaintiff and divers prostitutes in the defendant's brothel. The plaintiff sued for the re-delivery of the note. *Held*, the plaintiff's claim would fail as he had to base his claim upon an immoral transaction to which he was himself a party. (But see *Bowmakers Ltd v Barnet Instruments Ltd.*)

Thacker v Hardy (1878) 4 QBD 685 (Court of Appeal)   **[587]**

The plaintiff, a stock-broker, was employed by the defendant to speculate on his behalf on the Stock Exchange and to pay him the 'differences' between the cost of the stock and the amount for which it was sold. The plaintiff knew that the defendant was a mere speculator and quite unable to pay for stocks bought or to deliver those sold. The defendant sued to recover his commission on these transactions and also claimed an indemnity against such liability as he might incur. *Held*, the action would succeed as the agreement between the parties was not a wagering contract which was rendered void. (See also *Ellesmere (Earl) v Wallace*; but see *Universal Stock Exchange Ltd v David Strachan.*)

Thake v Maurice [1986] 1 All ER 497 (Court of Appeal)   **[588]**

The defendant surgeon carried out a vasectomy on the plaintiff husband but the plaintiff wife subsequently became pregnant and gave birth to a baby girl. *Held*, the defendant had not been in breach of contract because his obligation was to carry out the operation with reasonable skill and care rather than to sterilise the plaintiff husband. However, the defendant had been guilty of negligence in failing to give his usual warning that there was a slight risk that the first plaintiff might become fertile again. Damages were awarded for the birth and upkeep of the child and for distress, pain and suffering which were not cancelled out by the relief and joy felt after the birth of a healthy baby. (But see *Eyre v Measday.*)

Thomas v Thomas (1842) 2 QB 851 [589]

Before his death the plaintiff's husband said that he wished the plaintiff to have the use of a certain house. In deference to his wish the defendant and his co-executor entered into an agreement, the effect of which was to allow the plaintiff to occupy the house in consideration of the express desire of her husband and the payment of £1 pa towards the ground rent. *Held*, the husband's desire was not consideration but the agreement was binding as the undertaking to pay £1 pa was valuable consideration although by no means adequate. (See also *Rann v Hughes.*)

Thompson v Lohan (T.) (Plant Hire) Ltd [1987] 2 All ER 631 [590]
(Court of Appeal)

The first defendants, a plant hire company, hired an excavator with a driver to the third party for use at the third party's quarry. Condition 8 of certain standard conditions provided that drivers were to be regarded as the hirers' servants or agents and that they (the hirers) alone were responsible for all claims. Condition 13 stipulated that hirers would 'fully and completely' indemnify the owners. The plaintiff's husband was killed as a result of the driver's negligence and, having had damages awarded against them, the first defendants sought to be indemnified by the third party. *Held*, they were entitled to succeed. Section 2(1) of the Unfair Contract Terms Act 1977 did not apply to strike down condition 8 as that provision was not concerned with arrangements made by a wrongdoer with others for sharing or transferring the burden of compensating the victim. That condition was therefore effective and, under condition 13, the first defendants were entitled to their indemnity. (Distinguished: *Phillips Products Ltd v Hyland.*)

Thompson v London, Midland and Scottish Railway [591]
Co [1930] 1 KB 41 (Court of Appeal)

The plaintiff, who could not read, was handed an excursion ticket on the face of which were printed the words: 'Excursion. For conditions see back'. On the back was a notice that the ticket was issued subject to the conditions in the defendant company's time tables and excursion bills, and the excursion bills stated that excursion tickets were issued subject to the conditions in the company's time tables. The time tables, which cost 6*d* each, excluded liability 'in respect of . . . injury (fatal or otherwise)'. The plaintiff received injuries on the journey and claimed damages. *Held*, her action must fail. The fact that she could not read did not alter the legal position and she was bound by the contract which she made when she accepted the excursion ticket; the reference to the company's time tables was sufficient notice of the terms of that contract. (But see *Sugar v London, Midland & Scottish Railway Co.*)

Thornton v Shoe Lane Parking Ltd [1971] 1 All ER 686 [592]
(Court of Appeal)

The plaintiff parked his car at the defendants' automatic car-park. On entering the car-park he passed through an automatic barrier, taking a ticket from the machine at the barrier. On the ticket, in small print, it was stated that the ticket was issued subject to conditions displayed on the premises. To find where the conditions were displayed the plaintiff would have had to drive the car into the garage and walk around. The conditions were lengthy but included one exempting the defendants not only from liability for damage to cars but also from liability for any injury to a customer, howsoever caused, whilst his car was in the car-park. The plaintiff later returned to collect his car and there was an accident in which he was severely injured. *Held*, the defendants were not protected by the exemption clause. In order to show that the plaintiff was bound by it, it was necessary to show either that he knew of it or that the defendants had done what was reasonably necessary to draw it to his attention. For this purpose, where the clause was exceptionally wide and was one which was not usual in that class of contract, it was not enough to show that the plaintiff had been given notice that the ticket was issued subject to conditions. It must be shown that adequate steps had been taken to draw his attention in the most explicit way to the particular exempting condition relied on. Here the defendants had failed to show that the plaintiff knew of the condition or that they had taken sufficient steps to draw his attention to it. (Applied in *Interfoto Picture Library Ltd v Stiletto Visual Programmes Ltd*; see also *Parker v South Eastern Rail Co* and *Mendelssohn v Normand Ltd*.)

Thoroughgood's Case (1584) 2 Co Rep 9   [593]

A deed releasing all claims was read to an illiterate woman and she executed it on being told that it concerned arrears of rent. *Held*, the deed was null and void. (See also *Swan v North British Australasian Co Ltd*.)

Timmins v Moreland Street Property Co Ltd [1957]   [594]
3 All ER 265 (Court of Appeal)

The plaintiff and a Mr Chait, a director and authorised agent of the defendant company, orally agreed that the plaintiff should sell and the defendant company should buy certain freehold property at an agreed price. Chait gave the plaintiff a cheque, which he signed on behalf of the defendant company and drew in favour of the plaintiff's solicitors, and the plaintiff gave him a receipt in the following terms: 'Received of Moreland Street Property Co Ltd the sum of £3,900 as a deposit for the purchase of 6, 8 and 41 Boundary Street, (Shoreditch freehold), which I agree to sell at £39,000. Dated this 20th day of July, 1955. W. H. Timmins'. *Held*, the contract could not be enforced as there was no sufficient memorandum or note in writing signed on behalf of the party to be charged, the defendant company, to satisfy the requirements of s. 40 of the Law of Property Act 1925. The cheque could not be read with the receipt as it contained no reference to it. (See also *Hawkins v Price*.)

Tinn v Hoffmann & Co (1873) 29 LT 271   [595]

The plaintiff wrote to the defendant and asked him to quote his lowest price for 800 tons of iron. In reply to his inquiry the defendant offered the iron at 69*s* per ton and concluded the letter 'waiting your reply by return'. It was conceded that as the offer was not accepted by return there was no contract and the view was expressed that a requirement that acceptance should be by return of post would be satisfied if the reply was sent by any other method, such as a telegram or messenger, provided it reached its destination not later than a letter sent by return of post would have been delivered. (See also *Compagnie de Commerce, etc v Parkinson Stove Co Ltd*.)

Tiverton Estates Ltd v Wearwell [1974] 1 All ER 209   [596]
(Court of Appeal)

There was an oral agreement for the purchase of some leasehold property. A letter from the purchaser's solicitors to the vendor's solicitors referred to the 'proposed sale . . . subject to contract' and requested a draft contract. The vendor's solicitors acknow-ledged that letter and sent a draft contract for approval. Subsequently the vendor decided not to go ahead, and the question arose as to whether the letter enclosing the draft contract was a sufficient memorandum for the purposes of s. 40 of the Law of

Property Act 1925. *Held*, in order to satisfy the requirements of s. 40 it was necessary for the note or memorandum relied on to contain not only the terms of the contract but also an express or implied recognition that a contract had in fact been entered into. A document setting out the terms of the alleged contract which was expressed to be, or formed part of correspondence expressed to be, 'subject to contract' would not, therefore, constitute a sufficient memorandum. Since the vendor's solicitors' reply did not itself recognise the existence of a contract made orally, it did not, when read in isolation, constitute a sufficient memorandum nor could it do so when read in conjunction with the letter to which it was a reply. (See also *Cohen v Nessdale Ltd.*)

Tool Metal Manufacturing Co Ltd v Tungsten   [597]
Electric Co Ltd [1955] 2 All ER 657 (House of Lords)

The appellants granted the respondents a licence to import certain hard metal alloys for a period of 10 years from 1937 and thereafter until determined on six months' notice. The respondents agreed to pay a royalty in respect of such alloy as they used and an additional sum by way of 'compensation' if they used more than a specified amount, but payment of 'compensation' was suspended shortly after the outbreak of war in 1939. The appellants claimed compensation under the original agreement from 1 January 1947. *Held*, they were entitled to recover. Their promise to suspend payment of 'compensation' was binding upon them as it raised an equitable estoppel but they could resume their legal rights on giving reasonable notice to the respondents and this they had done when they delivered a counterclaim for 'compensation' from June 1945, in March 1946, in an action commenced by the respondents. (See also *Lyle-Miller v A. Lewis & Co (Westminster) Ltd.*)

Torrance v Bolton (1872) 8 Ch App 118   [598]

Certain property was put up for sale by auction and in the advertised particulars it was described as an immediate absolute reversion of a freehold estate which would fall into possession on the death of a lady who was then in her 70th year. Before the property was sold the auctioneer's clerk read aloud the particulars and conditions of sale, which were not printed or circulated among those present, and one of these conditions stated that the property was sold subject to three mortgages. The land was bought by the plaintiff who said that he was deaf and did not understand that he was buying an equity of redemption. *Held*, the plaintiff was entitled to have the contract rescinded and his deposit returned as the vendor had not discharged the burden of showing that the purchaser was not actually misled. (But see *Tamplin v James.*)

Townsend (Builders) Ltd v Cinema News and   [599]
Property Management Ltd [1959] 1 All ER 7 (Court of Appeal)

A builder carried out work which, when completed, infringed a London County Council bye-law. The contract required the work to be carried out in accordance with a specification and to the reasonable satisfaction of an architect and it was not until the work was far advanced that the builder knew that the requirements of the bye-law would not be satisfied. *Held*, the builder was entitled to recover payment for his work as there was no fundamental illegality pervading the whole contract. (But see *Chettiar v Chettiar.*)

Trollope and Colls Ltd v North West Metropolitan   [600]
Hospital Board [1973] 2 All ER 260 (House of Lords)

The respondents engaged the appellants to build a hospital and research centre, the work to be carried out in phases. The contract provided for the date of commencement of Phase III to be fixed by reference to the completion date of Phase I. The third phase was to be completed by a specified date. As a result of delays on Phase I for which the

139

contract provided extensions of time, an unreasonably short time was left to complete the final phase. *Held*, no term for extending the date for completion of Phase III could be implied. The express terms were clear and unambiguous. A term could only be implied if the court found that the parties must have intended it to form part of their contract, and it must be one necessary to give business efficacy to the contract. (See also *Brown and Davis Ltd v Galbraith*.)

Tsakiroglou & Co Ltd v Noblee and Thorl [601]
GmbH [1961] 2 All ER 179 (House of Lords)

By a contract dated 4 October 1956 the appellants agreed to sell to the respondents 300 tons of Sudanese groundnuts cif Hamburg, shipment during November/December 1956. As a result of the invasion of Egypt by Israel the Suez Canal was blocked to shipping from 2 November 1956 to April 1957. *Held*, the contract had not been frustrated as a term that the groundnuts were to be shipped via the Suez Canal would not be implied and shipping via the Cape of Good Hope did not render the contract fundamentally or radically different. 'An increase of expense is not a ground of frustration' (*per* Viscount SIMONDS). (See also *Ocean Tramp Tankers Corporation v V/O Sovfracht*; but see *Pioneer Shipping Ltd v BTP Tioxide Ltd, The Nema*.)

Tulk v Moxhay (1848) 2 Ph 774 [602]

The plaintiff, who owned several houses in Leicester Square, sold the gardens in the centre of the square to one Elms who covenanted, for himself, his heirs, and assigns, that he would keep the gardens and railings around them in their present condition and continue to allow the inhabitants of the square to have the use and enjoyment of the gardens. The land in question was sold to the defendant and the conveyance to him did not contain a covenant in similar terms although he knew of the restriction contained in the deed to which the plaintiff and Elms were parties. The defendant announced that he intended to build on the land and the plaintiff, who still remained the owner of several adjacent houses, sought an injunction to restrain him from doing so. *Held*, the injunction would be granted as the covenant would be enforced in equity against all subsequent purchasers with notice. (But see *Taddy & Co v Sterious & Co.*)

Turner v Green [1895] 2 Ch 205 [603]

Shortly before an interview between the parties' solicitors at which an action was compromised, the plaintiff's solicitor received a telegram informing him of the outcome of certain proceedings in the action which was favourable to the defendant. The plaintiff's solicitor did not disclose this information until the terms of the settlement had been agreed. *Held*, the defendant was bound by the terms of the settlement as there was no obligation on the plaintiff's solicitor to disclose all he knew. Mere silence as regards a material fact, which the solicitor was not bound to disclose, was not a ground for rescission of the compromise or a defence to specific performance. (But see *Tapp v Lee*.)

Tweddle v Atkinson (1861) 1 B & S 393 [604]

The plaintiff's father and father-in-law agreed with each other to pay the plaintiff £100 and £200 respectively in consideration of his then intended marriage and after the marriage had taken place they confirmed their agreement in writing. The £200 was not paid and the plaintiff sued his father-in-law's executor to recover this sum. *Held*, his action must fail as no stranger to the consideration can take advantage of a contract, although made for his benefit. A promisee cannot bring a successful action unless the consideration for the promise moved from him. (See also *Dunlop Pneumatic Tyre Co Ltd v Selfridge & Co Ltd*.)

UBAF Ltd v European American Banking Corp [605]
[1984] 2 All ER 226 (Court of Appeal)

The defendant New York bank invited the plaintiff English bank to participate in a syndicate loan to a Panamanian shipping group, the defendants' assistant secretary supplying the plaintiffs with information about the group. The plaintiffs duly participated, but the group encountered financial difficulties and defaulted on the loans. The plaintiffs sued, inter alia, for damages under s. 2(1) of the Misrepresentation Act 1967 and the defendants relied, inter alia, on s. 6 of the Statute of Frauds Amendment Act 1828, arguing that any representations had not been signed by 'the party to be charged'. *Held*, the defendants' contention would be rejected as the assistant secretary had been acting in the course of his duties. Further, any failure by the defendants to inform the plaintiffs that security for the loan was insufficient was a continuing breach of their fiduciary duty which would, for the purposes of s. 32(1)(b) of the Limitation Act 1980, prevent time from running until the plaintiffs discovered the concealment or could with reasonable diligence have done so.

United Dominions Trust Ltd v Western [606]
[1975] 3 All ER 1017 (Court of Appeal)

The defendant agreed to buy a car for £550 from dealers on hire-purchase. He paid £34 deposit and signed the plaintiffs' standard form in blank, leaving the dealers to fill in the figures. The form sent to the plaintiffs was in fact for a loan agreement and the figures inserted were £730 for the purchase price and £185 for the deposit. The plaintiffs accepted the document as containing figures agreed between the defendant and the dealers and as constituting a contract between them and the defendant. When the defendant received the copy document he realised that it was not in accordance with the agreement between himself and the dealers but he did nothing to rectify the mistake and paid no instalments. The plaintiffs claimed £750. *Held*, for the purposes of the doctrine of non est factum, to distinguish between the careless signing of a completed document and a document in blank was neither right on the authorities nor acceptable to common sense. In permitting the dealer to complete the intended contractual document the onus was on the defendant to show that he had acted carefully, and that onus had not been discharged. The transaction which the document purported to effect was not essentially different in substance or in kind from the transaction intended and therefore could not be considered void. (See also *Saunders v Anglia Building Society*.)

Universal Corporation v Five Ways Properties Ltd [607]
[1979] 1 All ER 552 (Court of Appeal)

Prospective purchasers of property paid a 10 per cent deposit of the purchase price. Due to a change in the exchange control regulations, the purchasers were unable to transfer funds from abroad. The vendors rescinded the contract and claimed to forfeit the deposit. The purchasers claimed repayment of the deposit on grounds, inter alia, of frustration. *Held*, although the purchasers had been unable to complete, the contract itself was not incapable of performance and had therefore not been frustrated. Even if the doctrine of frustration applies to sales of land, the mere inability of a purchaser to pay the purchase price on the completion date is not sufficient to frustrate the contract. (See also *National Carriers Ltd v Panalpina (Northern) Ltd*.)

Universal Stock Exchange Ltd v David Strachan [608]
[1896] AC 166 (House of Lords)

The parties contracted for the sale and purchase of stocks on the secret understanding that the stock should never be called for or delivered although the contract between them provided that either party could require completion of the purchase and delivery or receipt of the stocks. *Held*, such a contract was nevertheless void by reason of s. 18 of the Gaming Act 1845 as it was really a gambling transaction, but securities deposited to secure the payment of these 'differences' could be recovered.

Vanbergen v St. Edmund's Properties Ltd   [609]
[1933] 2 KB 223 (Court of Appeal)

The plaintiff owed £208 to the defendants whose solicitors agreed that if this amount was paid into a bank at Eastbourne to their account they would withhold service of a bankruptcy notice. The plaintiff paid the money as arranged but the bankruptcy notice was served; the plaintiff contended that this was a breach of contract and that consideration for the defendants' solicitors' promise not to serve the bankruptcy notice was to be found in his payment into a bank at Eastbourne to the solicitors' account, whereas in the normal course of events it would have been paid to the defendants directly. *Held*, the action must fail as the agreement as to the place and method of payment was to oblige the plaintiff and of no benefit to the defendants and therefore was not sufficient consideration to support the promise to withhold service of the bankruptcy notice. (See also *Neuchatel Asphalte Co Ltd v Barnett.*)

Vancouver Malt and Sake Brewing Co Ltd v   [610]
Vancouver Breweries Ltd [1934] AC 181 (Privy Council)

The appellants held a brewer's licence which entitled them to brew beer, but they had never brewed any liquor other than sake, a Japanese drink made from rice. The respondents, who held a similar licence but confined their activities to the brewing of beer, purported to purchase the goodwill of the appellants' brewer's licence for $15,000 and the appellants covenanted that they would not for 15 years engage in the manufacture or sale of beer. *Held*, the agreement was void as it was an agreement in restraint of trade. As the appellants did not in fact brew beer the contract contained in effect a bare covenant against competition which was not linked with any proprietary interest which would have justified the imposition of the restraint. (But see *Alec Lobb (Garages) Ltd v Total Oil (GB) Ltd.*)

Vandepitte v Preferred Accident Insurance   [611]
Corporation of New York [1933] AC 70 (Privy Council)

Mrs Vandepitte, the plaintiff, was being driven by her husband when their car was in collision with one driven by Jean Berry. Jean was driving her father's car with his permission and the plaintiff obtained a judgment, which was not satisfied, against her in respect of injuries which she received in the accident. Jean's father was insured with the defendants against third-party risks and the policy covered accidents which might occur while Jean was driving. The plaintiff sought to recover the amount of the judgment which she had previously obtained against Jean from the defendants and founded her claim on a local statute which enabled an injured person to avail himself of any rights possessed by the driver of the vehicle against the insurance company where an action against the negligent motorist had been unfruitful. *Held*, the plaintiff's action would fail as Jean was not a party to the contract of insurance and there was no evidence that her father had intended to create a trust in her favour. (See also *Re Schebsman.*)

Varley v Whipp [1900] 1 QB 513   [612]

The plaintiff agreed to sell a reaping machine to the defendant, stating that it was nearly new, and had been used only to cut 50 or 60 acres. The defendant had not seen the machine. On delivery, he returned it to the plaintiff as not answering to description, as it was extremely old. The plaintiff sued for the price, and the defendant pleaded that there had been a breach of the condition that goods will correspond with description, implied by what is now s. 13 of the Sale of Goods Act 1979. *Held*, this was a sale by description, and the defendant's argument prevailed. (See also *Beale v Taylor.*)

Varney v Hickman (1847) 5 CB 271   [613]

The action was brought to recover the sum of £20 deposited by the plaintiff with the defendant, as stakeholder, pending the outcome of a trotting match. Before the race was run, the plaintiff gave notice to the defendant that he repudiated the wager and demanded the return of his £20. *Held*, the plaintiff was entitled to recover the amount of the wager as at the time at which he asked for it to be refunded it was still in the hands of the defendant. (See also *Diggle v Higgs.*)

Victoria Laundry (Windsor) Ltd v Newman   [614]
Industries Ltd [1949] 1 All ER 997 (Court of Appeal)

The plaintiffs, who were launderers and dyers, agreed to buy a boiler from the defendants. The defendants knew that the boiler was wanted for immediate use but, as a result of an accident which occurred while the boiler was being dismantled for removal to the plaintiffs' premises, delivery actually took place five months after the date specified in the contract. The plaintiffs claimed damages for breach of contract. *Held*, the plaintiffs were entitled to recover the profit which might reasonably have been expected to result from the normal use of the boiler during the five months in question but no account could be taken of the exceptionally profitable character of some of the contracts which they lost. (See also *Hadley v Baxendale* and *Koufos v C. Czarnikow Ltd.*)

Wade v Simeon (1846) 2 CB 548   [615]

The plaintiffs sued the defendant to recover £2,000 but in consideration of the plaintiff forbearing to proceed with the action the defendant promised to pay the amount for which the action was instituted. In fact, the plaintiff did not have a cause of action and he knew this when he commenced his action and at the time when the defendant made the promise to pay him £2,000. *Held*, the promise was of no effect as forbearing to prosecute a claim which the plaintiff knew must fail was not consideration for the defendant's promise. (But see *Alliance Bank Ltd v Broom.*)

Wakeham v Mackenzie [1968] 2 All ER 783   [616]

B, a widower aged 72, orally agreed with the plaintiff that if she would move into his house and look after him, she should have the house and its contents after his death. It was a term of the agreement that the plaintiff would pay for her own board and coal. The plaintiff gave up the tenancy of her own flat, and moved in with B in accordance with the agreement. On B's death, it was found that B had not left the house and its contents to the plaintiff, and she sought specific performance of the agreement. *Held*, the plaintiff's giving up her flat in order to make her home with B, looking after him and paying for her board and coal, were acts of part performance referable to the alleged contract, and specific performance would be granted. (But see *Maddison v Alderson*; see also *Kingswood Estate Co Ltd v Anderson* and *Freevale Ltd v Metrostore (Holdings) Ltd.*)

Walker v Boyle [1982] 1 All ER 634   [617]

When dealing with the sale of his wife's property, in answer to a preliminary inquiry a husband stated that to the vendor's knowledge there were no boundary disputes. He genuinely believed, but without reasonable grounds, that this was the case: in fact there was a dispute with a neighbour and his statement therefore amounted to an innocent misrepresentation. Contracts were exchanged and one clause of the standard form provided that 'no error, mis-statement or omission in any preliminary answer concerning the property . . . shall annul the sale'. The purchaser sought rescission of the contract and the return of his deposit. *Held*, he was entitled to succeed as the vendor could not rely on the special condition, the true facts being within her knowledge. Even if the special condition had applied, it did not satisfy the requirements as to reasonableness set out in s. 11(1) of the Unfair Contract Terms Act 1977 and it was an exclusion clause within s. 3 of the Misrepresentation Act 1967. Further, s. 2(1) of the 1967 Act entitled the purchaser to loss of interest on his deposit.

Wallis, Son and Wells v Pratt and Haynes [1911]   [618]
AC 394 (House of Lords)

The defendants sold a quantity of seed to the plaintiffs, describing it as 'common English sainfoin'. The plaintiffs re-sold it to X, by whom it was sown. It was later discovered to be 'giant sainfoin'. In seed, the two plants were indistinguishable, but 'common English sainfoin' was more valuable than 'giant sainfoin'. The plaintiffs claimed damages for breach of the condition as to description implied by what is now s. 13 of the Sale of Goods Act 1979, while the defendants relied on an exemption clause exluding all 'warranties, express or implied, as to growth or description'. *Held*, the exemption clause was inadequate to protect the defendants, who were liable. (But see *Reardon Smith Line Ltd v Hansen-Tangen*.)

Wallington v Townsend [1939] 2 All ER 225   [619]

The defendant owned two adjoining freehold bungalows and contracted to sell one to the plaintiff. A misunderstanding arose as to the exact area of the land to be purchased and the defendant refused to convey a part of the land which, by the clear terms of the contract, he had agreed to sell. *Held*, the plaintiff was entitled to the return of her deposit and to recover her legal expenses but she would not, in this case, be awarded more as she had not shown that she had suffered damage by reason of her loss of bargain. (See also *Flureau v Thornhill*.)

Ward v Byham [1956] 2 All ER 318 (Court of Appeal)   [620]

The parents of an illegitimate child lived together for some years but the father then turned the mother out and later offered to let her have the child and to pay her an allowance of £1 per week, provided that the child was well looked after and happy. The mother took the child away and maintained it according to her promise but when, some months later, she married, the father discontinued the payments. When the mother sought to enforce the continuance of the payments the father contended that there was no consideration for his promise to pay £1 per week as the mother, in looking after the child, was only doing something that she was legally bound to do. *Held*, the agreement would be enforced as the mother, by undertaking that the child should be happy, had promised to do more than was required of her by statute. (See also *Williams v Williams*.)

Warlow v Harrison (1859) 29 LJQB 14   [621]

The defendant offered a horse for sale without reserve and the plaintiff made a bid for it which was the highest received apart from one from the owner upon whose instructions the horse was then withdrawn from the sale. *Held*, the plaintiff could not recover, but three of the judges took the view that if the plaintiff had argued that the highest bona fide bidder at an auction sale may sue the auctioneer upon his promise that the sale shall be without reserve, he would have been successful. (But see *Fenwick v Macdonald, Fraser & Co Ltd*.)

Warner Brothers Pictures Inc v Nelson [1936]   [622]
3 All ER 160

Bette Davis entered into a contract with the plaintiffs, initially for a term of one year, but giving the plaintiffs the option of extending it, whereby she agreed that she would not undertake other film work without obtaining their written consent. The plaintiffs sought an injunction to restrain her from doing film work for another in breach of this agreement. *Held*, the injunction would be granted for the period of the continuance of the contract or for three years, whichever was the shorter. (See also *Lumley v Wagner*.)

Watkins v Rymill (1883) 10 QBD 178   **[623]**

The plaintiff took his waggonette to the defendant's repository and left it to be sold. He was handed a printed receipt which stated that goods were received 'subject to the conditions as exhibited on the premises'. The conditions were displayed in conspicuous positions in many parts of the premises. *Held*, the plaintiff was bound by the conditions. (But see *Chapelton v Barry Urban District Council* and *Richardson, Spence & Co v Rowntree*.)

Watts v Spence [1975] 2 All ER 528   **[624]**

A husband and wife were joint owners of a house. The husband represented to the plaintiff that *he* owned the house and was in a position to sell. As a result, the plaintiff entered into a contract with the husband to buy the house. The wife, who had no knowledge of the discussions, refused to consent to the sale. The plaintiff claimed against the husband damages for misrepresentation under s. 2(1) of the Misrepresentation Act 1967. *Held*, the plaintiff's claim should succeed. The purchaser was not limited to damages measured by expenses incurred in consequence of the misrepresentation, but was entitled to damages for loss of bargain. (Distinguished: *Bain v Fothergill* and *Flureau v Thornhill*.)

Webber v Lee (1882) 9 QBD 315   **[625]**

There was an agreement by which the defendant orally promised to pay £100 for certain shooting rights and in return he was to receive one-quarter of the game killed. *Held*, the agreement came within the provisions of what is now s. 40 of the Law of Property Act 1925 in that the shooting rights were an interest in land and the plaintiff could not enforce payment of the amount promised unless the agreement complied with the requirements of that section.

Webster v Cecil (1861) 30 Beav 62   **[626]**

The defendant wrote to offer to sell some property to the plaintiff for £1,250. Although the defendant had already refused to sell this land to the plaintiff for £2,000, the plaintiff, who therefore had knowledge of the mistake, wrote to accept the offer contained in the defendant's letter. The defendant had intended that the price should be £2,250 and he immediately gave notice of the error. *Held*, a decree of specific performance would not be granted. (See also *Roberts (A.) & Co Ltd v Leicestershire County Council*.)

Welby v Drake (1825) 1 C & P 557   **[627]**

The defendant drew a bill for £18 odd which was returned unaccepted. The plaintiff agreed that if the defendant's father would pay him £9 he would accept that amount in full satisfaction of the debt. The £9 was duly paid. *Held*, the plaintiff could not recover the balance from the defendant because by suing the son he committed a fraud on the father, who paid £9 on the understanding that his son would be discharged from further liability. (See also *Hirachand Punamchand v Temple*.)

Welch v Royal Exchange Assurance [1939] 1 KB 294   **[628]**
(Court of Appeal)

An insurance policy provided that on making a claim the insured should 'give to the corporation all such proofs and information with respect to the claim as may reasonably be required'. The insured refused to furnish information with regard to certain bank accounts. *Held*, the insured could not recover in respect of his claim as compliance with the reasonable requirements of the insurance corporation was a condition precedent. (See also *Pym v Campbell.*)

Wells v Smith [1914] 3 KB 722 [629]

The plaintiff, the owner of a furnished house, wished to let her property and with this in view she put it in the hands of a firm of house agents who had not acted for her before. In a reference given to the agents in respect of a prospective tenant the defendant said that he would 'not hesitate to let it to her' if the house was his. In fact she was, as the agents and the defendant well knew, a woman of immoral character. The plaintiff let her house to the woman and when her tenant proved to be most undesirable she brought an action to recover damages for false and fraudulent misrepresentation. *Held*, the plaintiff would succeed as the agents' knowledge that the defendant's statement was untrue would not be imputed to her. (But see *Attwood v Small.*)

Wells (Merstham) Ltd v Buckland Sand and [630]
Silica Co Ltd [1964] 1 All ER 41

The plaintiffs were chrysanthemum growers and the defendants sellers of sand. The defendants produced a sample of their BW sand, and also a detailed analysis, and it appeared that this sand was of the quality required by the plaintiffs for use in their nursery. Upon being assured by the defendants that the sand delivered would conform to the analysis (as it later appeared, a misrepresentation which was made innocently), the plaintiffs decided to purchase some but, in order to reduce transport costs, placed the order through another firm. Thus the contract of sale was not between the plaintiffs and the defendants but between the plaintiffs and the other firm. The sand delivered purported to be BW sand but it contained an excess of iron oxide (i.e., it did not conform to the analysis) and, when it was used, it had a disastrous effect upon the plaintiffs' young chrysanthemums. The plaintiffs sued the defendants for damages for breach of warranty. *Held*, the plaintiffs were entitled to succeed as the warranty or collateral contract was enforceable notwithstanding the fact that the main contract was subsequently entered into between the plaintiffs and a third party. 'As between A (a potential seller of goods) and B (a potential buyer), two ingredients, and two only, are in my judgment required in order to bring about a collateral contract containing a warranty: (1) a promise or assertion by A as to the nature, quality or quantity of the goods which B may reasonably regard as being made animo contrahendi, and (2) acquisition by B of the goods in reliance on that promise or assertion' (*per* EDMUND DAVIES J). (See also *Shanklin Pier Ltd v Detel Products Ltd.*)

Wettern Electric Ltd v Welsh Development Agency [1983] [631]
2 All ER 629

In a letter dated 21 June 1979 the defendants offered the plaintiffs a licence to occupy a factory unit for 12 months from 25 June 1979. Without completing the acceptance portion of the letter, the plaintiffs moved in on 25 June. Structural defects appeared and, by 18 December, the plaintiffs were forced to evacuate the premises and on that day they commenced proceedings claiming damages for breach of an implied term that the unit was of sound construction and would be reasonably suitable for their purposes. On the following day they returned the acceptance portion of the letter, duly completed. *Held*, the plaintiffs' action would succeed. They had become occupants under a contract on the terms contained in the letter as, inter alia, by occupying the unit they had offered to enter into a contractual licence on the letter's terms and, by permitting them to occupy, the defendants had accepted their offer. A term would be implied as the plaintiffs claimed because it was necessary to give the contract business efficacy. Although such terms would not be implied into contracts for the sale of land or the grant of a lease, this was merely a contract granting a licence to occupy the land. (Applied: *The Moorcock* and *Liverpool City Council v Irwin.*)

White v John Warrick & Co Ltd [1953] 2 All ER 1021   [632]
(Court of Appeal)

The plaintiff contracted for the hire of a tradesmen's tricycle for use in the delivery of newspapers. The contract provided that 'Nothing in this agreement shall render the owners liable for any personal injuries to the riders of the machines hired' and another clause stipulated that the defendants agreed 'to maintain the machines in working order and condition'. *Held*, the clause which purported to exclude the defendants' liability would protect them from breach of their contractual obligation to maintain the machines but was not wide enough to exclude their liability in tort apart from contract should actual negligence be established. (See also *Alderslade v Hendon Laundry Ltd.*)

White and Carter (Councils) Ltd v McGregor   [633]
[1961] 3 All ER 1178 (House of Lords)

The respondent's sales manager, acting within his authority, entered into a contract with the appellants for the fixing to litter bins of plates advertising the respondent's business. On the same day upon hearing of the contract, the respondent wrote to the appellants to cancel the agreement, but the appellants refused to accept this cancellation. The contract was for a period of 156 weeks and, under the terms of the contract, if any instalment was unpaid for four weeks, the whole of the amount due for the 156 weeks, or the remainder of that period, became due and payable. The respondent did not pay the first instalment within the time allowed and the appellants sought to recover the whole price. *Held*, they were entitled to succeed. 'If one party to a contract repudiates it . . . the other party, the innocent party, has an option. He may accept that repudiation and sue for damages for breach of contract whether or not the time for performance has come; or he may if he chooses disregard or refuse to accept it and then the contract remains in full effect . . . It is . . . impossible to say that the appellants should be deprived of their right to claim the contract price merely because the benefit to them as against claiming damages and reletting their advertising space might be small in comparison with the loss to the respondent' (*per* Lord REID). (See also *Hoare v Rennie.*)

Whittington v Seale-Hayne (1900) 82 LT 49   [634]

The plaintiffs, who were lessees of certain premises which they used for breeding prize poultry, alleged that they had been induced to take up the lease by the representations of the defendant's agents, made during oral negotiations for the lease, that the premises were in a sanitary condition and in a good state of repair. The plaintiffs further alleged that in consequence of the insanitary condition of the premises their manager and his family became very ill and the poultry either died or became valueless for the purpose of breeding. The local authority declared that because of defective drainage the premises were unfit for human habitation. The plaintiffs contended that they were entitled to an indemnity against the consequences of entering into the contract which included losses in respect of stock and medical expenses. *Held*, their claim would fail as it was really a claim for damages which could not be awarded at that time in a case of innocent misrepresentation, but they were entitled to an indemnity in respect of those things which were required to be performed by the terms of the lease and this included rent, rates and repairs. (See also *Gilchester Properties Ltd v Gomm* and *Lamare v Dixon.*)

Whitwood Chemical Co v Hardman [1891] 2 Ch 416   [635]
(Court of Appeal)

The defendant, a manufacturing chemist, contracted to serve the plaintiffs for a period of 10 years and to give his whole time to their business. The defendant took steps to form a rival company and the plaintiffs wished to restrain him. *Held*, an injunction would not be granted and the plaintiffs should seek their remedy in damages. 'What injunction can be granted in this particular case which will not be, in substance, and effect, a decree for specific performance of this agreement?' (*per* LINDLEY LJ). (See also *Francis v Municipal Councillors of Kuala Lumpur* and *Scandinavian Trading Tanker Co AB v Flota Petrolera Ecuatoriana, The Scaptrade*.)

Wilkie v London Passenger Transport Board [1947]   **[636]**
1 All ER 258 (Court of Appeal)

The plaintiff was injured when attempting to board a bus. The accident was caused through the conductor's negligence. The plaintiff was himself a bus driver, and at the time of the accident was travelling on a free pass, issued and accepted on condition that neither the defendants nor their servants were liable to the holder for 'loss of life, injury or delay or other loss of or damage to property however caused'. *Held*, the pass was a mere licence and not a document conferring a contractual right, and the condition exempting liability prevailed. (But see *Gore v Van der Lann*.)

William Hill (Park Lane) Ltd v Hofman [1950]   **[637]**
1 All ER 1013

The defendant executed a deed of charge in favour of the plaintiffs in which it was recited that the defendant was justly and truly indebted to the plaintiffs in the sum of £7,451 odd for value received and by which the defendant covenanted with the plaintiffs that he would pay the amount of the debt on a certain date. In fact, the debt represented the amount which the defendant owed to the plaintiffs, who were bookmakers, in respect of unsuccessful betting. The plaintiffs sued on the deed of charge to recover the amount payable thereunder but the defendant took refuge behind s. 1 of the Gaming Act 1835. *Held*, the action would fail. The court was entitled to look behind the false recitals in the deed, discover that it was executed for an illegal consideration and declare it to be void. (See also *Carlton Hall Club Ltd v Laurence*.)

Williams v Bayley (1866) LR 1 HL 200 (House of Lords)   **[638]**

A son forged his father's signature on certain promissory notes. When the forgery, which the son did not deny, was discovered the bankers arranged a meeting with his father and issued veiled threats to the effect that if some settlement was not made the son would be prosecuted. The father thereupon executed an agreement to make an equitable mortgage of his property and the forged promissory notes were returned to him. *Held*, the agreement was invalid as in these circumstances the father could not be said to have entered into it freely and voluntarily. (See also *Davies v London and Provincial Marine Insurance Co.*)

Williams v Carwardine (1833) 5 C & P 566   **[639]**

The defendant had advertised that he would pay a reward of £20 to the person who gave information which led to the conviction of a certain murderer. The plaintiff knew of the reward but confessed that she gave the information required 'in consequence of her miserable and unhappy situation, and believing that she had not long to live . . . to ease her conscience, and in hopes of forgiveness hereafter.' *Held*, she was entitled to the reward although she did not give the information for the sake of £20 or because she had seen the advertisement, 'but from stings of conscience'. (See also *Lancaster v Walsh*.)

Williams v Williams [1957] 1 All ER 305   **[640]**
(Court of Appeal)

A wife deserted her husband and they later entered into an agreement whereby the husband undertook to pay the wife £1 10s per week during their joint lives 'so long as the wife shall lead a chaste life'. The wife agreed that out of the weekly sum she would support and maintain herself; that she would indemnify the husband against all debts which she incurred; that she would not pledge her husband's credit and that she would not so long as the husband made the payments punctually bring any matrimonial proceedings other than proceedings for divorce. The wife sued to recover arrears of maintenance but the husband contended that there was no consideration for his promise to pay and that for this reason the agreement could not be enforced against him. *Held*, the husband was liable to pay the arrears as the wife's promise to maintain herself and indemnify the husband and not to pledge his credit was consideration for the husband's promise to pay her maintenance. The clause relating to the bringing of matrimonial proceedings was void and was not therefore a bar to these proceedings. (Distinguished in *Sutton v Sutton*; but see *Stilk v Myrick.*)

Wilson v Wilson (1848) 1 HL Cas 538 (House of Lords) **[641]**

Differences arose between a husband and wife and the wife left the matrimonial home. A deed of separation was entered into and when the wife sued to enforce the agreement the husband contended that it was contrary to public policy for the courts to entertain such a suit. *Held*, the deed would be enforced as it was not contrary to public policy to make provision for the wife in the event of a present separation. (See also *Lurie v Lurie.*)

Winter Garden Theatre (London) Ltd v Millenium **[642]**
Productions Ltd [1947] 2 All ER 331 (House of Lords)

The appellants granted the respondents a licence for the use of their theatre for two periods of six months and thereafter the appellants agreed that the respondents were 'to have the option of further continuing the licence of the theatre on the payment each week of a flat rental of £300 per week and you will give us one month's notice of your intention of then terminating the licence'. The licence made no provision for its termination by the appellants but after more than three years from the date of the original licence they purported to give the respondents one month's notice to withdraw from the premises. *Held*, the notice was valid and effectual as the licence was not perpetual and could be determined by the appellants by giving sufficient notice, and in these circumstances notice of one month was sufficient. (But see *Sethia (K. C.) (1944) Ltd v Partabmull Rameshwar.*)

Woolf v Collis Removal Service [1947] 2 All ER 260 **[643]**
(Court of Appeal)

The parties entered into a contract whereby the defendants were to remove and store some of the plaintiff's furniture. The work was carried out in breach of this agreement and the plaintiff contended that, for this reason, he was no longer bound by the arbitration clause which the contract contained. *Held*, the defendants' breach of contract in relation to the place and mode of storing the goods did not displace the arbitration clause by which the parties continued to be bound. (But see *General Billposting Co Ltd v Atkinson.*)

Woolmer v Delmer Price Ltd [1955] 1 All ER 377 **[644]**

The defendants failed to return the plaintiff's fur coat which had been left with them for storage and were unable to explain its disappearance. A term of the contract provided that 'All goods are left at customer's risk'. *Held*, the plaintiff was entitled to damages unless the defendants could show that the loss was not due to their negligence, in which case they would not be liable, or that they had been negligent, in which case their liability was successfully excluded by the terms of the contract. As the defendants could not explain the loss of the coat they were liable to the plaintiff. (But see *Spurling (J.) Ltd v Bradshaw.*)

Wormell v RHM Agriculture (East) Ltd [1987] 3 All ER 75   **[645]**
(Court of Appeal)

The plaintiff, an experienced farmer, asked the defendant suppliers of agricultural products to recommend a weedkiller which, late in the season, would destroy wild oats. The defendants made a recommendation and the plaintiff purchased the recommended herbicide from them. On the cans, it was stated that late applications of the herbicide could damage crops and that spraying after specified growth stages was not recommended. The plaintiff applied the herbicide—after the specified growth stage— but it failed to destroy the wild oats. He sought damages for breach of the term implied by s. 14(3) of the Sale of Goods Act 1979. *Held*, his action would fail even though he had understood the warning to mean that late application could damage his crop (as opposed to failing to destroy the wild oats).

Wright v Carter [1903] 1 Ch 27 (Court of Appeal)   **[646]**

Colonel Wright executed a trust in favour of his solicitor. The solicitor advised him to obtain independent advice from another solicitor but this solicitor was not fully informed of the actual circumstances of the matter. *Held*, the deed was void as Colonel Wright had not received advice from an independent solicitor who was fully aware of all the facts. (But see *Howes v Bishop*.)

Wyatt v Kreglinger and Fernau [1933] 1 KB 793   **[647]**
(Court of Appeal)

When the plaintiff was 60 years of age and about to retire from the defendants' business they wrote to inform him that they would grant him a pension of £200 pa and that he would be at liberty to undertake any other employment, or enter into any business on his own account, except in the wool trade; the only other stipulation they attached to the continuance of the pension was that he did nothing at any time to their detriment (fair business competition excepted). The plaintiff acknowledged the receipt of this letter. Some nine years later the defendants purported to discontinue the payment of the pension and the plaintiff brought an action for damages for breach of contract. *Held*, assuming that there was a contract between the parties, it was a contract unreasonably in restraint of trade as it provided that if the plaintiff entered the wool trade at any time and in any place his pension would be lost. It was against public policy for the country to be deprived of the services of a man who was quite competent to enter into business and for this reason the contract was void and the plaintiff could not found a successful action upon it. (But see *Hitchcock v Coker*.)

Zamet v Hyman [1961] 3 All ER 933   **[648]**
(Court of Appeal)

Mr Zamet, a widower aged seventy-nine with assets of at least £10,000, became engaged to marry a widow aged seventy-one. Three days before the marriage the widow went to a solicitor employed by her fiancé and executed a deed whereby, contingent on the proposed marriage being solemnised, in consideration of the payment of £600 on the death of Zamet she agreed to relinquish 'all rights that she may have under . . . the Inheritance (Family Provision) Act 1938, or the Intestates' Estates Act 1952'. Although the terms of the deed were explained to her the solicitor did not make her aware of its full implications. Zamet died intestate and the widow maintained that the deed was not binding. *Held*, it was not and it should be delivered up for cancellation. On the facts of the case the widow had imposed on Zamet a duty of candour and protection and those claiming the estate on intestacy had not shown that the widow had executed the deed fully understanding its significance and after 'full, free and informed (and, particularly, informed) thought about it' (*per* Lord Evershed MR). (See also *Wright v Carter*.)

STATUTES

STATUTE OF FRAUDS 1677
(29 Car 2, c 3; 11 Halsbury's Statutes (4th edn) 205)

4. No action . . . upon a special promise . . . unless   **[649]**
agreement, etc, be in writing, and signed.

. . . no action shall be brought whereby to charge the defendant upon any special promise to answer for the debt default or miscarriages of another person . . . unless the agreement upon which such action shall be brought or some memorandum or note thereof shall be in writing and signed by the party to be charged therewith or some other person thereunto by him lawfully authorised.

[As amended by the Law Reform (Enforcement of Contracts) Act 1954.] (See also s. 40 of the Law of Property Act 1925 [**659**])

GAMING ACT 1710
(9 Anne, c 19; 5 Halsbury's Statutes (4th edn) 7)

1. Security given for money, etc, won by gaming or for **[650]**
repayment of money lent for gaming void.

. . . all notes bills bonds judgments mortgages or other securities or conveyances whatsoever given granted drawn or entered into or executed by any person or persons whatsoever where the whole or any part of the consideration of such conveyances or securities shall be for any money or other valuable thing whatsoever won by gaming or playing at cards dice tables tennis bowles or other game or games whatsoever or by betting on the sides or hands of such as do game at any of the games aforesaid or for the reimbursing or repaying any money knowingly lent or advanced for such gaming or betting as aforesaid or lent or advanced at the time and place of such play to any person or persons so gaming or betting as aforesaid or that shall during such play, so play or bett shall be utterly void frustrate and of none effect to all intents and purposes whatsoever any statute law or usage to the contrary thereof in any wise notwithstanding. (See also s. 1 of the Gaming Act 1835 [**652**])

STATUTE OF FRAUDS AMENDMENT ACT 1828
(9 Geo 4, c 14; 11 Halsbury's Statutes (4th edn) 206)

6. Action not maintainable on representations of **[651]**
character, etc, unless they be in writing signed by
the party chargeable.

No action shall be brought whereby to charge any person upon or by reason of any representation or assurance made or given concerning or relating to the character, conduct, credit, ability, trade, or dealings of any other person, to the intent or purpose that such other person may obtain credit, money, or goods upon, unless such representation or assurance be made in writing, signed by the party to be charged therewith.

GAMING ACT 1835
(5 & 6 Will 4, c 41; 5 Halsbury's Statutes (4th edn) 11)

1. Securities given for considerations arising out   **[652]**
of illegal transactions not to be void, but to be deemed
to have been given for an illegal consideration.

. . . Every note, bill or mortgage which if this Act had not been passed would, by virtue of the said several lastly herein-before mentioned Acts [including the Gaming Act 1710] or any of them, have been absolutely void, shall be deemed and taken to have been made, drawn, accepted, given or executed for an illegal consideration; and the said several Acts shall have the same force and effect which they would respectively have had, if, instead of enacting that any such note, bill, or mortgage should be absolutely void, such Acts had respectively provided that every such note, bill or mortgage should be deemed and taken to have been made, drawn, accepted, given, or executed for an illegal consideration: Provided always, that nothing herein contained shall prejudice or affect any note, bill, or mortgage which would have been good and valid if this Act had not been passed.

GAMING ACT 1845
(8 & 9 Vict, c 109; 5 Halsbury's Statutes (4th edn) 13)

18. Contracts by way of gaming to be void, and wagers   **[653]**
or sums deposited with stakeholders not to be
recoverable at law—Saving for subscriptions for prizes.

All contracts or agreements, whether by parole or in writing, by way of gaming or wagering, shall be null and void; and no suit shall be brought or maintained in any court of law and equity for recovering any sum of money or valuable thing alleged to have been won upon any wager, or which shall have been deposited in the hands of any person to abide the event on which any wager shall have been made: Provided always, that this enactment shall not be deemed to apply to any subscription or contribution, or agreement to subscribe or contribute, for or towards any plate, prize, or sum of money to be awarded to the winner or winners of any lawful game, sport, pastime, or exercise. (Excluded by the Financial Services Act 1986, ss. 1, 2, 63(1)(a), Sch 1, para 33.)

INFANTS' RELIEF ACT 1874
(37 & 38 Vict, c 62; 6 Halsbury's Statutes (4th edn) 12)

1. Contracts by [minors], except for necessaries, to be   **[654]**
void.

All contracts, whether by specialty or by simple contract, henceforth entered into by [minors] for the repayment of money lent or to be lent, or for goods supplied or to be supplied (other than contracts for necessaries), and all accounts stated with [minors], shall be absolutely void: Provided always, that this enactment shall not invalidate any contract into which a [minor] may, by any existing or future statute, or by the rules of common law or equity, enter, except such as now by law are voidable.

2. No action to be brought on ratification of minor's   **[655]**
contract.

No action shall be brought whereby to charge any person upon any promise made after full age to pay any debt contracted during [minority], or upon any ratification made after full age of any promise or contract made during [minority], whether there shall or shall not be any new consideration for such promise or ratification after full age.

(For contracts made by a minor after 9 June 1987, see Minors' Contracts Act 1987 [**745**])

Note: The age of majority was reduced from 21 to 18 by s. 1 of the Family Law Reform Act 1969.

BILLS OF EXCHANGE ACT 1882
(45 & 46 Vict, c 61; 5 Halsbury's Statutes (4th edn) 50)

27.   Value and holder for value.   **[656]**

(1) Valuable consideration for a bill may be constituted by,—
(a) Any consideration sufficient to support a simple contract;
(b) An antecedent debt or liability. Such a debt or liability is deemed valuable consideration whether the bill is payable on demand or at a future time.

(2) Where value has at any time been given for a bill the holder is deemed to be a holder for value as regards the acceptor and all parties to the bill who became parties prior to such time.

GAMING ACT 1892
(55 & 56 Vict, c 9; 5 Halsbury's Statutes (4th edn) 16)

1.   Promises to repay sums paid under contracts void by   **[657]**
the Gaming Act 1845 to be null and void.

Any promise, express or implied, to pay any person any sum of money paid by him under or in respect of any contract or agreement rendered null and void by the Gaming Act 1845, or to pay any sum of money by way of commission, fee, reward, or otherwise in respect of any such contract, or of any services in relation thereto or in connexion therewith, shall be null and void, and no action shall be brought or maintained to recover any such sum of money. (Excluded by the Financial Services Act 1986, ss. 1, 2, 63(1)(a), Sch 1, para 33.)

MARINE INSURANCE ACT 1906
(6 Edw 7, c 41; 22 Halsbury's Statutes (4th edn) 25)

18.   Disclosure by assured.   **[658]**

(1) Subject to the provisions of this section, the assured must disclose to the insurer, before the contract is concluded, every material circumstance which is known to the assured, and the assured is deemed to know every circumstance which, in the ordinary course of business, ought to be known by him. If the assured fails to make such disclosure, the insurer may avoid the contract.

(2) Every circumstance is material which would influence the judgment of a prudent insurer in fixing the premium, or determining whether he will take the risk.

LAW OF PROPERTY ACT 1925
(15 & 16 Geo 5, c 20; 37 Halsbury's Statutes (4th edn) 72)

40.   Contracts for sale, etc, of land to be in writing.   **[659]**

(1) No action may be brought upon any contract for the sale or other disposition of land or any interest in land, unless the agreement upon which such action is brought, or some memorandum or note thereof, is in writing, and signed by the party to be charged or by some other person thereunto by him lawfully authorised.

(2) This section applies to contracts whether made before or after the commencement of this Act and does not affect the law relating to part performance, or sales by the court.

41. Stipulations not of the essence of a contract. [660]

Stipulations in a contract, as to time or otherwise, which according to rules of equity are not deemed to be or to have become of the essence of the contract, are also construed and have effect at law in accordance with the same rules.

56. Persons taking who are not parties. [661]

(1) A person may take an immediate or other interest in land or other property, or the benefit of any condition, right of entry, covenant or agreement over or respecting land or other property, although he may not be named as a party to the conveyance or other instrument.

LAW REFORM (FRUSTRATED CONTRACTS) ACT 1943
(6 & 7 Geo 6, c 40; 11 Halsbury's Statutes (4th edn) 209)

1. Adjustment of rights and liabilities of parties to frustrated contracts. [662]

(1) Where a contract governed by English law has become impossible of performance or been otherwise frustrated, and the parties thereto have for that reason been discharged from the further performance of the contract, the following provisions of this section shall, subject to the provisions of section two of this Act, have effect in relation thereto.
(2) All sums paid or payable to any party in pursuance of the contract before the time when the parties were so discharged (in this Act referred to as 'the time of discharge') shall, in the case of sums so paid, be recoverable from him as money received by him for the use of the party by whom the sums were paid, and, in the case of sums so payable, cease to be so payable:
  Provided that, if the party to whom the sums were so paid or payable incurred expenses before the time of discharge in, or for the purpose of, the performance of the contract, the court may, if it considers it just to do so having regard to all the circumstances of the case, allow him to retain or, as the case may be, recover the whole or any part of the sums so paid or payable, not being an amount in excess of the expenses so incurred.
(3) Where any party to the contract has, by reason of anything done by any other party thereto in, or for the purpose of, the performance of the contract, obtained a valuable benefit (other than a payment of money to which the last foregoing subsection applies) before the time of discharge, there shall be recoverable from him by the said other party such sum (if any), not exceeding the value of the said benefit to the party obtaining it, as the court considers just, having regard to all the circumstances of the case and, in particular,—
  (a) the amount of any expenses incurred before the time of discharge by the benefited party in, or for the purpose of, the performance of the contract, including any sums paid or payable by him to any other party in pursuance of the contract and retained or recoverable by that party under the last foregoing subsection, and
  (b) the effect, in relation to the said benefit, of the circumstances giving rise to the frustration of the contract.
(4) In estimating, for the purposes of the foregoing provisions of this section, the amount of any expenses incurred by any party to the contract, the court may, without prejudice to the generality of the said provisions, include such sum as appears to be reasonable in respect of overhead expenses and in respect of any work or services performed personally by the said party.
(5) In considering whether any sum ought to be recovered or retained under the foregoing provisions of this section by any party to the contract, the court shall not take into account any sums which have, by reason of the circumstances giving rise to the

154

frustration of the contract, become payable to that party under any contract of insurance unless there was an obligation to insure imposed by an express term of the frustrated contract or by or under any enactment.

(6) Where any person has assumed obligations under the contract in consideration of the conferring of a benefit by any other party to the contract upon any other person, whether a party to the contract or not, the court may, if in all the circumstances of the case it considers it just to do so, treat for the purposes of sub-section (3) of this section any benefit so conferred as a benefit obtained by the person who has assumed the obligations as aforesaid.

2. Provision as to application of this Act.   [663]

(1) This Act shall apply to contracts, whether made before or after the commencement of this Act, as respects which the time of discharge is on or after the first day of July, nineteen hundred and forty-three, but not to contracts as respects which the time of discharge is before the said date.

(2) This Act shall apply to contracts to which the Crown is a party in like manner as to contracts between subjects.

(3) Where any contract to which this Act applies contains any provision which, upon the true construction of the contract, is intended to have effect in the event of circumstances arising which operate, or would but for the said provision operate, to frustrate the contract, or is intended to have effect whether such circumstances arise or not, the court shall give effect to the said provision and shall only give effect to the foregoing section of this Act to such extent, if any, as appears to the court to be consistent with the said provision.

(4) Where it appears to the court that a part of any contract to which this Act applies can properly be severed from the remainder of the contract, being a part wholly performed before the time of discharge, or so performed except for the payment in respect of that part of the contract of sums which are or can be ascertained under the contract, the court shall treat that part of the contract as if it were a separate contract and had not been frustrated and shall treat the foregoing section of this Act as only applicable to the remainder of that contract.

(5) This Act shall not apply—

(a) to any charterparty, except a time charterparty or a charterparty by way of demise, or to any contract (other than a charterparty) for the carriage of goods by sea; or

(b) to any contract of insurance, save as is provided by subsection (5) of the foregoing section; or

(c) to any contract to which section 7 of the Sale of Goods Act 1979 (which avoids contracts for the sale of specific goods which perish before the risk has passed to the buyer) applies, or to any other contract for the sale, or for the sale and delivery, of specific goods, where the contract is frustrated by reason of the fact that the goods have perished.

3. Interpretation.   [664]

(2) In this Act the expression 'court' means, in relation to any matter, the court or arbitrator by or before whom the matter falls to be determined.

CORPORATE BODIES' CONTRACTS ACT 1960
(8 & 9 Eliz 2, c 46; 11 Halsbury's Statutes (4th edn) 213)

1. Cases where contracts need not be under seal.   [665]

(1) Contracts may be made on behalf of any body corporate, wherever incorporated, as follows:—

(a) a contract which if made between private persons would be by law required to be in writing, signed by the parties to be charged therewith, may be made on behalf of the body corporate in writing signed by any person acting under its authority, express or implied, and

(b) a contract which if made between private persons would by law be valid although made by parol only, and not reduced into writing, may be made by parol on behalf of the body corporate by any person acting under its authority, express or implied.

(2) A contract made according to this section shall be effectual in law, and shall bind the body corporate and its successors and all other parties thereto.

(3) A contract made according to this section may be varied or discharged in the same manner in which it is authorised by this section to be made.

(4) Nothing in this section shall be taken as preventing a contract under seal from being made by or on behalf of a body corporate.

(5) This section shall not apply to the making, variation or discharge of a contract before the commencement of this Act but shall apply whether the body corporate gave its authority before or after the commencement of this Act.

[This Act came into force on 29 July 1960.]

2. Exclusion of companies under Companies Acts.   [666]

This Act shall not apply to any company formed and registered under the Companies Act, 1985, or an existing company as defined in that Act.

MISREPRESENTATION ACT 1967
(1967, c 7; 29 Halsbury's Statutes (4th edn) 724)

1. Removal of certain bars to rescission for innocent   [667]
misrepresentation.

Where a person has entered into a contract after a misrepresentation has been made to him, and—

(a) the misrepresentation has become a term of the contract; or

(b) the contract has been performed;

or both, then, if otherwise he would be entitled to rescind the contract without alleging fraud, he shall be so entitled, subject to the provisions of this Act, notwithstanding the matters mentioned in paragraphs (a) and (b) of this section.

2. Damages for misrepresentation.   [668]

(1) Where a person has entered into a contract after a misrepresentation has been made to him by another party thereto and as a result thereof he has suffered loss, then, if the person making the misrepresentation would be liable to damages in respect thereof had the misrepresentation been made fraudulently, that person shall be so liable notwithstanding that the misrepresentation was not made fraudulently, unless he proves that he had reasonable ground to believe and did believe up to the time the contract was made that the facts represented were true.

(2) Where a person has entered into a contract after a misrepresentation has been made to him otherwise than fraudulently, and he would be entitled, by reason of the misrepresentation, to rescind the contract, then, if it is claimed, in any proceedings arising out of the contract, that the contract ought to be or has been rescinded the court or arbitrator may declare the contract subsisting and award damages in lieu of rescission, if of opinion that it would be equitable to do so, having regard to the nature of the misrepresentation and the loss that would be caused by it if the contract were upheld, as well as to the loss that rescission would cause to the other party.

(3) Damages may be awarded against a person under subsection (2) of this section

whether or not he is liable to damages under subsection (1) thereof, but where he is so liable any award under the said subsection (2) shall be taken into account in assessing his liability under the said subsection (1).

3. Avoidance of provision excluding liability for   [669]
misrepresentation.

If a contract contains a term which would exclude or restrict—
(a) any liability to which a party to a contract may be subject by reason of any misrepresentation made by him before the contract was made; or
(b) any remedy available to another party to the contract by reason of such misrepresentation,
that term shall be of no effect except in so far as it satisfies the requirement of reasonableness stated in section 11(1) of the Unfair Contract Terms Act 1977[**691**]; and it is for those claiming that the term satisfies that requirement to show that it does.

5. Saving for past transactions.   [670]

Nothing in this Act shall apply in relation to a misrepresentation or contract of sale which is made before the commencement of this Act.
[As amended by the Unfair Contract Terms Act 1977.]

GAMING ACT 1968
(1968, c 65; 5 Halsbury's Statutes (4th edn) 98)

2. Nature of game.   [671]

(1) Subject to the following provisions of this section, no gaming to which this Part of this Act applies shall take place where any one or more of the following conditions are fulfilled, that is to say—
(a) the game involves playing or staking against a bank, whether the bank is held by one of the players or not;
(b) the nature of the game is such that the chances in the game are not equally favourable to all the players;
(c) the nature of the game is such that the chances in it lie between the player and some other person, or (if there are two or more players) lie wholly or partly between the players and some other person, and those chances are not as favourable to the player or players as they are to that other person.
(2) The preceding subsection shall not have effect in relation to gaming which takes place on a domestic occasion in a private dwelling, and shall not have effect in relation to any gaming where the gaming takes place in a hostel, hall of residence or similar establishment which is not carried on by way of a trade or business and the players consist exclusively or mainly of persons who are residents or inmates in that establishment.

16. Provision of credit for gaming.   [672]

(1) Subject to subsections (2) and (2A) of this section, where gaming to which this Part of this Act applies takes place on premises in respect of which a licence under this Act is for the time being in force, neither the holder of the licence nor any person acting on his behalf or under any arrangement with him shall make any loan or otherwise provide or allow to any person any credit, or release, or discharge on another person's behalf, the whole or part of any debt,—
(a) for enabling any person to take part in the gaming, or
(b) in respect of any losses incurred by any person in the gaming.
(2) Neither the holder of the licence nor any person acting on his behalf or under any arrangement with him shall accept a cheque and give in exchange for it cash or

tokens for enabling any person to take part in the gaming unless the following conditions are fulfilled, that is to say—

(a) the cheque is not a post-dated cheque, and

(b) it is exchanged for cash to an amount equal to the amount for which it is drawn, or is exchanged for tokens at the same rate as would apply if cash, to the amount for which the cheque is drawn, were given in exchange for them;

but, where those conditions are fulfilled, the giving of cash or tokens in exchange for a cheque shall not be taken to contravene subsection (1) of this section.

(2A) Neither the holder of a licence under this Act nor any person acting on his behalf or under any arrangement with him shall permit to be redeemed any cheque (not being a cheque which has been dishonoured) accepted in exchange for cash or tokens for enabling any person to take part in gaming to which this Part of this Act applies unless the following conditions are fulfilled, that is to say—

(a) the cheque is redeemed by the person from whom it was accepted giving in exchange for it cash, or tokens, or a substitute cheque, or any combination of these, to an amount equal to the amount of the redeemed cheque or (where two or more cheques are redeemed) the aggregate amount of the redeemed cheques;

(b) it is redeemed during the playing session in which it was accepted, or within thirty minutes after the end of the session;

(c) where a substitute cheque is given in whole or in part exchange for the redeemed cheque the substitute cheque is not a post-dated cheque; and

(d) where tokens are given in whole or in part exchange for the redeemed cheque, the value of each token is equal to the amount originally given in exchange for it or, if the token was won in the gaming, the value it represented when won;

but, where those conditions are fulfilled, the return of a redeemed cheque in exchange for cash, or tokens, or a substitute cheque, or any combination of these, shall not be taken to contravene subsection (1) of this section.

(3) Where the holder of a licence under this Act, or a person acting on behalf of or under any arrangement with the holder of such a licence, accepts a cheque in exchange for cash or tokens to be used by a player in gaming to which this Part of this Act applies or a substitute cheque, he shall not more than two banking days later cause the cheque to be delivered to a bank for payment or collection.

(3A) Subsection (3) of this section shall not apply to a redeemed cheque.

(4) Nothing in the Gaming Act 1710, the Gaming Act 1835, the Gaming Act 1845, or the Gaming Act 1892, shall affect the validity of, or any remedy in respect of any cheque which is accepted in exchange for cash or tokens to be used by a player in gaming to which this Part of this Act applies or any substitute cheque.

(5) In this section 'banking day' means a day which is a business day in accordance with section 92 of the Bills of Exchange Act 1882.

'playing session' means a continuous period during one day, or two consecutive days, throughout which gaming is permitted by or under this Act to take place on premises in respect of which a licence under this Act is for the time being in force;

'redeemed cheque' means a cheque accepted in fulfilment of the conditions specified in subsection (2) of this section and returned to the person from whom it was accepted in fulfilment of the conditions specified in subsection (2A) of this section;

'substitute cheque' means a cheque accepted in accordance with subsection (2A) of this section by either the holder of a licence under this Act or a person acting on behalf of or under any arrangement with the holder of such a licence.

[As amended by the Gaming (Amendment) Act 1986.]

52. Interpretation. [673]

(1) 'Gaming' means (subject to subsections (3) to (5) of this section) [which exclude certain lotteries, pool betting and certain games played by machines] the playing of a game of chance for winnings in money or money's worth, whether any person playing the game is at risk of losing any money or money's worth or not.

SUPPLY OF GOODS (IMPLIED TERMS) ACT 1973
(1973, c 13; 11 Halsbury's Statutes (4th edn) 8)

8. Implied terms as to title.   **[674]**

(1) In every hire-purchase agreement, other than one to which subsection (2) below applies, there is—
(a) an implied condition on the part of the creditor that he will have a right to sell the goods at the time when the property is to pass; and
(b) an implied warranty that—
  (i) the goods are free, and will remain free until the time when the property is to pass, from any charge or encumbrance not disclosed or known to the person to whom the goods are bailed or (in Scotland) hired before the agreement is made, and
  (ii) that person will enjoy quiet possession of the goods except so far as it may be disturbed by any person entitled to the benefit of any charge or encumbrance so disclosed or known.
(2) In a hire-purchase agreement, in the case of which there appears from the agreement or is to be inferred from the circumstances of the agreement an intention that the creditor should transfer only such title as he or a third person may have, there is—
(a) an implied warranty that all charges or encumbrances known to the creditor and not known to the person to whom the goods are bailed or hired have been disclosed to that person before the agreement is made, and
(b) an implied warranty that neither—
  (i) the creditor; nor
  (ii) in a case where the parties to the agreement intend that any title which may be transferred shall be only such title as a third person may have, that person; nor
  (iii) anyone claiming through or under the creditor or that third person otherwise than under a charge or encumbrance disclosed or known to the person to whom the goods are bailed or hired, before the agreement is made;
will disturb the quiet possession of the person to whom the goods are bailed or hired.

9. Bailing or hiring by description.   **[675]**

(1) Where under a hire-purchase agreement goods are bailed or (in Scotland) hired by description, there is an implied condition that the goods will correspond with the description, and if under the agreement the goods are bailed or hired by reference to a sample as well as a description, it is not sufficient that the bulk of the goods corresponds with the sample if the goods do not also correspond with the description.
(2) Goods shall not be prevented from being bailed or hired by description by reason only that, being exposed for sale, bailment or hire, they are selected by the person to whom they are bailed or hired.

10. Implied undertakings as to quality or fitness.   **[676]**

(1) Except as provided by this section and section 11 below and subject to the provisions of any other enactment, including any enactment of the Parliament of Northern Ireland or the Northern Ireland Assembly, there is no implied condition or warranty as to the quality or fitness for any particular purpose of goods bailed or (in Scotland) hired under a hire-purchase agreement.
(2) Where the creditor bails or hires goods under a hire-purchase agreement in the course of a business, there is an implied condition that the goods supplied under the agreement are of merchantable quality, except that there is no such condition—
(a) as regards defects specifically drawn to the attention of the person to whom the goods are bailed or hired before the agreement is made; or

159

(b) if that person examines the goods before the agreement is made, as regards defects which that examination ought to reveal.

(3) Where the creditor bails or hires goods under a hire-purchase agreement in the course of a business and the person to whom the goods are bailed or hired, expressly or by implication, makes known—

(a) to the creditor in the course of negotiations conducted by the creditor in relation to the making of the hire-purchase agreement, or

(b) to a credit-broker in the course of negotiations conducted by that broker in relation to goods sold by him to the creditor before forming the subject matter of the hire-purchase agreement,

any particular purpose for which the goods are being bailed or hired, there is an implied condition that the goods supplied under the agreement are reasonably fit for that purpose, whether or not that is a purpose for which such goods are commonly supplied, except where the circumstances show that the person to whom the goods are bailed or hired does not rely, or that it is unreasonable for him to rely, on the skill or judgment of the creditor or credit-broker.

(4) An implied condition or warranty as to quality or fitness for a particular purpose may be annexed to a hire-purchase agreement by usage.

(5) The preceding provisions of this section apply to a hire-purchase agreement made by a person who in the course of a business is acting as agent for the creditor as they apply to an agreement made by the creditor in the course of a business, except where the creditor is not bailing or hiring in the course of a business and either the person to whom the goods are bailed or hired knows that fact or reasonable steps are taken to bring it to the notice of that person before the agreement is made.

(6) In subsection (3) above and this subsection—

(a) 'credit-broker' means a person acting in the course of a business of credit brokerage.

(b) 'credit brokerage' means the effecting of introductions of individuals desiring to obtain credit—

    (i) to persons carrying on any business so far as it relates to the provision of credit, or

    (ii) to other persons engaged in credit brokerage.

[As amended by the Supply of Goods and Services Act 1982.]

11. Samples.   [677]

Where under a hire-purchase agreement goods are bailed or (in Scotland) hired by reference to a sample, there is an implied condition—

(a) that the bulk will correspond with the sample in quality; and

(b) that the person to whom the goods are bailed or hired will have a reasonable opportunity of comparing the bulk with the sample; and

(c) that the goods will be free from any defect, rendering them unmerchantable which would not be apparent on reasonable examination of the sample.

12. Exclusion of implied terms and conditions.   [678]

(1) An express condition or warranty does not negative a condition or warranty implied by this Act unless inconsistent with it.

14. Special provisions as to conditional sale agreements.   [679]

(1) Section 11(4) of the Sale of Goods Act 1979 (whereby in certain circumstances a breach of a condition in a contract of sale is treated only as a breach of warranty) shall not apply to a conditional sale agreement where the buyer deals as consumer within Part I of the Unfair Contract Terms Act 1977 . . .

(2) In England and Wales and Northern Ireland a breach of a condition (whether express or implied) to be fulfilled by the seller under any such agreement shall be treated as a breach of warranty, and not as grounds for rejecting the goods and

treating the agreement as repudiated, if (but only if) it would have fallen to be so treated had the condition been contained or implied in a corresponding hire-purchase agreement as a condition to be fulfilled by the creditor.

15. Supplementary. [680]

(1) In sections 8 to 14 above and this section—
'business' includes a profession and the activities of any government department (including a Northern Ireland department), [or local or public authority];
'buyer' and 'seller' includes a person to whom rights and duties under a conditional sale agreement have passed by assignment or operation of law;
'condition' and 'warranty', in relation to Scotland, mean stipulation, and any stipulation referred to in sections 8(1)(a), 9, 10 and 11 above shall be deemed to be material to the agreement.
'conditional sale agreement' means an agreement for the sale of goods under which the purchase price or part of it is payable by instalments, and the property in the goods is to remain in the seller (notwithstanding that the buyer is to be in possession of the goods) until such conditions as to the payment of instalments or otherwise as may be specified in the agreement are fulfilled;
'creditor' means the person by whom the goods are bailed or (in Scotland) hired under a hire-purchase agreement or the person to whom his rights and duties under the agreement have passed by assignment or operation of law; and
'hire-purchase agreement' means an agreement, other than a conditional sale agreement, under which—
(a) goods are bailed or (in Scotland) hired in return for periodical payments by the person to whom they are bailed or hired, and
(b) the property in the goods will pass to that person if the terms of the agreement are complied with and one or more of the following occurs—
   (i) the exercise of an option to purchase by that person,
   (ii) the doing of any other specified act by any party to the agreement,
   (iii) the happening of any other specified event.
(2) Goods of any kind are of merchantable quality within the meaning of section 10(2) above if they are as fit for the purpose or purposes for which goods of that kind are commonly bought as it is reasonable to expect having regard to any description applied to them, the price (if relevant) and all the other relevant circumstances; and in section 11 above 'unmerchantable' shall be construed accordingly.
(3) In section 14(2) above 'corresponding hire-purchase agreement' means, in relation to a conditional sale agreement, a hire-purchase agreement relating to the same goods as the conditional sale agreement and made between the same parties and at the same time and in the same circumstances and, as nearly as may be, in the same terms as the conditional sale agreement.
(4) Nothing in sections 8 to 13 above shall prejudice the operation of any other enactment including any enactment of the Parliament of Northern Ireland or the Northern Ireland Assembly or any rule of law whereby any condition or warranty, other than one relating to quality or fitness, is to be implied in any hire-purchase agreement.
[The above provisions were substituted by the Consumer Credit Act 1974 as from 19 May 1985.]

MATRIMONIAL CAUSES ACT 1973
(1973, c 18; 27 Halsbury's Statutes (4th edn) 746)

34. Validity of maintenance agreements. [681]

(1) If a maintenance agreement includes a provision purporting to restrict any right to apply to a court for an order containing financial arrangements, then—
(a) that provision shall be void; but

(b) any other financial arrangements contained in the agreement shall not thereby be rendered void or unenforceable and shall, unless they are void or unenforceable for any other reason (and subject to sections 35 and 36 below [which apply to the alteration of agreements by the court during the lives of parties and after the death of one party]), be binding on the parties to the agreement.

(2) In this section and in section 35 below—

'maintenance agreement' means any agreement in writing made, whether before or after the commencement of this Act, between the parties to a marriage, being—

(a) an agreement containing financial arrangements, whether made during the continuance or after the dissolution or annulment of the marriage; or

(b) a separation agreement which contains no financial arrangements in a case where no other agreement in writing between the same parties contains such arrangements;

'financial arrangements' means provisions governing the rights and liabilities towards one another when living separately of the parties to a marriage (including a marriage which has been dissolved or annulled) in respect of the making or securing of payments or the disposition or use of any property, including such rights and liabilities with respect to the maintenance or education of any child, whether or not a child of the family.

UNFAIR CONTRACT TERMS ACT 1977
(1977, c 50; 11 Halsbury's Statutes (4th edn) 214)

Part I

Amendment of Law for England and Wales and Northern Ireland

Introductory

1. Scope of Part I. [682]

(1) For the purposes of this Part of this Act, 'negligence' means the breach—

(a) of any obligation, arising from the express or implied terms of a contract, to take reasonable care or exercise reasonable skill in the performance of the contract;

(b) of any common law duty to take reasonable care or exercise reasonable skill (but not any stricter duty);

(c) of the common duty of care imposed by the Occupiers' Liability Act 1957 or the Occupiers' Liability Act (Northern Ireland) 1957.

(2) This Part of this Act is subject to Part III; and in relation to contracts, the operation of sections 2 to 4 and 7 is subject to the exceptions made by Schedule 1.

(3) In the case of both contract and tort, sections 2 to 7 apply except where the contrary is stated in section 6(4)) only to business liability, that is liability for breach of obligations or duties arising—

(a) from things done or to be done by a person in the course of a business (whether his own business or another's);

(b) from the occupation of premises used for business purposes of the occupier;

and references to liability are to be read accordingly but liability of an occupier of premises for breach of an obligation or duty towards a person obtaining access to the premises for recreational or educational purposes, being liability for loss or damage suffered by reason of the dangerous state of the premises, is not a business liability of the occupier unless granting that person such access for the purposes concerned falls within the business purposes of the occupier.

(4) In relation to any breach of duty or obligation, it is immaterial for any purpose of this part of this Act whether the breach was inadvertent or intentional, or whether liability for it arises directly or vicariously.

[As amended by the Occupiers' Liability Act 1984.]

Avoidance of liability for negligence, breach of contract, etc.

2. Negligence liability.   [683]

(1) A person cannot by reference to any contract term or to a notice given to persons generally or to particular persons exclude or restrict his liability for death or personal injury resulting from negligence.

(2) In the case of other loss or damage, a person cannot so exclude or restrict his liability for negligence except in so far as the term or notice satisfies the requirement of reasonableness.

(3) Where a contract term or notice purports to exclude or restrict liability for negligence a person's agreement to or awareness of it is not of itself to be taken as indicating his voluntary acceptance of any risk.

3. Liability arising in contract.   [684]

(1) This section applies as between contracting parties where one of them deals as consumer or on the other's written standard terms of business.

(2) As against that party, the other cannot by reference to any contract term—

(a) when himself in breach of contract, exclude or restrict any liability of his in respect of the breach; or

(b) claim to be entitled—

　　(i) to render a contractual performance substantially different from that which was reasonably expected of him, or

　　(ii) in respect of the whole or any part of his contractual obligation, to render no performance at all,

except in so far as (in any of the cases mentioned above in this subsection) the contract term satisfies the requirement of reasonableness.

4. Unreasonable indemnity clauses.   [685]

(1) A person dealing as consumer cannot by reference to any contract term be made to indemnify another person (whether a party to the contract or not) in respect of liability that may be incurred by the other for negligence or breach of contract, except in so far as the contract term satisfies the requirement of reasonableness.

(2) This section applies whether the liability in question—

(a) is directly that of the person to be indemnified or is incurred by him vicariously;

(b) is to the person dealing as consumer or to someone else.

Liability arising from sale or supply of goods

5. 'Guarantee' of consumer goods.   [686]

(1) In the case of goods of a type ordinarily supplied for private use or consumption, where loss or damage—

(a) arises from the goods proving defective while in consumer use; and

(b) results from the negligence of a person concerned in the manufacture or distribution of the goods,

liability for the loss or damage cannot be excluded or restricted by reference to any contract term or notice contained in or operating by reference to a guarantee of the goods.

(2) For these purposes—

(a) goods are to be regarded as 'in consumer use' when a person is using them, or has them in his possession for use, otherwise than exclusively for the purposes of a business; and

(b) anything in writing is a guarantee if it contains or purports to contain some promise or assurance (however worded or presented) that defects will be made good by complete or partial replacement, or by repair, monetary compensation or otherwise.

163

(3) This section does not apply as between the parties to a contract under or in pursuance of which possession or ownership of the goods passed.

6. Sale and hire-purchase. [687]

(1) Liability for breach of the obligations arising from—
(a) section 12 of the Sale of Goods Act 1979 (seller's implied undertakings as to title, etc);
(b) section 8 of the Supply of Goods (Implied Terms) Act 1973 (the corresponding thing in relation to hire-purchase);
cannot be excluded or restricted by reference to any contract term.
(2) As against a person dealing as consumer, liability for breach of the obligations arising from—
(a) section 13, 14 and 15 of the 1979 Act (seller's implied undertakings as to conformity of goods with description or sample, or as to their quality or fitness for a particular purpose);
(b) section 9, 10 or 11 of the 1973 Act (the corresponding things in relation to hire-purchase),
cannot be excluded or restricted by reference to any contract term.
(3) As against a person dealing otherwise than as consumer, the liability specified in subsection (2) above can be excluded or restricted by reference to a contract term, but only in so far as the term satisfies the requirement of reasonableness.
(4) The liabilities referred to in this section are not only the business liabilities defined by section 1(3), but include those arising under any contract of sale of goods or hire-purchase agreement.

7. Miscellaneous contracts under which goods pass. [688]

(1) Where the possession or ownership of goods passes under or in pursuance of a contract not governed by the law of sale of goods or hire-purchase, subsections (2) to (4) below apply as regards the effect (if any) to be given to contract terms excluding or restricting liability for breach of obligation arising by implication of law from the nature of the contract.
(2) As against a person dealing as consumer, liability in respect of the goods' correspondence with description or sample, or their quality or fitness for any particular purpose, cannot be excluded or restricted by reference to any such term.
(3) As against a person dealing otherwise than as consumer, that liability can be excluded or restricted by reference to such a term, but only in so far as the term satisfies the requirement of reasonableness.
(3A) Liability for breach of the obligations arising under section 2 of the Supply of Goods and Services Act 1982 (implied terms about title etc in certain contracts for the transfer of the property in goods) cannot be excluded or restricted by references to any such term.
(4) Liability in respect of—
(a) the right to transfer ownership of the goods, or give possession; or
(b) the assurance of quiet possession to a person taking goods in pursuance of the contract,
cannot (in a case to which subsection (3A) above does not apply) be excluded or restricted by reference to any such term except in so far as the term satisfies the requirement of reasonableness.
(5) This section does not apply in the case of goods passing on a redemption of trading stamps within the Trading Stamps Act 1964 or the Trading Stamps Act (Northern Ireland) 1965.
[As amended by the Supply of Goods and Services Act 1982.]

Other provisions about contracts

9. Effect of breach. [689]

(1) Where for reliance upon it a contract term has to satisfy the requirement of reasonableness, it may be found to do so and be given effect accordingly notwithstanding that the contract has been terminated either by breach or by a party electing to treat it as repudiated.

(2) Where on a breach the contract is nevertheless affirmed by a party entitled to treat it as repudiated, this does not of itself exclude the requirement of reasonableness in relation to any contract term.

10. Evasion by means of secondary contract. [690]

A person is not bound by any contract term prejudicing or taking away rights of his which arise under, or in connection with the performance of, another contract, so far as those rights extend to the enforcement of another's liability which this Part of this Act prevents that other from excluding or restricting.

Explanatory provisions

11. The 'reasonableness' test. [691]

(1) In relation to a contract term, the requirement of reasonableness for the purposes of this Part of this Act, section 3 of the Misrepresentation Act 1967 and section 3 of the Misrepresentation Act (Northern Ireland) 1967 is that the term shall have been a fair and reasonable one to be included having regard to the circumstances which were, or ought reasonably to have been, known to or in the contemplation of the parties when the contract was made.

(2) In determining for the purposes of section 6 or 7 above whether a contract term satisfies the requirement of reasonableness, regard shall be had in particular to the matters specified in Schedule 2 to this Act; but this subsection does not prevent the court or arbitrator from holding, in accordance with any rule of law, that a term which purports to exclude or restrict any relevant liability is not a term of the contract.

(3) In relation to a notice (not being a notice having contractual effect), the requirement of reasonableness under this Act is that it should be fair and reasonable to allow reliance on it, having regard to all the circumstances obtaining when the liability arose or (but for the notice) would have arisen.

(4) Where by reference to a contract term or notice a person seeks to restrict liability to a specified sum of money, and the question arises (under this or any other Act) whether the term or notice satisfies the requirement of reasonableness, regard shall be had in particular (but without prejudice to subsection (2) above in the case of contract terms) to—

(a) the resources which he could expect to be available to him for the purpose of meeting the liability should it arise; and

(b) how far it was open to him to cover himself by insurance.

(5) It is for those claiming that a contract term or notice satisfies the requirement of reasonableness to show that it does.

12. 'Dealing as consumer'. [692]

(1) A party to a contract 'deals as consumer' in relation to another party if—

(a) he neither makes the contract in the course of a business nor holds himself out as doing so; and

(b) the other party does make the contract in the course of a business; and

(c) in the case of a contract governed by the law of sale of goods or hire-purchase, or by section 7 of this Act, the goods passing under or in pursuance of the contract are of a type ordinarily supplied for private use or consumption.

(2) But on a sale by auction or by competitive tender the buyer is not in any circumstances to be regarded as dealing as consumer.

(3) Subject to this, it is for those claiming that a party does not deal as consumer to show that he does not.

13. Varieties of exemption clause. [693]

(1) To the extent that this Part of this Act prevents the exclusion or restriction of any liability it also prevents—

(a) making the liability or its enforcement subject to restrictive or onerous conditions

(b) excluding or restricting any right or remedy in respect of the liability, or subjecting a person to any prejudice in consequence of his pursuing any such right or remedy;

(c) excluding or restricting rules of evidence or procedure; and (to that extent) sections 2 and 7 also prevent excluding or restricting liability by reference to terms and notices which exclude or restrict the relevant obligation or duty.

(2) But an agreement in writing to submit present or future differences to arbitration is not to be treated under this Part of this Act as excluding or restricting any liability.

14. Interpretation of Part I. [694]

In this Part of this Act—

'business' includes a profession and the activities of any government department or local or public authority;

'goods' has the same meaning as in the Sale of Goods Act 1979;

'hire-purchase agreement' has the same meaning as in the Consumer Credit Act 1974;

'negligence' has the meaning given by section 1(1);

'notice' includes an announcement, whether or not in writing, and any other communication or pretended communication; and

'personal injury' includes any disease and any impairment of physical or mental condition.

SCHEDULES

SCHEDULE 1 [695]

Section 1(2)

Scope of sections 2 to 4 and 7

1. Sections 2 to 4 of this Act do not extend to—

(a) any contract of insurance (including a contract to pay an annuity on human life);

(b) any contract so far as it relates to the creation or transfer of an interest in land, or to the termination of such an interest, whether by extinction, merger, surrender, forfeiture or otherwise;

(c) any contract so far as it relates to the creation or transfer of a right or interest in any patent, trade mark, copyright, registered design, technical or commercial information or other intellectual property, or relates to the termination of any such right or interest;

(d) any contract so far as it relates—

(i) to the formation or dissolution of a company (which means any body corporate or unincorporated association and includes a partnership), or

(ii) to its constitution or the rights or obligations of its corporators or members;

(e) any contract so far as it relates to the creation or transfer of securities or of any right or interest in securities.

2. Section 2(1) extends to—

(a) any contract of marine salvage or towage;

(b) any charterparty of a ship or hovercraft; and

(c) any contract for the carriage of goods by ship or hovercraft;

but subject to this sections 2 to 4 and 7 do not extend to any such contract except in favour of a person dealing as consumer.

. Where goods are carried by ship or hovercraft in pursuance of a contract which
ither—
a) specifies that as the means of carriage over part of the journey to be covered, or
b) makes no provision as to the means of carriage and does not exclude that means,
hen sections 2(2), 3 and 4 do not, except in favour of a person dealing as consumer,
xtend to the contract as it operates for and in relation to the carriage of the goods by
hat means.
. Section 2(1) and (2) do not extend to a contract of employment, except in favour of
he employee.
. Section 2(1) does not affect the validity of any discharge and indemnity given by a
person, on or in connection with an award to him of compensation for pneumoconiosis
ttributable to employment in the coal industry, in respect of any further claim arising
rom his contracting that disease.
Note In para. 1(c), the reference to a trade mark includes a reference to a service mark
Patents, Designs and Marks Act 1986) and the reference to copyright includes a
reference to topography right (Semiconductor Products (Protection of Topography)
Regulations 1987).

SCHEDULE 2 [696]
Sections 11(2) and 24(2)

'GUIDELINES' FOR APPLICATION OF REASONABLENESS TEST
The matters to which regard is to be had in particular for the purposes of sections 6(3),
7(3) and (4), 20 and 21 are any of the following which appear to be relevant—
(a) the strength of the bargaining positions of the parties relative to each other, taking
into account (among other things) alternative means by which the customer's
requirements could have been met;
(b) whether the customer received an inducement to agree to the term, or in accepting it
had an opportunity of entering into a similar contract with other persons, but
without having to accept a similar term;
(c) whether the customer knew or ought reasonably to have known of the existence and
extent of the term (having regard, among other things, to any custom of the trade
and any previous course of dealing between the parties);
(d) where the term excludes or restricts any relevant liability if some condition is not
complied with, whether it was reasonable at the time of the contract to expect that
compliance with that condition would be practicable;
(e) whether the goods were manufactured, processed or adapted to the special order of
the customer.
[As amended by Sale of Goods Act 1979.]

SALE OF GOODS ACT 1979
(1979, c 54; 39 Halsbury's Statutes (4th edn) 106)

Contract of sale

2. Contract of sale. [697]
(1) A contract of sale of goods is a contract by which the seller transfers or agrees to
transfer the property in goods to the buyer for a money consideration, called the price.
(2) There may be a contract of sale between one part owner and another.
(3) A contract of sale may be absolute or conditional.
(4) Where under a contract of sale the property in the goods is transferred from the seller
to the buyer the contract is called a sale.
(5) Where under a contract of sale the transfer of the property in the goods is to take
place at a future time or subject to some condition later to be fulfilled the contract is
called an agreement to sell.

(6) An agreement to sell becomes a sale when the time elapses or the conditions are fulfilled subject to which the property in the goods is to be transferred.

3. Capacity to buy and sell.   [698]

(1) Capacity to buy and sell is regulated by the general law concerning capacity to contract and to transfer and acquire property.
(2) Where necessaries are sold and delivered to a minor or to a person who by reason of mental incapacity or drunkenness is incompetent to contract, he must pay a reasonable price for them.
(3) In subsection (2) above 'necessaries' means goods suitable to the condition in life of the minor or other person concerned and to his actual requirements at the time of the sale and delivery.

Formalities of contract

4. How contract of sale is made.   [699]

(1) Subject to this and any other Act, a contract of sale may be made in writing (either with or without seal), or by word of mouth, or partly in writing and partly by word of mouth, or may be implied from the conduct of the parties.
(2) Nothing in this section affects the law relating to corporations.

Conditions and warranties

11. When condition to be treated as warranty.   [700]

(1) (*Applies to Scotland.*)
(2) Where a contract of sale is subject to a condition to be fulfilled by the seller, the buyer may waive the condition, or may elect to treat the breach of the condition as a breach of warranty and not as a ground for treating the contract as repudiated.
(3) Whether a stipulation in a contract of sale is a condition, the breach of which may give rise to a right to treat the contract as repudiated, or a warranty, the breach of which may give rise to a claim for damages but not to a right to reject the goods and treat the contract as repudiated, depends in each case on the construction of the contract; and a stipulation may be a condition, though called a warranty in the contract.
(4) Where a contract of sale is not severable and the buyer has accepted the goods or part of them, the breach of a condition to be fulfilled by the seller can only be treated as a breach of warranty, and not as a ground for rejecting the goods and treating the contract as repudiated, unless there is an express or implied term of the contract to that effect.
(5) (*Applies to Scotland.*)
(6) Nothing in this section affects a condition or warranty whose fulfilment is excused by law by reason of impossibility or otherwise.

12. Implied terms about title, etc.   [701]

(1) In a contract of sale, other than one to which subsection (3) below applies, there is an implied condition on the part of the seller that in the case of a sale he has a right to sell the goods, and in the case of an agreement to sell he will have such a right at the time when the property is to pass.
(2) In a contract of sale, other than one to which subsection (3) below applies, there is also an implied warranty that—
(a) the goods are free, and will remain free until the time when the property is to pass, from any charge or encumbrance not disclosed or known to the buyer before the contract is made, and

(b) the buyer will enjoy quiet possession of the goods except so far as it may be disturbed by the owner or other person entitled to the benefit of any charge or encumbrance so disclosed or known.

(3) This subsection applies to a contract of sale in the case of which there appears from the contract or is to be inferred from its circumstances an intention that the seller should transfer only such title as he or a third person may have.

(4) In a contract to which subsection (3) above applies there is an implied warranty that all charges or encumbrances known to the seller and not known to the buyer have been disclosed to the buyer before the contract is made.

(5) In a contract to which subsection (3) above applies there is also an implied warranty that none of the following will disturb the buyer's quiet possession of the goods, namely—

(a) the seller;

(b) in a case where the parties to the contract intend that the seller should transfer only such title as a third person may have, that person;

(c) anyone claiming through or under the seller or that third person otherwise than under a charge or encumbrance disclosed or known to the buyer before the contract is made.

13. Sale by description. [702]

(1) Where there is a contract for the sale of goods by description, there is an implied condition that the goods will correspond with the description.

(2) If the sale is by sample as well as by description it is not sufficient that the bulk of the goods corresponds with the sample if the goods do not also correspond with the description.

(3) A sale of goods is not prevented from being a sale by description by reason only that, being exposed for sale or hire, they are selected by the buyer.

14. Implied terms about quality or fitness. [703]

(1) Except as provided by this section and section 15 below and subject to any other enactment, there is no implied condition or warranty about the quality or fitness for any particular purpose of goods supplied under a contract of sale.

(2) Where the seller sells goods in the course of a business, there is an implied condition that the goods supplied under the contract are of merchantable quality, except that there is no such condition—

(a) as regards defects specifically drawn to the buyer's attention before the contract is made; or

(b) if the buyer examines the goods before the contract is made, as regards defects which that examination ought to reveal.

(3) Where the seller sells goods in the course of a business and the buyer, expressly or by implication, makes known—

(a) to the seller, or

(b) where the purchase price or part of it is payable by instalments and the goods were previously sold by a credit-broker to the seller, to that credit-broker,

any particular purpose for which the goods are being bought, there is an implied condition that the goods supplied under the contract are reasonably fit for that purpose, whether or not that is a purpose for which such goods are commonly supplied, except where the circumstances show that the buyer does not rely, or that it is unreasonable for him to rely, on the skill or judgment of the seller or credit-broker.

(4) An implied condition or warranty about quality or fitness for a particular purpose may be annexed to a contract of sale by usage.

(5) The preceding provisions of this section apply to a sale by a person who in the course of a business is acting as agent for another as they apply to a sale by a principal in the course of a business, except where that other is not selling in the course of a business and

either the buyer knows that fact or reasonable steps are taken to bring it to the notice of the buyer before the contract is made.

(6) Goods of any kind are of merchantable quality within the meaning of subsection (2) above if they are as fit for the purpose or purposes for which goods of that kind are commonly bought as it is reasonable to expect having regard to any description applied to them, the price (if relevant) and all the other relevant circumstances.

(8) In subsection (7) above and paragraph 5 of Schedule 1 below references to the appointed day are to the day appointed for the purposes of those provisions by an order of the Secretary of State made by statutory instrument.

Sale by sample

15. Sale by sample. [704]

(1) A contract of sale is a contract for sale by sample where there is an express or implied term to that effect in the contract.

(2) In the case of a contract for sale by sample there is an implied condition—

(a) that the bulk will correspond with the sample in quality;

(b) that the buyer will have a reasonable opportunity of comparing the bulk with the sample;

(c) that the goods will be free from any defect, rendering them unmerchantable, which would not be apparent on reasonable examination of the sample.

(3) In subsection (2)(c) above 'unmerchantable' is to be construed in accordance with section 14(6) above.

Transfer of property as between seller and buyer

17. Property passes when intended to pass. [705]

(1) Where there is a contract for the sale of specific or ascertained goods the property in them is transferred to the buyer at such time as the parties to the contract intend it to be transferred.

(2) For the purpose of ascertaining the intention of the parties regard shall be had to the terms of the contract, the conduct of the parties and the circumstances of the case.

18. Rules for ascertaining intention. [706]

Unless a different intention appears, the following are rules for ascertaining the intention of the parties as to the time at which the property in the goods is to pass to the buyer.

Rule 1.—Where there is an unconditional contract for the sale of specific goods in a deliverable state the property in the goods passes to the buyer when the contract is made, and it is immaterial whether the time of payment or the time of delivery, or both, be postponed.

Rule 2.—Where there is a contract for the sale of specific goods and the seller is bound to do something to the goods for the purpose of putting them into a deliverable state, the property does not pass until the thing is done and the buyer has notice that it has been done.

Rule 3.—Where there is a contract for the sale of specific goods in a deliverable state but the seller is bound to weigh, measure, test, or do some other act or thing with reference to the goods for the purpose of ascertaining the price, the property does not pass until the act or thing is done and the buyer has notice that it has been done.

Rule 4.—When goods are delivered to the buyer on approval or on sale or return or other similar terms the property in the goods passes to the buyer:—

(a) when he signifies his approval or acceptance to the seller or does any other act adopting the transaction;

(b) if he does not signify his approval or acceptance to the seller but retains the goods without giving notice of rejection, then, if a time has been fixed for the return of the goods, on the expiration of that time, and, if no time has been fixed, on the expiration of a reasonable time.

Rule 5.—(1) Where there is a contract for the sale of unascertained or future goods by description, and goods of that description and in a deliverable state are unconditionally appropriated to the contract, either by the seller with the assent of the buyer or by the buyer with the assent of the seller, the property in the goods then passes to the buyer; and the assent may be express or implied, and may be given either before or after the appropriation is made.

(2) Where, in pursuance of the contract, the seller delivers the goods to the buyer or to a carrier or other bailee or custodier (whether named by the buyer or not) for the purpose of transmission to the buyer, and does not reserve the right of disposal, he is to be taken to have unconditionally appropriated the goods to the contract.

34. Buyer's right of examining the goods. [797]

(1) Where goods are delivered to the buyer, and he has not previously examined them, he is not deemed to have accepted them until he has had a reasonable opportunity of examining them for the purpose of ascertaining whether they are in conformity with the contract.

(2) Unless otherwise agreed, when the seller tenders delivery of goods to the buyer, he is bound on request to afford the buyer a reasonable opportunity of examining the goods for the purpose of ascertaining whether they are in conformity with the contract.

35. Acceptance. [708]

(1) The buyer is deemed to have accepted the goods when he intimates to the seller that he has accepted them, or (except where section 34 above otherwise provides) when the goods have been delivered to him and he does any act in relation to them which is inconsistent with the ownership of the seller, or when after the lapse of a reasonable time he retains the goods without intimating to the seller that he has rejected them.

55. Exclusion of implied terms. [709]

(1) Where a right, duty or liability would arise under a contract of sale of goods by implication of law, it may (subject to the Unfair Contract Terms Act 1977) be negatived or varied by express agreement, or by the course of dealing between the parties, or by such usage as binds both parties to the contract.

(2) An express condition or warranty does not negative a condition or warranty implied by this Act unless inconsistent with it.

57. Auction sales. [710]

(1) Where goods are put up for sale by auction in lots, each lot is prima facie deemed to be the subject of a separate contract of sale.

(2) A sale by auction is complete when the auctioneer announces its completion by the fall of the hammer, or in other customary manner; and until the announcement is made any bidder may retract his bid.

(3) A sale by auction may be notified to be subject to a reserve or upset price, and a right to bid may also be reserved expressly by or on behalf of the seller.

(4) Where a sale by auction is not notified to be subject to a right to bid by or on behalf of the seller, it is not lawful for the seller to bid himself or to employ any person to bid at the sale, or for the auctioneer knowingly to take any bid from the seller or any such person.

(5) A sale contravening subsection (4) above may be treated as fraudulent by the buyer.
(6) Where, in respect of a sale by auction, a right to bid is expressly reserved (but not otherwise) the seller or any one person on his behalf may bid at the auction.

LIMITATION ACT 1980
(c 58; 24 Halsbury's Statutes (4th edn) 629)

Time limits under Part I subject to extension or exclusion under Part II

1. Time limits under Part I subject to extension or   **[711]**
exclusion under Part II.

(1) This Part of this Act gives the ordinary time limits for bringing actions of the various classes mentioned in the following provisions of this Part.
(2) The ordinary time limits given in this Part of this Act are subject to extension or exclusion in accordance with the provisions of Part II of this Act.

Actions founded on simple contract

5. Time limit for actions founded on simple contract.   **[712]**

An action founded on simple contract shall not be brought after the expiration of six years from the date on which the cause of action accrued.

6. Special time limit for actions in respect of certain   **[713]**
loans

(1) Subject to subsection (3) below, section 5 of this Act shall not bar the right of action on a contract of loan to which this section applies.
(2) This section applies to any contract of loan which—
(a) does not provide for repayment of the debt on or before a fixed or determinable date; and
(b) does not effectively (whether or not it purports to do so) make the obligation to repay the debt conditional on a demand for repayment made by or on behalf of the creditor or on any other matter;
except where in connection with taking the loan the debtor enters into any collateral obligation to pay the amount of the debt or any part of it (as, for example, by delivering a promissory note as security for the debt) on terms which would exclude the application of this section to the contract of loan if they applied directly to repayment of the debt.
(3) Where a demand in writing for repayment of the debt under a contract of loan to which this section applies is made by or on behalf of the creditor (or, where there are joint creditors, by or on behalf of any one of them) section 5 of this Act shall thereupon apply as if the cause of action to recover the debt had accrued on the date on which the demand was made.
(4) In this section 'promissory note' has the same meaning as in the Bills of Exchange Act 1882.

7. Time limit for actions to enforce certain awards.   **[714]**

An action to enforce an award, where the submission is not by an instrument under seal, shall not be brought after the expiration of six years from the date on which the cause of action accrued.

General rule for actions on a specialty

8. Time limit for actions on a specialty.   [715]

(1) An action upon a specialty shall not be brought after the expiration of twelve years from the date on which the cause of action accrued.
(2) Subsection (1) above shall not affect any action for which a shorter period of limitation is prescribed by any other provision of this Act.

Disability

28. Extension of limitation period in case of disability.   [716]

(1) Subject to the following provisions of this section, if on the date when any right of action accrued for which a period of limitation is prescribed by this Act, the person to whom it accrued was under a disability, the action may be brought at any time before the expiration of six years from the date when he ceased to be under a disability or died (whichever first occurred) notwithstanding that the period of limitation has expired.
(2) This section shall not affect any case where the right of action first accrued to some person (not under a disability) through whom the person under a disability claims.
(3) When a right of action which has accrued to a person under a disability accrues, on the death of that person while still under a disability, to another person under a disability, no further extension of time shall be allowed by reason of the disability of the second person.
(4) No action to recover land or money charged on land shall be brought by virtue of this section by any person after the expiration of thirty years from the date on which the right of action accrued to that person or some person through whom he claims.
(5) If the action is one to which section 10 of this Act applies, subsection (1) above shall have effect as if for the words 'six years' there were substituted the words 'two years'.
(6) If the action is one to which section 11 or 12(2) of this Act applies, subsection (1) above shall have effect as if for the words 'six years' there were substituted the words 'three years'.
(7) If the action is one to which section 11A of this Act applies or one by virtue of section 6(1)(a) of the Consumer Protection Act 1987 (death caused by defective product), subsection (1) above—
(a) shall not apply to the time limit prescribed by subsection (3) of the said section 11A or to that time limit as applied by virtue of section 12(1) of this Act; and
(b) in relation to any other time limit prescribed by this Act shall have effect as if for the words 'six years' there were substituted the words 'three years'.
[As amended by the Consumer Protection Act 1987.]

Acknowledgment and part payment

29. Fresh accrual of action on acknowledgment or   [717]
part payment.

(1) Subsections (2) and (3) below apply where any right of action (including a foreclosure action) to recover land or an advowson or any right of a mortgagee of personal property to bring a foreclosure action in respect of the property has accrued.
(2) If the person in possession of the land, benefice or personal property in question acknowledges the title of the person to whom the right of action has accrued—
(a) the right shall be treated as having accrued on and not before the date of the acknowledgment; and
(b) in the case of a right of action to recover land which has accrued to a person entitled to an estate or interest taking effect on the determination of an entailed interest against whom time is running under section 27 of this Act, section 27 shall thereupon cease to apply to the land.

(3) In the case of a foreclosure or other action by a mortgagee, if the person in possession of the land, benefice or personal property in question or the person liable for the mortgage debt makes any payment in respect of the debt (whether of principal or interest) the right shall be treated as having accrued on and not before the date of the payment.

(4) Where a mortgagee is by virtue of the mortgage in possession of any mortgaged land and either—

(a) receives any sum in respect of the principal or interest of the mortgage debt; or

(b) acknowledges the title of the mortgagor, or his equity of redemption;

an action to redeem the land in his possession may be brought at any time before the expiration of twelve years from the date of the payment or acknowledgment.

(5) Subject to subsection (6) below, where any right of action has accrued to recover—

(a) any debt or other liquidated pecuniary claim; or

(b) any claim to the personal estate of a deceased person or to any share or interest in any such estate;

and the person liable or accountable for the claim acknowledges the claim or makes any payment in respect of it the right shall be treated as having accrued on and not before the date of the acknowledgment or payment.

(6) A payment of a part of the rent or interest due at any time shall not extend the period for claiming the remainder then due, but any payment of interest shall be treated as a payment in respect of the principal debt.

(7) Subject to subsection (6) above, a current period of limitation may be repeatedly extended under this section by further acknowledgements or payments, but a right of action, once barred by this Act, shall not be revived by any subsequent acknowledgment or payment.

30. Formal provisions as to acknowledgments and part payments. [718]

(1) To be effective for the purposes of section 29 of this Act, an acknowledgment must be in writing and signed by the person making it.

(2) For the purposes of section 29, any acknowledgment or payment—

(a) may be made by the agent of the person by whom it is required to be made under that section; and

(b) shall be made to the person, or to an agent of the person, whose title or claim is being acknowledged or, as the case may be, in respect of whose claim the payment is being made.

Fraud, concealment and mistake

32. Postponement of limitation period in case of fraud, concealment or mistake. [719]

(1) Subject to subsection (3) below, where in the case of any action for which a period of limitation is prescribed by this Act, either—

(a) the action is based upon the fraud of the defendant; or

(b) any fact relevant to the plaintiff's right of action has been deliberately concealed from him by the defendant; or

(c) the action is for relief from the consequences of a mistake;

the period of limitation shall not begin to run until the plaintiff has discovered the fraud, concealment or mistake (as the case may be) or could with reasonable diligence have discovered it.

References in this subsection to the defendant include references to the defendant's agent and to any person through whom the defendant claims and his agent.

(2) For the purposes of subsection (1) above, deliberate commission of a breach of duty

in circumstances in which it is unlikely to be discovered for some time amounts to deliberate concealment of the facts involved in that breach of duty.

(3) Nothing in this section shall enable any action—

(a) to recover, or recover the value of, any property; or

(b) to enforce any charge against, or set aside any transaction affecting, any property;

to be brought against the purchaser of the property or any person claiming through him in any case where the property has been purchased for valuable consideration by an innocent third party since the fraud or concealment or (as the case may be) the transaction in which the mistake was made took place.

(4) A purchaser is an innocent third party for the purposes of this section—

(a) in the case of fraud or concealment of any fact relevant to the plaintiff's right of action, if he was not a party to the fraud or (as the case may be) to the concealment of that fact and did not at the time of the purchase know or have reason to believe that the fraud or concealment had taken place; and

(b) in the case of mistake, if he did not at the time of the purchase know or have reason to believe that the mistake had been made.

36. Equitable jurisdiction and remedies. [720]

(1) The following time limits under this Act, that is to say—

(a) the time limit under section 2 for actions founded on tort;

(b) the time limit under section 5 for actions founded on simple contract;

(c) the time limit under section 7 for actions to enforce awards where the submission is not by an instrument under seal;

(d) the time limit under section 8 for actions on a specialty;

(e) the time limit under section 9 for actions to recover a sum recoverable by virtue of any enactment; and

(f) the time limit under section 24 for actions to enforce a judgment;

shall not apply to any claim for specific performance of a contract or for an injunction or for other equitable relief, except in so far as any such time limit may be applied by the court by analogy in like manner as the corresponding time limit under any enactment repealed by the Limitation Act 1939 was applied before 1 July 1940.

(2) Nothing in this Act shall affect any equitable jurisdiction to refuse relief on the ground of acquiescence or otherwise.

38. Interpretation. [721]

(1) In this Act, unless the context otherwise requires—

'action' includes any proceeding in a court of law, including an ecclesiastical court;

'land' includes corporeal hereditaments, tithes and rentcharges and any legal or equitable estate or interest therein, including an interest in the proceeds of the sale of land held upon trust for sale, but except as provided above in this definition does not include any incorporeal hereditament;

'personal estate' and 'personal property' do not include chattels real;

'personal injuries' includes any disease and any impairment of a person's physical or mental condition, and 'injury' and cognate expressions shall be construed accordingly;

'rent' includes a rentcharge and a rentservice;

'rentcharge' means any annuity or periodical sum of money charged upon or payable out of land, except a rent service or interest on a mortgage on land;

'settled land', 'statutory owner' and 'tenant for life' have the same meanings respectively as in the Settled Land Act 1925;

'trust' and 'trustee' have the same meanings respectively as in the Trustee Act 1925; and

'trust for sale' has the same meaning as in the Law of Property Act 1925.

(2) For the purposes of this Act a person shall be treated as under a disability while he is an infant, or of unsound mind.

(3) For the purposes of subsection (2) above a person is of unsound mind if he is a person who, by reason of mental disorder within the meaning of the Mental Health Act 1983, is incapable of managing and administering his property and affairs.

(4) Without prejudice to the generality of subsection (3) above, a person shall be conclusively presumed for the purposes of subsection (2) above to be of unsound mind—

(a) while he is liable to be detained or subject to guardianship under the Mental Health Act 1983 (otherwise than by virtue of section 35 or 89); and

(b) while he is receiving treatment as an in-patient in any hospital within the meaning of the Mental Health Act 1983 or mental nursing home within the meaning of the Nursing Homes Act 1975 without being liable to be detained under the said Act of 1983 (otherwise than by virtue of section 35 or 89), being treatment which follows without any interval a period during which he was liable to be detained or subject to guardianship under the Mental Health Act 1959, or the said Act of 1983 (otherwise than by virtue of section 35 or 89) or by virtue of any enactment repealed or excluded by the Mental Health Act 1959.

PUBLIC PASSENGER VEHICLES ACT 1981
(c 14; 51 Halsbury's Statutes (3rd edn) 1344)

29. Avoidance of contracts so far as restrictive of liability   **[722]**
in respect of death of or injury to passengers in public
service vehicles.

A contract for the conveyance of a passenger in a public service vehicle shall, so far as it purports to negative or to restrict the liability of a person in respect of a claim which may be made against him in respect of the death of, or bodily injury to, the passenger while being carried in, entering or alighting from the vehicle, or purports to impose any conditions with respect to the enforcement of any such liability, be void.

SUPREME COURT ACT 1981
(c 54; 11 Halsbury's Statutes (4th edn) 808)

50. Power to award damages as well as, or in substitution   **[723]**
for, injunction or specific performance.

Where the Court of Appeal or the High Court has jurisdiction to entertain an application for an injunction for specific performance, it may award damages in addition to or in substitution for an injunction for specific performance.

SUPPLY OF GOODS AND SERVICES ACT 1982
(c 29; 39 Halsbury's Statutes (4th edn) 161)

PART I

SUPPLY OF GOODS

Contracts for the transfer of property in goods

1. The contracts concerned.   **[724]**

(1) In this Act a 'contract for the transfer of goods' means a contract under which one person transfers or agrees to transfer to another the property in goods, other than an excepted contract.

(2) For the purposes of this section an excepted contract means any of the following—
(a) a contract of sale of goods;
(b) a hire-purchase agreement;
(c) a contract under which the property in goods is (or is to be) transferred in exchange for trading stamps on their redemption;
(d) a transfer or agreement to transfer which is made by deed and for which there is no consideration other than the presumed consideration imported by the deed;
(e) a contract intended to operate by way of mortgage, pledge, charge or other security.
(3) For the purposes of this Act a contract is a contract for the transfer of goods whether or not services are also provided or to be provided under the contract, and (subject to subsection (2) above) whatever is the nature of the consideration for the transfer or agreement to transfer.

2. Implied terms about title, etc. [725]

(1) In a contract for the transfer of goods, other than one to which subsection (3) below applies, there is an implied condition on the part of the transferor that in the case of a transfer of the property in the goods he has a right to transfer the property and in the case of an agreement to transfer the property in the goods he will have such a right at the time when the property is to be transferred.
(2) In a contract for the transfer of goods, other than one to which subsection (3) below applies, there is also an implied warranty that—
(a) the goods are free, and will remain free until the time when the property is to be transferred, from any charge or encumbrance not disclosed or known to the transferee before the contract is made, and
(b) the transferee will enjoy quiet possession of the goods except so far as it may be disturbed by the owner or other person entitled to the benefit of any charge or encumbrance so disclosed or known.
(3) This subsection applies to a contract for the transfer of goods in the case of which there appears from the contract or is to be inferred from its circumstances an intention that the transferor should transfer only such title as he or a third person may have.
(4) In a contract to which subsection (3) above applies there is an implied warranty that all charges or encumbrances known to the transferor and not known to the transferee have been disclosed to the transferee before the contract is made.
(5) In a contract to which subsection (3) above applies there is also an implied warranty that none of the following will disturb the transferee's quiet possession of the goods, namely—
(a) the transferor;
(b) in a case where the parties to the contract intend that the transferor should transfer only such title as a third person may have, that person;
(c) anyone claiming through or under the transferor or that third person otherwise than under a charge or encumbrance disclosed or known to the transferee before the contract is made.

3. Implied terms where transfer is by description. [726]

(1) This section applies where, under a contract for the transfer of goods, the transferor transfers or agrees to transfer the property in the goods by description.
(2) In such a case there is an implied condition that the goods will correspond with the description.
(3) If the transferor transfers or agrees to transfer the property in the goods by sample as well as by description it is not sufficient that the bulk of the goods corresponds with the sample if the goods do not also correspond with the description.
(4) A contract is not prevented from falling within subsection (1) above by reason only that, being exposed for supply, the goods are selected by the transferee.

177

4. Implied terms about quality or fitness.   [727]

(1) Except as provided by this section and section 5 below and subject to the provisions of any other enactment, there is no implied condition or warranty about the quality or fitness for any particular purpose of goods supplied under a contract for the transfer of goods.

(2) Where, under such a contract, the transferor transfers the property in goods in the course of a business, there is (subject to subsection (3) below) an implied condition that the goods supplied under the contract are of merchantable quality.

(3) There is no such condition as is mentioned in subsection (2) above—

(a) as regards defects specifically drawn to the transferee's attention before the contract is made; or

(b) if the transferee examines the goods before the contract is made, as regards defects which that examination ought to reveal.

(4) Subsection (5) below applies where, under a contract for the transfer of goods, the transferor transfers the property in goods in the course of a business and the transferee, expressly or by implication, makes known—

(a) to the transferor, or

(b) where the consideration or part of the consideration for the transfer is a sum payable by instalments and the goods were previously sold by a credit-broker to the transferor, to that credit-broker,

any particular purpose for which the goods are being acquired.

(5) In that case there is (subject to subsection (6) below) an implied condition that the goods supplied under the contract are reasonably fit for that purpose, whether or not that is a purpose for which such goods are commonly supplied.

(6) Subsection (5) above does not apply where the circumstances show that the transferee does not rely, or that it is unreasonable for him to rely, on the skill or judgment of the transferor or credit-broker.

(7) An implied condition or warranty about quality or fitness for a particular purpose may be annexed by usage to a contract for the transfer of goods.

(8) The preceding provisions of this section apply to a transfer by a person who in the course of a business is acting as agent for another as they apply to a transfer by a principal in the course of a business, except where that other is not transferring in the course of a business and either the transferee knows that fact or reasonable steps are taken to bring it to the transferee's notice before the contract concerned is made.

(9) Goods of any kind are of merchantable quality within the meaning of subsection (2) above if they are as fit for the purpose or purposes for which goods of that kind are commonly supplied as it is reasonable to expect having regard to any description applied to them, the price (if relevant) and all the other relevant circumstances.

5. Implied terms where transfer is by sample.   [728]

(1) This section applies where, under a contract for the transfer of goods, the transferor transfers or agrees to transfer the property in the goods by reference to a sample.

(2) In such a case there is an implied condition—

(a) that the bulk will correspond with the sample in quality; and

(b) that the transferee will have a reasonable opportunity of comparing the bulk with the sample; and

(c) that the goods will be free from any defect, rendering them unmerchantable, which would not be apparent on reasonable examination of the sample.

(3) In subsection (2)(c) above 'unmerchantable' is to be construed in accordance with section 4(9) above.

(4) For the purposes of this section a transferor transfers or agrees to transfer the property in goods by reference to a sample where there is an express or implied term to that effect in the contract concerned.

Contracts for the hire of goods

6. The contracts concerned.   [729]

(1) In this Act a 'contract for the hire of goods' means a contract under which one person bails or agrees to bail goods to another by way of hire, other than an excepted contract.

(2) For the purposes of this section an excepted contract means any of the following:—

(a) a hire-purchase agreement;

(b) a contract under which goods are (or are to be) bailed in exchange for trading stamps on their redemption.

(3) For the purposes of this Act a contract is a contract for the hire of goods whether or not services are also provided or to be provided under the contract, and (subject to subsection (2) above) whatever is the nature of the consideration for the bailment or agreement to bail by way of hire.

7. Implied terms about right to transfer possession, etc.   [730]

(1) In a contract for the hire of goods there is an implied condition on the part of the bailor that in the case of a bailment he has a right to transfer possession of the goods by way of hire for the period of the bailment and in the case of an agreement to bail he will have such a right at the time of the bailment.

(2) In a contract for the hire of goods there is also an implied warranty that the bailee will enjoy quiet possession of the goods for the period of the bailment except so far as the possession may be disturbed by the owner or other person entitled to the benefit of any charge or encumbrance disclosed or known to the bailee before the contract is made.

(3) The preceding provisions of this section do not affect the right of the bailor to repossess the goods under an express or implied term of the contract.

8. Implied terms where hire is by description.   [731]

(1) This section applies where, under a contract for the hire of goods, the bailor bails or agrees to bail the goods by description.

(2) In such a case there is an implied condition that the goods will correspond with the description.

(3) If under the contract the bailor bails or agrees to bail the goods by reference to a sample as well as a description it is not sufficient that the bulk of the goods corresponds with the sample if the goods do not also correspond with the description.

(4) A contract is not prevented from falling within subsection (1) above by reason only that, being exposed for supply, the goods are selected by the bailee.

9. Implied terms about quality or fitness.   [732]

(1) Except as provided by this section and section 10 below and subject to the provisions of any other enactment, there is no implied condition or warranty about the quality or fitness for any particular purpose of goods bailed under a contract for the hire of goods.

(2) Where, under such a contract, the bailor bails goods in the course of a business, there is (subject to subsection (3) below) an implied condition that the goods supplied under the contract are of merchantable quality.

(3) There is no such condition as is mentioned in subsection (2) above—

(a) as regards defects specifically drawn to the bailee's attention before the contract is made; or

(b) if the bailee examines the goods before the contract is made, as regards defects which that examination ought to reveal.

(4) Subsection (5) below applies where, under a contract for the hire of goods, the bailor bails goods in the course of a business and the bailee, expressly or by implication, makes known—

(a) to the bailor in the course of negotitions conducted by him in relation to the making of the contract, or

179

(b) to a credit-broker in the course of negotiations conducted by that broker in relation to goods sold by him to the bailor before forming the subject matter of the contract,
any particular purpose for which the goods are being bailed.

(5) In that case there is (subject to subsection (6) below) an implied condition that the goods supplied under the contract are reasonably fit for that purpose, whether or not that is a purpose for which such goods are commonly supplied.

(6) Subsection (5) above does not apply where the circumstances show that the bailee does not rely, or that it is unreasonable for him to rely, on the skill or judgment of the bailor or credit-broker.

(7) An implied condition or warranty about quality or fitness for a particular purpose may be annexed by usage to a contract for the hire of goods.

(8) The preceding provisions of this section apply to a bailment by a person who in the course of a business is acting as agent for another as they apply to a bailment by a principal in the course of a business, except where that other is not bailing in the course of a business and either the bailee knows that fact or reasonable steps are taken to bring it to the bailer's notice before the contract concerned is made.

(9) Goods of any kind are of merchantable quality within the meaning of subsection (2) above if they are as fit for the purpose or purposes for which goods of that kind are commonly supplied as it is reasonable to expect having regard to any description applied to them, the consideration for the bailment (if relevant) and all the other relevant circumstances.

10. Implied terms where hire is by sample.   [733]

(1) This section applies where, under a contract for the hire of goods, the bailor bails or agrees to bail the goods by reference to a sample.

(2) In such a case there is an implied condition—

(a) that the bulk will correspond with the sample in quality; and

(b) that the bailee will have a reasonable opportunity of comparing the bulk with the sample; and

(c) that the goods will be free from any defect, rendering them unmerchantable, which would not be apparent on reasonable examination of the sample.

(3) In subsection (2)(c) above 'unmerchantable' is to be construed in accordance with section 9(9) above.

(4) For the purposes of this section a bailor bails or agrees to bail goods by reference to a sample where there is an express or implied term to that effect in the contract concerned.

Exclusion of implied terms, etc

11. Exclusion of implied terms, etc.   [734]

(1) Where a right, duty or liability would arise under a contract for the transfer of goods or a contract for the hire of goods by implication of law, it may (subject to subsection (2) below and the 1977 Act) be negatived or varied by express agreement, or by the course of dealing between the parties, or by such usage as binds both parties to the contract.

(2) An express condition or warranty does not negative a condition or warranty implied by the preceding provisions of this Act unless inconsistent with it.

(3) Nothing in the preceding provisions of this Act prejudices the operation of any other enaçtment or any rule of law whereby any condition or warranty (other than one related to quality or fitness) is to be implied in a contract for the transfer of goods or a contract for the hire of goods.

Part II

Supply of Services

12. The contracts concerned. [735]

(1) In this Act a 'contract for the supply of a service' means, subject to subsection (2) below, a contract under which a person ('the supplier') agrees to carry out a service.

(2) For the purposes of this Act, a contract of service or apprenticeship is not a contract for the supply of a service.

(3) Subject to subsection (2) above, a contract is a contract for the supply of a service for the purposes of this Act whether or not goods are also—

(a) transferred or to be transferred, or

(b) bailed or to be bailed by way of hire,

under the contract, and whatever is the nature of the consideration for which the service is to be carried out.

(4) The Secretary of State may by order provide that one or more of sections 13 to 15 below shall not apply to services of a description specified in the order, and such an order may make different provision for different circumstances.

(5) The power to make an order under subsection (4) above shall be exercisable by statutory instrument subject to annulment in pursuance of a resolution of either House of Parliament.

13. Implied term about care and skill. [736]

In a contract for the supply of a service where the supplier is acting in the course of a business, there is an implied term that the supplier will carry out the service with reasonable care and skill.

14. Implied term about time for performance. [737]

(1) Where, under a contract for the supply of a service by a supplier acting in the course of a business, the time for the service to be carried out is not fixed by the contract, left to be fixed in a manner agreed by the contract or determined by the course of dealing between the parties, there is an implied term that the supplier will carry out the service within a reasonable time.

(2) What is a reasonable time is a question of fact.

15. Implied term about consideration. [738]

(1) Where, under a contract for the supply of a service, the consideration for the service is not determined by the contract, left to be determined in a manner agreed by the contract or determined by the course of dealing between the parties, there is an implied term that the party contracting with the supplier will pay a reasonable charge.

(2) What is a reasonable charge is a question of fact.

16. Exclusion of implied terms, etc. [739]

(1) Where a right, duty or liability would arise under a contract for the supply of a service by virtue of this Part of this Act, it may (subject to subsection (2) below and the 1977 Act) be negatived or varied by express agreement, or by the course of dealing between the parties, or by such usage as binds both parties to the contract.

(2) An express term does not negative a term implied by this Part of this Act unless inconsistent with it.

(3) Nothing in this Part of this Act prejudices—

(a) any rule of law which imposes on the supplier a duty stricter than that imposed by section 13 or 14 above; or

(b) subject to paragraph (a) above, any rule of law whereby any term not inconsistent with this Part of this Act is to be implied in a contract for the supply of a service.

(4) This Part of this Act has effect subject to any other enactment which defines or restricts the rights, duties or liabilities arising in connection with a service of any description.

PART III

SUPPLEMENTARY

18. Interpretation: general.   [740]

(1) In the preceding provisions of this Act and this section—

'bailee', in relation to a contract for the hire of goods means (depending on the context) a person to whom the goods are bailed under the contract, or a person to whom they are to be so bailed, or a person to whom the rights under the contract of either of those persons have passed;

'bailor', in relation to a contract for the hire of goods, means (depending on the context) a person who bails the goods under the contract, or a person who agrees to do so, or a person to whom the duties under the contract of either of those persons have passed;

'business' includes a profession and the activities of any government department or local or public authority;

'credit-broker' means a person acting in the course of a business of credit brokerage carried on by him;

'credit brokerage' means the effecting of introductions—

(a) of individuals desiring to obtain credit to persons carrying on any business so far as it relates to the provision of credit; or

(b) of individuals desiring to obtain goods on hire to persons carrying on a business which comprises or relates to the bailment of goods under a contract for the hire of goods; or

(c) of individuals desiring to obtain credit, or to obtain goods on hire, to other credit-brokers;

'enactment' means any legislation (including subordinate legislation) of the United Kingdom or Northern Ireland;

'goods' include all personal chattels (including emblements, industrial growing crops, and things attached to or forming part of the land which are agreed to be severed before the transfer or bailment concerned or under the contract concerned), other than things in action and money;

'hire-purchase agreement' has the same meaning as in the 1974 Act;

'property', in relation to goods, means the general property in them and not merely a special property;

'quality', in relation to goods, includes their state or condition;

'redemption', in relation to trading stamps, has the same meaning as in the Trading Stamps Act 1964 or, as respects Northern Ireland, the Trading Stamps Act (Northern Ireland) 1965;

' trading stamps' has the same meaning as in the said Act of 1964 or, as respects Northern Ireland, the said Act of 1965;

'transferee', in relation to a contract for the transfer of goods, means (depending on the context) a person to whom the property in the goods is transferred under the contract, or a person to whom the property is to be so transferred, or a person to whom the rights under the contract of either of those persons have passed;

'transferor', in relation to a contract for the transfer of goods, means (depending on the context) a person who transfers the property in the goods under the contract, or a person who, agrees to do so, or a person to whom the duties under the contract of either of those persons have passed.

(2) In subsection (1) above, in the definitions of bailee, bailor, transferee and transferor,

a reference to rights or duties passing is to their passing by assignment, operation of law or otherwise.

19. Interpretation: references to Acts.   [741]

In this Act—
'the 1973 Act' means the Supply of Goods (Implied Terms) Act 1973;
'the 1974 Act' means the Consumer Credit Act 1974;
'the 1977 Act' means the Unfair Contract Terms Act 1977; and
'the 1979 Act' means the Sale of Goods Act 1979.

COMPANIES ACT 1985
(c 6; 8 Halsbury's Statutes (4th edn) 107)

35. Company's capacity: power of directors to bind it.   [742]

(1) In favour of a person dealing with a company in good faith, any transaction decided on by the directors is deemed to be one which is within the capacity of the company to enter into, and the power of the directors to bind the company is deemed to be free of any limitation under the memorandum or articles.
(2) A party to a transaction so decided on is not bound to enquire as to the capacity of the company to enter into it or as to any such limitation on the powers of the directors, and is presumed to have acted in good faith unless the contrary is proved.

36. Form of company contracts.   [743]

(1) Contracts on behalf of a company may be made as follows—
(a) a contract which if made between private persons would be by law required to be in writing, and if made according to the law of England and Wales to be under seal, may be made on behalf of the company in writing under the company's common seal;
(b) a contract which if made between private persons would be by law required to be in writing, signed by the parties to be charged therewith, may be made on behalf of the company in writing signed by any person acting under its authority, express or implied;
(c) a contract which if made between private persons would by law be valid although made by parol only, and not reduced into writing, may be made by parol on behalf of the company by any person acting under its authority, express or implied.
(2) A contract made according to this section—
(a) is effectual in law, and binds the company and its successors and all other parties to it;
(b) may be varied or discharged in the same manner in which it is authorised by this section to be made.
(3) (*Applies to Scotland only.*)
(4) Where a contract purports to be made by a company, or by a person as agent for a company, at a time when the company has not been formed, then subject to any agreement to the contrary the contract has effect as one entered into by the person purporting to act for the company or as agent for it, and he is personally liable on the contract accordingly.

INSOLVENCY ACT 1986
(c 45; 4 Halsbury's Statutes (4th edn) 980)

345. Contracts to which bankrupt is a party.   [744]

(1) The following applies where a contract has been made with a person who is subsequently adjudged bankrupt.

(2) The court may, on the application of any other party to the contract, make an order discharging obligations under the contract on such terms as to payment by the applicant or the bankrupt of damages for non-performance or otherwise as appear to the court to be equitable.

(3) Any damages payable by the bankrupt by virtue of an order of the court under this section are provable as a bankruptcy debt.

(4) Where an undischarged bankrupt is a contractor in respect of any contract jointly with any person, that person may sue or be sued in respect of the contract without the joinder of the bankrupt.

MINORS CONTRACTS ACT 1987
(c 13; Halsbury's Statutes (4th edn) 6 (S) 89)

1. Disapplication of Infants Relief Act 1874 etc.   [745]

The following enactments shall not apply to any contract made by a minor after the commencement of this Act—

(a) the Infants Relief Act 1874 (which invalidates certain contracts made by minors and prohibits actions to enforce contracts ratified after majority); and

(b) section 5 of the Betting and Loans (Infants) Act 1892 (which invalidates contracts to repay loans advanced during minority).

2. Guarantees.   [746]

Where—

(a) a guarantee is given in respect of an obligation of a party to a contract made after the commencement of this Act, and

(b) the obligation is unenforceable against him (or he repudiates the contract) because he was a minor when the contract was made,

the guarantee shall not for that reason alone be unenforceable against the guarantor.

3. Restitution.   [747]

(1) Where—

(a) a person ('the plaintiff') has after the commencement of this Act entered into a contract with another ('the defendant'), and

(b) the contract is unenforceable against the defendant (or he repudiates it) because he was a minor when the contract was made,

the court may, if it is just and equitable to do so, require the defendant to transfer to the plaintiff any property acquired by the defendant under the contract or any property representing it.

(2) Nothing in this section shall be taken to prejudice any other remedy available to the plaintiff.

4. Consequential amendment and repeals.   [748]

(1) In section 113 of the Consumer Credit Act 1974 (that Act not to be evaded by use of security) in subsection (7)—

(a) after the word 'indemnity', in both places where it occurs, there shall be inserted 'or guarantee';

(b) after the words 'minor, or' there shall be inserted 'an indemnity is given in a case where he'; and

(c) for the word 'they' there shall be substituted 'those obligations'.

(2) The Infants Relief Act 1874 and the Betting and Loans (Infants) Act 1892 are hereby repealed (in accordance with section 1 of this Act).

[NB This Act same into force on 9 June 1987.]

CONSUMER PROTECTION ACT 1987
(c 43; 39 Halsbury's Statutes (4th edn) 197)

7. Prohibition on exclusions from liability. [749]

The liability of a person by virtue of this Part to a person who has suffered damage caused wholly or partly by a defect in a product, or to a dependant or relative of such a person, shall not be limited or excluded by any contract term, by any notice or by any other provision.

GLOSSARY

OF LATIN AND OTHER WORDS AND PHRASES

Words are Latin unless otherwise indicated

Ab extra. From outside.

Ab inconvenienti. *See* ARGUMENTUM.

Ab initio. From the beginning.

Accessio. Addition; appendage. The combination of two chattels belonging to different persons into a single article.

Acta exteriora indicant interiora secreta. A man's outward actions are evidence of his innermost thoughts and intentions.

Actio personalis moritur cum persona. A personal right of action dies on the death of the person by or against whom it could be enforced.

Actus no facit reum, nisi mens sit rea. The act itself does not make a man guilty, unless he does it with a guilty intention.

Ad hoc. Arranged for this purpose; special.

Ad idem. *See* CONSENSUS.

Ad infinitum. To infinity; without limit; for ever.

Ad litem. For the purpose of the law suit.

Adversus extraneos vitiosa possessio prodesse solet. Possession, though supported only by a defective title, will prevail over the claims of strangers other than the true owner.

A fortiori (ratione). For a stronger reason; by even more convincing reasoning.

Aliter. Otherwise; the result would be different, if . . .; (also, used of a judge who thinks differently from his fellow judges).

Aliunde. From elsewhere; from other sources.

A mensa et thoro. A separation from the 'table and bed' of one's spouse.

Animo revocandi. With the intention of revoking.

Animus deserendi. The intention of deserting.

Animus possidendi. The intention of possessing.

Animus revertendi. The intention of returning.

Animus testandi. The intention of making a will.

Ante. Before; (also used of a case referred to earlier on a page or in a book).

A posteriori. From effect to cause; inductively; from subsequent conclusions.

A priori. From cause to effect; deductively; from previous assumptions or reasoning.

Argumentum ab inconvenienti. An argument devised because of the existence of an awkward problem so as to provide an explanation for it.

Asportatio. The act of carrying away.

Assensus. *See* CONSENSUS.

Assumpsit (super se). He undertook.

Ats. (ad sectam). At the suit of. (The opposite of VERSUS.)

187

Bona fide. In good faith; sincere.

Bona vacantia. Goods without an owner.

Brutum fulmen. A silent thunderbolt; an empty threat.

Cadit quaestio. The matter admits of no further argument.

Caeterorum. Of the things which are left.

Capias ad satisfaciendum. A writ commanding the sheriff to take the body of the defendant in order that he may make satisfaction for the plaintiff's claim.

Caveat emptor. The buyer must look out for himself.

Cessante ratione legis, cessat lex ipsa. When the reason for its existence ceases, the law itself ceases to exist.

Cestui(s) que trust. A person (or persons) for whose benefit property is held on trust; a beneficiary (beneficiaries). (*Norman-French*)

Chose in action. Intangible personal property or rights, which can be enjoyed or enforced only by legal action, and not by taking physical possession (e.g. debts). (*Norman-French*)

Colore officii. Under the pretext of a person's official position.

Confusio. A mixture; union. The mixture of things of the same nature, but belonging to different persons so that identification of the original things becomes impossible.

Consensu. By general consent; unanimously.

Consensus ad idem. Agreement as to the same thing.

Consortium. Conjugal relations with and companionship of a spouse.

Contra. To the contrary. (Used of a case in which the decision was contrary to the doctrine or cases previously cited; also of a judge who delivers a dissenting judgment.)

Contra bonos mores. Contrary to good morals.

Contra proferentem. Against the party who puts forward a clause in a document.

Cor. (coram). In the presence of; before (a judge).

Coram non judice. Before one who is not a judge.

Corpus. Body; capital.

Coverture. Marriage. (*Norman-French*)

Cri de coeur. Heartfelt cry. (*French*)

Cujus est solum, ejus est usque ad coelum et ad inferos. Whosoever owns the soil also owns everything above it as far as the heavens and everything below it as far as the lower regions of the earth.

Culpa. Wrongful default.

Cum testamento annexo. With the will annexed.

Cur. adv. vult. (curia advisari vult). The court wishes time to consider the matter.

Cy-près. For a purpose resembling as nearly as possible the purpose originally proposed. (*Norman-French*)

Damage feasant. *See* DISTRESS.

Damnosa hereditas. An insolvent inheritance.

Damnum. Loss; damage.

Damnum fatale. Damage resulting from the workings of fate for which human negligence is not to blame.

Damnum sine (or **absque**) **injuria.** Damage which is not the result of a legally remediable wrong.

De bene esse. Evidence or action which a court allows to be given or done provisionally, subject to further consideration at a later stage.

Debitor non praesumitur donare. A debtor is presumed to give a legacy to a creditor to discharge his debt and not as a gift.

Debitum in praesenti. A debt which is due at the present time.

Debitum in futuro solvendum. A debt which will be due to be paid at a future time.

De bonis asportatis. Of goods carried away.

De bonis non administratis. Of the assets which have not been administered.

De die in diem. From day to day.

De facto. In fact.

De futuro. Regarding the future; in the future; about something which will exist in the future.

Dehors. Outside (the document or matter in question); irrelevant. (*French*)

De integro. As regards the whole; entirely.

De jure. By right; rightful.

Del credere agent. An agent who for an extra commission guarantees the due performance of contracts by persons whom he introduces to his principal. (*Italian*)

Delegatus non potest delegare. A person who is entrusted with a duty has no right to appoint another person to perform it in his place.

De minimis non curat lex. The law does not concern itself with trifles.

De novo. Anew; starting afresh.

Deus est procurator fatuorum. God is the protector of the simpleminded.

Devastavit. Where an executor 'has squandered' the estate.

Dictum. Saying. *See* OBITER DICTUM.

Dissentiente. Delivering a dissenting judgment.

Distringas. That you may distrain.

Dolus qui dat locum contractui. A deception which clears the way for the other party to enter into a contract.

Dominium. Ownership.

Dominus pro tempore. The master for the time being.

Donatio mortis causa. A gift made in contemplation of death and conditional thereon.

Dubitante. Doubting the correctness of the decision.

Durante absentia. During an executor's absence abroad.

Durante minore aetate. While an executor remains an infant.

Ei incumbit probatio qui dicit, non qui negat. The onus of proving a fact rests upon the man who asserts its truth, not upon the man who denies it.

Ejusdem generis. General words following a list of specific things are construed as relating to things 'of the same kind' as those specifically listed.

Eodem modo quo oritur, eodem modo dissolvitur. What has been created by a certain method may be extinguished by the same method.

Eo instanti. At that instant.

Escrow. A document delivered subject to a condition which must be fulfilled before it becomes a deed. (*English*)

Estoppel. A rule of evidence which applies in certain circumstances and stops a person from denying the truth of a statement previously made by him. (*English*)

Et cetera. (Etc.) And other things of that sort.

Et seq. (et sequentes). And subsequent pages.

Ex. From; by virtue of.

Ex abundanti cautela. From an abundance of caution.

Ex aequo et bono. According to what is just and equitable.

Ex concessis. In view of what has already been accepted.

Ex contractu. Arising out of contract.

Ex debito justitiae. That which is due as of right; which the court has no discretion to refuse.

Ex delicto. Arising out of a wrongful act or tort.

Ex dolo malo non oritur actio. No right of action arises out of a fraud.

Ex facie. On the face of it; ostensibly.

Ex gratia. Out of the kindness. Gratuitous; voluntary.

Ex hypothesi. In view of what has already been assumed.

Ex officio. By virtue of one's official position.

Ex pacto illicito non oritur actio. No action can be brought on an unlawful contract.

Ex parte. Proceedings brought on behalf of one interested party without notice to, and in the absence of, the other.

Ex post facto. By reason of a subsequent act; acting retrospectively.

Expressio unius est exclusio alterius. When one thing is expressly specified, then it prevents anything else being implied.

Expressum facit cessare tacitum. Where terms are expressed, no other terms can be implied.

Ex turpi causa non oritur actio. No action can be brought where the parties are guilty of illegal or immoral conduct.

Faciendum. Something which is to be done.

Factum. Deed; that which has been done; statement of facts or points in issue.

Fait accompli. An accomplished fact. (*French*)

Feme covert. A married woman. (*Norman-French*)

Feme sole. An unmarried woman. (*Norman-French*)

Fieri facias. A writ addressed to the sheriff: 'that you cause to be made' from the defendant's goods the sum due to the plaintiff under the judgment.

Force majeure. Irresistible compulsion. (*French*)

Fructus industriales. Cultivated crops.

Fructus naturales. Vegetation which grows naturally without cultivation.

Functus officio. Having discharged his duty; having exhausted its powers.

Genus numquam perit. Particular goods which have been identified may be destroyed, but 'a category or type of article can never perish'.

Habeas corpus (ad subjiciendum). A writ addressed to one who detains another in custody, requiring him 'that you produce the prisoner's body to answer' to the court.

Habitué. A frequent visitor to a place. (*French*)

Ibid. (ibidem). In the same place, book, or source.

Id certum est quod certum reddi potest. That which is capable of being reduced to a certainty is already a certainty.

Idem. The same thing, or person.

Ignorantia juris haud (neminem) (non) excusat, ignorantia facti excusat. A man may be excused for mistaking facts, but not for mistaking the law.

Ignorantia juris non excusat. Ignorance of the law is no excuse.

Imperitia culpae adnumeratur. Lack of skill is accounted a fault.

In aequali jure melior est conditio possidentis. Where the legal rights of the parties are equal, the party with possession is in the stronger position.

In bonis. In the goods (or estate) of a deceased person.

In consimili casu. In a similar case.

In custodia legis. In the keeping of the law.

Indebitatus assumpsit. A form of action in which the plaintiff alleges the defendant 'being already indebted to the plaintiff undertook' to do something.

In delicto. At fault.

Indicia. Signs; marks.

Indicium. Indication; sign; mark.

In esse. In existence.

In expeditione. On actual military service.

In extenso. At full length.

In forma pauperis. In the character of a poor person.

Infra. Below; lower down on a page; later in a book.

In futuro. In the future.

In jure non remota causa sed

proxima spectatur. In law it is the immediate and not the remote cause which is considered.

Injuria. A wrongful act for which the law provides a remedy.

Injuria sine damno. A wrongful act unaccompanied by any damage yet actionable at law.

In lieu of. In place of. (*Anglo-French*)

In limine. On the threshold; at the outset.

In loco parentis. In the place of a parent.

In minore delicto. A person who is 'less at fault'.

In omnibus. In every respect.

In pari delicto, potior est conditio defendentis (or possidentis). Where both parties are equally at fault, the defendant (or the party in possession) is in the stronger position.

In pari materia. In an analogous case or position.

In personam. *See* JUS IN PERSONAM.

In pleno. In full.

In praesenti. At the present time.

In propria persona. In his own capacity.

In re. In the matter of. In rem. *See* JUS IN REM.

In situ. In its place.

In specie. In its own form; not converted into anything else.

In statu quo ante. In the condition in which it, or a person, was before.

Inter alia. Amongst other things.

Inter alios. Amongst other persons.

Interest reipublicae ut sit finis litium. It is in the interests of the community that every law suit should reach a final conclusion (and not be reopened later).

Interim. In the meanwhile; temporary.

Inter partes. Between (the) parties.

In terrorem. As a warning; as a deterrent.

Inter se. Between themselves.

Inter vivos. Between persons who are alive.

In toto. In its entirety; completely.

In transitu. In passage from one place to another.

Intra vires. Within the powers recognised by law as belonging to the person or body in question.

In vacuo. In the abstract; without considering the circumstances.

Ipsissima verba. 'The very words' of a speaker.

Ipso facto. By that very fact.

Jus. A right which is recognised in law.

Jus in personam. A right which can be enforced against a particular person only.

Jus in rem. A right which can be enforced over the property in question against all other persons.

Jus naturale. Natural justice.

Jus quaesitum tertio. A right vested in a third party (who is not a party to the contract).

Jus tertii. *See* JUS QUAESITUM TERTIO.

Laches. Slackness or delay in pursuing a legal remedy which disentitles a person from action at a later date. (*Norman-French*)

Laesio fidei. Breach of faith.

Laissez faire. 'Let him do what he likes'; permissive. (*French*)

Lex fori. The law of the court in which the case is being heard.

Lex loci contractus. The law of the place where the contract was made.

Lex loci delicti. The law of the place where the wrong was committed.

Lex loci situs. *See* LEX SITUS.

Lex loci solutionis. The law of the place where the contract is to be performed.

Lex situs. The law of the place where the thing in question is situated.

Loc. cit. (loco citato). In the passage previously mentioned.

Locus classicus. Authoritative passage in a book or judgment; the principal authority or source for the subject.

Locus in quo. Scene of the event.

Locus poenitentiae. Scope or opportunity for repentance.

Locus standi. Recognised position or standing; the right to appear in court.

Magnum opus. A great work of literature.

Mesne. Intermediate; middle; dividing. (*English*)

Mesne profits. Profits of land lost by the plaintiff while the defendant remained wrongfully in possession. (*English*)

Mobilia sequuntur personam. The domicile of movable property follows the owner's personal domicile.

Molliter manus imposuit. Gently laid his hand upon the other party.

Mutatis mutandis. With the necessary changes of detail being made.

Natura negotii. The nature of the transaction.

Negotiorum gestio. Handling of other people's affairs.

Nemo dat quod non habet. No one has power to transfer the ownership of that which he does not own.

Nemo debet bis vexari, si constat curiae quod sit pro una et eadem causa. No one ought to be harassed with proceedings twice, if it appears to the court that it is for one and the same cause.

Nemo est haeres viventis. No one can be the heir of a person who is still living.

Nexus. Connection; bond.

Nisi. Unless; (also used of a decree or order which will later be made absolute 'unless' good cause be shown to the contrary); provisional.

Nisi prius. Cases which were directed to be tried at Westminster only if the justices of assize should 'not' have tried them in the country 'previously'.

Non compos mentis. Not of sound mind and understanding.

Non constat. It is not certain.

Non est factum. That the document in question was not his deed.

Non haec in foedera veni. This is not the agreement which I came to sign.

Non omnibus dormio. I do not turn a blind eye on every instance of misconduct.

Non sequitur. It does not follow; an inconsistent statement.

Noscitur a sociis. The meaning of a word is known from the company it keeps (i.e. from its context).

Nova causa interveniens. An independent cause which intervenes between the alleged wrong and the damage in question.

Novus actus interveniens. A fresh act of someone other than the defendant which intervenes between the alleged wrong and the damage in question.

Nudum pactum. A bare agreement (unsupported by consideration).

Obiter dictum (dicta). Thing(s) said by the way; opinions expressed by judges in passing, on issues not essential for the decision in the case.

Obligatio quasi ex contractu. An obligation arising out of an act or event, as if from a contract, but independently of the consent of the person bound.

Omnia praesumuntur contra spoliatorem. Every presumption is raised against a wrongdoer.

Omnia praesumuntur rite et solemniter esse acta donec probetur in contrarium. All things are presumed to have been performed with all due formalities until it is proved to the contrary.

Omnis ratihabitio retrotrahitur et mandato priori aequiparatur. Every ratification of a previous act is carried back and made equivalent to a previous command to do it.

Op. cit. (opere citato). In the book referred to previously.

Par delictum. Equal fault.

Parens patriae. Parent of the nation.

Pari passu. On an equal footing; equally; in step with.

Pari ratione. By an equivalent process of reasoning.

Parol. By word of mouth, or unsealed document. (*Norman-French*)

Pendente lite. While a law suit is pending.

Per. By; through; in the opinion of a judge.

Per capita. Divided equally between all the persons filling the description.

Per curiam. In the opinion of the court.

Per incuriam. Through carelessness or oversight.

Per quod. By reason of which.

Per quod consortium et servitium amisit. By reason of which he has lost the benefit of her company and services.

Per quod servitium amisit. By reason of which he has lost the benefit of his service.

Per se. By itself.

Plus quam tolerabile. More than can be endured.

Post. After; mentioned in a subsequent passage or page.

Post mortem. After death.

Post obitum. After the death of a specified person.

Pour autrui. On behalf of another. (*Norman-French*)

Prima facie. At first sight.

Primae impressionis. Of first impression.

Profit a prendre. The right to enter the land of another and take part of its produce. (*Norman-French*)

Pro hac vice. For this occasion.

Pro rata. In proportion.

Pro rata itineris. At the same rate per mile as was agreed for the whole journey.

Pro tanto. So far; to that extent.

Pro tempore. For the time being.

Publici juris. Of public right.

Puisne. Inferior; lower in rank; not secured by deposit of deeds; of the High Court.

Punctum temporis. Moment, or point of time.

Pur autre vie. During the life of another person.

q.v. (quod vide). Which see.

Qua. As; in the capacity of.

Quaere. Consider whether it is correct.

Quaeritur. The question is raised.

Quantum. Amount; how much.

Quantum meruit. As much as he has earned.

Quantum valebant. As much as they were worth.

Quare clausum fregit. Because he broke into the plaintiff's enclosure.

Quasi. As if; seemingly.

Quasi ex contractu. *See* OBLIGATIO.

Quatenus. How far; in so far as; since.

Quia timet. Because he fears what he will suffer in the future.

Quid pro quo. Something for something; consideration.

Qui facit per alium facit per se. He who employs another person to do something does it himself.

Quoad. Until; as far as; as to.

Quoad hoc. As far as this matter is concerned.

Quo animo. With what intention.

Ratio decidendi. The reason for a decision; the principle on which a decision is based.

Ratione domicilii. By reason of a person's domicile.

Re. In the matter of; by the thing or transaction.

Res. Thing; affair; matter; circumstance.

Res extincta. The thing which was intended to be the subject matter of a contract but had previously been destroyed.

Res integra. A point not covered by the authority of a decided case which must therefore be decided upon principle alone.

Res inter alios acta alteri nocere

non debet. A man ought not to be prejudiced by what has taken place between other persons.

Res judicata. A matter on which a court has previously reached a binding decision; a matter which cannot be questioned.

Res nova. A matter which has not previously been decided.

Res nullius. Nobody's property.

Respondeat superior. A principal must answer for the acts of his subordinates.

Res sua. Something which a man believes to belong to another when it in fact is 'his own property'.

Restitutio in integrum. Restoration of a party to his original position; full restitution.

Res vendita. The article which was sold.

Rigor aequitatis. The inflexibility of equity.

Sc. *See* SCILICET.

Sciens. Knowing.

Scilicet. To wit; namely; that is to say.

Scintilla. A spark; trace; or moment.

Scire facias. A writ; that you cause to know.

Scriptum praedictum non est factum suum. A plea that the aforesaid document is not his deed.

Secus. It is otherwise; the legal position is different.

Sed. But.

Sed quaere. But inquire; look into the matter; consider whether the statement is correct.

Semble. It appears; apparently. (*French*)

Seriatim. In series; one by one; point by point.

Serivitium. Service.

Sic. So; in such a manner; (also used to emphasise wording copied or quoted from another source: 'such was the expression used in the original source').

Sic utere tuo ut alienum non laedas. So use your own property as not to injure the property of your neighbour.

Similiter. Similarly; in like manner.

Simplex commendatio non obligat. Mere praise of goods by the seller imposes no liability upon him.

Simpliciter. Simply; merely; alone; without any further action; without qualification.

Sine animo revertendi. Without the intention of returning.

Sine die. Without a day being appointed; indefinitely.

Solatium. Consolation; relief; compensation.

Specificatio. The making of a new article out of the chattel of one person by the labour of another.

Spes successionis. The hope of inheriting property on the death of another.

Spondes peritiam artis. If skill is inherent in your profession, you guarantee that you will display it.

Status quo (ante). The previous position; the position in which things were before; unchanged position.

Stet. Let it stand; do not delete.

Sub colore officii. Under pretext of someone's official position.

Sub modo. Within limits; to a limited extent.

Sub nom. (sub nomine). Under the name of.

Sub silentio. In silence.

Sub tit. (sub titulo). Under the title of.

Suggestio falsi. The suggestion of something which is untrue.

Sui generis. Of its own special kind; unique.

Sui juris. Of his own right; possessed of full legal capacity.

Suppressio veri. The suppression of the truth.

Supra. (Sup.) Above; referred to higher up the page; previously.

Talis qualis. Such as it is.

Toties quoties. As often as occasion

shall require; as often as something happens.

Transit in rem judicatam. A right of action merges in the judgment recovered upon it.

Turpis causa. Immoral conduct which constitutes the subject matter of an action.

Uberrima fides. Most abundant good faith.

Ubi jus ibi remedium. Where there is a legally recognised right there is also a remedy.

Ubi supra. In the passage or reference mentioned previously.

Ultra vires. Outside the powers recognised by law as belonging to the person or body in question.

Uno flatu. With one breath; at the same moment.

Ut res magis valeat quam pereat. Words must be construed so as to support the validity of the contract rather than to destroy it.

v. (versus). Against.

Verba fortius accipiuntur contra proferentem. Ambiguous wording is construed adversely against the party who introduced it into the document.

Verbatim. Word by word; exactly; word for word.

Vice versa. The other way round; in turn.

Vide. See.

Vi et armis (et contra pacem domini regis). By force of arms (and in breach of the King's peace).

Vigilantibus et non dormientibus jura subveniunt (or jus succurrit). The law(s) assist(s) those who are vigilant, not those who doze over their rights.

Vinculum juris. Legal tie; that which binds the parties with mutual obligations.

Virtute officii. By virtue of a person's official position.

Vis-à-vis. Face to face; opposite to. (*French*)

Vis major. Irresistible force.

Viz. (videlicet). Namely; that is to say.

Voir dire. Examination of a witness before he gives evidence, to ascertain whether he is competent to tell the truth on oath. (*French*)

Volens. Willing.

INDEX

Acceptance, 66, 93, 206, 217, 459, 602
  advertised offer, 99, 267
  condition as to method of, 133, 188
  posting of letter, 1, 94, 282, 305, 372, 595
  telegram, etc., by, 145, 194, 562
  withdrawal, 94, 372, 562
Act of God, 70
Ad idem. *See also* MISTAKE.
  parties must be, 527, 546
Advertisement, 99, 109, 267
  See also TICKET.
Agent,
  contracting in own name, 160
  impersonation by, 463
Agreement, 37, 64, 119, 234, 243, 256, 357,
    462, 616
  breach of, 106, 371
  failure to perform, 106
  impliedly terminable, 557
  maintenance, 559, 681
  set aside, 243
  subsidiary, cancellation of, 446
  training service agreement, frustration of,
    536
  under threat, 430, 637
Agricultural Holdings Act 1948,
  protection of, 329
Arbitration,
  award, time limit for enforcement of, 5
Arbitration clause, 286, 643
Assignment,
  absolute prohibition on, 13
  lease, of, 463
Auction, 220, 621, 710
  contract, when complete, 168, 207, 359,
    455, 710
  Sale of Goods Act 1979 . . . 710
Awards,
  time limit for actions to enforce certain, 5,
    714

Bailment, 44, 364, 556
Bank interest
  entitlement to, 28
Betting. *See* GAMING.
Bill of lading,
  exemptions and immunities, 425
  limitation of liability under, 10, 528
  stranger to, protection of, 528
Bills of Exchange Act 1882 . . . 656
Binding in honour only, 26, 325, 506

Breach of promise to marry, 231
Building contract, 25, 102, 155, 351, 442,
    451
  illegality, 599
  implied term, 49
  term of, 600

Carriage, contract of,
  conditions, 384
  exclusion of liability, 384
  risk note, 384
Carriage of goods, 27
  breach of agreement, 199
  collateral contract, under, 27
  liability, exclusion of, 384
  negligence of carrier, 384
  Road and Rail Traffic Act 1933, licence
    under, 27
  special contract, 312
Charter voyage,
  deviation, 342
  implied terms, 572
Cheque,
  dishonoured, 238
  forged signature on, 128
Clauses. *See* CONDITIONS.
Commission, 80, 356
Companies Act 1985 . . . 742, 743
Company
  form of contract, 743
  power of directors to bind, 742
Completion, 86, 168, 710
Concealment,
  limitation period in case of postponement
    of, 719
Conditions, 51, 258, 564, 636, 700–703
  acceptance of, 93
  ambiguous clauses, 295
  carriage of, 156
  charter party, breach of, 10, 208, 436, 519
  exclusion clause, 156, 617
  exemption clause in, 296
  fairly and reasonably brought to other
    party's attention, 316
  forfeiture clause, 564
  implied, 89, 114, 222, 260, 338, 381, 531,
    703, 709
  incorporated subsequently, cannot be, 156
  indemnity clause, 548
  merchantable quality, of, breach of, 33, 61,
    502, 537

Conditions—*continued*
not part of contract, 384
precedent, 54, 116, 473
price variation clause, 93
printed, 400, 592
reading of, 69, 363, 579
reasonableness, 268, 544, 617, 691, 696
subsequent, 278
ticket, etc., on, 3, 109, 156, 280, 449, 571, 591
unknown, 384, 437, 449, 598
unreasonable, 316
versions of, 548
warranty, when to be treated as, 700
Conduct, 117, 380
Consideration, 113, 125, 303, 486, 511
benefit, 115, 178, 241, 522
binding promise, 107, 131, 532, 563, 597
danger, 273, 563
detriment, 38, 218, 532
forbearance to sue, etc., 18, 82, 97, 119, 609, 615
immoral. *See* IMMORAL AGREEMENT.
moral obligation, 182, 620
obligation, promisee under, 129, 532, 620
party, stranger to. *See* PRIVITY.
past, 52, 346, 383, 434, 505
price void for lack of, 430
value of, 589
Consumer goods,
guarantee of, 686
prohibition on exclusions from liability, 749
Consumer Protection Act 1987 . . . 749
Contract,
already performed, 441
booking ticket, running from, 156
breach of, 50, 79, 90, 92, 264, 315, 318, 320, 332, 354, 364, 467, 481, 534, 570
compensation for, 147, 318, 320, 354
contractual warranty, 50
contributory negligence, 225
damages for, 10, 28, 31, 79, 90, 199, 201, 287, 315, 390, 410, 534
effect of, 689
inducing, 255
liability arising in, 6, 684
statutory duty, 548
cancellation provision, 208
company, 742, 743
condition, 42
consideration, 112, 430, 511
constitution of, 203
consumer, dealing as, 692
court's jurisdiction, whether made within, 79
covenant, not contained in, 367
defective—
design, 315
product, liability for, 749
workmanship, 73
description, compliance with, 489

Contract—*continued*
discharge of, 511
disclaimer, 268
employment, of, breach of, 147, 202, 264.
See also EMPLOYMENT.
evasion by means of secondary, 690
exchange of, 269
exclusion clause, 364
exemption clauses, 295, 332, 400, 467, 592, 693
expenditure after conclusion of, 23
frustration of. *See* FRUSTRATION.
guarantees, clauses excluding, 42
implied—
obligation, 367
terms, 5, 33, 89, 114, 235, 481
warranty, 261
indemnification, 111, 685
inducing clause, 400
inequality of bargaining power, 364
licence—
contractual, 631
contrasted with, 247, 636
lump sum, 73
minors', 745–748
miscellaneous, under which goods pass, 688
mutual obligations, change in significance of, 433
negotiate, to, 306
oral, 127, 187, 235, 295, 574
performance, 73, 607
price increase, 430
reasonableness test, 268, 544, 617, 691, 696
rectification, 326
repudiation of, 90, 208, 236, 354, 417
rescission, 28, 98, 266, 460, 463, 497, 567, 603, 607, 617
sale, of—
capacity to buy and sell, 698
formalities of, 699
nature of, 697
not legally enforceable, where, 239
sale subject to, 19, 34, 127
secondary, 690
service of. *See* SERVICE, CONTRACT OF.
severed, 101
side letter, 360
simple, time limit for actions founded on, 712
specific performance. *See* SPECIFIC PERFORMANCE.
terminate—
entitled to, 371
threatening to, 430
time of payment of the essence, 265
ultra vires, 324
undue influence. *See* UNDUE INFLUENCE.
Unfair Contract Terms Act 1977 . . . 268, 466, 617, 682–696
voidability of, 53, 430
warranty, 50, 478

Contributory negligence,
  breach of contract, where, 225
Conversion,
  tort of, 56, 235, 365
Copyright,
  breach of, 112, 121, 521
Corporations,
  Corporate Bodies' Contracts Act 1960 . . .
    665, 666
Covenant,
  contract, not contained in, 367
  restraint of trade in. *See* RESTRAINT OF
    TRADE.
  restrictive, 39, 162, 202, 333, 403, 602
  transfer, 549, 601, 602
Custom, 4, 251, 445
  agricultural, 313
  maritime, 445, 461
Customs duty,
  avoidance of, 198

Damage, 456, 468, 619, 749
  See also REMOTENESS OF DAMAGE.
Damages, 110, 164, 354, 456
  adverse claim, where, 488
  assessment of, 110, 539
  breach of—
    contract for, 10, 28, 31, 79, 90, 199, 201,
      287, 315, 390, 410, 534
    implied obligation, for, 367
    implied term, 631
    warranty, for, 298
  deceit, in, 28
  exemplary, 28
  expenditure where contract partially
    performed, 95
  expenses, limited to, 488, 534
  hire-purchase agreement, under. *See* HIRE-
    PURCHASE.
  income tax, 304
  injunction, award as well as or in
    substitution for, 723
  injured feelings, for, 28
  loss—
    employment, of, 28
    profit, of, 106, 259, 534
    transaction, of, 371
  misrepresentation for, 306
  negligence, 27, 38, 315, 357, 425, 548
  nominal, 238
  quantum, 317, 468
  reasonable consideration of, 259
  recovery of, under charterparty, 436
  special circumstances, 259
  specific performance—
    award as well or in substitution for, 723
    order discharged, where, 454
  tax liability taken account of, 539
  wasted expenditure, for, 106
Deadfreight,
  claim for, 208

Debt,
  part payment of. *See* PART PAYMENT.
  suing for balance, 627, 637
Deed, 232, 233, 434
  cancellation of, 644
  signature induced by fraudulent
    misrepresentation, 334
  signed under duress, 48
Defamation, 111
Defective workmanship, 73
Delay,
  frustration of adventure by, 470
Description,
  hire of goods by, 731
  transfer of goods by, 726
Detinue, 516
Diligence,
  reasonable, 460
Disability,
  limitation period in cases of, extension of,
    716
Disclaimer,
  preventing duty of care arising, 268
  requirement of reasonableness under
    Unfair Contracts Terms Act, 268, 544
Disclosure, 202, 299, 577, 622
Documents,
  signed without reading, 517
  wording, construction of, 9
Drunk,
  incompetent to contract, 698
Duress, 215, 638
Duty of care,
  disclaimer, 268

Employment, 2, 181
  See also SERVICE, CONTRACT OF.
  breach of contract of, 147, 202, 264
  duty of fidelity, 202
  wrongful dismissal, 236
  wrongful termination of contract, 539
Equitable jurisdiction,
  Limitation Act 1980 . . . 720
Estoppel, 34, 235, 329, 463, 564, 597
  See also QUASI-ESTOPPEL.

Fidelity,
  duty of, 202
Fixed bidding sale,
  referential bid in, 275
Football pool, 325
Forged signature,
  cheque, on, 128
Fraud, 98, 577, 719
Frauds, statutes of, 187, 351, 493, 605,
    649, 651
  See also NOTE OR MEMORANDUM.
Fraudulent misrepresentation. *See*
    MISREPRESENTATION.
Frustration, 135, 209, 213, 285, 319, 393,
    414

Frustration—*continued*
adventure, of, by delay, 470
cancellation of event, 285, 343
compulsory purchase order, 290
failure to establish, 418, 436, 607
fire, destruction by, 399, 585
fundamental difference, 601
Government, by, 45, 148, 200, 402, 580
Law Reform (Frustrated Contracts) Act
    1943 . . . 662–664
property, loss of use, 421, 447, 583
third party, by, 40, 583
training service agreement, of, 536
war. *See* WAR.

Gaming, 100, 137, 637
agency, 78, 126, 166, 352, 582
Betting and Gaming Act 1960 . . . 15
collateral undertaking, 140, 288, 385, 637
Gaming Acts—
    1710 . . . 650
    1835 . . . 652
    1845 . . . 653
    1892 . . . 657
    1968 . . . 671–673
loan for, 388, 440
losses, promise to pay, 385
recovery from stakeholder, 174, 613
Stock Exchange, on, 587, 608
unlawful, 15
wagers, 190, 587
Good faith,
duty of, 202
Goodwill,
protection of, 162, 333
Guarantee, 144, 262, 344, 369, 446, 575
consumer goods, of, 686
minors, 746

***High Trees House* doctrine**, 107, 131, 311,
    501, 597
Hire, 317, 322, 632
conditions of, 81, 519
goods, of—
    contracts concerned, 729
    description, by, 731
    quality or fitness, implied terms about,
        732
    right to transfer possession, 730
    sample, by, 733
illegal, 27
Hire-purchase, 350, 518, 564, 606
breach of, 606, 687
damages—
    breach, for, 212
    recovery of, 179
default of payment, 212
determination of, 136
Hire-Purchase and Credit Sale Agreements
    (Control) Order 1960 . . . 550
illegality, 56, 516, 550

Hire-purchase—*continued*
implied conditions and warranties,
    674–680, 687
liability for breach of obligations, 687
merchantable quality, breach of condition
    of, 537
offer, 212
option under, 77
ownership, right of, 554
penalty clause, 24, 32, 77, 136, 179, 211
promissory estoppel, 7
termination of, 32, 77, 179, 211
    compensation for, 77
    written notice of, 77

Illegality, 14, 17, 53, 56, 60, 75, 139, 210,
    394
agreement of, not relevant, 408
hire-purchase, 56
ignorance of the law, 15
immorality. *See* IMMORAL AGREEMENT.
marriage, 85, 231, 284, 379
money, revenue, etc., 67, 328, 405
mortgage, 101
payment, not recoverable. *See* PAYMENT.
prosecution, suppression of, 123, 327, 330,
    638
public policy. *See* PUBLIC POLICY.
statute, etc., contrary to, 21, 71, 167
understated invoice, 198
Immoral agreement,
adultery, 49, 89, 434
blasphemy, obscenity, etc., 144, 224
prostitution, etc., 368, 457, 586
Impersonation,
agent, by, 463
Implied term, 5, 33, 89, 114, 222, 235, 253,
    260, 338, 381, 453, 481, 483, 531, 631,
    645, 674–680, 725–728, 730–734,
    736–739
Impossibility, 260
    See also FRUSTRATION.
Indemnity, 53, 257, 446, 483, 548, 634, 685
unreasonable clauses, 685
Inducement, 57, 400
Infants. *See* MINORS.
Influence,
personal, use of, contrary to public policy,
    360
undue. *See* UNDUE INFLUENCE.
Injunction. *See also* RESTRAINT OF TRADE.
damages awarded as well as, or in
    substitution for, 723
granted, 162, 333, 377, 378, 403, 497, 542,
    602, 622
refused, 397, 513, 519, 635
Instalments,
failure to pay, 564, 633
recovery of payment, 211, 564
Insurance,
breach of contract, 225

Insurance—*continued*
claim, 11
conditions, 628
contributory negligence, 225
damages for, 11
fire, 370
life, 331, 374, 524
marine, 53, 299, 523, 529
Marine Insurance Act 1906 . . . 658
material fact. *See* UBERRIMAE FIDEI.
mistake, 392
motor, 611
proposal inaccurately completed, 392
reinsurance, 53
repayment, 11
Intention,
informal agreement, 554
legal relations. *See* LEGAL RELATIONS.
Interest in land, 351, 625
Intoxication, 246, 398

Laches, 13, 16, 355
Laundry, cleaning, etc., 12, 152, 158, 364, 368, 614
Lease. *See* TENANCY.
Legal charge,
independent advice before executing, 46
voidable in equity, 38
Legal relations,
husband and wife, agreement between, 542
intention to create—
express terms, 26, 325, 506
letters of comfort, 339
negative, 43
positive, 99, 448, 540
Letters of comfort, 339
Liability. *See also* NEGLIGENCE
condition exempting from, 636
prohibition on exclusions from, 749
restrictive, 722
Limitation Act 1980 . . . 605, 711–721
Liquidated damages, 176, 188, 292
See also PENALTY.
Loans,
fraudulent misrepresentation to obtain, 334
letters of comfort as part of agreement, 339
liability on husband and wife's joint account, 404
postponement of limitation period, 605, 719
secured by charge on house, 128
security transaction voidable in equity, 38
time limit for actions in respect of certain, 713

Marine insurance, 53, 299, 523, 529
Marine Insurance Act 1906 . . . 658
Marriage, 85, 231, 284, 379
See also SEPARATION AGREEMENT.
Matrimonial Causes Act 1973 . . . 681
Memorandum. *See* NOTE OR MEMORANDUM.

Mental disability, 272, 411, 698
Merchantable quality,
breach of condition of, 33, 61, 502, 537
Minors, 91, 205
apprenticeship, 70, 189, 543
benefit of, 119, 163, 179, 499, 543
contracts, 745–748
guarantees, 746
hiring, etc., 322
Infants' Relief Act 1874 . . . 654, 745
loan to, 362
necessaries, 113, 124, 420, 698
promise—
ratification when of age, 182
repudiation when of age, 184
restitution, 559, 747
tort, suing in, 322
trading contract, 146, 538
Minors' Contracts Act 1987 . . . 745–748
Misdescription, 240, 270, 279
Misrepresentation, 46, 210, 355, 368, 375, 629
Act 1967 . . . 28, 443, 493, 605, 624, 667–670
fraudulent, 28, 306, 334, 356, 362, 404, 431, 435, 545, 547, 582
honest belief, 8, 68, 170, 439
innocent, 57, 277, 424, 439, 510, 526, 617, 634
liability attaching to principal, 493
not relied on, 36, 321, 431
onus of proofs as to, 306
possibility of discovering truth, 108, 302, 490
prospectus, in, 170, 183, 431, 435, 491, 545
puffing, 99, 525
Misstatement,
negligent, damages for, 315
Mistake, 274, 444, 579
compensation not recoverable, due to, 55
fact, of, 256, 460, 577
fundamental, 392
identity of parties, 151, 232, 335, 465, 553
limitation period in case of, postponement of, 719
material fact, 55, 310, 524, 552, 568
money paid, 432, 530
nature of subject matter, 271, 484, 507, 526, 527, 546
position of parties, 138
rectification of—
contract, 500
parties, 138, 497
written instrument, 227, 307, 593, 626
Mortgage,
advice as to effect of, 141
covenants in restraint of trade, 196
Limitation Act 1980, application of, to, 717
second, 141, 334
security, as, 101
survey report, disclaimer in, 268, 544

Necessaries, See MINORS.
Negligence, 247, 384
  contributory, 225
  damages for, 27, 50, 268, 315, 357, 425,
    544, 548
  honest mistake, 296
  liability—
    for, 9, 295, 410, 466, 493, 683
    in tort for, 50
    limitation of, 6, 410, 528
  personal injury, 548
  professional, 137
Non est factum, 38, 517
Note or memorandum, 105, 204, 245, 361,
  596
  agreement for sale or lease, 277, 361, 376,
    448, 458, 594
  Law of Property Act 1925 . . . 351, 559,
    596, 659–661
  Statute of Frauds, 649, 651
  two documents, in, 309, 376, 458, 594

Offer, 66, 252, 314, 376, 555, 626
  acceptance, 93, 203, 212, 239, 297, 631
  conditional, 212
  counter-offer, 93
  display not offer, 214
  firm, 239
  invitation only, 214
  preliminaries to, 99, 122, 250, 276, 464,
    504
  Restriction of Offensive Weapons Act 1959,
    exclusion, 214
  retraction by conduct, 103, 172
  revocation of, 212
  reward, of, 192, 217, 237, 349, 482, 639
  train time-table, 169, 449
  withdrawal, 455, 509
Option,
  purchase, to, 289, 488, 570
  specific performance of, 570
Oral agreement, 81, 199, 235, 249, 596
  collateral, 29, 142, 152, 345, 569
  implied term, 535
  part performance under, 336
  variation, 63, 248
Order,
  acknowledgment of, 93

Parol evidence, 251
Part payment, 154, 221
  formal provisions as to, 718
  fresh accrual of action of, on, 717
  'full settlement', in, 291, 423, 469
  suing for balance, 150, 469, 494, 627
Part performance,
  acceptance of new accommodation, 336
  act unequivocally referable, 157, 389, 391,
    487
  improvement to property, 88, 487
  payment for. *See* QUANTUM MERUIT.

Part performance—*continued*
  separation agreement, of, 574
Partnership, 219, 424
Party to contract,
  identity must be known, 514
  stranger. *See* PRIVITY.
Payment,
  deposit, of, as fundamental term, 407
  excess, 430
  Exchange Control Act 1947, under, 535
  ex gratia, 185
  for goods received, 401
  hire, of, conditions, 519
  illegal, not recoverable, 535
  part. *See* PART PAYMENT.
  prompt, as condition of agreement, 371
  refusal, 93
  security, 18
Penalty, 133, 176, 223, 350
  See also LIQUIDATED DAMAGES.
Possession,
  claim for, 329, 334, 367, 422
Post,
  acceptance by, 1, 94, 282, 305, 372, 595
  ticket containing conditions sent by, 156
Pre-emption,
  right of, 234
Privity,
  non-party suing, 149, 178, 377, 406, 477,
    549, 611, 623
  trade practices, 177, 578
Promise, 185, 446
Property,
  Law of Property Act 1925 . . . 596,
    659–661
  passes when intended to pass, 705
  transfer of, between seller and buyer,
    705–710
Prosecution,
  suppression of, 123, 327, 330, 638
Provisional agreement, 76, 116
Public Passenger Vehicles Act 1981 . . .
  722
Public policy. *See also* ILLEGALITY.
  attainment of title of honour, 186, 450
  international comity, 226, 492
  marriage. *See* MARRIAGE; SEPARATION
    AGREEMENT.
  personal influence contrary to, 360
  restraint of trade, 74, 386, 508, 610, 647
  restrictive covenant not contrary to, 333

Quantum meruit, 104, 118, 161, 316, 573
Quasi-estoppel, 107, 131, 311, 501, 597

Reasonable care, 38, 164, 413
  breach of contract for, 164
Reasonable diligence, 460
Reasonable notice, 396, 496
Reasonableness,
  requirement of, 268, 544, 617, 691, 696

Receivership,
specific performance and, 230
Rectification, 326, 497
Referential bid,
fixed bidding sale, in, 275
Remoteness of damage,
contemplation of parties, 171, 259, 301, 468, 541
fraudulent misrepresentation, after, 419
loss flowing from breach, 134, 137, 301, 419, 541
special circumstances unknown, 259
tax liability, 539
time element, 614
Repudiation, 47, 54, 294, 435, 446, 633
part performance, after, 229, 401
Rescission, 28, 98, 266, 460, 463, 497, 567, 603, 607, 617
Restitution, 173, 228, 441, 565, 584, 619, 747
Restraint of trade,
covenants, 20, 120, 196, 236
employee, retention of, 181, 561
goodwill, protection of, 333
lease and sublease, 13
public policy, 74, 386, 508, 610, 647
reasonable, 193, 216, 292, 347, 427, 429, 503
reciprocal agreements, 341
sale, 397
service agreement, unlawful, 566
severance of covenant, 35, 242
solus agreements, 462
trade secrets, 283, 459
unreasonable, 83, 185, 191, 255, 283, 361, 382, 397, 459, 521, 566
wrongful dismissal, 236, 340
Restrictive trade practices, 156, 177, 193, 610
Unfair Contract Terms Act 1977 . . . 682–196
Reward,
offer of, 192, 217, 237, 349, 482, 639

Sale of Goods, 377
acceptance, 708
Act 1979 . . . 33, 61, 453, 483, 502, 645, 698–710
breach—
condition of, 51
implied term, of, 645
buyer's rights, 707
condition as to warranty, 700
conditional sale agreements, 679
contract of sale, 697–699
description—
compliance with, 489
sale by, 428, 612, 618, 702
fitness, implied conditions as to, 33, 453, 481, 483, 703
guarantee of consumer goods, 686

Sale of Goods—*continued*
hire-purchase, by. *See* HIRE-PURCHASE.
intention, rules to ascertain, 706
liability for breach of obligations, 687
merchantable quality, breach of condition of, 33, 61, 502, 537
price variation clause, 93
property passes when intended to pass, 705
sale or return transaction, 198
sample, sale by, 704
stolen, 198
title, implied undertaking as to, 687, 701
Sample,
sale by, 526, 527, 546, 687, 688, 704
transfer of goods by, 728
Seal,
not required, 303
Secondary contract,
evasion by means of, 690
Separation agreement, 62, 232, 233, 244, 387, 574, 640, 641
future, 85, 379
Service, contract of. *See also* EMPLOYMENT; RESTRAINT OF TRADE
armed forces, joining, effect, 395, 414, 538
enforcement of, 566
frustration of, 433
implied term, 253, 293, 474, 498
new agreement, 566
part performance of, 153, 438
restrict provision, 132, 566
termination—
notice of, 185
of employment, 228
theatrical, 65, 378, 473, 585, 622
training service agreement, frustration of, 536
Services, supply of. *See* SUPPLY OF SERVICES.
Settlement of action, 84, 416
Severance of clauses, 426, 479
Shipping, 342, 572
Side letter, 360
Solus agreements, 462
Specialty,
time limit for actions on a, 715
Specific performance, 19, 64, 66, 160, 254, 256, 269, 277, 407, 443, 472, 519, 542, 616, 626
building contract, 102, 389
damages awarded as well as, or in substitution for, 723
failure to claim, 37
misrepresentation, 87, 240
option, of, 570
oral contract, of, 127, 187
order discharged, 454
part performance, 127, 389, 391, 574
receivership, where, 230
separation agreement, 574
unforeseeable changes, 454

Stamp,
  omission of, 356
Sterilisation,
  no implied warranty, 201
Stranger to contract. *See* PRIVITY.
Supply of Goods,
  Act 1973 . . . 674–680
  and Services Act 1982 . . . 724–741
  exclusion of implied terms, 734
  hire of goods—
    contracts concerned, 729
    description, by, 731
    quality or fitness, implied terms about,
      732
    right to transfer possession, 730
    sample, by, 733
  transfer of property in goods—
    contracts concerned, 724
    description, by, 726
    quality or fitness, implied terms about,
      727
    sample, by, 728
    title, 725
Supply of services,
  care and skill, 736
  consideration, 738
  contracts concerned, 735
  exclusion of implied terms, etc., 739
  time for performance, 737
Supreme Court Act 1981 . . . 723
Survey report,
  disclaimer of responsibility, 268, 544

Tax liability,
  taken into account for assessment of
    damages, 539
Telegraph,
  acceptance by, 145, 194, 562
Tenancy, 167, 323, 373, 444, 642
  agreement, 9, 487
  assignment of lease, 463
  covenant—
    not contained in contract, 367
    unclear, 200
  damages, liability for, 357, 367
  frustration of lease, 421
  High Trees House doctrine, 107, 131, 311,
    501, 597
  illegal agreement, 408
  Law of Property Act 1925 . . . 336, 351
  maintain, obligation to, 367
  protection of Agricultural Holdings Act
    1948 . . . 329
  regulations, 337, 552
  Rent Restriction Acts, 336
  repairing, 200, 311, 367
  restraint of trade doctrine, 13
  sale of lease 'subject to contract', 127

Tenancy—*continued*
  specific performance of obligation in lease,
    472
  statutory, 336
Termination,
  implied, 557
Terms. *See* CONDITIONS.
Ticket,
  booking of, contract running from, 156
  conditions, 3, 109, 156, 280, 449, 571, 591
Time-barred action, 460
Title, 365
Tort,
  conversion, of, 56, 235, 365
  measure of damages in, 342
  minor suing in, 322
  negligence, for, 50
Transfer of property in goods. *See* SUPPLY
  OF GOODS.
Trust, 520

Uberrimae fidei, 299, 370, 374
Ultra vires, 30, 324
Undue influence, 16, 141, 243, 409, 415,
  441
  bank's duty, 422
  family relationship, 128, 308, 348, 404
  solicitor's duty, 412, 476, 646
Unfair Contracts Terms Act 1977 . . .
  268, 466, 617, 682–696
Unsoundness of mind. *See* MENTAL
  DISABILITY.

Variation, 63, 82, 248
  price variation clause, 93

Wagering. *See* GAMING.
War,
  effect of—
    frustration, 195, 209
    no frustration, 373, 447, 597, 601
Warranty,
  breach of—
    consequences, 453
    damages for, 197, 315
    remedy for, 298
  condition treated as, 700
  contractual, 50, 478
  enforceable, 630
  implied, 201, 261, 701, 703, 709
  less than condition, 298
  mere representation not, 266, 300
  misrepresentation, 57
  nature of goods, 630
  oral, 10, 142, 152, 165, 345, 569
  quality, as to, 533, 567
  unqualified collateral, 201
Withdrawal. *See* ACCEPTANCE; OFFER.